DEMOCR
LEGACY
IN TRAN

Perspectives

Democratic Legacy in Transition

Perspectives on American Education

Edited by

John E. Sturm

John A. Palmer

State University College of New York at Buffalo

Van Nostrand Reinhold Company

New York / Cincinnati / Toronto / London / Melbourne

Van Nostrand Reinhold Company Regional Offices:
New York / Cincinnati / Chicago / Millbrae / Dallas
Van Nostrand Reinhold Company International Offices:
London / Toronto / Melbourne
Copyright © 1971 by Litton Educational Publishing, Inc.
Library of Congress Catalog Card Number 70-140103
Published by **Van Nostrand Reinhold Company**
450 West 33rd Street, New York, N.Y. 10001
Published simultaneously in Canada by
Van Nostrand Reinhold Ltd.
10 9 8 7 6 5 4 3 2 1

This book is affectionately dedicated to our wives,
Jean M. Sturm and Elaine A. Palmer,
and to our students
at the State University College of New York at Buffalo.

Our nation stands at a crossroads. As we face the future, we must make a choice on which road we will travel. One leads to that plural society to which we rededicate ourselves whenever we repeat the Pledge of Allegiance. . . . That road leads to unity of the purpose and action which will make life meaningful for all. The other road would divide us into segments of discontented people with a divisiveness that leaves no room for the happiness and contentment of the children of any of us in the foreseeable future.

—former Chief Justice Earl Warren in an address to the N.A.A.C.P. Legal Defense and Educational Fund, Inc. (May 15, 1970)

DEMOCRATIC LEGACY IN TRANSITION

Perspectives on American Education

Contents

Preface

Like so many of our colleagues now teaching introductory, foundations, and problems courses in education, we have found it necessary in recent seasons to reassess the objectives and the content of such courses. How does one introduce a new generation of American educators to the "basics" of their profession when no one knows what shape that profession will assume in the years ahead? And what "foundations" can we give the as-yet uncommitted student who thinks he *might* want to teach but isn't sold on the idea?

In facing these questions within our own professional education program, we have had to temper our old assumptions in the heat of the public debate and professional reexamination that dominates today's educational arena. Some of our earlier assumptions have fallen away. Others seem stronger today after their trial by fire amid present problems. It is because of subsequent realignments in our governing assumptions and associated revisions in our course content that we have compiled, in conjunction with our students, the present assemblage of materials as an introduction to American education.

Briefly, our concept is that people new to the profession find it meaningful to view education less as a fixed institution than as an evolving product of American historical, sociocultural, psychological, and economic forces.

We chose to begin with the historical, in Part I (although it is possible to begin equally effectively at any of the other Parts), where we open with a spotlight on the nineteenth century one-room school. A flashback to school objectives and practices from the colonial through the modern period follows, with particular attention given to the status of minority group members and the growing role of the federal government. The section closes with a provocative reinterpretation of American educational history.

A sociocultural view is the organizing concept in Part II. Here the anthropological insights of Kluckhohn and Mead provide a base from which to explore the effects of social change upon curriculum, students, and the educational environment as a whole, including the response of higher education to recent American foreign policy.

The more individualistic perspective of Part III focuses on alternative *goals of education* as expounded by psychologists and philosophers ranging from Comenius to Dewey, Piaget, and others, and on alternative *means of education* as put forward more recently by Bruner and other present-day researchers.

A closer look at students least easily accommodated by the schools, the so-called disadvantaged, is provided in Part IV, which treats poor, black, Indian, and migrant children in particular and also investigates specific modifications in methodology, curriculum, and educational assumptions that might be effective in reversing the plight of these students.

The book concludes with a roundup of new directions emerging in the profession: teacher organizations for collective bargaining, new self-images that teachers—especially urban teachers and black teachers—hold, and the new behavior repertoire of today's administrators.

In arranging selections under the five rubrics sketched above, it was decided to avoid the practice of summarizing each article for the student or of following each article with questions emphasizing specific recall. On the assumption that today's instructors and students are concerned about larger issues, each Part begins with a brief general inquiry into the subject at hand, culminating in a few broad questions which we hope will help illuminate the truly fundamental issues inherent in the study of education—with these and other materials, in this or any age.

J. E. S.
J. A. P.

Acknowledgments

Grateful acknowledgment is made to the following publishers and individuals who graciously granted permission to reprint material for which they hold copyright or of which they are the authorized publishers:

AMERICAN ECONOMIC ASSOCIATION: for passages by Alan Batchelder from *American Economic Review,* May 1965, Vol. 55, No. 2. Reprinted by permission of the author and the American Economic Association. This article appeared originally as "Poverty: The Special Case for the Negro."

ASSOCIATION FOR SUPERVISION AND CURRICULUM DEVELOPMENT: for passages by Galen Saylor and Kimball Wiles from *Educational Leadership,* October 1965, Vol 23, and May 1960, Vol. 17. Reprinted with permission of the Association for Supervision and Curriculum Development and the authors. Copyright © 1965 and 1960 by the Association for Supervision and Curriculum Development. Mr. Saylor's article appeared originally as "The Federal Colossus in Education—Threat or Promise?" Mr. Wiles' article appeared originally as "Education of Adolescents: 1985."

JAMES BALDWIN: for "A Talk to Teachers" which appeared originally in *Saturday Review,* December 21, 1963. Reprinted by permission.

DEMOCRATIC LEGACY IN TRANSITION

Perspectives on American Education

Part I

The Historical View

I want the children to be at good schools
and without loss of time. If you cannot
make suitable arrangements in St. Louis
you may go where you think best,
East or West.

Ulysses S. Grant
in a letter to his wife Julia during the siege of
Petersburg, 1864

We live at one of the most critical junctures in the history of education in America. Many schools and colleges are in ferment—in response not only to larger issues facing society as a whole, but to new conditions and tensions within the educational community itself. It is tempting at periods of "live" transition such as this to want to cease the study of history, on the grounds that our present situation is unprecedented, that the past is "dead" and has no meaning for us, that the present demands our attention so urgently that we have no time to consider anything else.

And yet, yesterday's student demonstration is already "history." So is the Supreme Court's "historic" desegregation ruling. So, of course, is the concept of a meaningful education for every citizen regardless of his origin. Where, then, does the past cease and the present begin? It is difficult to say, precisely. The more we learn of history, the more we find that events of the present are but continuations of forces set in motion long ago. The more we come to know our institutions—social, political, legal, religious, economic—the more they emerge not so much as products of this age as the offspring of earlier systems.

To opt for a purely "now" view of American education, or of any current phenomenon, is to remain unaware of how much the present is but a metamorphosis of preexisting conditions—and how much the outlines of the future, though certainly amenable to the effects of present action, have already begun to be shaped.

What factors caused early American schools to develop along lines different from those of their European counterparts?

3

What precedents are there in our educational system for community control of schools?

How did the present pattern of elementary-secondary-higher education organization develop in America?

What provisions have been made for the education of ethnic and racial minority groups and for women during the course of American education?

What sorts of moral and ethical motivations have guided American educators during our history?

Does the advent of federal funding to education portend a shift in authority for our educational system?

Country Schoolmaster of the Nineteenth Century

Thomas Woody

Change in culture is always confronted by society as a mixed blessing. There are those who would have us believe the "good old days" were golden and present day life is wracked by decadence. Thomas Woody (1891–1960), who was a professor of education at the University of Pennsylvania, believed this nostalgia is a common human affliction which has a special meaning to teachers when the remembrance is turned back to the little red schoolhouses of yesteryear and the teachers who "kept" school in them. This is a story based upon the recollections of a nineteenth century schoolmaster, as personally told to Professor Woody. In addition to vividly recounting memorable experiences in his teaching career, the old schoolmaster also tells about his own education as a child during the 1870's and 1880's.

It is now [in 1929] fifty-five years ago that I first entered the public schools of Pennsylvania, in the little village of Springville, now Florin. The experiences related of going to school in the early seventies and eighties, the trials of teaching, the methods, discipline, buildings, mode of recitation, the teachers who taught me, and other matters, are vivid memories and can be verified.[1]

5

The village was mainly Pennsylvania Dutch, of whom I am a descendant. At the age of six I was scarcely able to speak a word of English. We lived about a block from the school. The building was an old moss-covered structure, built long before my entry. It was of brick and had three windows on each side and a door at one end. There were no cloak rooms, but a row of hooks to the right and left of the door, where hats and coats were hung, often three deep. If one kept his own wearing apparel for the whole term, he was lucky.

The seats were plain pine board benches; the desks, of the same material, had plain tops, with backs raised about two inches above the top. Legs were two by four uprights, fastened to the floor. Two sat at each desk; a partition inside it was designed to keep books and materials of pupils separate. The floor was oak boards, split and rough hewn. Walls were partly wainscoting. The "blackboard" was painted on the walls; slate, just coming into use, was opposed as a too expensive luxury. The rest of the walls and the ceiling were plastered with a mixture of lime, sand and clay, and white-washed about twice a year, at the beginning of the term in autumn and again at holidays. There were no blinds; but outside shutters, partly closed, kept out sun-glare; when entirely closed, to keep out cold and wind, the room was so dark, it was almost impossible to see to work, unless the oil lamps hanging on the wall were lit.

The school had forty or fifty pupils. The boys sat on one side of a wide aisle, the girls on the other. A platform ran across the front of the room. Long benches stood against the wall, where the class reciting was seated. The teacher usually turned his back to the recitation he was hearing; it was not safe to turn his back to the rest of the school, for some culprit would try "heathen tricks" on him; and if he went to the other end of the room, the reciting class would make trouble. Teaching by moral influence had not yet superseded the hickory rod.

Little pedagogy and less psychology were used. A recitation—geography, for example, covering the United States, its location, extent, and development—was conducted as follows: the lesson was assigned; questions, numbering often twenty or thirty, came at the end of the chapter. If the class had ten pupils, it was easy for us to learn the lesson. The pupil at the head of the class learned No. 1, the next one No. 2, and so on to the tenth; the first then studies No. 11, and so on through the entire list. Each had his question and answer well studied, and a perfect recitation could be recorded. It seems not to have occurred to the teacher to vary the order of the recitation. Routine dominated method; it went over big, it was easiest for teacher and pupil alike; it was followed in all subjects having questions and answers. That was the day of formal teaching. Variations were avoided. Originality was frowned upon. Promiscuous asking of questions was taboo; the child had no right to think; he was to do just what the teacher said.

In a school where thirty-one classes were heard in about 300 minutes—an average of about ten minutes to a class—little more could be expected than a rapid question and answer period. The same routine obtained in all classes. In arithmetic the pupil solved his problem, read it from the board, was excused, another was called on, and so on to the end; a new lesson was assigned, and the class was dismissed, either by taps on a bell or counting one, two, three—stand, pass, sit. Seldom did the teacher explain the lesson; his object was to get through the day and cover all the ground. This continued throughout the year; at the end of six months we had often "gone through" the book twice. In one term we even "went through" the same book three times.

Until I was fifteen, while I was at this type of school, I had "gone through" my grammar, arithmetic, geography, speller, and the rest, a dozen times or more. There were no "grades" or "promotions" then. You were placed by the book you were reading. In my first three years I had completed my Third Reader; at twelve or thirteen I reached the Fifth and Sixth. We used Sander's, McGuffey's and Swinton's readers; Appleton's were more difficult, and I read the Fifth Reader several years. Tests or examinations were never held. If we did what was in the book, it was a mark of perfect scholarship, and that was all that was required.

When eight years old, I was afflicted with a malady which crippled me badly, so I could not play games, or move rapidly. It grew worse; I had to use crutches; for seven years there seemed no prospect of recovery, and I was threatened with spinal paralysis. Finally, after much deliberation and opposition, an operation at Jefferson Hospital saved me from the blighting effects of deformity, and enabled me to carry on my profession, though always incapacitated for physical labor.

Due to poverty, I was compelled to learn some trade; and my illness dictated that it should be something I could do with my hands while my body remained quiet. My cousin, A. B. Kreider, was both teacher and cigar-maker—which was not contrary to the ethics of that time. After long consultation with my mother, it was decided I should become his ward, attend his school, and learn cigar-making at the same time. I began the trade in the spring of 1884, and entered his school that fall. I worked morning, noon, and night, attending school from nine to twelve and one to four. After supper I applied myself to my books by the kitchen stove, with the aid of a kerosene lamp, often till one and two o'clock next morning. Summers, I spent the day in the shop, and read at night, chiefly history, for my benefactor had a good library for that time. Thus I was occupied from 1884 to 1888.

It was at Salunga Public School, under the solicitous teaching of my cousin, that I prepared, during the winter of 1887–1888, to become a teacher. I remained in his school till I was twenty. For three months I went to night school. In day school I studied the common branches; [2] at night school, I read and recited pedagogy and several advanced studies. After school closed in March, I was tutored for my first county teachers examination, which came in June, 1888.[3]

On my way to the examination I met the County Superintendent, M. J. Brecht. We walked a half mile together from the train, and I have no doubt I won his sympathy, which may have stood me in good stead. There were then no uniform State examinations. The County Superintendent, chosen by the trustees of the school district, was the sole authority. At nine o'clock, the mill began to grind—operated by one-man power, the Superintendent. The first subject was arithmetic. The Superintendent read a set of questions, prepared in advance in his office or propounded extemporaneously. About forty minutes were allowed to solve them. There were problems in mental arithmetic, to be solved on the spot, and on one's feet. Sometimes only the method of solution was called for. When each candidate finished one examination, his papers were taken up, read, and graded then and there by the official. All the nine common branches were treated the same way during the day.

At last the end approached. At four o'clock we would know our fate. If one passed, his name was called, and a certificate was handed him. If he failed, his name was not called, which saved some embarrassment. The subjects were rated 1, very good; 2, good; 3, middling.[4] If the sum total were more than twenty-four, no certificate could be issued. Percent grades were not then popularized in Lancaster County. Later, when I followed Greeley's advice and went West, my Ohio certificate, issued in 1891, used percents. My total the first time was 23¾. If I had added a quarter to my total, my hopes would have received a rude shock; but I lowered my integers and raised my standard enough so that I was on the road I longed to travel. I still treasure my first three certificates.

Thus armed, I was ready, whether "qualified" or not, to enter upon the noblest work of man. The preparation I then had at the age of twenty might now be matched by a pupil in Junior High School. My first school was a man's job—sixty-four pupils, ranging from six to twenty, more than half being under ten years of age—but I set to work with serious intent to apply my little store of pedagogy and psychology.

Getting my first school proved to be an experience never to be forgotten. After receiving a certificate, one looked for a school—unless it had been promised earlier on condition of passing. I had no such promise, but the County Superintendent suggested several places to look up. I selected one and notified the Board I would present myself.

A word on the administration of common schools may be useful. Lancaster County had township organization. The township I first taught in had forty districts, all under the direction of six school trustees, chosen annually. Each trustee had an area, or number of schools under his oversight, and he reported to the Board each month. At such meetings the trustees also examined teachers' reports and paid their salaries. The Board could be quite autocratic, might disregard even the suggestions of the County Superintendent, for he himself held office at their pleasure.

The Board I approached wanted a "man" teacher. They met on a Saturday in August (1888), twenty days before the beginning of school, to hire the teacher. These six representatives of the community were indeed an august body—but their names are all forgotten now, save those of the president and one other. It was with some trepidation that I came before this body, for they met in the back end of a barroom in the village of Schoeneck. As I entered the room, I met the gaze, the inspection, and then the quiz of these patriarchs of education.

I had applied in writing for a school a short way from the village, and the application was filed here with others. When I was seated at one end of the long table around which the Board sat,

I was asked by the chairman whether I believed in the "three
R's"; but he, to relieve me of any fear, at once assured me they
stood for "Radcliffe's Ready Relief." Of course, they had already
read the applications and had really decided by a previous vote to
let me have the school at the munificent salary of $28.00 [5] a
month for a term of six months. I was to be my own janitor, sweep
out, and keep fires going. But before I was to sign the contract, a
surprise awaited me.

"Mr. Domer," the President began, "we have decided to give you
the M—— School, and we think you are all right. Now since one
good turn deserves another, we think you ought to set up the
drinks to us for the favor; so if you want to sign the contract,
go and bring a bottle of whiskey and six glasses for us, and we
will then close the deal." The Almighty was witness to such an
act, no doubt. With disgust and dejection I acted on the suggestion
of the venerable President of the Board. That a body of men
could be so enslaved to drinking on all occasions, and to bind a
contract by treating a set of men in the deal, was indeed dumb-
founding to me, an incident in my young life that I can never
erase. For I had been under the tutelage of a radical prohibition-
ist, and had signed the temperance pledge on the sixth of May,
1886, which I have kept all these years.

Nevertheless, I turned on my heel and went to the barroom;
there, across the bar were handed me a bottle and six small
glasses. Returning to the room with the loaded tray, I placed
it on the table in front of the President of the Board. He acted as
host to the rest of them, poured six glasses full, passed one to
each of the members, and all drank to my success as a teacher,
swallowing all at one gulp, without even a twitch of the mouth, so
habituated to liquor were these men. When they had all drunk,
I took the tray-load back to the bartender, who took my word for
it that only six glasses full were used. I paid him sixty cents for
the drinks, the price of my contract. When I returned, they told
me I was a good sport, and could now sign the contract, as they
had already done. Seating myself next to the clerk of the Board,
I attached my signature. Many reflections have come and gone
since I traded six glasses of whiskey for a teacher's contract.
Nothing like it has happened to me from that day to this. Whether
it happened so to other young men who sought positions, I do not
know. The moral effect on me was profound. Raised in a home
which was opposed to strong drink of any kind, and tutored by a
man who was a leader in the anti-whiskey forces, I felt I had

done wrong; but as I was not a professing Christian at the time, and I was anxious to get a school, I soon cleared my conscience and started on the first Monday in September to teach school.

I chose a place to room and board a few days in advance of opening school. It was about three-fourths of a mile away, and I covered the distance, walking, or catching a ride when possible. In sloppy weather I wore high top rubber boots, changed to shoes at school, and wore the boots home in the evening. Board, room, and washing cost $10.00 a month.[6] It was an old-fashioned farm home, and one lived with the family. There was plenty to eat, a good bed (a wooden bedstead, rope springs, straw mattress, feather ticks, and blankets), and woven carpets on the floor. Wood and an old-fashioned cookstove furnished heat for kitchen, dining room, and all the rest of the house, upstairs and down. Hot water was provided by a tea kettle and a reservoir in the stove itself.

I went to the schoolhouse alone the Saturday before school began. The building, located on an acre for a playground, was not significantly different from the one where I first went to school. It was of brick, dirt cheap, burned in a nearby kiln for the purpose. Aesthetics had not yet taken root among patrons, trustees, or teachers. The inside was as dull as a leaden sky in December, save as it was sometimes brightened by leaves in autumn, or some pictures that could be borrowed from the pupils' homes. The desks were a little better than I had first used at school, but single seats had not yet appeared. The double-seated desks were a source of trouble: they induced whispering, idle mischief, neglect and dishonesty in studies; books got mixed up, articles were stolen, and property destroyed. I counted the seats, made up a tentative programme, set the clock, put shoe mats in place, had two water buckets (one for waste, for there was no drain) and two tin cups ready for thirsty children. Sanitary rules were then unknown in country districts, and often in small towns, too. Water was brought from the nearest farmer's well. With sixty children, a bucket full would not last long. Sometimes trustees paid a monthly tax to the farmer for the water used at school. Toilets were outdoors, and exposed to public view. A partition separated boys and girls. Obscenity was bound to result from such conditions. More than one problem arose from this source to confront me in my early teaching.

Monday, the first day of school, came. It was with no little emotion that I faced a small army of motley-dressed boys and girls. They had arranged themselves in two rows of about equal length along the pathway, and I had to run the gauntlet of inspection. No sooner was the door opened than a rush for seats was made; for it was customary there, that the first arrivals should have the choice of seats. One can imagine the tumult: about sixty pupils, six to twenty, dashing through the door before I could say "Stop!" Such a scramble meant that half the seats were unsuitable to those who first claimed them, so teacher's job, and a lot of trouble it was, too, loomed before him. But with a show of being master, after an hour's work the "seating" of the school was completed, the small ones up front, the rest according to size, reaching back to the rear.

Classifying pupils was the next task that taxed my ingenuity. I had them write their names, if they could, and the Reader they were "in" at the previous school term. This showed me at once who were the writers. Some who could not write, printed their names. The beginners were interviewed personally, to get their names. These would be the A B C class. Placing the others was more difficult. Some brought an advanced Reader, but could not read it at all, when put to the test. The promotions and demotions made some parents glad and others mad; mothers came and wanted their children changed. I made enemies the first day. I was obdurate; I was running the school, and I would not change pupils unless I was convinced they could do the work that was assigned them. I handled some cases by calling the pupils to read in the presence of their parents, who could then see and hear the child could not read, or do the other work of the class they had wanted to enter. The oldest pupils, whose records I could learn from the register left by my predecessor, I simply directed to the programme placed earlier on the blackboard.

The programme went like this: I opened with Bible reading, repeating the Lord's Prayer, and singing a familiar song. Then came, first, the beginners; then arithmetic; reading classes; grammar, elementary and advanced; geography; history; physiology; and finally three or four spelling classes. The beginners recited three or four times a day; altogether thirty-three classes were heard in about 310 minutes, an average of less than ten minutes to each.

Rules, all of which I thought very necessary at the time, were posted in a conspicuous place for the observation of all. Among them were: no whispering, sharpening pencils, throwing stones, name-calling. They were to raise their hands when anything was wanted; they were to stand, pass, and be seated, as I counted one, two, three, or tapped a small bell. All seemed sensible then, but they appear nonsensical now. The most ridiculous rule I made was that no German should be spoken on the playground at recess; and no swearing, either in German or English, would be permitted. My intentions were good, I tried to enforce the rules I made; but my pedagogy was bad. I went at teaching character the wrong way. I soon saw my entire code was out of place, and I learned to put children on their honor more and more, charging them with only two things: do right, and make life worth while. These I tried to exemplify before them. But the public moral atmosphere was very much lower then than it is today. Children's conduct was not so well looked after as it is now; and pupils were not so independent and self-reliant as they are today.

The school classified, programme and rules posted, I was ready to teach. One of my first difficult problems was due to the community, which was Pennsylvania Dutch. More than half the children were unable to speak a word of English, and did not understand English words even when they read them. How could it be otherwise? They spoke Dutch or German at home; and all the religion they knew was in German. Doubtless many a Pennsylvania German felt as did the old man who insisted, *Der Herr Gott war ja deutsch*—The Lord God was indeed German. To the beginners, then, I was the interpreter of a foreign tongue, not just a teacher of written forms for a language already known by daily use. I devised my own method. As I happened to be a good artist, I would draw pictures on the "board"—a hat, a fly, a moth, a ball, a knife, etc., write the Pennsylvania Dutch names shouted by the pupils (they seemed to like the pictures) and then the English terms. Thus I helped each one to the English for various objects, increasing their vocabulary.[7]

As for other teaching, I followed a method my mother had used forty years earlier, the same by which I had myself been taught. We memorized the alphabet and the "a–b's"—combining all the vowels with the twenty-two consonants, thus: *ab, eb, ob, ub; ac, ec, ic, oc, uc; ad, ed, id, od, ud;* and so on through the alphabet. However nonsensical it may seem now, it was then considered a splendid method, and was exhibited on the pages of many a textbook. This was formal discipline with a vengeance; if a child could remember this, he could very well remember a lesson in spelling, reading, history, or any other fundamental subject. As a good method, it had the stamp of approval of the County Superintendent and other pedagogical leaders of the day, though it seems "devilish" to critics now.

When *ab, eb, ec,* and so on had been learned, pupils went to the First Reader, and learned to use words in sentences. The name of the letter was essential then. When *A* was put on the "board" it meant *A,* and not another sound. *O, Y, T* meant *O, Y,* and *T.* If a child saw *TOY* on the board, he spelled it out, naming the letters, and then pronounced the word. Phonics were unknown; if we had tried to introduce such "tomfoolery," it would have brought the wrath of parents on our heads. In every word he built, the pupil must know the letters; no one was allowed to read unless he knew his letters forward, backward, and crosswise. Reading was not dramatized, one read to increase vocabulary, and to see who could read farthest without a mistake, noticing all the *marks.*

In geography the question and answer method was thought the best. Map study was an art. Every town, city, river, mountain peak, bay, gulf, lake, island, straight, isthmus, peninsula, and sea were hunted up. It was a contest in acquiring information. "Trapping" was a game in every class; the one who could stand at the head of the class longest was the best scholar. History was a matter of chronology, as many old textbooks show. Arithmetic was extremely formal; the one who got the answers to the most problems was the best mathematician. I myself committed almost all the problems of a Mental Arithmetic to memory, together with the answers for each. It was a feat to be proud of! It was a day of memorizing; not much reasoning was sought or developed.

Grammar was chiefly the committing of the parts of speech, conjugations, and paradigms to memory. We went through the modes and tenses of every regular and irregular verb. Parsing [8] and diagramming were a mental acrobatic stunt. It was pure memory drill. Writing compositions was a Friday afternoon exercise, not a regular curriculum subject. It was chiefly to increase vocabulary, not for literary value. No one thought of having children read good books, tell stories, write narratives, or descriptions, or dramatize a scene from life. Such things, if tried, would have been criticized violently and reported to the School Board as proof of a lack of sense and the qualifications of a good teacher. Children went to school to "learn," not to be entertained.

Penmanship was simply drill in following a copy. Each pupil had a Spencerian copybook, or the teacher wrote a "copy" to follow—often a very fine model, expressing good moral precepts to be followed in later life. The Palmer system came into use later, then the vertical system—and a ruinous system it was. Finally there came scales to measure the quality of writing.

Thus my first three years were spent practicing what I thought was common sense in teaching: committing the rules of grammar, the rules of arithmetic and of spelling, and the location of every mountain and molehill in the United States to memory. I knew little or nothing of principles of pedagogy or laws of psychology, except the little gained from reading a few books. While pedagogy classes were offered in Normal School,[9] I had not attended such an institution before beginning to teach. Hence my knowledge was extremely limited. I passed from the rural school to the small town school, where "grades," "method," and "psychological teaching" were unknown. It was just a question of the smartest pupil going on to higher classes as fast as he could make them.

Discipline was a large part of the old school. No other phase of teaching has undergone such a thorough change. Discipline, when I began teaching, depended more on physical strength, the ability and the will to give punishment, than any other thing. One of the first questions I was asked upon applying for the school, was whether I believed in "licking," and whether I was afraid of the boys in school. A negative answer to the first question, or an affirmative answer to the second, would have ended my career then and there.

The kind of school one had was a reflection of the government and discipline he employed. In my own school days it was not uncommon to see a large bundle of "hickories" behind the teacher's desk ready for use. I cannot even estimate the number of punishments I received with the "rod"; but I can well remember some of them, administered by a strong arm, justly or unjustly. It was not uncommon forty or fifty years ago for a master to wear out a heavy "hickory" on an obstreperous boy, or even a girl, as I have seen. I vividly recall one occasion, a real fight between a teacher and a pupil, resulting from the teacher's attempting to thrash a large boy. Teacher and pupil both "went to the mat," and fought from the desk to the door, while smaller children crouched in fright under seats, or ran to the older ones for protection. The teacher came out second best, with bruised face and torn clothes, while the bully walked out of the room with an oath on his lips. Nothing was done to either pupil or teacher; it was purely a matter of discipline. If the teacher could not "handle" the boys, he must resign; and if a boy did not like the teacher's rule he could take a licking or leave school. But sometimes he did neither. This particular young ruffian never came back to school.

As for my own school, much of my time was spent showing boys, and girls too, how strong I was, and what feats of strength I could perform. It was a day of weight-lifting! I became adept at lifting with my arms and gripping with teeth and hands. It was no small trick to place a twenty-five pound bag of shot on my left shoulder, and then reach my right hand over my head and lift the weight single-handed to the right shoulder. I moved the big stove around the schoolroom, held pupils in or out of the room by bracing myself against them in the doorway; let the pupils hang on my arm, extended against the wall; had pupils strike my chest; lifted heavy objects on the school grounds, and did feats of strength at neighborhood gatherings, such as lifting bags of wheat with my teeth, and wheeling heavy loads in a wheelbarrow. These I did when "living round" with patrons of a district.

By such demonstrations I showed I would be physically able to punish boys as old and big as I was, and the girls too, for they were sometimes hard to keep obedient to the rules laid down. It was sometimes necessary to demonstrate competence. I did not hold to the notion that it was always necessary to thrash pupils to make them mind, but it was sometimes necessary, seemed a fairly effective remedy, and, in fact, was mandatory from headquarters. Several teachers had been run out before I came. Laws governing conduct of pupils in the late eighties, save by such means as have been named, were not thought of, and the teacher had to be a law unto himself when emergencies demanded quick action.

The last school I taught at in Pennsylvania was chiefly of boys, and they were hard to handle. Coming, as they did, from a community that had little culture,[10] and composed mostly of pioneers and sons of first and second generations, it was necessary for me to do more fighting and to use more physical punishments in this school than I had in the two years before. Some boys came from homes of veriest ruffians. Belligerent and rebellious towards school discipline, I could not have dared to show the white feather.

They would not hesitate to "double team" the teacher, as they had the year before. But I was on guard. With vigilant eye, I was constantly on watch for any concerted action of these fellows.

One day, towards the middle of the term, I saw a move was on foot to play horse with me in a spelling class. Every word that came to a group of boys was misspelled; after the second round, I pronounced the same word to the same boys, and they all misspelled it again. I then told them that if they missed another word during that recitation, I would thrash every one of them individually. I meant what I said. I placed a large "gad" [11] where I could reach it, and I put the stove-poker next to it, to let them know that I would be boss, even if I had to kill some of them. Things moved along very quietly after that, and I finished the term "to the satisfaction of the trustees."

But I could not reconcile myself to such teaching, where one had to declare war on incorrigibles. Patrons offered to make up five dollars extra pay, over the regular salary of forty dollars; but I had "Western fever," and turned down all inducements. I exercised such discipline for three years in the public schools of Pennsylvania, never lacking the courage to put it into execution when needed. But times have now changed; no more does a teacher have to be a branch of the War Department to teach successfully.

Search for Freedom: The Story of American Education

R. Freeman Butts

What kind of education will best develop the free citizen and the free person? This is the persistent question that runs through the story of American education. It has been answered in different ways at different times in our history. It is still being debated vigorously, and sometimes angrily, today.

This question is so important that every American—and above all, every student and teacher—should make it his business to learn all he can about it. The first requirement is a knowledge of the history of American education. Here are some of the fundamental questions that mark the highlights of the story:

What kind of schools and colleges will promote maximum freedom in society?

To what extent should a free society encourage public schools in contrast to private schools?

Is freedom better served by religious schools or by secular schools?

Is a free society better served by local control or by central control of schools?

Should a free society maintain common schools and colleges open equally to all, or should it divide students into separate schools and colleges according to their race, religion, social class, prospective vocation, or intellectual ability?

What kind of educational program will promote maximum freedom for all individuals?

Should schools and colleges stress practical training or purely intellectual studies?
Should schools and colleges offer students preparation for many vocations or for just a few?
Should educational methods stress learning by direct experience or by reading books?
Should a liberal education be designed for a few or for the many?

If we can understand some of the major answers given to these questions during our history, we shall be on the way to understanding the central idea of American education.

Education Under Colonial Rule (1600 to 1770's)

For nearly 175 years the source of governmental authority for the American colonies was the crown and parliament of England. The colonists were, however, ruled locally by legislative assemblies or by individual proprietors, or by royal governors who received their authority from the English government in London.

This authority included jurisdiction over education. From the very beginning of American history, education was a function of government. It continued to be so after the states were independent.

The various colonies, however, handled educational matters differently. In the New England colonies, the governing bodies not only exerted general authority over education but also established, supported, and directly administered their own schools.

For example, the colonial legislature of Massachusetts passed a law founding Harvard College in 1636; in the following years it took hundreds of actions concerning the college. In the 1630's, the governments of several towns in New England established schools under their direct jurisdiction and supervision.

In 1642 the colonial legislature of Massachusetts passed a general educational law applying to all parts of the colony. It required all parents to see that their children were taught to read, learn the major laws, know the catechism, and learn a trade. It authorized and required the town officials to see that parents obeyed the law and to levy fines upon those parents who disobeyed.

In 1647 the Massachusetts legislature passed a second law, this time requiring all towns of fifty or more families to appoint a teacher and permitting the towns to pay him out of public taxes if the people so voted. Such a teacher was to teach reading and writing. (We would call him an elementary-school teacher.) Furthermore, the law of 1647 required towns of one hundred or more families to appoint a teacher of Latin grammar. (We would call him a secondary-school teacher.)

The New England version of state authority in education came to this: The colonial government could require parents to have their children educated; the central government of the colony could require local towns to appoint teachers (establish schools) ; public funds could be raised by taxation to pay the teachers; and public teachers were subject to direct supervision and control by governmental authorities (either the town meeting as a whole or the selectmen or the education committee).

In the Southern colonies the colonial governments had the same legal authority to legislate on educational matters, but they did not pass laws requiring *all* children to be educated. They rather assumed, as in England, that any parent who could afford to educate his own children should do so by making individual arrangements with a private tutor or by sending them to a private school.

The Southern legislatures, however, did pass laws requiring that poor children and orphaned children be apprenticed to a trade and taught the rudiments of reading and religion by their masters.

The governmental attention in the South was directed mainly at lower-class underprivileged children who had no parents or whose parents could not care for them. Even so, the parish or county governments sometimes legislated on educational matters through their boards of vestrymen or magistrates.

Some efforts were even made in the colonial legislatures of Maryland, South Carolina, and Virginia to establish colony-wide systems of public schools. These were unsuccessful, not because there was no governmental authority for education, but because the people at that time did not believe they were necessary.

In the Middle Colonies the same governmental authority was used by the Dutch to establish public schools in New Netherland and by the Quakers in Pennsylvania. But a more tolerant policy toward religion had attracted several different religious denominations to these colonies.

Each group wanted its own religious principles taught in its own school. It was consequently more difficult to teach a single religious outlook in a public school open to children of different faiths than it had been in New England, where most people were Congregationalists, or in the South, where most people were Anglicans.

In the eighteenth century the colonial governments began to permit the different religious groups to establish their own schools in which they could teach their own religious doctrines and their own languages (whether German, Dutch, French, or Swedish). In this way the state gave to religious and charitable bodies the right to conduct schools.

In like manner the colonial governments began to grant charters to small groups of businessmen or landowners. An educational charter gave these groups the right to incorporate as a board of trustees. They could then buy land, build buildings, appoint teachers, and generally manage a school.

Some of these corporate schools came to be known as "academies." One of the most famous was the Philadelphia Academy founded in 1751 by Benjamin Franklin. Others were the Newark Academy in Delaware, the Washington Academy in New Jersey, and the Dummer Academy and Phillips Academy in Massachusetts.

These incorporated academies made education attractive and available to children of middle-class merchants who could afford the tuition. At first it was unclear whether these denominational schools and incorporated academies were private or public schools, but eventually they came to be known as "private" schools in American terminology.

Other private schools were run by individual teachers as profit-making, business enterprises. In the seacoast cities of the eighteenth century these private teachers began to give young people direct preparation for jobs in commerce and trade. In general, the private-school teacher accepted or rejected students as he pleased. He charged what fees he could get, and he managed his affairs as he saw fit—so long as he had enough students to stay in business.

By contrast, the "public" school in the eighteenth century was a nonprofit school under the supervision of a governmental agency or a corporate board of control. The parents had the right to send their children to it; the governing body set the fees and employed the teacher. Hence a "public" school was not run for the teacher's private profit.

The standards of curriculum were established and the achievement of pupils evaluated by the board of control, whether governmental or corporate. Later on, the corporate school came to be known as a "private" school because it was not operated directly by a governmental board.

In the seventeenth century the "public" or town schools of Massachusetts, Connecticut, and New Hampshire taught the doctrines of a specific religion, that is, Congregational Calvinism. This was so because the Congregational church was established by the law of the legislature in those colonies.

This practice, known as "an establishment of religion," was common throughout Europe in the sixteenth and seventeenth centuries. The laws of the state required all people to accept the doctrines and rituals of the established church and authorized punishment for those who objected. The law levied taxes on everyone to support the ministers of the established church or churches. The Church of England, for example, was the established church in several of the Southern colonies; therefore, orthodox Anglicanism was taught in their schools.

But in the course of the eighteenth century, the idea of religious freedom gained great headway in the American colonies. This meant that such minority religious groups as Quakers, Presbyterians, Baptists, Dutch Reformed, Lutherans, Methodists, Mennonites, and others gained freedom to worship as they pleased. As a result, such groups did not wish to send their children to town schools where the children would be obliged to accept a religion in which they did not believe. The established churches would not at first consent to the removal of their religion from the public schools.

The solution in the eighteenth century was to permit the minority religious groups to establish their own schools. This meant that private religious schools could operate alongside the public schools. Although the public schools were weakened, this arrangement contributed to freedom at a time when the majority religious groups insisted that the public schools teach *their* religion and *only* their religion.

A few voices began to argue that if public schools did *not* teach a sectarian religion then all children could attend them freely. This was argued by William Smith in Pennsylvania, by William Livingston in New York, and by Thomas Jefferson in Virginia.

But the time was not yet ripe for such a solution. Although it was a gain for freedom to permit people to pursue their own way in religion and education, most people were not yet convinced that *others* should have the same freedoms *they* had. Nor were they convinced that an education separated from specific religious doctrines was desirable. The search for freedom continued.

Meanwhile, as people moved out of the New England towns and cities into the unsettled lands of the country, they could no longer send their children long distances back to the town schools. They therefore began to set up their own local schools. This was the origin of the "district" school.

Representing the ultimate in local control, the district system reflected a decline in central state control of schools as the eighteenth century came to a close. This system had the advantage that it kept the schools close to the people, but it had the disadvantage that some districts ran low-quality schools or none at all. Local control was no guarantee that the quality of schools would be uniformly high.

At the end of colonial rule, common schools in which children of different religions or races learned together were still the exception. It was generally felt that schools should perpetuate the religious or cultural beliefs of the sponsoring agency. Some groups did go so far as to try to set up schools for Indians. Few but Quakers tried to do so for Negroes.

Seldom was it argued in colonial times that the aim of education was to empower every individual to make the most of himself as a person. The first system of education set up in America served to maintain the class distinctions imported from Europe.

Children of poor, lower-class parents had no education at all or were bound out as apprentices to learn a trade. Children of upper-class parents (public officials, clergymen, wealthy landowners) were expected to have an education appropriate to their station in life. The New England colonies broke this pattern somewhat when they required the towns to provide a minimum amount of education for *all* children.

Not all children actually received an education, but the principle was established that a commonwealth must rest upon an educated citizenry even if the education amounted only to bare literacy. Added to this was the Protestant belief that all adherents to the true faith should be able to read the Bible for themselves so that they could know the grounds and reasons for their faith. In any case, the New England town schools went a long way in seeing that a large number of their children received some education. This was the first step toward an education for freedom.

Learning to read, write, recite the catechism, and possibly do some arithmetic was the essence of a beginning or elementary education. In the earliest days, school books were rare and materials were scarce. A common device for teaching reading was a hornbook, a piece of wood with the alphabet and *The Lord's Prayer* on it. The child could carry this around with him until he had learned everything on it.

Somewhat later in the seventeenth century books began to be used; the most famous was *The New England Primer*. This consisted of the alphabet, simply syllables, words, sentences, and stories, all of a religious and moral character. A child may have spent two or three years obtaining this kind of elementary education. Taking the thirteen colonies as a whole, probably only one child in ten went to school at all.

What we would call secondary education was offered in Latin grammar schools. The immediate reason for stress on Latin was that Harvard College required it for admission because the main bodies of knowledge throughout Europe since the days of the Roman Republic and the Roman Empire had been written in Latin.

Even though the common languages of the people (vernaculars) were being used more widely by the sixteenth and seventeenth centuries, it was still the custom for an educated person to know Latin—and some Greek, if possible.

So the Latin grammar school was designed to prepare sons of the privileged classes for college in order that they might eventually enter one of the "higher" professions, such as the ministry, law, medicine, teaching, or simply that of "gentleman." Relatively few in the total population were expected to attain these callings in life. Most were expected to be tradesmen, farmers, workers, mechanics, or servants. For these an elementary education was considered sufficient—or even more than necessary.

In the course of the eighteenth century, however, cities and towns grew rapidly in size, trade and commerce increased, immigration rose, and goods and services were much more in demand than in the seventeenth century.

The cry was heard that the old classical Latin education was no longer appropriate for preparing young people to engage in these new important occupations of making goods, distributing them, and selling them. Education, some said, should become more practical, not solely intellectual or literary.

Two types of intermediate or secondary schools tried to meet this need. Some were "English" schools, so called because they were taught in English rather than in Latin. The instructors tried to offer whatever studies the young people desired, for example, English language; French, German, Spanish, Italian (languages useful for trade) ; mathematics (useful for navigation and surveying) ; commercial arithmetic and bookkeeping (useful in business) ; geography, history, and drawing (useful for leisure).

In the early decades of the eighteenth century these private-venture schools responded to the needs of the growing middle classes (merchants and tradesmen). They gave an education directly aimed at occupations other than the learned professions, and they catered to girls as well as to boys.

A second type of practical school was the academy, which was usually residential and often under the auspices of a religious denomination or a nonsectarian board of control. The curriculum of these schools, at least as proposed by Benjamin Franklin, was likely to be much broader than that of the Latin grammar school. It might include geography, history, science, modern languages, and the arts and music, as well as the classical languages and mathematics.

Both of these types of schools contributed to freedom by increasing the range of occupations for which they gave preparation. In this way an increasing number of young people from all social classes could gain a larger measure of self-direction and improve their position in society. Both types of schools were frowned upon by the classicists, but the academy survived the opposition because it met the needs of the middle classes. It eventually drove the Latin grammar school out of existence.

Meanwhile, the opportunities for college education were expanding. Eight colleges besides Harvard were founded prior to the Revolutionary War. Most of them reflected specific denominational outlooks, and their courses of study were largely linguistic, mathematical, and bookish.

Some outstanding leaders tried to change the character of college studies by stressing the new sciences and social sciences. Among these were William Smith at the College of Philadelphia, William Livingston and Samuel Johnson at the founding of Kings College (Columbia), and Thomas Jefferson at the College of William and Mary.

But the tradition of classical studies supported by religious discipline was too strong for these reformers. Harvard (1636), Yale (1701), and Dartmouth (1769) remained Congregational in outlook; William and Mary (1693) and Columbia (1754), Anglican; Princeton (1746), Presbyterian; Brown (1764), Baptist; and Rutgers (1766), Dutch Reformed. The College at Philadelphia, the only college to be nondenominational at the outset (1755), was a forecast of the future, but it soon came under Anglican denomination.

In general, then, the colonial period saw gains for freedom in the growth of representative government, the spread of religious freedom, and the rise of energetic middle classes of free men in town and country alike. Education tried to respond to these social movements as well as to a growing liberalism in thought and belief.

At the beginning of the colonial period, orthodoxies in theology, philosophy, and politics dominated the schools. Children were looked upon as sinful creatures who could be ruled only by harsh discipline, fear, and unrelenting obedience. By the end of the period, a growing liberalism meant that, here and there, children and adults alike were treated more humanely and less brutally. Human dignity and respect for persons were safer than they had been.

During most of the colonial period, education for developing a free person moved slowly and haltingly. For the most part, education at all levels was concerned as much with moral training as with intellectual training. If anything, the moral was considered more important and closely bound up with orthodox religion. Teachers were expected to conform in their beliefs to the dictates of whatever group controlled the schools. It was seldom argued that the teacher had a claim to deal freely with ideas even though they might be distasteful to the immediate managers of the school.

The founding of nine colleges of liberal arts in the thirteen colonies was a remarkable achievement by men who would be free, but the dominant view was definitely that a liberal education (and thus the educational basis for freedom) was for the few, not for the many. There was reluctance to expand the range of liberal studies beyond the traditional classics, mathematics, and philosophy, even though the explosion of knowledge was already beginning to crackle and pop in the seventeenth and eighteenth centuries.

The notion that education had a clear responsibility for enabling each individual to develop himself to the utmost was beginning to be stated but was not yet widely accepted. Building schools for a colonial society prior to the Revolutionary War was a dress rehearsal for freedom, not the main performance.

A Century of Republican Education [1] (1770's to 1870's)

From the 1770's to the 1870's Americans planned, built, changed, argued about, and fought over the kinds of free institutions that should replace colonial rule. One of these institutions was education. As they set up and operated a republican form of government dedicated to equality, democracy, and freedom, they found that they needed an educational system appropriate to such a government.

In many different ways they said that if a republican government—or society—were to prosper and endure, then the people who elected the government, held office, made laws, enforced laws, and consented to be ruled must be educated as responsible citizens.

James Madison, father of the Constitution and author of the Bill of Rights, put it this way:

A popular Government, without popular information, or the means of acquiring it, is but a Prologue to a Farce or Tragedy; or, perhaps both. Knowledge will forever govern ignorance; and a people who mean to be their own Governors must arm themselves with the power which knowledge gives.

But this was not easy to do. The people who had won the Revolutionary War—these so-called Americans—were not really Americans, at least *not yet*. They were English, Scottish, French,

German, Dutch, Swedish, and a good many more. And they were soon to be Irish, Italian, Hungarian, Polish, and Russian as well. They spoke different languages and they had different customs. Some had no tradition of self-government and others were fiercely proud or jealous of rule by others.

When it was finally decided that they should all learn the same language and the same principles of republican government, how was this to be done?

The answer was that it could best be done by a common school, taught in English, to which all the children of all the people could go together and learn how to live together and govern themselves.

But some people were poorer and some richer; some had good manners and others were coarse and rude. Should *all* these people really be educated?

Yes, they must be—if free government is to endure.

Well, but who is to pay for the poor ones?

Everyone must pay for all. If there are weak spots anywhere, the whole community of freedom is weakened. So the common schools must be supported by taxes paid by all.

All right, but who is to control these schools?

The only institution of a free society which serves everyone equally and is controlled by everyone is the government. So the government should control the common schools. And to keep the schools close to the people, the state and local governments, rather than the national government, should control the schools.

But won't the schools be subject to political and partisan prejudice?

Well, they might be, so we must create something genuinely new, something that will give all the people their say but keep the schools free of narrow, partisan politics. This can be done by a series of local boards of education subject to but separate from the executive, legislative, and judicial branches of government.

These school boards, often elected directly by the people, could constitute a kind of "fourth branch of government." They would exert direct control over local education under the general authority set up by the state governments and subject to guarantees of equality and freedom laid down in the United States Constitution and applying to all Americans.

So far so good, but what about religious education? Don't all these Americans with different religions have freedom to run their own schools under the First Amendment of the Constitution and under their state constitutions?

Yes, indeed, they do. But each American will have to decide for himself whether the education that supports a free society should be conducted in separate schools in which religion provides the fundamental framework for all studies or in common schools devoted primarily to the whole range of free institutions in America. If they decide the first way, the children will be divided into separate schools for their entire education and this division will be along religious lines. If the second way, the children will attend the same public school together for their common education and only be separated for their religious education, which can be conducted as may be desired by the home or by the church or by the synagogue.

In the century of republican education most Americans chose the common school, controlled and supported in common, and embracing a nonsectarian religious outlook.

Their primary concern was to design a universal, free, public school that would promote free institutions and free citizenship. For the first one hundred years of the Republic, the need for creating the common bonds and loyalties of a free community was paramount.

Less attention was given to the claims of diversity and difference as the essence of freedom for individuals. This came later when the Union had been established, made secure against internal opposition, defended against outside invaders, and preserved despite a war between the states themselves.

The republican ideal of the first century of nationhood gave the following answers regarding the control of education: a free society required public elementary schools to provide the basic information, literacy, and moral teachings required by every free man. For most Americans the term "free" was limited to white men, until the Civil War legally introduced Negroes to citizenship. Private elementary schools continued to exist but they were declining in numbers and in importance by the 1870's.

Under the effective and determined leadership of an extraordinary galaxy of "public-school men," the idea of universal common schooling was widely accepted in the new United States during the first half of the nineteenth century. Outstanding among these were Horace Mann and James G. Carter in Massachusetts, Henry Barnard in Connecticut, Calvin Stowe in Ohio, Caleb Mills in Indiana, John D. Pierce in Michigan, Ninian Edwards in Illinois, Calvin Wiley in North Carolina, and Charles F. Mercer in Virginia. These men and others made speeches before thousands of people; wrote hundreds of pamphlets, articles, and reports; organized scores of groups and societies to agitate for common schools; and held dozens of positions in state governments or school systems.

They argued that the payment of tuition for schooling was unfair to children of poor parents, who could not pay for an education. They argued that the older forms of public support, like land grants from the federal Land Ordinances of 1785 and 1787, would not support schools on the vast scale now necessary.

They argued that the term "free school" should no longer mean a school in which only the poor children were given free education and all others paid tuition.

They argued that class distinctions could be lessened only when a "free school" meant that *all* children were given a free education together and when the entire school system was supported by taxes levied upon everyone.

Aiding their efforts were the newly formed labor unions, which demanded that the public schools provide universal education.

The states gradually accepted this idea of a free public school. The state legislatures passed laws *permitting* local school districts to tax themselves for such schools; they sometimes gave state funds to *encourage* local districts to tax themselves; and they finally *required* all local districts to tax themselves and establish public schools.

By these means, the local freedom of districts to ignore schooling for their children gave way to the larger freedom to be gained by a total population enlightened by education of all. Local control by districts was gradually limited by requirements set by state constitutions, state legislatures, state boards of education, and state superintendents of schools. It was decided that a free society would be better served if education were planned by the central authority of the states rather than left wholly to the completely decentralized control of local school boards. This was not done without bitter conflict, for many believed that state, as opposed to local, control would be undemocratic and destroy freedom.

But in the 1820's, 1830's, and 1840's it was decided that a state government, responsive to public control, could serve freedom as well as, if not better than, the hundreds of local school districts could do. If a local district were left free to provide a poor education or no education at all for its children, those children would be deprived of their birthright to an education that would prepare them for free citizenship. Thereby, the state's own freedom would be endangered.

A smaller freedom must be limited in the interests of a greater freedom. And to guarantee the larger freedom, the state must exert its authority to see to it not only that schools were available to all but that all children actually attended school. Massachusetts led the way by passing its compulsory attendance law in 1852.

The solution was a genuinely creative one. Authority for providing education was defined in state constitutions and in state laws. State authority for education was carried out by state superintendents of schools responsible to a state board of education, elected by the people or appointed by the governor. New York State created the office of state superintendent of schools in 1812. Massachusetts established a state board of education in 1837 with Horace Mann as secretary, and Connecticut did likewise in 1839 with Henry Barnard as secretary. Other states followed.

These state agencies could then set minimum standards for all the schools of the state. Meanwhile, the direct management of schools would be left in the hands of locally elected school boards, local superintendents, and locally appointed teachers. Local management served the cause of flexibility, diversity, and freedom.

This arrangement was designed to assure that schools would serve the whole *public* and would be controlled by the *public* through special boards of education, not through the regular agencies of the state or local governments. This is why in America we use the term "public school," not simply "state schools" or "government schools," as they are often called in those countries that have centralized systems of education.

Since the United States Constitution had not mentioned education as a function of the federal government, the free states after the Revolution reclaimed the authority over education that had been the prerogative of the colonial legislatures.

But the United States Constitution and the state constitutions *did* proclaim freedom of religion and separation of church and state as one of the essentials of republican government. That is, neither the federal government nor state governments could interfere in the affairs of churches or use public funds to support them. Therefore, the states could not give public money to schools under the control of churches.

But what about religious instruction in the common public schools? It was soon evident that if common schools taught the doctrines of a particular church they would violate the freedom of conscience of all those who did not agree.

Could the common schools find a common religious outlook

and teach that? Many Protestants thought so. They tried to find the common religious doctrines of Christianity and they found them in the Bible. If the schools would teach only nonsectarian principles of Christianity as contained in the Bible, they argued, all sects would be satisfied. This might have been the case if America had remained exclusively Protestant.

But immigration had brought increased numbers of Roman Catholics and Jews. Besides, many Americans had never officially belonged to any church. Catholics charged that the so-called "nonsectarian" schools were really Protestant in character and that they were therefore sectarian. So Catholics established their own schools and many demanded a share in the public tax funds to support them. Most Protestants and Jews opposed the giving of public money to parochial schools.

Most states finally decided to prohibit any sectarian control over common schools and to prohibit use of public money for private schools under sectarian control. Especially bitter struggles between Protestants and Catholics were decided for the time being by legislation in New York in 1842 and by constitutional amendment in Massachusetts in 1855. Nearly every state had a similar struggle and enacted similar laws.

By the end of the first century of republican education the general decision was that a free society was better served if the majority of children went to common, nonsectarian schools than if they went to separate, sectarian religious schools. This made it possible for the United States to build a universal system of free elementary schools sooner than any other country in the world.

The line of argument went like this: nonsectarianism would provide a greater measure of national unity than could be achieved when each sectarian group shepherded its own children into its own schools. The range of communication among children would be restricted if each group continued to run its own schools differently in religion and language from others. Separate schools would create and perpetuate divisions among the people—thus narrowing their outlooks and reducing free interchange of ideas. Free common schools would more certainly serve the cause of free institutions.

At the end of the first century of the Republic, secondary schools, however, were still largely in private and religious hands. This fact did not seem undesirable to most Americans of that particular period.

The private academies provided considerable opportunity to

those who could afford some education beyond the essentials. Likewise, most of the 200 colleges were under private and religious control. This, too, seemed reasonable to the majority of Americans at that time: Elementary education for all at public expense would be sufficient to guarantee the basic security of a republican government; advanced education for *leadership* in the state and in the professions could then be obtained privately by those who could afford it.

A few spokesmen, however, began to argue that a free society needed "free" secondary and higher institutions as well as free elementary schools. The public high school, for example, appeared as early as 1821 in Boston. The idea spread rapidly, but the public high schools did not dominate the secondary-school field till the late nineteenth century.

Advocates of free higher education tried to transform some of the private colleges into state institutions. This happened at the College of William and Mary in Virginia, at Columbia in New York, and at the College of Philadelphia.

The most notable attempt, however, occurred when the New Hampshire legislature tried to transform Dartmouth College into a state university. But the United States Supreme Court in 1819 (*Trustees of Dartmouth College v. Woodward*) decided that the college was a private corporation and that its charter was a contract which the state could not change unless "the funds of the college be public property."

Following the Dartmouth College decision, private colleges increased in numbers, most of them sponsored by religious denominations. Especially active were Presbyterians, Congregationalists, Episcopalians, Methodists, and Roman Catholics. But the advocates of public higher education also redoubled their efforts. State universities were established in twenty states before the Civil War. The earliest universities to be set up under state control (but not free of tuition) were in Georgia, North Carolina, and Vermont.

The ideal of freedom as a basis for a state university was most eloquently proclaimed by Thomas Jefferson at the University of Virginia, which opened in 1825. In Virginia, as elsewhere, religious groups were bitterly opposed to the state university and tried to prevent its establishment or to divert public funds to their own institutions.

Federal land grants authorized by the Morrill Act in 1862 gave a significant boost to the state-university movement. Funds from these grants were used by the states to establish agricultural and engineering colleges or to strengthen their state universities.

Despite the advocates of free and equal education for all, the era of republican education tried to get along with common schools at the elementary level, but with secondary and higher institutions divided along denominational lines. In general, while the elementary schools served everyone, the academies and colleges and universities catered to the wealthier and upper social classes rather than to the ordinary people.

The major failure to achieve the reformers' goal of a common universal school was the system of segregated schools for Negroes, which appeared occasionally in the North as well as generally in the South. In fact, it was the Roberts case in the Massachusetts Supreme Court in 1849 which set forth the principle that separate schools for Negroes were permissible so long as their facilities were equal to those of the white schools. Charles Sumner's argument that separate schools violated the equal rights of Negroes was rejected by the court, but, even so, Massachusetts and other Northern states moved soon thereafter to abolish their segregated schools by law.

Turning now to the kind and quality of education achieved in the first century of the Republic, we find that the main elements of the common-school curriculum continued to be reading, writing, and arithmetic. These three R's were supposed to give the elements of literacy and the intellectual tools necessary for acquiring the knowledge and "popular information" of which Madison spoke.

But, said the school reformers, the citizen of the new Republic needed more than this—much more. He needed a knowledge of history and geography to instill feelings of patriotism, loyalty, and national pride. He needed moral teachings to instill habits of "republican" character. And he needed some practical studies, like bookkeeping or manual training, so that he could get and keep a job.

The common school was designed to do more than give intellectual training. It was to provide citizenship training, character education, and a means by which every child might advance up the economic and social scale as far as his talents would carry him.

By providing such equal opportunity, the common school would protect free institutions. It would promote progress and prosperity; it would reduce poverty and prevent crime. This was a big order to hand to the schools, but the optimism, energy, and faith of the times all prodded the schools to try to do their share—sometimes more than their share—in making the American dream come true.

The "new" school had to have new methods as well as new subjects. Such school reformers as Joseph Neef and Horace Mann argued that the customary strict discipline, corporal punishment, and slavish memorizing of textbooks were not good enough to carry the burden the school must carry. They therefore argued for the enthusiasm, excitement, interest, and eager learning that could come with a more humane and sympathetic attitude toward children.

Of course, the conservatives charged that the reformers would spoil the children if they spared the rod, but the reformers persisted despite the opposition.

The main trouble was that the teachers were not trained to deal with small children constructively. Would the liberal-arts colleges provide this training? Some proposals were made—at Amherst, at Brown, at Michigan, and elsewhere—that they should do so, but the colleges were not interested. So, entirely new institutions called normal schools were created to give their whole attention to the training of elementary-school teachers.

The first of these were founded as private normal schools in the 1820's by Samuel R. Hall at Concord, Vermont, and by James G. Carter at Lexington, Massachusetts. The first state normal school was opened in 1839 at Lexington, and the idea eventually spread throughout the country.

The normal schools taught young people of high-school age how to teach the elementary-school subjects. Compared with the better colleges of the day, their quality was low, but they made possible the rapid building of the common school systems in the several states. They raised school teaching above the level of incidental apprenticeship and began the process of making it a profession, narrow though the training was in the beginning. If the colleges of liberal arts had been as much interested in school teaching as they were in law, medicine, or other professions, the quality and status of the elementary-school teacher might have been higher much sooner than they were.

The curriculum of the secondary schools also began to respond to the political and economic progress of the times. The academies, replacing the Latin grammar schools, taught a wider range of subjects. Thus, students began to have some freedom of choice of studies. And some academies opened their doors to girls, a notable victory for freedom. By the 1870's some 6000 academies dotted the educational landscape.

But the common-school reformers felt that the private academies could never do the job that needed to be done. They therefore argued that free public high schools should be created to provide a practical education for those boys and girls who would not or could not go on to college.

Offering a practical nonclassical curriculum to youth who could live at home while attending secondary school, the public high school was destined to become ever more popular after the Civil War. It added to the range of vocations for which the schools prepared and in this way opened up possibilities of self-improvement through careers that had never before been within reach of the majority of youth.

Reformers such as George Ticknor at Harvard and Henry Tappan at Michigan also tried to broaden the curriculum of the colleges to make them serve the commercial, business, and political needs of the rapidly growing nation. They wanted to make real universities out of the small colleges.

Classicists put up great resistance against such reforms. Especially powerful was the report of the Yale faculty in 1828, which condemned practical courses and argued that the colleges would continue to stress the mental discipline to be acquired by strict study of Greek, Latin, mathematics, and philosophy.

Colleges should give a *liberal* education, said the Yale faculty, not a vocational education. Colleges should lay the *foundation* for later professional study; they should not give the professional study itself.

By the 1870's the dominant view of higher education came down to this: Liberal education was the only proper education for a free man, but relatively few young men (and no young women) could profit from such a training. Universal education may be all right for the common man, but college education should be reserved for the uncommon man.

The republican ideal of free universal education had not yet been applied to secondary schools or to colleges. The second century of the Republic, the century of democracy in education, did just this.

Nearly a Century of Democratic Education (1870's to 1960)

Whereas the republican ideal had been to provide *some* education for all and *much* education for a few, the democratic goal was to provide *as much education as possible for all*. The keynote of the century of democratic education was "more education for more people." It had its drawbacks, its setbacks, and its ups and downs, but nothing seemed able to stop for long the surge to education as the essence of the search for freedom.

The march to the schools came faster, the lines stretched longer, and the students grew older as the second century of the Republic moved the 1870's to the 1960's. By 1900 the great majority of children aged six to thirteen were in elementary schools; by 1960 over 99 percent were in attendance. Universal elementary schooling for all children had been won.

More remarkable, however, was the march to the secondary schools. By 1900 about 10 percent of children aged fourteen to seventeen were actually in school; in 1930 more than 50 percent attended; and by 1960 nearly 90 percent were attending. This comes close to universal secondary education, something not dreamed of by the republican leaders of the first century of nationhood.

In 1760 the average colonist may have had two to three years of schooling; by 1960 the average American had ten to eleven years of schooling. And the end has not been reached. The average years of schooling will probably go to twelve or even to fourteen within a decade or two.

Still more remarkable was the stepped-up tempo of the march to college. In 1910 about 5 percent of all youth aged eighteen to twenty-one were attending college; by 1960 nearly 40 percent of all such youth were attending institutions beyond high school. Millions more were attending adult-education classes and courses of instruction being offered by business, industry, labor, the armed services, churches, and voluntary agencies. And education by television and other automatic devices had scarcely begun. The potentials were staggering.

How did all this happen and why? The story is complicated, but a few elements are clear. Republican education may have been sufficient for a society marked by a relatively small population scattered over large areas of rich land and relying mainly upon farming and trading for subsistence. But in a society that relied on science and technology, the situation was radically different.

Not only did the leaders, scholars, experts, and professional men need more and better education, but also the kind of education that *everyone* needed grew steadily greater in quantity and higher in quality. For *this* kind of industrial society, a democratic education would be necessary if freedom were to be maintained.

A society based on steam power, electric power, or nuclear power can be managed and controlled by relatively few people. Technical power leads to political and economic power. To prevent autocratic, dictatorial use of political and economic power by a few, everyone must have an education devoted to freedom. There is no other satisfactory way to limit political or economic power.

So it became increasingly clear that the opportunity to acquire an expanded and extended education must be made available to *all,* to the poor as well as to the rich, to the slow student as well as to the bright, to the South and West as well as to the North and East, to girls as well as to boys, to Negroes as well as to whites, to immigrants as well as to the native-born, to Catholic and Jew as well as to Protestant and non-churchgoer.

The century of democratic education took the doctrines of the common school and applied them almost completely to the secondary school and in part to the college. Equality of opportunity stood alongside freedom as the prime goals of education.

Let us see what happened to the organization and control of education in the age of democratic education:

The nineteenth-century solution to the problem of public and private schools came to this: A system of public institutions ranging from primary school to university, open for everyone as long as his abilities justify, is the best guarantor of a free society based upon equality of opportunity. Private institutions are free to operate alongside the public institutions, but these should be supported voluntarily and should not be given public funds.

In the 1870's a series of court cases (especially the Kalamazoo case in Michigan) agreed that the people of the states could establish and support public high schools with tax funds if they so desired. Thereupon the public high-school movement spread rapidly, and the private academy shrank in importance. Furthermore, all states passed compulsory attendance laws requiring attendance to at least age sixteen. Provision of public secondary schools thereupon became an *obligation* of the states, not just a voluntary matter for the local districts to decide.

Children were permitted to attend properly approved non-public schools as a way of meeting state attendance laws. This principle was affirmed by the United States Supreme Court in the Oregon case of 1925 (*Pierce v. Society of Sisters*).

States had the right to supervise, inspect, and set minimum standards for *all* schools and to require children to attend *some* school, but the state could not compel students to attend public schools if their parents preferred private schools. Freedom to have a say in the education of their children was a constitutional right of parents under the Fourteenth Amendment. Besides, private schools were valuable property which could not be destroyed by action of the state without due process of law.

By 1930 the preference of most Americans for public schools was clear; only about 9 percent of children attended nonpublic schools. The public policy hammered out in the nineteenth century was also clear: Public funds should not be used to support private schools. Beginning in the 1930's, however, the clamor began to rise again that the private schools should be given some public aid. Campaigns to get parents to send their children to private schools began to show results.

Today more than 16 percent of children are in nonpublic schools, a gain so spectacular that the American people have to face up to certain questions more directly than at any time since the 1830's: Shall we encourage private schools as well as public schools with public money? Is the present balance among public and private schools about right? If not, should we favor private or public schools?

Through the years, much of the controversy over public and private schools has been basically sectarian. Today more than 90 percent of children attending nonpublic schools are enrolled in parochial schools conducted by the Roman Catholic Church. A whole series of laws and court cases in the nineteenth century decided that religious freedom and separation of church and state meant that the states could not give tax money to support private education. But from 1930 onward, exceptions began to be made.

The Cochran case in 1930 permitted Louisiana to spend tax funds to give free textbooks to children in private as well as public schools; the Everson case in 1947 permitted New Jersey to provide bus transportation for parochial-school pupils; in 1948 the School Lunch Act gave federal money to parochial schools even though state funds could not be so used. Advocates of parochial schools were now arguing that public funds should be used to pay for auxiliary services that benefited the child but were not direct aid to the school as such.

In recent decades, the arguments for diverting public funds to private schools have changed. It is now argued that the states should aid all parents to send their children to the kind of school they wish. This would not aid *schools;* it would aid parents to exercise their freedom of educational choice. So if parents want their children to go to religious schools, they should receive their fair share of tax funds. If they want their children to go to all-white schools, they should receive tax funds to help them do this. Obviously, the whole idea of a common school is now under severe attack.

What the American people will decide in the years to come is in doubt. In fact, the whole idea inherited from republican days that a free society rests upon a common school system maintained and controlled by the free government is in peril.

"Freedom" may come to mean that parents can divide up among themselves the public funds which had originally been designed to support a free educational system which in turn was designed to perpetuate the free society itself. Does freedom of choice for parents mean that the state is obligated to support and pay for that choice?

Such questions as these came to focus sharply in the problem of central and local control. If some towns or regions in a state could not or would not provide good schools for their children, should the children suffer, or should the state try to equalize the burden by giving financial aid to those towns? The answer turned out to be clear: Equalize the burden in fairness to the children.

Most states use tax money, raised all over the state, to support schools in all parts of the state wherever and whenever local property taxes did not provide enough money to operate good schools. Central control in state hands seemed desirable for the purpose.

But what about the federal government? Will the same answer be given? If some *states* cannot or will not provide good schools for their children, should the federal government try to equalize the burden by giving financial aid to the states? If all states try hard, and still some states cannot provide acceptable educational opportunity for all children, should the federal government step in and help out? By and large, the answer thus far has been no; a qualified no, but still no.

To be sure, the Land Ordinances of 1785 and 1787 and other

grants gave millions of acres of land to the states for education; the Morrill Act of 1862 helped establish land-grant colleges; the Smith-Lever Act of 1914 supported agricultural and home-economics instruction; the Smith-Huges Act of 1917 aided vocational education in high schools.

Emergency aid was given in the 1930's, and the National Youth Administration and Civilian Conservation Corps helped youth in the depression; a bill was passed to provide aid for federally impacted school districts; the G. I. Bill of Rights helped millions of veterans of World War II and the war in Korea to get an education; and the National Defense Education Act of 1958 gave loans to students and supported specific programs in foreign-language training, science, guidance, and audio-visual methods.

But up to the [recent] present, the idea of federal-state partnership in public-school support [was] not . . . squarely faced by the federal government.[2] For nearly a hundred years a whole series of bills had been introduced in Congress to achieve this purpose. Beginning with the Hoar bill, Perce bill, and Burnside bill of the 1870's and the several Blair bills in the 1880's, Republicans were the chief advocates of federal aid, but Democrats of the South were afraid that the federal government was trying to punish them and impose Northern ideas upon them.

In the decade between 1950 and 1960 it was the liberal Democrats from the North and West who tried to achieve federal aid, but were thwarted by economy-minded Republicans and by some Southern Democrats who feared federal imposition of integrated schools upon the South. Throughout the century many Roman Catholic leaders opposed federal aid unless it would help parochial as well as public schools.

The race issue, the religious issue, and the economy issue successfully blocked federal aid for decades. After the close of the Civil War, it was touch and go for a while whether federal action would result in equal educational opportunity for Negroes in the South.

The Fourteenth Amendment (1866) guaranteed "equal protection of the laws" to all citizens, but the federal education bills failed and the Civil Rights Act of 1875 was declared unconstitutional. The Southern states proceeded to set up segregated school systems, one system for Negroes and one for whites. The United States Supreme Court decision in *Plessy v. Ferguson* (1896) was taken to mean that separate school systems were permissible provided they had equal facilities.

In the 1940's a whole series of court cases began the process of gaining access for Negroes to the public institutions of the South —first to the universities and then to the schools. The historic decisions headed by the Brown case of May 17, 1954, reversed the "separate but equal" doctrine of Plessy and declared that segregated schools were inherently unequal even if each had "equal" amounts of money spent on it.

In the following years, case after case was taken to court to require boards of education to admit Negroes to the public schools on an unsegregated basis.

Violence, often instigated by outside agitators, broke out in Clinton, Tennessee, and a number of other places; and federal troops were called to Little Rock, Arkansas, when the governor interfered with a federal court order to integrate the schools. Gradually, however, desegregation spread through the border states and by 1960 was being faced in the Deep South.

Some Southern governors and legislatures tried to prevent integration by legal devices. Laws were passed to close the public schools, to give public money to parents so they could send their children to segregated private schools, and even to abolish the public-school system itself.

These actions posed the most serious threat to the ideals of both republican and democratic education it was possible to pose. Does a state have the right to abolish its "fourth branch of government"? What *is* essential to a "republican form of government" (as guaranteed in the United States Constitution) if public education is not? Could the principles of a free society withstand this onslaught safely?

If the demands for private religious education and the demands for private segregated education were joined by economy demands for reducing public-school budgets, the result could be a repudiation of the public-school idea itself and a return to the "voluntary" principle of the sixteenth and seventeenth centuries in Europe: let those have an education who can pay for it; let education be fully private. Or, alternatively: let us divide up the public moneys among competing racial and religious groups so they can set up their own private schools; let us have many free *private* educational systems.

In either of these cases, the central idea of American education would disappear. An unlimited role for free private enterprise in education would take the place of a limited role for free public enterprise. The freedom of segmented voluntary groups to work at cross purposes would replace the freedom of the people as a whole to work through a system of public schools. . . .

Just as the keynote to *quantity* in education for the century of democratic education has been "more education for more people," so the keynote to *quality* in education has been "better education for all." Each decade had its reformers who demanded better education than the schools were then offering, but there has been little agreement concerning what is "better."

Different reformers have demanded different measures at different times. As the times changed, the schools were behind the times for different reasons. Nowhere else in the world have so many people been so much concerned about education so much of the time—and almost never has everyone been satisfied.

No sooner had the elementary schools been established to start six-year-olds on the road to formal schooling than reformers began to argue that we ought to have a pre-school school called the kindergarten. So, borrowing ideas from Friedrich Froebel in Europe, we began to attach kindergartens to the public schools, beginning in the 1870's. The idea was to help children of four to six years learn by directed play activities.

By 1960 most American cities had kindergartens, and some of them had even established nursery schools for two-to-four-year-olds.

The elementary school itself was subject to recurring reforms. No sooner did it make headway in teaching the three R's to every child than someone, outside the schools or in, would urge it to broaden its curriculum: Add drawing and the arts; add geography and history; add nature study; hygiene and physical training; domestic science. And these all seemed reasonable.

The famous Swiss educator, Pestalozzi, had said so; Edward A. Sheldon, founder of the Oswego (New York) Normal School, said so; Francis W. Parker, superintendent of schools in Quincy, Massachusetts, said so. And so said a host of others, including such diverse characters as the presidents of Harvard (Charles W. Eliot) and of Columbia (Nicholas Murray Butler), publicists like Joseph Mayer Rice, social workers like Jane Addams and Lilian Wald, reformers like Jacob Riis and Walter Hines Page.

Social reformers, humanitarians, and philanthropists, especially in the cities of the 1890's, were indignant about the endless memory work that marked most schools. Schools, they said, were far too intellectualistic—they dealt almost exclusively with words and numbers that did not mean very much to the children. They felt that schools should be alive, interesting, exciting, practical, and useful.

This seemed fair enough. John Dewey took up the ideas in his experimental school at the University of Chicago, and Teachers College at Columbia University applied them in its experimental Lincoln School. Eventually "progressive" schools mushroomed on the landscape, and "progressive" ideas became popular in the 1920's and 1930's. Chief among the spokesmen after John Dewey was William H. Kilpatrick at Teachers College, Columbia University.

All sorts of plans were devised to loosen up the formal curriculum and give it life and vitality—units, projects, activities, excursions and visits, handicrafts, gardens, laboratories, audio-visual aids, and much else—anything to overcome the slavish drill on the textbook or notebook. There was little doubt that the general quality of learning for most children was raised as the school added vitality and zest to the learning process.

But in the 1940's and 1950's a new set of "reformers" began to charge that the schools were too soft. Schools, they said, were just letting children play and not teaching them anything. Elementary schools were exhorted to return to the three R's and stiffen up discipline and concentrate on intellectual studies.

Many of the criticisms were overdrawn and unfair, but many had some truth in them. Progressive methods *had* been carried to an extreme by a few spokesmen and by a few teachers who assumed that all children learned better by "direct" experiences, by visits, or by physical activities than they did by reading or writing. A general tightening of school methods was evident by 1960.

Sputnik and Russian education strengthened the critics' hands. But how long would it be before "loosening" and flexibility in the curriculum would again be necessary and a new wave of progressive reform to overcome excessive academic formalism be desirable?

Meanwhile, the controversy over religion in the public schools continued. By the beginning of the twentieth century, most public schools had not only dropped sectarian religious teaching but also much of the nonsectarian religious instruction they had attempted in the early nineteenth century. In other words, although the public schools dealt with moral and spiritual values, they no longer tried to deal with religion at all; they were secular. But after World War II the demand arose again that the public schools restore some kind of religious instruction.

Some Protestants proposed that the Bible be read without comment by the teacher, but Catholics and Jews opposed this as really sectarian. It was proposed that students be given time off from regular classes to receive sectarian instruction from their own religious teachers (released time).

In 1948 the United States Supreme Court in the McCollum decision said that released-time religious instruction could not be given inside public-school buildings, but in 1952 (the Zorach decision) the Supreme Court said it could be done outside schools if the public teachers did not coerce or persuade students to go to the religious classes. Neither of these decisions has satisfied many people. Some educators have proposed that public schools avoid religious instruction as such but undertake factual study about religion right along with the study of 'other regular school subjects, but most religious groups have been cool to this proposal. The formula for honoring religious diversity while still promoting social unity through common schools had not been satisfactorily found.

Reform movements stirred through secondary as well as elementary schools. Most revolutionary reform was the very idea of a secondary school which would accept students of the whole range of ability and try to give all a course of study suited to their abilities and their possible vocations in life.

Most other countries divide children at age eleven or twelve, send a few to academic (college preparatory) schools, others to vocational schools, and the majority directly to work. The American high school, however, has tried to be a comprehensive school, one in which students from all walks of life would study and work and play together. This meant that many new subjects and courses have been added periodically to the high-school curriculum.

The resulting number of elective studies has worried the colleges. As early as 1893 the National Education Association tried to encourage a standardized high-school curriculum. Noteworthy were the efforts of the Committee of Ten (1893) and the Committee on College Entrance Requirements (1899).

These "reforms" stressed those academic studies which should be required for college entrance; namely, four units in foreign language, two in mathematics, two in English, one in history, and one in science. (The relative inattention to science is at least sixty years old.) It was assumed that such studies would be good for all students whether they were headed for college or not. This was fair enough at a time when 75 percent of high-school graduates were going on to college.

But after 1900 the pressures of enrollment on the high schools grew stronger. By 1918 an NEA Committee formulated *The Seven Cardinal Principles of Secondary Education,* in which preparations for college was definitely less important than it had been twenty years before. Now, the high school's aims were to give attention to health, command of the fundamental processes, worthy home membership, vocational preparation, citizenship, leisure-time activities, and ethical character.

This note continued to be emphasized in the 1930's and 1940's. By 1950 about 30 percent of high-school graduates were going to college. Preparation for college had actually become a minor function of the high schools.

However, a new wave of reaction (or was it reform?) began to criticize secondary schools for permitting low academic standards, for not stimulating youth to rigorous study, for letting youth take so-called "easy" courses instead of working hard at the regular academic subjects. The success of Russian space flights and the threat of falling behind in the armament race raised fears that American high schools were not doing their jobs.

Many of the critics did not know what they were talking about, but some did. There was little doubt that many high schools could do a better job for college-bound youth than they were doing. Some high-school educators were still assuming that only a small minority of high-school graduates were headed for college. They had not noticed that by 1960 many more high-school students were expecting to go to college.

It might not be long until we would be back where we were in 1900 with 75 percent of high-school graduates bound for college, but with this vast difference: In 1900 only 10 percent of youth were in high school; today 90 percent are there.

The potential enrollments called for a drastic new look at the secondary school, at both the junior-high and senior-high levels. The first thing the schools did was to give more attention to the academic subjects, especially to the foreign languages, science, and mathematics. The time was ripe, however, for a complete overhauling of the junior-high school, which was just about fifty years old and born in a very different age from that of the 1960's.

Undoubtedly the pressure of high-school graduates upon college doors would lead to even further drastic expansion of junior colleges and other two-year institutions. They too were just about half a century old and, in some ways, the epitome of the democratic movement in American education.

It was being estimated that by the decades following 1970 all students with an IQ of one hundred or over would be finishing at least a two-year college. If this proved to be true, standards of admission to some colleges would go up and in others they were bound to go down.

Finally, the upward push of the educational surge left its unmistakable mark on the four-year colleges and universities. In the 1870's most institutions of higher education were relatively small undergraduate colleges. Their curriculums were still largely devoted to the liberal arts of Greek and Latin, mathematics, and philosophy; and these courses were all required of all students.

In a relatively short time, however, new studies, like the modern languages, English, modern history and the social sciences, modern science, and the fine arts found a place in the curriculum. Students had to be given a choice because they could not possibly study all these subjects in four years. So the elective system was instituted.

Meanwhile, graduate study began to change the whole character of higher education. When Johns Hopkins University opened its doors in 1876, it helped to set the pattern for graduate schools devoted to the advancement of knowledge and research in the entire range of the arts and sciences. Professional schools of medicine, law, education, engineering, agriculture, business administration, and the like began to flourish.

This meant that universities were now devoted to direct professional preparation for an ever larger number of vocations rather than for just a few. Some liberal-arts colleges tried to maintain their nonvocational and nonprofessional character, but most were not able or did not care to do so. The democratic surge was too strong.

In the 1920's and 1930's a number of experimental colleges tried to grapple with the overcrowded curriculum and to design new patterns of liberal education. Bennington, University of Wisconsin, Sarah Lawrence, Bard, University of Minnesota were among them.

Critics arose, such as Robert Hutchins and Alexander Meikle-john, to call for preservation of the liberal-arts college free from professionalism and vocationalism. They were struggling against the tide. Nevertheless, undergraduate colleges did institute a wide variety of programs which, in one way or another, tried to assure that all students would have some acquaintance with the humanities, the social sciences, the sciences and mathematics, and the fine arts. Whatever a liberal education or a general education was supposed to be, it was to deal with these fields of knowledge.

Much criticism was directed at the professional schools for not giving enough attention to the liberal arts. They began to give heed. As the 1960's opened, considerable ferment was evident in medical schools, business schools, engineering schools, and schools of education.

It seemed likely that the teachers college, as a separate institution devoted exclusively to the training of teachers, would disappear. Normal schools had become teachers colleges, and now teachers colleges were becoming state colleges and even state universities. These changes were signs on the road of the march of democratic education.

Higher education was no longer confined to the few nor to the upper classes of wealth or privilege. It was on the way to becoming financially free, as secondary and elementary education had become before it. The opportunity was great.

The question was whether all this educational activity could measure up to the intellectual and moral demands of a free society in the modern world. If individuals used the vast resources of American higher education simply to further their own interests, this was one kind of small freedom all right, but in the long run would it serve the cause of the free society? How to enable American education to serve the cause of the larger freedoms was the paramount question. The answer to this question cannot be rigged. The fate of the nation rides upon it.

At the heart of the answer to the fateful question is the scholarship, the wisdom, the vitality and the freedom of American teachers. If teachers are weak, timorous, or poorly trained, the American idea of education has little chance of success. If powerful or selfish groups demand that teachers conform to *their* ways of thinking or to *their* beliefs, education will be a narrow little thing. And our history here is not too reassuring.

Orthodoxy of belief in colonial days was a prime requirement for teaching. Oaths of loyalty to the crown and to the doctrines of the church were familiar trappings of colonial rule. The American Revolution in its turn demanded that teachers be faithful to the Revolution rather than the crown; and, similarly, Congress exacted loyalty oaths to the Union in the Reconstruction Period after the Civil War.

Conformity of economic belief, faith in private business enterprise, and opposition to any radical movements were expected of teachers in the nineteenth century. State laws required special loyalty oaths from teachers as early as the 1920's, and as late as 1958 the National Defense Education Act required such oaths from students applying for federal loans.

After World Wars I and II, thirty states passed laws requiring teachers to sign special loyalty oaths. Other laws (notably the Feinberg law of 1949 in New York State) were passed to hunt down and dismiss teachers suspected of belonging to subversive organizations. Many patriotic organizations served as self-appointed censors of school textbooks and complained about outspoken teachers.

The frantic search for communist teachers and others suspected vaguely of "leftist" leaning was fired up by McCarthyism and the wave of legislative investigations that swept the country in the early 1950's.

As a result, a cloud of timidity, suspicion, and fear settled down upon the schools and colleges in what the *New York Times* called "a subtle, creeping paralysis of freedom of thought." Classroom teachers and school administrators tended to avoid acts or ideas that might "cause any trouble" or arouse any criticism.

This general atmosphere of caution and anxiety affecting millions of students did infinitely more damage to the cause of freedom in education than the handful of communist teachers could possibly do. Fortunately, the most active "Red hunts" have now passed, but their revival is an ever-present danger, especially if teachers and students are fearful or are indifferent to the importance of freedom in education.

The first defenses of freedom in education are strong professional organizations of teachers like the American Association of University Professors and the National Education Association. If they do their jobs, they will insist upon high-quality training for teachers, upon fearless and competent scholarship in the classroom, and upon freedom to seek the truth in research and in the publication of findings. They will defend those qualified teachers who come under attack.

The ultimate defenses of freedom in education, however, are the people themselves who will realize that education's main function is to free the minds of the younger generation and to equip them as free citizens and free persons.

The schools and colleges must therefore generate a spirit of intellectual, political, and personal freedom throughout the land. To do this, they must in turn have a genuine measure of self-government resting upon the competent scholarship of the teachers.

The most distinctive mark of a free society is that it specifically delegates to its educational institutions the task of constant study and criticism of the free society itself. No other kind of society dares to permit such a thing. No other kind of society prevents its government from endangering the liberties of the people and at the same time entrusts the government with the obligation to guarantee the rights of the people against attack by powerful groups or individuals in the community.

Just as a free government guarantees the freedom of the press, of association, of religion, and of trial by jury, so must a free government guarantee the freedom of teaching and learning.

A free society knows that its surest foundation rests upon the liberal education of the people—a liberal education available freely and equally to all, beginning with the earliest stages of the elementary school, extending to the highest reaches of the university, and limited only by considerations of talent.

As the fourth century of American history reaches its midpoint and as the second century of the American Republic draws to a close, the search for freedom in American education has just well begun. That is why the story of American education must continue to be, in the future even more than in the past, the unflagging search for freedom.

Milestones in the Education of the Negro in America

Joseph S. Roucek

Much has been written, especially lately, both in the United States and abroad, about the problems connected with the education of the American Negro. [Much] of it is influenced by strong emotions [and is] presented along ideological lines, although the issues concerning segregated education lie within the framework of a wider pressing problem in America: the need to provide adequate educational opportunities for all American citizens.[1]

Furthermore, the problem of the American Negro is inseparable from other sociological factors relating to the Negro's existence in the United States as a citizen born in the United States; it is not just a problem of the South, as often supposed, since racial tensions that exist in Northern cities have often burst also into violence. The fact remains that the problem of the American Negro looms large in the United States, and America's most enduring moral, social, and political issues have been shaped, or at least influenced, by its mere presence—and they remain unsolved. Yet, until recent years, the unintegrated Negro minority has been only an abstraction to the American white man, much on his mind, it is true, but, in human terms, largely beyond his notice.

[This despite the fact that] the Negroes, as America's most conspicuous minority group, constituting a full 10 percent of the population, have influenced not only a large part of America's historical development [and] its politics, but also its relations with other nations, and . . . its internal culture.

The . . . majority of American Negroes have been concentrated in the Southern states. . . . Thus, until recently, the Negro problem [tended to be viewed] mainly within the framework of Southern traditions. We must note that [and many historians have written that] the Civil War was not fought on the issue of the freeing of the Negro, although it culminated with his Emancipation; the step taken on his behalf by President Lincoln was one of the emergency measures designed to weaken the fighting power of the South. (The basic issue of the Civil War, according to this view, was what we might call the "self-determination of the states" within the Federal Union; another issue was rivalry between the slave-owning South and the "capitalist"—industrialized—North.) . . .

The Generation Between 1900 and 1936

The Negro generation of 1900–1936 began with the Tuskegee idea in the ascendancy: purchasing peace for their time by deferring social and political aspirations. In the Negro institutions, the standards were still low, and a "college" was still mostly an elementary and "normal" school with a "collegiate department" plus a few feeble theology courses. Courses were largely taught by self-taught Negro "professors" and white missionary teachers "who (with notable exceptions) had more zeal than competence." But among the fifty-odd church leaders were also some of the earliest Negro Ph.D.'s: J. W. E. Bowen, Sr., [from] Boston University (1882) [and] Richard Robert Wright, [whose] degree [was] in sociology [from] Pennsylvania. But such higher academic and professional degrees were unusual, "for education of most of the group fell short of junior-college levels and theological training was even more modest." [2]

. . .

About fifty persons in the period between 1900 and 1936 were in the category of educators identified with Negro higher education.[3]

By 1900, institutions calling themselves colleges or universities numbered about ninety-nine; in 1936 the number was about the same. Founded in the post-Civil War decades by Northern philanthropy, missionary enterprise, the Freedmen's Bureau, and state authority, as well as by denominations, one group was under public control, another under white sectarian boards, and one cluster in the hands of Negro denominations.

As of 1922, 85 percent of the enrollment in the so-called "colleges" was in the elementary and secondary department, for all but three or four of the colleges were in the South, where common-school provision for Negro children was still minimal and public high schools wholly absent. But at the end of the period (1936), more than three fourths of the enrollment was in the collegiate departments (which often afforded only a two-year course).[4]

Opportunities for Negroes to rise to prominence as educators were extremely small. There were only 23,000 students, most of them . . . ill-prepared, in the Negro colleges in 1932, and the supply of adequately trained professors and administrators was microscopic. Most of the best Negro colleges were in the hands of white trustees, faculties and administrators; the most notable exceptions were the schools founded by Negro denominations. Howard, [then] sixty years old, acquired its first Negro president in 1926; Hampton was still run by whites in the early 1940's; Fisk, then eighty years old, inaugurated its first Negro president in 1947.

Of the fifty-two educators in the roster, all but a tiny minority were college presidents (or, in a few cases, deans), and residents in the South. All but two were born in the South (the only exceptions being [W. E. B.] Du Bois and [Alain L.] Locke). Negroes distinguished in fields other than religion and education, by contrast, were nearly all residents of the North.

Concludes one historian:

At the end of the era (1936), the [Negro] institutions were still seriously deficient as to library facilities, equipment, preparation of instructors, administrative skill, and all the other indices of academic status. Their symbol was the begging bowl; they were from the beginning dependent upon alms, first from religious and relatively unorganized benefactors, and then from foundations and philanthropic agencies.[5]

The Changing Educational Pattern

[Following] the Reconstruction period, Negro education suffered from the handicap of starting from nowhere. Literacy was estimated at about 5 percent among Negroes in 1860; by 1890 nearly 60 percent were still illiterate; by 1910 illiteracy had been reduced to 30 percent. While a few lower schools in four or five Southern states had been opened on a mixed basis by the Negro "carpetbag" governments of the immediate postwar era, most of the Southern states established separate schools for whites and Negroes. For many years, there were no local school taxes in the South, the funds being distributed from state sources to counties on a per capita basis; thus the heavily populated counties with large numbers of Negroes received more money than those counties with smaller Negro populations. White groups in smaller counties were angered by these provisions, but it was not long before funds due to Negro schools were being diverted in various ways to white schools. By 1930 Negro schools were still on the average getting only 37 percent of the amount due to them on a per capita basis. Having no political voice, being a particularly weak economic force, and remaining largely uneducated, Negroes were the unfortunate victims of one of America's greatest national tragedies and blights.

Although a considerable amount of aid was given Negro education by private foundations during the late 1890's and early twentieth century (Peabody, Slater, Jeanes, Rosewald, Carnegie, Phelps-Stokes funds and the General Education Board), they made only a limited dent, important though it was, in the [problem]. By 1900, according to a report of the U.S. Commissioner of Education, out of over 1,000 public high schools in the South, less than seventy were provided for Negroes. The years of the Great Depression further strained Negro education as increased thousands of Negro youngsters, squeezed from the labor market, bulged the schools. Generally in the South, the Negroes still had ramshackle buildings, more poorly trained teachers, near-starvation salaries, and "benefit[s]" from discarded white school desks, books, and decrepit buses.[6]

Several key factors brought the long overdue improvements that have marked the recent history of Negro education.

An important factor was the changing "climate of opinion" developing among the Negro leaders.

Booker T. Washington, in essence, wanted Negroes to prepare

for jobs which were open to them. The Negro must first become literate and learn skills which might help him to be economically independent. Then, perhaps, he would be ready for political and social equality.[7]

Dr. W. E. B. Du Bois, a Negro sociologist and educator, attacked Washington for accepting the Negro caste position and for remaining silent and asking other Negroes to remain silent in the face of injustice. Du Bois and his group demanded no less than equality of opportunity in education at the higher levels as well as in elementary and vocational training. They argued that, in the struggle for equality, training for inferior positions will not be of much help. What was needed was a large number of highly literate and capable Negro leaders who could only come into existence if equal opportunities in higher education became a reality. He led the "Niagara Movement," the spiritual ancestor of the National Association for the Advancement of Colored People.[8]

The controversy between Washington and Du Bois continued until Washington's death in 1915.

A great migration of Negroes from the farm to Southern and Northern cities came after Washington's death. "In an important sense the movement was flight from poverty, oppression, and the boll weevil. The unprecedented urbanization and individualization of the Negro was thus under way." [9]

In spite of disenfranchisement, discrimination, poverty, and lack of opportunity, which had been the black man's lot, the Negro's situation had improved in many ways after 1900.

In 1910, 30 percent of the Negroes had been illiterate; only 8 percent were thus handicapped in 1940.[10]

As late as 1915 there had been only sixty-four Negro high schools in this country; by 1940, the number had risen to 2,500. Almost 20,000 Negroes were graduated from colleges during the decade of the 1930's—more than twice the number of the more prosperous twenties. After World War II, these educational trends were accelerated.

More specifically, between World War I and World War II, there was a significant growth of Negro public high schools, especially in large urban areas, both in North and South; there were enormous increases in both the relative and actual sizes of the enrollment, supply of teachers, number of graduates, and capital outlay; many Negro colleges dropped their high school programs, added graduate instruction, and many degree-conscious Negroes graduated in ever-increasing numbers from Negro and

Northern colleges; state supported and land grant institutions surpassed the private Negro colleges in enrollment and financial support; and "the most profound change was the quest for equality." [11]

The Modern Federal Colossus in Education: Threat or Promise?

Galen Saylor

That the federal government is contributing in a colossal manner to the support of education from the nursery school level through the graduate college is, of course, a fact. A mere listing of some of the important acts that provide federal funds for the support of education reveals the tremendous scope of federal participation in the educational endeavors of this country.[1]

GI Rights Act (education for veterans), 1944
Aid to Federally Impacted Areas, 1950
Library Services Act, 1956
National Defense Education Act, 1958
Juvenile Delinquency and Youth Offenses Control Act, 1961
Manpower Training and Development Act, 1962
Health Professions Educational Assistance Act, 1963
Mental Retardation Facilities and Community Health Centers Act, 1963
Higher Education Facilities Act, 1963
Vocational Education Act, 1963
National Defense Education Act—Extension and Amendments, 1963-64

Library Services and Construction Act and Amendments, 1964
Civil Rights Act—Title IV and VI, 1964
Amendments to Juvenile Delinquency Act of 1961, 1964
Economic Opportunity Act, 1964
Elementary and Secondary Education Act, 1965
Higher Education Act, 1965

There are many other federal assistance programs, such as the school lunch program, the educational phases of the National Science Foundation Act, and a multitude of other forms of federal aid for education, broadly conceived.

The increase in appropriations of federal funds for education is even more revealing of the extent to which the federal government is making a gigantic effort in the support of education. The comparative report prepared each year by the U.S. Office of Education entitled, "Federal Funds for Education," shows that in 1945, $291,500,000 was appropriated by the Congress for the direct support of education and related activities; in 1955, this sum had increased to $1,523,700,000; in 1960, the amount was $2,324,-100,000; in 1965, it was $6,328,907,000; and . . . [in the fiscal year ending June 30, 1970 was $12,757,000,000. This is to say that in a period of twenty-five years, federal appropriations for the support of educational programs and projects have increased over forty-fold.]

A further revealing fact is the increase in the amount of direct appropriations to the United States Office of Education for support of that office and the aid programs directly administered by it; the office received $34,336,483 in 1950; in 1960, it was granted $474,280,893; and . . . [in 1970, $3,583,000,000 was dispersed through the United States Office of Education.] This constitutes . . . [an enormous] increase in . . . [allocation of federal funds for education through] the U.S. Office of Education.

The best estimates made available to the House Appropriations Committee indicate that federal support for education, nursery school level through graduate college, this year constitutes one-sixth of all funds spent for education in this country, and that in 1965–66 it will constitute one-fifth of all such expenditures.[2] The federal government is indeed a major source of support for education and the programs and activities which it subsidizes are widespread and far-flung.

Threat or Promise?

This stupendous amount of federal support for education is indeed both a threat and a promise to good education for children, youth and young adults in America. Let us explore both possibilities more fully.

The Promise

Federal programs for the support of education in the United States show great promise for the development and advancement of the total opportunities for the education of children, youth and adults in this country for these reasons:

1. *Much greater sums of money become available for the support of the educational effort of this nation.* Obviously, the appropriation of more than six billion dollars directly for the support of education in this country is a huge sum of money and it represents a major contribution to our effort. If such sums of money were not available, the total program would of course be curtailed, or the citizens through local or state units of government would have to raise these large sums of money to maintain even our present effort.

2. *Extensive national effort of this size provides programs and services not possible or feasible through local and state efforts.* Generally speaking, the program of elementary, secondary and collegiate education as it exists in this country is inadequately supported now by local and state agencies. The pressure everywhere on these units of government is to appropriate ever expanding sums of money for the support of our regular program of education. Little, if any, of their revenues can be used for new services, new programs, and new ventures of an educational nature even if it is generally agreed that such an expansion is desirable.

Moreover, some aspects of educational development, by their very natures, should be undertaken on a larger base than is possible by local or state authorities. Many of the existing programs of federal support are of this nature, such as the programs and services provided by the mental retardation act, the cooperative research program, the research and development centers, the various curriculum projects and commissions that are extensively engaged in the formulation of new instructional materials and plans for various areas of the curriculum, the establishment of educational service centers, and many other endeavors of this kind.

3. *The federal government is able to support and foster the development of new programs and new types of educational undertakings that generally would not be undertaken by local educational authorities.* Generally local boards of education, state departments of education, and the power structure of local communities would not countenance or approve the undertaking of the types of new educational programs that the federal government frequently fosters and supports. Examples are the entire program being developed under the Economic Opportunity Act and most of the activities that will be possible under the Elementary and Secondary Education Act of 1965.

4. *Federal support for the existing educational enterprise frequently stimulates local and state agencies to increased effort in support of the regular and traditionally accepted program of education.* Good examples of such nudging are the Higher Education Facilities Act, which provides a portion of the cost of new facilities for higher education, Title III of the National Defense Education Act, which provided partial federal subsidy for the improvement of facilities and teaching resources in science, mathematics, and foreign languages, and the Vocational Education Act of 1963. Similarly, Title II of the Elementary and Secondary Education Act will induce many school districts throughout the United States to expand and improve library service, and to develop much more rapidly than they would be inclined to do otherwise, their library resources for elementary and secondary schools.

5. *The federal government has clearly demonstrated that it can rapidly initiate the development and support of new programs in areas of urgent need that become evident because of new economic, social and cultural conditions.* In my belief, the Congress of the United States and the educational agencies established by it have shown dexterity and willingness to move rapidly when great need for new kinds of programs is evident. Examples of this, of course, are the Manpower Training and Development Act, the National Defense Education Act, and the redesigning and expansion of the vocational education programs.

6. *Federal efforts in education serve to prod the pedantic, nudge the lethargic, and inspire the imaginative school officials and boards of education of local educational agencies throughout the nation.* Of course, we do have highly imaginative, creative,

and aggressive educators and members of local boards of education throughout the nation, for it is such professional educators and scholars that advise the Congress of the United States and our national leaders on new developments and new programs that should be undertaken. Nevertheless it is evident that far too many of our local educational officials simply lack the professional qualifications to invent new programs needed to serve adequately all of the educational needs of their localities. But once the federal government provides support for new types of educational endeavors, a political climate is created in which the pedantic are prodded, although sometimes reluctantly, into action.

7. *Federal efforts in support of education clearly demonstrate a desire on the part of the Congress to develop a total program for the education of all Americans regardless of any economic, social, cultural, or racial factors that may under existing local programs deny or curtail the equality of access to educational opportunity.* The widespread nature of the federal programs clearly indicates that the Congress is insistent that every American have the privilege of participating in the types of schooling and in educational programs that will enable him personally and individually to realize the maximum of his full potentialities regardless of any factors that in the past have restricted or curtailed these opportunities.

8. *The total federal effort in behalf of schools, colleges, and all educational agencies has fostered a new national interest in education and has made education a matter of great national concern.* Everyone is well aware of the fact that the presidents of the United States in recent administrations, with the support of Congress, have been responsible for a reawakening and a revival of the American interest and concern for the education of its people.

The Threat

Yet there are also some threats evident in our present national efforts in support of education. Chief among these I detect the following:

1. *The stifling of the creativeness, inventiveness, and skill of discovery of local educational leaders and officials.* It is not, in my opinion, an inevitable corollary of federal participation in education that creativeness and inventiveness of individual practitioners, researchers, and scholars is stifled. Such an outcome, how-

ever, certainly is always a threat and such a possibility should be clearly recognized not only by the Congress of the United States and federal officials, but by the educators and citizens themselves so that conditions will be maintained that encourage stimulation of such inventiveness by everyone concerned with the educational enterprise.

The very nature of federal support itself makes possible if not encourages a situation in which those who administer the federal programs approve and support only those things that appeal to them or that carry out their ideas and desires. For example, in the cooperative research program decisions obviously must be made about what proposals to approve.

Similarly, in the establishment of research and development centers now under way in this country, someone must make a decision as to which proposal for a center shall receive federal support and which proposal shall be rejected. Whose philosophy of education, whose concept of what is good and what is not good, whose concept of what should receive the blessing of the federal government, and what should be denied its support are to prevail? Although these types of programs are at present only one small aspect of the federal participation, the possibilities here are very serious and indicate the nature of the problems that face us.

2. *Invidious control over the program of education itself.* Here I point to direct federal control of education through the acts that provide support for these programs. I believe that the actual curriculum and other types of educational programs provided children in the classrooms and schools of this nation must be determined by the teachers and their fellow staff members who guide and direct the development of learning opportunities and plan the total program of education for the children of a particular school and school system. Lessening the responsibility for such decisions by the staff of the individual school system reduces the possibilities for adaptability, flexibility, experimentation, innovation, and, most seriously of all, administration to the educational needs of each child enrolled in school.

The threat that such decisions will be curtailed as a result of federal support is a serious one. I see no threat in the national curriculum projects that have been substantially subsidized by the National Science Foundation and the U.S. Office of Education. The local school authorities and teachers still have complete freedom insofar as those programs are concerned to decide whether they want to use the instructional materials, plans, and the recommendations formulated by these commissions and curriculum development centers, modify them, use some aspects and reject others, or completely reject the whole project itself. These projects represent one of the very rich resources being made available through federal support for the upgrading of various aspects of the educational programs of the schools and are indeed to be lauded and encouraged.

The real threat, I believe, comes from control by federal officials over the educational aspects of the plans developed for carrying out some of these acts, particularly the Elementary and Secondary Education Act. *This act gives the United States Commissioner of Education authority to approve plans for carrying out the act and hence the conditions within provisions of the law under which grants will be made.* The Economic Opportunity Act, Title II, prescribes the nature of community action plans and further states that "The Director is authorized to prescribe such additional criteria for programs carried on under this part as he shall deem appropriate." This is the title under which many of the educational activities can be established for children.

Now being proposed to carry out provisions of the Elementary and Secondary Education Act are testing programs and programs for the assessment of educational outcomes that indeed, in my opinion, constitute a serious threat to the prerogatives of the teachers and local school officials in each school district, and hence to sound educational planning and administration. It is a very alarming development in the history of federal support for education that for the first time in its history the federal government is demanding that evidence be submitted by local school systems on the effectiveness of these programs.

Title II of the Elementary and Secondary Education Act requires that the local educational agency include in its plans, "effective procedures, including provision for proper objective measurements of educational achievement, will be adopted for evaluating at least annually the effectiveness of the programs in meeting the special education needs of educationally deprived children." Further, the Act requires that the local education agency report annually to the state educational agency "information relating to the educational achievement of students participating in programs carried out under this title." In turn, the state educational agency must "make to the commissioner periodic reports (including the results of the objective measurements required by

Section 205 [A] [5]) evaluating the effectiveness of payments under this title and of particular programs assisted under it in improving the educational attainments of educationally deprived children."

If this is not direct federal control over the curriculum of the schools, I do not know what federal control is. When you require a school system to report on the effectiveness of the program, you are requiring that school to report on its curriculum. Pure and simple. If the purpose of such a report is not to control the program, then why make it? It is presumed by the very wording of the Act that the Congress of the United States will use these reports on the measurement of educational attainment to determine what the nature of the programs shall be in subsequent legislation by Congress. And it should be pointed out that this Title of the Act is only authorized for one year and hence will be subject to scrutiny by Congress next year, at which time Congress will determine whether it wants to extend this program, modify it, or terminate it. Presumably, then, if the schools want to continue to receive such aid, they will have to establish programs that within even the next few months would demonstrate to Congress that they are "effective" with "effectiveness" in no way being defined or described.

As I state, it is to me a terrifying development that such provisions were written into the most recent federal program for the support of education. I remind the reader that *no such provisions requiring objective evidence of effectiveness were ever written into any other acts for the federal support of education in the entire history of the United States.* The land grant universities were not required under the Morrill Act to report to the Commissioner of Education and hence to the Congress of the United States on their effectiveness in carrying out the provisions of that Act; the Smith-Hughes law in 1917 made no such requirements of any kind on the secondary schools of the United States that accepted federal support for vocational education and neither does the new Vocational Education Act of 1963. No one, local schools, colleges who administer institutes, or any agency that receives grants for research projects or other types of money under the National Defense Education Act is required to report to the United States Commissioner of Education on the effectiveness of these programs.[3]

Any one who has had such grants or worked with such programs knows that the federal government in the past had relied on the imagination, creativeness, and integrity of the local agencies to provide outstanding programs under the provisions of these acts. Why has the Congress of the United States suddenly written into its most recent federal subsidy bill provisions that require the local school to gather evidence on the effectiveness of the program and then to submit this evidence directly to the United States Commissioner of Education through the state educational agency?

Title IV of the Civil Rights Act, moreover, requires the U.S. Commissioner of Education to gather evidence on the lack of availability of educational opportunities because of race, color, religion or national origin—a provision that gives the Commissioner authority to study schools at the local level.

3. *Development of attitudes and modes of operation of dependency and indifference, of kowtowing to entrenched bureaucrats.* A third threat of federal support correlative to the other two is the possibility of the gradual evolvement on the part of local citizens, boards of education, and school officials of an attitude of indifference to educational matters in the local communities and lethargy in doing anything to improve the quality of the program. There is a serious possibility of a decline in local interest and concern for education as support and control from sources beyond the local community increase. Anyone who has studied closely schools and educational programs in European countries, most of which have highly centralized and nationalized systems of education, is well aware of the almost total apathy and indifference of the citizens of the local community about the state and conditions of the educational programs of the community. Certainly, there is a gross lack of any effort to introduce change, to experiment, and to innovate.

Although such a threat, obviously, is one of long-term development, I nevertheless fear a gradual weakening of the concern local citizens in many communities now have about their schools as federal involvement increases.

The Future

For the future, I believe the following things should be done:

1. Much greater support for the total program of education should be provided by the federal government. Federal support for education should double and then triple and then continue to increase in the years immediately ahead.

2. Federal support should be provided for a great variety of programs, projects and other educational undertakings of all kinds. The total effort of the federal government should reach out into all aspects of education and the funds should in large part be used to stimulate and support more comprehensive and extensive educational efforts than are carried out as a part of our traditional program of schooling in local districts.

3. A large part of the program of the federal government should constitute research and development activities of broad scope, such as would not be feasible for local educational systems or even state departments of education to undertake. A part of these research efforts should consist of broadly conceived and widespread efforts to assess educational outcomes and evaluation of the effectiveness of educational programs, but only on a basis that ensures integrity of local control over the curriculum provided pupils.

4. In providing categorical aid, the federal government should be certain that it supports only those aspects of the total educational program that represent a wise investment of funds. Philosophically and educationally, programs supported by the federal government should offer great promise for major advances in the education of this country.

5. All educational efforts should be correlated and unified through a common administrative agency at all levels, federal, state, and local. This is not to say that the school district or the school system itself must carry out and administer all programs, but rather that all programs whether receiving federal support or not should be part of a comprehensive and planned program of total education for all children, youth and young adults.

6. The administration of and carrying out of federally-supported educational programs should under no circumstances be placed in the hands of persons who lack extensive and adequate professional preparation for such positions. There should be no place in such federal programs for politicians not fully qualified by training and experience to administer such programs.

How the School System Is Rigged for Failure

Paul Lauter and Florence Howe

There has hardly been a time during the last 150 years when Americans were not being told that the schools were at a "turning point," "confronted with a crucial challenge," "entering an era of new importance." At the same time, they have forever been at the edge of failure. Indeed, one major enterprise of educators in every generation has been to analyze that failure and propose new remedies. In the 1840's, industrialization, urbanization, and immigration produced conflict and dislocation in most cities of the North. Educational innovators envisioned public high schools as the means for unifying and civilizing communities, as well as promoting economic growth and social mobility. According to Joseph White, fourth secretary of the Massachusetts Board of Education during this period, in the high schools,

The children of the rich and poor, of the honored and the unknown, meet together on common ground. Their pursuits, their aims and aspirations are one. No distinctions find place, but such as talent and industry and good conduct create. In the competitions, the defeats, and the successes of the schoolroom, they meet each other as they are to meet in the broader fields of life before them; they are

67

taught to distinguish between the essential and true, and the frac-
tious and false, in character and condition. . . . Thus a vast and
mutual benefit is the result. Thus, and only thus, can the rising
generation be best prepared for the duties and responsibilities of
citizenship in a free commonwealth. No foundation will be laid in
our social life for the brazen walls of caste; and our political life,
which is but the outgrowth of the social, will pulsate in harmony
with it, and so be kept true to the grand ideals of the fathers and
founders of the republic.[1]

The aspirations of mid-nineteenth-century America [were] thus
to be fulfilled in the schoolroom.

Similarly, Sputnik launched the demand, in the 1950's, for a new
high-school curriculum to save the national honor and restore
military superiority. Vice-Admiral Hyman Rickover and President James Bryant Conant of Harvard proposed more rigorous
mathematics and science courses, better preparation of teachers,
and special attention to the "gifted." Schools all over the country
adopted the slogan "Quality Education."

During the 1960's, the focus of agitation shifted to the "disadvantaged" student, and the byword became "equality of educational opportunity." No major school system is now without
some special project for the children of the poor. Nor has there
been any shortage of federally sponsored programs: Head Start,
Follow-through, Upward Bound, NDEA Institutes, Model Cities
colloquia, Titles I–IV. During the single fiscal year ending June,
1967, the federal government alone provided over one billion
dollars, supposedly for educating poor children, under Title I of
the Elementary and Secondary Education Act. Another $100
million was authorized under Title III for experimental and model
programs, many of which could be directed to the problems of the
"disadvantaged." Private foundations have invested very heavily
in "educational innovation." And during the last year or more,
dozens of books have offered new hopes and desires to straining
educational bureaucracies and a public impatient to solve the
continuing and deepening "crisis."

There are a few common threads in these diverse and sometimes
contradictory efforts: that the schools play crucial roles in
achieving transcendent national goals, and especially in breaking
the "cycle" of ignorance, joblessness, and poverty; and that the
educational system has, for the most part, failed to achieve these
objectives. The goals and assumptions to which most writers on
education, congressmen, and parents would subscribe have been

stated, for example, by the Committee for Economic Development, a very influential organization of financial and corporate executives:

> The well-being of individual citizens, the integrity of the nation's social institutions, the strength of the economy, and the long-term national security depend on the effectiveness of the schools. Unless schooling keeps pace with the large demands that will be made on it in the years ahead, the American people will not achieve their personal, community, and national goals. A free society must always depend on the capacity of its schools to provide the kind of education that produces rational, responsible, and effective citizens.[2]

If these are, indeed, the goals of our educational system, it has surely failed, especially in the urban ghetto. The statistics bear witness to the fact that schools in Harlem, Watts, the District of Columbia do not impart even basic skills to their pupils. Nearly 81 percent of sixth-grade Harlem pupils score below grade level in reading comprehension, 77.5 percent in word knowledge, 83.3 percent in arithmetic. Often these poor and black children are two or three years behind in achievement scores,[3] and in the years since Kenneth Clark publicized these statistics, the situation has not materially improved. But, of course, defective schools are not confined to the ghettos. In the Elementary and Secondary Education Act of 1965 the failures of the schools are noted, with somewhat more down-to-earth insights about the objectives of the educational system than those posited by the Committee for Economic Development:

> A national problem . . . is reflected in draft rejection rates because of educational deficiencies. It is evidenced by the employment and manpower retraining problems aggravated by the fact that there are over 8 million adults who have completed less than 5 years of school. It is seen in the 20% unemployment rate of our 18 to 24 year olds.[4]

Surely, the proposers of the 1965 Act seem to be saying; if the schools fail to prepare men for the Army and for industry, they have failed altogether.

This litany over the failure of the schools is repeated in almost every new book on the subject. Mario Fantini and Gerald Weinstein, who have had much to do with shaping the Ford Foundation's broad program of educational support, cite Kenneth Clark and the ESEA in their *The Disadvantaged: Challenge to Educa-*

tion. They add their own variations on the theme: the schools have not only failed the poor and the black, but they have not taught "adult maturity" or necessary skills to many children from comfortable, middle-class families.

> . . . it becomes all too clear that our education has been severely deficient in achieving its purpose, quantitatively and qualitatively. Yet education is the only institution upon which we, as a nation, can rely to provide us with a population which has a significant proportion of truly democratic, socially oriented, dedicated adults who will contribute to our country's welfare.[5]

Thus Fantini and Weinstein join their hopes to those of Joseph White a hundred years ago, to those of the Committee for Economic Development, to those of the Elementary and Secondary Education Act. And they devote their 455 pages to strategies for helping educators achieve these presumed—and traditional—objectives.

But are the schools "failures"? If they do not accomplish the goals which educators have laid out for them, it may well be that all they need—as the CED, Congress, and Fantini and Weinstein urge—is more money, more innovation, more machines, more specialization. It may also be, however, that the stated goals of American education are deceptive and irrelevant ones, that their grand rhetoric clouds the character and social objectives of the schools. A review of the alleged "failures" of the Selective Service System—the uncertainty it has engendered, its unfairness, its apparently arbitrary and harebrained procedures—reveals features that have been built in because they are necessary to its function of channeling young men into what are thought to be socially desirable activities.[6] Looking at what the schools *do* rather than at what they should or might do may tell a similar story. What if the apparent "failures" of the American educational system have served necessary functions in American society? Perhaps the schools, like almost all other American institutions, have been very, indeed horrifyingly, successful.

Such a proposition may seem shocking, if not perverse, since Americans have traditionally believed in the virtues of schooling as much as in motherhood or a balanced budget. The black and Jewish communities in New York City continue to quarrel bitterly about the control of education, yet they agree about the fundamental importance of keeping children in schools. Recently, however, observing conditions in Harlem, Kenneth Clark suggested that schools function in a manner precisely contrary to their acclaimed ideals:

> . . . American public schools have become significant instruments in the blocking of economic mobility and in the intensification of class distinctions rather than fulfilling their historic function of facilitating such mobility.
>
> In effect, the public schools have become captives of a middle class who have failed to use them to aid others also to move into the middle class—it might even be possible to interpret the role of the controlling middle class as that of using the public schools to block further mobility.[7]

Although Clark's analysis of the present situation is accurate, he accepts too readily the historical claims, rather than the performance, of American education.

Michael B. Katz has compared in some detail such historical claims with what the schools really accomplished. High schools in the nineteenth century were presented by their promoters as mechanisms for achieving social mobility and economic development, for democratizing society, for eliminating class distinctions, and for producing, as Fantini and Weinstein put it more than a century later, "truly democratic, socially oriented, dedicated adults who will contribute to our country's welfare." In fact, however, as Katz shows, the innovation called high schools achieved none of these goals. Few poor and working-class children actually attended, and before very long, those who did were channeled off into vocational programs "more suitable to their interests and capacities." The pressure for schools originated in response to economic growth, but, as Katz suggests, there is little evidence to demonstrate that continued industrial development depended in any sense on the expansion of education.

This is not to say that the public educational system had *no* functions. On the contrary, some of its achievements seem to have been inversely related to the claims made for it. For the middle-class children who made up the bulk of high-school students, schools helped to maintain their status and position in the community. Schools were an entree for boys into business (though they taught little of major importance to enterprise) and for girls into teaching. And teaching, as Katz says, "was undoubtedly the most attractive vocational goal for the middle-class girl who wanted to earn some money because all the other occupations populated by large numbers of females were manual, arduous, and decidedly lower-class." [8] The public high school also served middle-class parents, because "they could spread among the population at large the [fiscal] burden of educating their children." [9] Thus, far from pulling down "the brazen walls of caste," as Joseph White had asserted, the high schools reinforced them.

Though the schools did not function to the advantage of poor and working-class children, they did not ignore them. Katz quotes a contributor to the *Massachusetts Teacher* who in 1861 explained the value of education to business: "The habit of prompt action in the performance of the duty required of the boy, by the teacher at school, becomes in the man of business confirmed; thus system and order characterize the employment of the day laborer." [10] Katz quotes a Lowell manufacturer, one H. Bartlett, who insisted, in 1841, that:

Workers with more education possessed "a higher and better state of morals, [were] more orderly and respectful in their deportment, and more ready to comply with the wholesome and necessary regulations of an establishment." Perhaps most important, "in times of agitation, on account of some change in regulations or wages, I have always looked to the most intelligent, best educated and the most moral for support." . . . The educated, in short, were seen as company men.[11]

In their conscious attempt to impose personal habits of restraint, self-control, diligence, promptness, and sobriety on their students, particularly those from "loose," "shiftless" (or "disadvantaged") backgrounds, schoolmen served the desires of business for a disciplined and acquiescent work force. In this sense, too, schools served the dominant interests of the middle-class community; and, not surprisingly, such businessmen and industrialists were among the major promoters of school reforms.

This history is important, for it contradicts the easy assumptions we have usually made about the uniform virtues of schooling. And it suggests that earlier "failings" in the educational system can better be understood as contradictions between the professed objectives of educators—their ideology—and the real social and economic forces to which the educational system was in fact responding. Such forces continue to operate: a recent Harris poll shows that 62 percent of parents questioned thought that in school "maintaining discipline is more important than student self-inquiry." [12] A *Life* reporter, commenting on the study, wrote that "the parents in the *Life* poll know exactly what *they* want from the schools: 'Teach the kids to understand our existing values,' they say; 'discipline them to conform.' . . . They think the schools should keep the children passive and disciplined, and provide them with the tools that lead to college and a job." [13] To what extent does our educational system today continue, not to "fail," but to succeed in serving these by now traditional objectives?

II

In 1927 many Americans were troubled about their society. Morals seemed to be disintegrating, crime increasing. Indeed, some felt there was a "legal bias in favor of the criminal." He "is petted and pampered and protected to a degree which makes the punishment of crime relatively rare." Educators were quick to rise to this social crisis. They urged their fellow Americans to look to the schools to train citizens not to "set themselves against the state." After all, there was "no other organized force which aims primarily at citizenship and at the same time represents the state. Schools could, moreover, satisfy the demands of industry for "the type of help that knows something, that has social graces arising from extended social experience" of the sort provided by high schools.

There was one problem, however: how to keep children *in* school. Many dropped out because their main experience in the classroom was one of frustration. A new way of organizing schools had to be found that would not forever be confronting those most in need of schooling with failure, that might more fully "individualize" their instruction in order to prepare children more efficiently for the kinds of jobs they would get. This way was "ability grouping."

> Ability grouping in the junior high school is to be defined as the classification of the pupils of the school into groups which, within reasonable limits, are homogeneous in ability to perform the kind of task which confronts those pupils in the classroom. It is not a social segregation. It is not a caste stratification. It is not an attempt to point out those who are worth while and those who are not. It is not a move to separate the leaders from the followers.[14]

Despite the best intentions of its promoters, ability grouping—or tracking, or streaming, as it is variously called—has unfortunately become all that they asserted it would not be. What it has *not* been is either a means of keeping children in school or of improving their performance while they attend.

In Washington, D.C., for example, where an elaborate track system reached far down into the elementary schools, 54 percent of the classes of 1965 and 1966 dropped out before graduation. The most extensive and careful study of ability grouping, moreover, concludes "that ability grouping, *per se,* produces no improvement in achievement for any ability level and, as an administrative device, has little merit." [15] The study indicates further that children may learn better in strongly heterogeneous groups. Arthur W. Foshay . . . suggests also that evidence from Sweden and England "raises the dark possibility that ability grouping functions . . . as selective deprivation." [16] Tracking may actually *prevent* children from learning, the study indicates, because "teachers generally underestimate the capability of pupils in lower track classes, expect less of them, and consequently the pupils learn less." [17] None of this is surprising, since teachers generally concentrate on students who respond. But why, then, if tracking has not succeeded in keeping most kids in school and has succeeded in creating for those lower-tracked kids the "self-fulfilling prophecy" that they won't learn anything in school— why, then, has it persisted for more than forty years?

In the first place, tracking is to schools what channeling is to the draft. Its function is identical, namely, the control of manpower "in the National Interest." In democratic societies like that of the United States, individuals are encouraged to believe that opportunities for social advancement are unlimited; such beliefs are part of the national myth, and also necessary to encourage young people to achieve and get ahead. Yet opportunities are, in fact, limited. Not everyone with the talent can, for example, become a scientist, industrial manager, engineer, or even a college professor; the economy has greater need for technologists, technicians, salesmen, white-collar workers, not to speak of men on production lines. It has been estimated that industry demands five semiprofessionals and technicians to enable every professional to function.[18]

There must be "valves" which can help to control the flow of manpower into the economy. "Tracking" is one of those important valves; it helps to ensure that the American work force is not "overeducated" (as has been the case, for example, in India, where there are far too few jobs "suitable" for college graduates). It also helps to ensure that unpopular industries, like the Army, or less prestigious occupations, like sanitation work, are supplied with manpower.

Indeed, sociologist Theodore Caplow has argued that:

> . . . the principal device for the limitation of occupational choice is the education system. It does this in two ways: first, by forcing the student who embarks upon a long course of training to renounce other careers which also require extensive training; second, by excluding from training and eventually from the occupations themselves those students who lack either the intellectual qualities (such as intelligence, docility, aptitude) or the social characteristics (such as ethnic background, wealth, appropriate conduct, previous education) which happen to be required.[19]

Tracking is one of the educational system's major techniques for thrusting forward students with the necessary qualities of school-measured intelligence, docility, background, and the rest; and for channeling the others into "appropriate" slots. James Bryant Conant is explicit about this practice. "I submit," he writes in *Slums and Suburbs*, "that in a heavily urbanized and industrialized free society, the educational experiences of youth should fit their subsequent employment." Accomplishing this goal in cities is difficult, Conant continues, given the limitations of guidance personnel and parental indifference; therefore, "the system of rigid tracks may be the only workable solution to a mammoth guidance problem."[20]

The "valves" of ability grouping, some economists complain,[21] have become sticky, and have slowed economic growth by limiting the flow of students with middling talent and motivation, particularly those from lower-class backgrounds. In fact, however, from another point of view one might argue that the valves have been operating effectively to limit competition with the children of white, middle-class parents who, on the whole, have controlled the schools.[22] In New York City in 1967, for example, nonwhites, the vast majority of them poor, made up 40 percent of the high-school population; they constituted about 36 percent of students in the "academic" high schools and about 60 percent of those tracked into "vocational" high schools. In the Bronx High School of Science and in Brooklyn Tech, elite institutions for which students must qualify by examination, "nonwhites" totaled only 7 and 12 percent of the students respectively.

But the real effects of tracking can better be seen in the statistics of students in the academic high schools. A majority of blacks and Puerto Ricans fill lower tracks, which lead them—if they stay at all—to "general" rather than "academic" diplomas. Only 18 percent of academic high-school graduates were black or Puerto Rican (though they were, as we said, 36 percent of the academic student population); and only one-fifth of that 18 percent went on to college, as compared with 63 percent of whites who graduated. In other words, only 7 percent of the graduates of New York's academic high schools who went on to college were black or Puerto Rican. The rest, for the most part tracked into non-college-preparatory programs, left school with what amounted to a ticket into the Army.[23]

The statistics for Washington, D.C., are even more striking, in part because figures are available on the basis of income as well as race and ethnic background. In the nation's capital, where, in 1966, 91 percent of the students were black, 84 percent of those black children were in schools *without any honors track*. In areas with a median income of $3,872 a year, 85 percent of the children were in a basic or general track, neither of them college-bound; while in areas where the income was $10,374 or better, only 8 percent of the children were in the general track, and in such areas there was *no basic track at all*. Theoretically, tracking ranks students according to their ability to achieve. Yet Washington's statistics suggest that the children of the poor have less than one-tenth of the ability of the children of the well-to-do—an obvious absurdity. Indeed, tracking in Washington was more than absurd: in 1967 Federal Judge J. Skelly Wright declared that the system unconstitutionally discriminated against poor and black children and ordered it abolished.[24] But although it has officially been disbanded in the District's schools, it lingers on subtly in placement and curriculum, and more openly in the way teachers teach.

If one studies the means by which students are selected into tracks, one discovers a further layer of discrimination against the children of the poor. It is on the basis of reading scores, IQ, and other standard achievement tests—as well as teachers' recommendations—that children are determined "slow" or "superior." Yet Herbert Kohl reports that he was able to help his students raise their reading scores from one to three years, within a period of months, simply by teaching them how to take tests. Middle-class children, Kohl points out, learn about tests early in their school careers; indeed, a "predominantly white school located less than a mile down Madison Avenue [from Kohl's Harlem school] even gave after-school voluntary classes in test preparation." But in the Harlem schools it was "against the rules" to provide copies of old tests so that teachers could help their pupils prepare for them; Kohl had to obtain such copies from friends who taught in white, middle-class schools, where back files were kept and made available.[25] Recent studies have suggested, moreover, that the content of "standardized" tests conforms to the experience and norms of white, middle-class children, thereby discriminating in still another manner against able children of poor or black parents.

Thus, just as the establishment of high schools in the nineteenth century promoted the interests of middle-class parents, so ability grouping has become an elaborate mechanism for ensuring those same interests. In this respect the track system has joined with "the ordinary operations of educational institutions," which, deliberate discrimination aside, by themselves tend to deny poor and working-class children equal opportunities for social mobility. Experienced teachers transfer out of schools in poor neighborhoods, seeking better-paying and less exacting assignments.[26] Schools develop studied institutional defenses of secrecy and professional mystification against criticism or even inquiry by lower-class parents. But they are, of course, much more responsive to wealthier parents, who often control PTAs and school boards and whom, in any case, schoolteachers and administrators emulate.

Thus, as the sociologist Howard Becker has written, "The schools, organized in terms of one of the subcultures [that of the middle class] of a heterogeneous society, tend to operate in such a way that members of subordinate groups of differing culture do not get their fair share of educational opportunity, and thus of opportunity for social mobility." [27] Which is an elaborate way of saying that schools institutionalize and maintain privilege in America.

But statistics and abstractions may obscure the lives of children trapped in what has been called "programmed retardation." A group of New York City parents, whose children have been tracked into the special "600" schools for allegedly "difficult" children, has begun to prepare a suit to challenge the compulsory-attendance law. While the state has the right to make laws for the health, welfare, or safety of children, they claim, it has no right to subject children to a system that deprives and injures them. Their point is that tracking is not simply a neutral "valve" to control manpower flow, as our initial image might at first have suggested. Rather, tracking harms some children, depriving those we call "deprived," making them less competent, less able to reach, let alone to use, the instruments of power in US society. In the light of tracking, schools become for such children not the means to democratization and liberation, but to oppression.

On the other hand, tracking is also one means of controlling middle-class students. The Selective Service's "channeling" system benefits the young man who can afford to go to college, and whose culture supports both higher education and avoiding the draft if he can. Channeling helps him, however, only so long as he lives up to the draft board's standards of behavior and work. Just as the threat of loss of deferment drives draft registrants into college or jobs in the "National Interest," so the threat of losing privileged status within the school system is used to drive students to fulfill upper-track, college-bound requirements. In a school in which students are tracked from, say, "12-1"—the twelfth-grade class for college-bound students—down to "12-34" —the class for alleged unteachables—demotion not only would threaten a student's social position, but his entire future life. Having a child placed in a lower track is a stigma for a college-oriented family, as every principal faced with angry parents pushing to have their children in the "best" classes will testify. Moreover, entry into prestige colleges, or even into college at all, normally depends upon track and other measures of school status. Thus though the threat, like that of channeling in the past, has been largely unspoken, it continues to push students to behaving and achieving as required by the system.

These operations of tracking and channeling (and of racial segregation, for which tracking is often an administrative substitute) [28] help to explain why, contrary to popular American mythology, this society has more and more rapidly become stratified, structured by class. Increasingly, Americans follow the occupations of their fathers or, at any rate, enter occupations of roughly the same prestige and income. [29] Level of education— which must be distinguished both from what a student has learned and from how competent he might be—is a major determinant of what kind of job he can get. [30] The more education attained, on the whole, the better the job; and, of course, the more prestigious the college the better. There is a direct correlation between a student's social and economic class and the likelihood that he will enter *or* graduate from college. A recent study by the Carnegie Commission of Higher Education found that children from families whose income is above the national median have a chance of getting into college three times greater than that of children from families below the median. And only 7 percent of college students come from families in the bottom quarter of national income.[31] "The passage from school to college, in fact, seems to depend more upon socialization, life experience, and opportunity than upon intellective factors." [32]

The track system provides a formal basis for translating these class-based factors into academic criteria for separating students into different groups: those who will drop out; those whose diplomas will not admit them to college; those who will be able to enter only two-year or junior colleges; and the lucky few in the honors classes who will go on to elite institutions and to graduate or professional schools. Thus while tracking may assure the "failure" of lower-class students, as a system it allows the schools to "succeed" in serving middle-class interests by preparing their children to fill the technological and professional needs of corporate society.

In several cities during the past few years, as the contradictions between systems of tracking and the rhetoric of social mobility have become especially apparent, some groups have begun to pressure for the abolition of tracking and others, in the meantime, for "open" admissions to colleges. It is clear enough to students and their parents that there are fewer jobs available for young men who have not completed high school or who have emerged from "basic" or other lower tracks. Jobs requiring no secondary education have decreased 25 percent in the past ten years; and white-collar workers, who made up 15 percent of the work force in 1900 and 28.5 percent in 1940, will make up about 48 percent in 1970. Schools with tracking systems have not been particularly responsive to a job market changed by automation and "upgrading" (an economist's term for saying that you now need more educational credentials to get the same level of job). Manpower specialists, often writing under the auspices of major foundations, have therefore called on school systems to change their practice so that their products will suit a modernizing industrial economy.[33] But of course, the pressure to maintain a system segregated by class has not abated.

The clash between those upholding tracking and those wishing to end it has taken particularly dramatic forms in several cities.

In Washington, D.C., for example, tracking was a primary issue in the battle over former Superintendent Carl Hansen's job. In New York City, the issue of whom the schools will serve has been fought over "community control." Experiments designed to make schools more responsive to the needs of blacks and Puerto Ricans by giving them direct control over the education of their children through the creation of community school boards have been financed by the Ford Foundation and supported by politicians, including Mayor Lindsay and Governor Rockefeller, who have been sensitive to the changing needs of large industry as well as the demands of black voters.

In opposition to community-controlled decentralization, the New York Teachers' Union and much of the white, middle-class electorate correctly understand the demand for community control as a demand that the schools help the children of poor blacks and Puerto Ricans to compete with their own children instead of preventing them from doing so. Jewish teachers remember their battle against WASPs and Irish Catholics entrenched in the schools before them. Odd alliances between the Ford Foundation and the Ocean Hill-Brownsville local board, on the one hand, and the liberal Jewish and conservative Italian communities, on the other, as well as the bitterness of the struggle in New York City suggest how fundamental are the social and economic stakes at issue in the control of the schools.

The issue is also powerful and divisive for higher education. Encouraged by US society to believe that young people can rise to the top, whatever their race or class, blacks, Chicanos, Puerto Ricans, and some working-class white students are beginning to press into colleges. Higher education in the United States has had to manage an elaborate and delicate technique for diverting many of these students from goals toward which they have been taught to aspire, but which a stratified society cannot allow them all to reach. "Cooling" them "out," the term openly used in higher education and now beginning to become as familiar to students as "channeling," means that certain students are deliberately and secretively discouraged from aspirations middle-class youth take for granted. Working-class students are tracked into second-class or "junior" colleges, "cooled out" and counseled into substitute curricula (a medical technician's program rather than a premedical course), or, if they get to a university, programmed for failure in large "required" courses.[34]

California's three-tiered system of higher education has provided a model for other states: the "top" eighth of high-school graduates may be admitted to the university system, the "top" third to the state colleges; the rest are relegated to what one writer has described as "those fancied-up super high schools, the local two-year 'community colleges.' " [35] Factors closely related to race and economic class—students' high-school track, grades, and College Board scores—determine placement into a particular level of higher education, though the fees students pay are relatively similar wherever they may go in the state.[36] Like tracking in high schools, state-subsidized higher education channels students into distinctly inequitable systems. In Maryland, for example, the average per pupil expenditure during fiscal year 1966 was $802 in community colleges, $1,221 in the state colleges, and $1,724 (excluding research funds) in the University of Maryland.[37]

Another significant index of discrimination is the relative teaching load of faculties: at the University of Maryland, an English professor teaches three courses, at state colleges four, and at community colleges five. Theoretically, at least, university students are taught by professors with better credentials, higher salaries, and lighter teaching loads than at state or community colleges. It is not surprising, therefore, as Todd Gitlin has pointed out, that from the university campuses come "high professionals and managers for the great corporations. At the bottom, the two-year junior colleges take on all comers, and process them into clerks, punch-card operators, foremen—the dregs of the white-collar labor force." [38]

But it is not only that the student attending a junior college will have far less public money spent on his education than the student attending Berkeley, Michigan, or the University of Maryland. It is rather that tracking at public colleges also benefits the children of the rich at the expense of the children of the poor. Patricia Cayo Sexton has stated the case: "In general the more money a student's parents make, the more money will be spent on his education, despite some efforts at public 'compensatory' expenditures for the disadvantaged." [39] In New York City, for example, tuition-free colleges with " 'high standards' . . . have . . . subsidized many middle-income students and virtually excluded most impoverished ethnic groups." "Low college tuition," Mrs. Sexton writes, "offers few opportunities to lower-income students if entrance 'standards' are too high to hurdle."

Significantly, her statistics bear out the relationship between income and admission: at the University of Michigan, only 25 percent of the fathers of entering freshmen had less than a college education, only 4.8 percent less than a high-school diploma; consequently, only 1.8 percent of the students were from families with incomes under $4,000.[40] The circular process is obvious: just as the economic class of a student's family largely determines his admission to a particular college or university in the first place, so does his placement at that college determine his future. Indeed, money is destiny![41] Given the process of "upgrading" jobs, one might find suitable the image of a squirrel in a circular cage: the faster he runs, the more firmly does he remain bound to his position. While the admission of working-class students to community colleges may seem to be serving their desire for upward mobility, in fact it may barely be keeping the lid on potentially explosive campuses.

Demonstrations throughout the nation during the spring of 1969 arose from students' increasing awareness that tracking, and its methods of cheating and controlling the poor, have been translated into new campus forms. Demands for "open admissions" of black and "third-world" students, prominent first at San Francisco State College, attempt to strike at the heart of the tracking system by negating the streaming process of earlier school years. Students at San Francisco State, at City College in New York, and elsewhere, in lengthy strikes and demonstrations, have first paralyzed the institution, then divided it irrevocably on principles similar to those we have described with relation to high schools.

In the official catalogue of San Francisco State, a passage claims that the curriculum ought to satisfy "existing student interests" and "the technical and professional manpower requirements of the State." [42] But interests of students and those of manpower specialists often diverge fundamentally: they are obviously most divergent with respect to working-class students' aspirations for the alleged room at the top and industry's needs for a highly differentiated work force.

Can the track system survive this new and deeply outraged onslaught of college students? The "valves" of tracking in high school may be sticky, at once denying both reasonable opportunity to poor and black students and better trained manpower to industry. But the demand for dividing the work force by some tracking mechanism remains. To be sure, it doesn't much matter, at least abstractly, to the corporation manager just *who* fills what slots —so long as young people are channeled and prepared to fill them. In this respect, the need for a class-based track system diminishes. But a particular John D. Executive—not to speak of Jack Salesman—wants to maintain *his* privilege for *his* kids. Thus the pressure to maintain the present social and class divisions has hardly diminished. Colleges are, on the one hand, pressed from below by poor, black, and radical students to end discriminatory admissions practices. On the other hand, they are pressed from above by politicians, trustees, and contributors to "maintain standards," not to "capitulate to the demands of demonstrators." [43] Implicitly, they are of course urged to maintain the present system of class and economic privilege embodied in those "standards."

In March, 1969, Rutgers University agreed to an "open admissions" policy for disadvantaged students from the three cities in which its campuses are located. Almost at once, opposition to the program developed in the New Jersey legislature, partly because the plan would reduce the number of students eligible to enter the state university who were not from those lucky three cities. Similarly, an announcement by New York City's Board of Higher Education that it would attempt to implement an "open admissions policy by 1970 was greeted with opposition by key state legislators." [44]

More sensitive to the complexities of New York City's educational politics, a conservative Democratic candidate for mayor in 1969, Mario A. Procaccino, "hoped" that money could be found so that all city youths would have access to "free education," but warned "against any lowering of academic standards at the university." The New York City plan by no means envisaged an end to tracking. As initially presented, it pictured only 19 percent of graduating high-school seniors entering the senior colleges, some 26 percent going on to community colleges, and another 20 percent or more being channeled into "educational skills centers," where, presumably, they would be trained to fill vacancies in low-paying hospital, teaching-aid, and clerical positions.

The revised plan now being implemented considerably increased the proportion of high-school graduates entering senior colleges. But more ingeniously, it changed the standard of admission to the senior colleges from high-school grade-point average alone, adding as an alternative criterion a student's rank in his high-school class. Thus the student from ghetto schools, where grade-point averages are notoriously low, will be able to enter one of the senior colleges by finishing in the top half or so of his class.

The competition for places in the city's colleges will thus be increased even for middle-class students, since the compromise tries to placate white, middle-class advocates of "standards" by saying to them that their children can be admitted to a senior college if they maintain high standards. At the same time, the compromise attempts to placate ghetto residents by opening the senior colleges to more of their children—those, on the whole, perhaps, with middle-class aspirations. What the plan does, rather neatly, is to turn a threatening racial and ethnic crisis into a division of students by class; it is precisely such school-maintained divisions that Americans have in the past chosen not to contest.

New York City's response to the pressure for open admissions and an end to tracking seems a likely harbinger. It shifts part of the burden of tracking upward to "education beyond high school," now available for "all who want it," and held out as a carrot for disaffected minorities. The plan expands Upward Bound and SEEK programs to permit more individuals of "high potential but weak background" to flow into higher educational streams. In short, it places the valves higher in the educational system and lets them function a bit more freely. It gives the needs of the economy for a screened, differentiated, and controllable work force somewhat higher priority than the wishes of white middle-class parents that the schools perpetuate their privilege. But it by no means destroys the mechanisms by which schools have maintained class privilege. Now students will be separated—according to grades and class standing—into senior college, community college, and "other" categories.

Not surprisingly: for the systems of tracking are so closely tied to those who control American education and to the qualities of American schools that it is hard to imagine their replacement altogether—certainly not by a system which would permit children to develop according to their own needs and abilities.

Notes

COUNTRY SCHOOLMASTER OF THE NINETEENTH CENTURY/ WOODY

[1] Mr. Domer showed me documents which he had preserved, to vouch for some of them.

[2] *Editors' Note:* Common "branches" of the "tree of knowledge" generally included the various aspects of reading, writing, history, geography, mathematics, and in many cases philosophy and classical languages.

[3] Mr. Domer's memory slipped here; his first certificate shows May.

[4] Mr. Domer's memory varied from the documents later shown me, which are followed here.

[5] The County Superintendent rated teachers "1 plus, 1, 1—, 2 plus, 2, and 2—." From "2—" up each grade meant a $5.00 raise. I was raised to $33.00 the second year, and received $40.00 the third.

[6] The salary of $28.00 was really far more than it seems now, for prices were low; a suit cost $8.00 to $10.00; hat $1.00 to $1.50; shoes, made to order, $4.50 to $5.00.

[7] Mr. Domer seems not to have known Sander's *Bilder Fibel.* This book (1846) showed pictures, gave German and English in parallel columns and pages, and thus facilitated transition from the tongue of family and community to the idiom of the schoolroom. It was to be an introduction to Sander's First Reader.

[8] *Editors' Note: Parsing* (from the Latin *pars orationis* for *part of speech*) was a common term—and activity—throughout much of American education, when it was believed that identifying parts of speech was one of the most important abilities acquired in school.

[9] *Editors' Note:* the forerunner of the modern "teachers college," which appears, in turn, to be merging with the more broadly based "state college." The term derived from the French *école normale*, signifying the offering of standard professional training, usually for educators.

[10] *Editors' Note:* Mr. Domer here uses the term *culture* in its more limited sense, referring to refined artistic and cultivated activities, rather than all the characteristic features of a given group. Certainly the Pennsylvania "Dutch" had a particularly rich cultural heritage in the latter sense of the term.

[11] *Editors' Note:* a heavy metal rod.

SEARCH FOR FREEDOM: THE STORY OF AMERICAN EDUCATION/BUTTS

[1] *Editors' Note:* The terms *republican* and *democratic* are used in their general sense in this selection and do not refer to the specific political parties with which we associate them today.

[2] *Editors' Note:* The massive federal funding stemming from the Elementary and Secondary Education Act of 1965 represented an additional step toward a nationwide educational effort.

MILESTONES IN THE EDUCATION OF THE NEGRO IN AMERICA/ ROUCEK

[1] Among the best recent studies of Negro education in the United States is: Virgil A. Clift; Archibald W. Anderson and H. Gordon Hullfish (eds.) *Negro Education in America: Its Adequacy, Problems and Needs* (New York: Harper, 1962), and especially: W. A. Low, "The Education of Negroes Viewed Historically," pp. 27–59; William H. Martin, "Unique Contributions of Negro Educators," pp. 69–92; Regina M. Goff, "Culture and the Personality Development of Minority Peoples," pp. 124–152. Cf. also the quarterly *The Journal of Negro Education*, Howard University, Washington 1, D.C.

Among numberless valuable studies, see: Robert M. Frumkin and Joseph S. Roucek, "Contributions from Minorities, Elites, and Special Educational Organizations" in Richard Gross (ed.) *Heritage of American Education* (Boston: Allyn & Bacon, 1962), chapter X, pp. 365–422; Francis J. Brown and Joseph S. Roucek (eds.) *One America* (Englewood Cliffs, N.J.: Prentice-Hall, 1952); Harry S. Ashmore, *The Negro and the Schools* (Chapel Hill, N.C.: University of North Carolina Press, 1954); Margaret Just Butcher, *The Negro in American Culture* (New York: Mentor Books, 1956); E. Franklin Frazier, *The Negro in the United States* (New York: Macmillan, 1957); Eli Ginsberg et al., *The Negro Potential* (New York: Columbia University Press, 1956); Gunnar Myrdal et al., *An American Dilemma* (New York: Harper, 1944); Edward A. Suchman et al., *Desegregation* (New York: B'nai B'rith, 1958).

[2] Richard Bardolph, *The Negro Vanguard* (New York: Rinehart, 1959), p. 115.

[3] For their list, see Bardolph, *op. cit.*, p. 120.

[4] *Ibid.*, p. 120.

[5] Bardolph, *op. cit.*, p. 121. For more details, see pp. 121–135.

[6] Among the well-documented histories, see especially: Edgar W. Knight, *Public Education in the South* (Boston: Ginn, 1922); Truman M. Pierce et al., *White and Negro Schools in the South* (Englewood Cliffs, N.J.; Prentice-Hall, 1955); Horace M. Bond, *The Education of the Negro in the American Social Order* (Englewood Cliffs, N.J.: Prentice-Hall, 1945).

[7] Booker T. Washington, *Up from Slavery* (New York: Doubleday, 1901).

[8] W. E. B. Du Bois, *The Souls of Black Folk* (Chicago: McClurg, 1928).

[9] W. A. Low, "The Education of Negroes Viewed Historically," in Virgil A. Clift, pp. 27–59; Archibald W. Anderson and H. Gordon Hullfish (eds.) *Negro Education in America: Its Adequacy, Problems, and Needs* (New York: Harper, 1962), p. 52.

[10] Oscar Barek, Heedore, Jr., and Nelson Manfred Blake, *Since 1900: A History of the United States in Our Times* (New York: Macmillan, 1959), p. 747.

[11] Low, *op. cit.*, pp. 53–54.

THE MODERN FEDERAL COLOSSUS IN EDUCATION: THREAT OR PROMISE/SAYLOR

[1] *Editors' Note:* Legislation providing federal funds for the support of education since the Higher Education Act of 1965 include the following:
Head Start Program (Introduced through Office of Economic Opportunity), 1965
National Teacher Corps Act, 1965
Permanent G.I. Rights Act, 1966

International Education Act, 1967
Head Start Program extension, 1967
Education Professions Development Act, 1967
Amendments to National Defense Education Act and Elementary and
 Secondary Education Act, 1967
2 *Editors' Note:* Statistics from the U.S. Office of Education show that
federal funds for education in 1969–1970 made up about 18% of all monies
spent on education in the U.S. by all levels of government combined.
3 *Editors' Note:* Evaluation of the effectiveness of Title I ESEA programs is
handled through state and local evaluation agency reports. In this way the
U. S. Office of Education obtains data which enable it to determine the types
of programs which are functioning well and should be continued or expanded.

HOW THE SCHOOL SYSTEM IS RIGGED FOR FAILURE/LAUTER AND HOWE

1 *The 28th Report of the Massachusetts Board of Education,* pp. 83–84.
Quoted in Michael B. Katz, *The Irony of Early School Reform* (Cambridge,
1968), pp. 44–45.
2 "Innovation in Education: New Directions for 'the American School," a
statement by the Research and Policy Committee, July, 1968, pp. 9, 10.
3 Kenneth Clark, *Dark Ghetto* (New York, 1965), pp. 120–21.
4 *Elementary and Secondary Education Act of 1965,* Report #143. House of
Representatives, 89th Congress.
5 Mario D. Fantini and Gerald Weinstein, *The Disadvantaged: Challenge to
Education* (New York, 1968), pp. 172–73.
6 See our article in *NYR* (June 20, 1968) and Chapter 7 of our forthcoming
book, *The Conspiracy of the Young.*
7 Kenneth Clark, in a paper for a conference sponsored by the US Commission on Civil Rights in November, 1967.
8 Katz, *op. cit.*, p. 91.
9 *Ibid.*, p. 92.
10 *Ibid.*, p. 87.
11 *Ibid.*, p. 88.
12 *Life,* 66 (May 16, 1969), p. 29.
13 Bayard Hooper, "The Task Is to Learn What Learning Is For," *Life,* 66
(May 16, 1969), pp. 34, 39.
14 All quotations from Heber Hinds Ryan and Philpine Crecelius, *Ability
Grouping in the Junior High School* (New York, 1927), pp. 1–10.
15 Miriam L. Goldberg, et al., *The Effects of Ability Grouping* (New York,
1966), p. 163. "Differences in achievement growth over the two-grade span,"
the authors found, "did not support the common wisdom that narrowing the
ability range or separating the extreme groups from the intermediate groups
enables teachers to be more effective in raising the pupils' achievement level.
. . . On the contrary, although the achievement differences among patterns
of varying ability range were small, overall observed increments tended to
favor the *broad range*" (p. 160).
 See also Joseph Justman, "Ability Grouping—What Good Is It?" *The
Urban Review,* 2 (February, 1967), pp. 2–3: ". . . homogeneous grouping is
not a panacea for educational ills. . . . Grouping by itself, without curricular modification as a concomitant, will not give rise to the desired outcome
of improved pupil performance." Unfortunately, no one has shown, either,
that grouping with "curricular modifications" would make real differences,

or just what "curricular modifications" there might be that would not, for example, strait-jacket and limit "slow learners."

[16] The *Times* of London reported August 12, 1966, on a set of samples being taken by the British Foundation for Educational Research: "Most of the existing research of streaming [tracking] has come to the conclusion that children get better results in unstreamed schools. One notable piece of work was that of Dr. J. C. Daniels (1961). . . . Dr. Daniels compared academic progress in two streamed and two unstreamed schools in detail. He reported that progress in reading, English and arithmetic was more rapid for all children in unstreamed schools, but particularly for the weakest children. These findings have not as yet been seriously challenged by later research. . . ."

Dr. J. W. B. Douglas examined the "school careers of 5,000 children in the Medical Research unit's permanent sample." He showed that "although children in higher streams all made good progress, the IQs of children in lower streams actually deteriorated during the later years of primary school. This deterioration was most marked in children of working class background. Dr. Douglas' general conclusion was that 'streaming by ability tends to reinforce the process of social selection.' The initial act of streaming was, in Dr. Douglas' view, heavily influenced by social and nonacademic factors."

[17] Goldberg, *op. cit.*, p. 165. The study "reinforces the conclusion that what pupils learn is at least as much a function of what teachers teach and expect of them as it is a function of pupil attitudes, self-percepts, or, within limits, even tested intellectual ability" (p. 164). See, in this regard, Robert A. Rosenthal, *Pygmalion in the Classroom* (Cambridge, 1968). Rosenthal relates the results of an experiment in which teachers were told that certain of their students were revealed through "tests" as having superior, though hidden, ability. Though the students were not, in fact, special, they began to perform better, apparently in response to teachers' special ministrations.

[18] See, for example, Maryland Council for Higher Education, *Master Plan for Higher Education in Maryland* (Baltimore, 1968), section 2, p. 36.

[19] Theodore Caplow, *The Sociology of Work* (Minneapolis, 1954), p. 216.

[20] *Slums and Suburbs* (New York: McGraw-Hill, 1961), pp. 40, 66. Conant's comments on tracking help to explain some of the mistrust felt by black communities for liberal educational reformers. He writes: "In short, my recommendation in both my senior high report and my junior high report still stands. In these subjects [English, social studies, mathematics, science —in short, in all the academic curriculum] there ought to be subject-by-subject grouping in three groups—fairly small top and bottom groups and a large middle group. Such an arrangement may well isolate Negroes in some schools in the bottom group, but surely there will be considerable mixing in the large middle group if not in the top group. Moreover, with an integrated staff and with frank discussions of the problem I should think a workable solution might be arrived at in good faith" (p. 64). What is one to say in the face of such naïve optimism?

[21] See, for example, John Vaizey and Michael Debeauvais, "Economic Aspects of Educational Development," in *Education, Economy, and Society*, ed. A. H. Halsey, Jean Floud, and C. H. Anderson (Glencoe, 1961), p. 43.

[22] See, for example, Patricia Cayo Sexton, *Education and Income* (New York, 1962), pp. 228, 234.

[23] These figures were obtained by Columbia University SDS from the records of the N.Y.C. Board of Education through the office of the Reverend Milton Galamison, then a member of the board.

[24] The figures cited in this paragraph are contained in the briefs filed by the

plaintiff in *Hobson vs. Hansen*, the case decided by Judge Wright. See our article on "The Washington School Mess." *NYR*, February 1, 1968.

Hansen's own description of Washington's track system, printed in the November, 1960, *Atlantic Monthly*, is worth quoting at length.

Honors Level: ". . . To protect the quality of instruction, the honors curriculum is selective. A student is enrolled in this curriculum only if he has demonstrated ability to do superior work by his previous grades, by test scores, and by teacher judgment. . . ."

Regular College Preparatory: ". . . While the program is designed as preparatory for college, it offers excellent general background for able students not planning college careers. If I could be, or wanted to be, fully authoritarian on this point, I would require every capable pupil, college bound or not, to choose this or the honors curriculum. The intellectual development most needed for general citizenship can best be obtained through study of the great and significant disciplines taught at a demanding and invigorating level . . . many capable students are under-achieving, and maximum persuasion, short of authoritative controls, should be used to motivate them to move up to the more difficult but richer curriculums. . . ."

General Curriculum: ". . . cafeteria-type election of subjects with bargain-basement rummaging for good grades at reduced prices. . . ."

Basic Curriculum: ". . . This curriculum is for the academically delayed high school student, as indicated by standardized test scores in reading and mathematics, academic grades, and teacher opinion. . . . Teacher opinion is of first importance. . . . The two objectives of the basic curriculum are to upgrade the academic achievement of retarded pupils and to provide education for those whose innate endowments, so far as they are reflected in performance, limit the range and difficulty of learning. . . ."

Small wonder passions in the black community ran rather high against the superintendent.

25 See Herbert Kohl, *36 Children* (New York, 1968), p. 178.

26 In forty schools in New York City with more than 90 percent black and Puerto Rican enrollment, for example, 46.8 percent of the teachers had three years of experience or less, whereas only a quarter of the teachers in similar schools with predominantly white enrollment were similarly inexperienced. In Washington, where the median income is under $4,000, about 46 percent of the teachers are "temporary"—that is, they cannot, for one reason or another, achieve permanent certification.

27 Howard S. Becker, "Schools and Systems of Stratification," *Education, Economy and Society, op. cit.*, p. 103. See also August Hollingshead's classic study, *Elmtown's Youth* (New York, 1949), which describes how schools give rewards to students based on their families' class position.

28 Because assignment to track reflects so closely class and racial factors, it is still not unusual to observe in theoretically "integrated" schools predominantly white "advanced" classes and predominantly (more often, all) black "slower" classes.

29 See, for example, J. W. Bennett and Melvin M. Tumin, *Social Life* (New York, 1949), p. 587. In his study, *Wealth and Power in America*, Gabriel Kolko shows that despite the New Deal and higher levels of government spending on welfare, there has been no change in basic distribution of income and wealth in the United States since 1910.

30 See, for example, Patricia Cayo Sexton, *The American School* (Englewood Cliffs, N.J., 1967), p. 51: "There is, in fact, an absence of evidence that the most able in performance of jobs or other real-life tasks are selected or produced by the standards set and training offered by higher education. Employers often hire from among the degree elite because of the prestige

rather than the superior training or job performance skill attached to a college degree."

[31] See *Chronicle of Higher Education*, Dec. 9, 1968.

[32] Bruce K. Eckland, "Social Class and College Graduation: Some Misconceptions Corrected," *American Journal of Sociology*, 70 (July, 1964), p. 36.

[33] See, for example, John Vaizey and Michael Debeauvais, "Economic Aspects of Educational Development," *Education, Economy, and Society, op. cit.*, pp. 38–39, 43.

[34] See, for example, Burton R. Clark, "The 'Cooling-Out' Function in Higher Education," *American Journal of Sociology*, LXV (May, 1960): "In summary, the cooling-out process in higher education is one whereby systematic discrepancy between aspiration and avenue is covered over and stress for the individual and the system is minimized. The provision of readily available alternative achievements in itself is an important device for alleviating the stress consequent on failure and so preventing anomic and deviant behavior. The general result of cooling-out processes is that society can continue to encourage maximum effort without major disturbance from unfulfilled promises and expectations. . . .

"For an organization and its agents one dilemma of a cooling-out role is that it must be kept reasonably away from public scrutiny and not clearly perceived or understood by prospective clientele. Should it become obvious, the organization's ability to perform it would be impaired. If high school seniors and their families were to define the junior college as a place which diverts college-bound students, a probable consequence would be a turning-away from the junior college and increased pressure for admission to the four-year colleges and universities that are otherwise protected to some degree. This would, of course, render superfluous the part now played by the junior college in the division of labor among the colleges."

[35] Kingsley Widmer, "Why Colleges Blew Up," *The Nation*, 208 (Feb. 24, 1969), p. 238.

[36] Bowdoin College recently eliminated College Board scores as an entrance requirement. Richard M. Moll, the director of admissions, explained that "there is a widespread feeling and convincing evidence today that standardized aptitude and achievement tests cannot escape cultural bias and that they thereby work in favor of the more advantaged elements of our society, while handicapping others." *The Chronicle of Higher Education*, February 2, 1970, p. 1.

[37] *Master Plan for Higher Education in Maryland*, section 2, p. 19.

[38] "On the Line at S. F. State," *Mayday* (now *Hard Times*), 18 February 10–17, 1969).

[39] *The American School*, p. 54.

[40] *Ibid.*, p. 52.

[41] Race is obviously also a factor of exclusion: even the most casual observation of campuses in Maryland bears out the same kind of racial divisions that Mrs. Sexton documents for other states. Indeed, so few blacks attend the university that it is under orders from the US Office of Education to implement a plan for integration.

[42] Todd Gitlin called this passage to our attention in his "On the Line at S. F. State."

[43] See, for example, Leonard Buder, "On Open Admissions." *The New York Times*, July 11, 1969.

[44] See "Open Admissions in City U. Opposed by Albany Chiefs," *The New York Times*, July 11, 1969.

Further Reading

In addition to references cited by authors in this Part the following texts may be useful.

Butts, R. Freeman, and Lawrence A. Cremin. *A History of Education in American Culture.* New York, N.Y.: Holt, Rinehart and Winston, 1953.

In this basic work on the history of American education, the student is referred to chapters 2, 4, 7, and 10 especially, for discussions of the development of early American education patterns.

Cubberly, Ellwood P. *Readings in Public Education in the United States.* Boston, Mass.: Houghton Mifflin, 1934.

Providing background material on the early development of our educational institutions, this older reference is especially useful in tracing the growth of our common schools (pages 89–114).

DeYoung, Chris A., and Richard Wynn. *American Education.* New York, N.Y.: McGraw-Hill, 1968.

The student is referred to chapter 16 for an exceptionally thorough treatment of the financing of American public schools from colonial times to the present.

Tyack, David B. (ed). *Turning Points in American Educational History.* Waltham, Mass.: Ginn, Blaisdell, 1967.

Chapter 5 provides an excellent discussion of Horace Mann's influence upon the common school movement in America. The student is also referred to Chapter 8 for an interesting treatment of early efforts in Negro education.

Films of Related Interests *

"Education in America" Coronet Films, 16 min. each

A series of 3 films depicting the historical development of American schools from the 16th to the 20th centuries.

"Horace Mann" Emerson Film Corporation, 19 min.

Portrays the influence of the American educator on the development of our schools.

"Satellites, Schools and Survival" National Education Association, 28 min.

Depicts the development of our school system from early days, presenting challenges and significant problems.

* All films are 16mm unless otherwise noted.

Part II

Social and Cultural Concerns

There is only one subject-matter for education, and that is Life in all its manifestations.

Alfred North Whitehead
Philosopher and Educator
from **The Aims of Education,** 1929

Everybody knows that American society is changing—that a lot of things aren't like they were last year, that people are growing up differently, that new things are happening fast, and that some things aren't happening at all any more.

One could keep busy—many people and whole industries do—just staying in tune with the shifting scene: the new life-styles, the breakdown of old taboos, the changing family and residential patterns, the continuing wonders of our labor-saving age. If one is particularly interested in any of society's institutions, however—its legal system, its political sphere, organized religion, education—just "keeping up" isn't fully satisfying. The minute the scene changes, click! one is back at zero and must figure it all out again from scratch. And all one's views about the Church or the law or the schools must be reassembled out of the new material.

An alternate way of viewing rapid social change is from the standpoint of the institution itself. In the case of education, this means that we note not only modifications in student behavior, or in curriculum, but anything that bears upon the fundamental tasks performed by education for the society which it serves. Viewed through this sociological lens, events such as modifications in teachers staffing patterns or in enrollment figures are more than just interesting, or baffling, in and of themselves. They expand our awareness of education as an institution evolved by society to discharge certain functions: whether it be handing on values, skills, and information, or acting as custody agent for the younger members of the society until they become adults, acting as a "melting pot," or perpetuating the old order. The broader sociological perspective casts considerable light, in turn, on society itself, for once we note differences in the functions being discharged, or not discharged, by the schools, we have a greater insight into societal trends.

What functions do American junior and senior high schools perform for students today? Are these services likely to be required by students in forthcoming years?

Have American schools undergone sufficient change in recent years to serve our rapidly evolving modern society?

What specific social problems face American schools today? What, if anything, is being done about each?

How do—and how can—teachers from middle-class socioeconomic backgrounds relate to students from lower socioeconomic milieu?

How might shifting patterns of authority in a society affect its educational activities?

Culture as a Force: Mirroring Modern Man

Clyde Kluckhohn

Why do the Chinese dislike milk and milk products? Why should the Japanese die willingly in a Banzai charge [1] that seemed senseless to Americans? Why do some nations trace descent through the father, others through the mother, still others through both parents? Not because they were destined by God or Fate to different habits, not because the weather is different in China and Japan and the United States. Sometimes shrewd common sense has an answer that is close to that of the anthropologist: "because they were brought up that way." By "culture" anthropology means the total life way of a people, the social legacy the individual acquires from his group. Or culture can be regarded as that part of the environment that is the creation of man.

This technical term has a wider meaning than the "culture" of history and literature. A humble cooking pot is as much a cultural product as is a Beethoven sonata. In ordinary speech a man of culture is a man who can speak languages other than his own, who is familiar with history, literature, philosophy, or the fine arts. In some cliques that definition is still narrower. The cultured person is one who can talk about James Joyce, Scarlatti, and Picasso.

To the anthropologist, however, to be human is to be cultured. There is culture in general, and then there are the specific cultures such as Russian, American, British, Hottentot, Inca. The general abstract notion serves to remind us that we cannot explain acts solely in terms of the biological properties of the people concerned, their individual past experience, and the immediate situation. The past experience of other men in the form of culture enters into almost every event. Each specific culture constitutes a kind of blueprint for all of life's activities.

One of the interesting things about human beings is that they try to understand themselves and their own behavior. While this has been particularly true of Europeans in recent times, there is no group which has not developed a scheme or schemes to explain man's actions. To the insistent human query "why?" the most exciting illumination anthropology has to offer is that of the concept of culture. Its explanatory importance is comparable to categories such as evolution in biology, gravity in physics, disease in medicine. A good deal of human behavior can be understood, and indeed predicted, if we know a people's design for living. Many acts are neither accidental nor due to personal peculiarities nor caused by supernatural forces nor simply mysterious. Even those of us who pride ourselves on our individualism follow most of the time a pattern not of our own making. We brush our teeth on arising. We put on pants—not a loincloth or a grass skirt. We eat three meals a day—not four or five or two. We sleep in a bed—not in a hammock or on a sheep pelt. I do not have to know the individual and his life history to be able to predict these and countless other regularities, including many in the thinking process, of all Americans who are not incarcerated in jails or hospitals for the insane.

To the American woman a system of plural wives seems "instinctively" abhorrent. She cannot understand how any woman can fail to be jealous and uncomfortable if she must share her husband with other women. She feels it "unnatural" to accept such a situation. On the other hand, a Koryak woman of Siberia, for example, would find it hard to understand how a woman could be so selfish and so undesirous of feminine companionship in the home as to wish to restrict her husband to one mate.

Some years ago I met in New York City a young man who did not speak a word of English and was obviously bewildered by American ways. By "blood" he was as American as you or I, for his parents had gone from Indiana to China as missionaries.

Orphaned in infancy, he was reared by a Chinese family in a remote village. All who met him found him more Chinese than American. The facts of his blue eyes and light hair were less impressive than a Chinese style of gait, Chinese arm and hand movements, Chinese facial expression and Chinese modes of thought. The biological heritage was American, but the cultural training had been Chinese. He returned to China.

Another example of another kind: I once knew a trader's wife in Arizona who took a somewhat devilish interest in producing a cultural reaction. Guests who came her way were often served delicious sandwiches filled with a meat that seemed to be neither chicken nor tuna fish yet was reminiscent of both. To queries she gave no reply until each had eaten his fill. She then explained that what they had eaten was not chicken, not tuna fish, but the rich, white flesh of freshly killed rattlesnakes. The response was instantaneous—vomiting, often violent vomiting. A biological process is caught in a cultural web.

A highly intelligent teacher with long and successful experience in the public schools of Chicago was finishing her first year in an Indian school. When asked how her Navaho pupils compared in intelligence with Chicago youngsters, she replied, "Well, I just don't know. Sometimes the Indians seem just as bright. At other times they just act like dumb animals. The other night we had a dance in the high school. I saw a boy who is one of the best students in my English class standing off by himself. So I took him over to a pretty girl and told them to dance. But they just stood there with their heads down. They wouldn't even say anything." I inquired if she knew whether or not they were members of the same clan. "What difference would that make?"

"How would you feel about getting into bed with your brother?" The teacher walked off in a huff, but actually, the two cases were quite comparable in principle. To the Indian the type of bodily contact involved in our social dancing has a directly sexual connotation. The incest taboos between members of the same clan are as severe as between true brothers and sisters. The shame of the Indians at the suggestion that a clan brother and sister should dance and the indignation of the white teacher at the idea that she should share a bed with an adult brother represent equally nonrational responses, culturally standardized unreason.

All this does not mean that there is no such thing as raw human nature. The very fact that certain of the same institutions are found in all known societies indicates that at bottom all human beings are very much alike. The files of the Cross-Cultural Survey at Yale University are organized according to categories such as "marriage ceremonies," "life crisis rites," "incest taboos." At least seventy-five of these categories are represented in every single one of the hundreds of cultures analyzed. This is hardly surprising. The members of all human groups have about the same biological equipment. All men undergo the same poignant life experiences such as birth, helplessness, illness, old age, and death. The biological potentialities of the species are the blocks with which cultures are built. Some patterns of every culture crystallize around focuses provided by the inevitables of biology: the difference between the sexes, the presence of persons of different ages, the varying physical strength and skill of individuals. The facts of nature also limit culture forms. No culture provides patterns for jumping over trees or for eating iron ore.

There is thus no "either-or" between nature and that special form of nurture called culture. Cultural determinism is as one-sided as biological determinism. The two factors are interdependent. Culture arises out of human nature, and its forms are restricted both by man's biology and by natural laws. It is equally true that culture channels biological processes—vomiting, weeping, fainting, sneezing, the daily habits of food intake and waste elimination. When a man eats, he is reacting to an internal "drive," namely, hunger contractions consequent upon the lowering of blood sugar, but his precise reaction to these internal stimuli cannot be predicted by physiological knowledge alone. Whether a healthy adult feels hungry twice, three times, or four times a day and the hours at which this feeling recurs is a question of culture. What he eats is of course limited by availability but is also partly regulated by culture. It is a biological fact that some types of berries are poisonous; it is a cultural fact that, a few generations ago, most Americans considered tomatoes to be poisonous and refused to eat them. Such selective, discriminative use of the environment is characteristically cultural. In a still more general sense, too, the process of eating is channeled by culture. Whether a man eats to live, lives to eat, or merely eats and lives is only in part an individual matter, for there are also cultural trends. Emotions are physiological events. Certain situations will evoke fear in people from any culture. But sensations of pleasure, anger, and lust may be stimulated by cultural cues that would leave unmoved someone who has been reared in a different social tradition.

Except in the case of newborn babies and of individuals born with clear-cut structural or functional abnormalities we can observe innate endowments only as modified by cultural training. In a hospital in New Mexico where Zuni Indian, Navaho Indian, and white American babies are born, it is possible to classify the newly arrived infants as unusually active, average, and quiet. Some babies from each "racial" group will fall into each category, though a higher proportion of the white babies will fall into the unusually active class. But if a Navaho baby, a Zuni baby, and a white baby—all classified as unusually active at birth—are again observed at the age of two years, the Zuni baby will no longer seem given to quick and restless activity—*as compared with the white child*—though he may seem so as compared with the other Zunis of the same age. The Navaho child is likely to fall in between as contrasted with the Zuni and the white, though he will probably still seem more active than the average Navaho youngster.

It was remarked by many observers in the Japanese relocation centers [2] that Japanese who were born and brought up in this country, especially those who were reared apart from any large colony of Japanese, resemble in behavior their white neighbors much more closely than they do their own parents who were educated in Japan.

I have said "culture channels biological processes." It is more accurate to say "the biological functioning of individuals is modified if they have been trained in certain ways and not in others." Culture is not a disembodied force. It is created and transmitted by people. However, culture, like well-known concepts of the physical sciences, is a convenient abstraction. One never sees gravity. One sees bodies falling in regular ways. One never sees an electromagnetic field. Yet certain happenings that can be seen may be given a neat abstract formulation by assuming that the electromagnetic field exists. Similarly, one never sees culture as such. What is seen are regularities in the behavior or artifacts of a group that has adhered to a common tradition. The regularities in style and technique of ancient Inca tapestries or stone axes from Melanesian islands are due to the existence of mental blueprints for the group.

Culture is a *way* of thinking, feeling, believing. It is the group's knowledge stored up (in memories of men; in books and objects) for future use. We study the products of this "mental" activity: the overt behavior, the speech and gestures and activities of people, and the tangible results of these things such as tools, houses, cornfields, and what not. It has been customary in lists of "culture traits" to include such things as watches or law books. This is a convenient way of thinking about them, but in the solution of any important problem we must remember that they, in themselves, are nothing but metals, paper and ink. What is important is that some men know how to make them, others set a value on them, are unhappy without them, direct their activities in relation to them, or disregard them.

It is only a helpful shorthand when we say, "the cultural patterns of the Zulu were resistant to Christianization." In the directly observable world, of course, it was individual Zulus who resisted. Nevertheless, if we do not forget that we are speaking at a high level of abstraction, it is justifiable to speak of culture as a cause. One may compare the practice of saying "syphilis caused the extinction of the native population of the island." Was it "syphilis" or "syphilis germs" or "human beings who were carriers of syphilis"?

"Culture," then, is a "theory." But if a theory is not contradicted by any relevant fact and if it helps us to understand a mass of otherwise chaotic facts, it is useful. Darwin's contribution was much less the accumulation of new knowledge than the creation of a theory which put in order data already known. An accumulation of facts, however large, is no more a science than a pile of bricks is a house. Anthropology's demonstration that the most weird set of customs has a consistency and an order is comparable to modern psychiatry's showing that there is meaning and purpose in the apparently incoherent talk of the insane. In fact, the inability of the older psychologies and philosophies to account for the strange behavior of madmen and heathens was the principal factor that forced psychiatry and anthropology to develop theories of the unconscious and of culture.

Since culture is an abstraction, it is important not to confuse culture with society. A "society" refers to a group of people who interact more with each other than they do with other individuals —who cooperate with each other for the attainment of certain ends. You can see and indeed count the individuals who make up a society. A "culture" refers to the distinctive ways of life of such a group of people. Not all social events are culturally patterned. New types of circumstances arise frequently.

A culture constitutes a storehouse of the pooled learning of the group. A rabbit starts life with some innate responses. He can learn from his own experience and perhaps from observing other rabbits. A human infant is born with fewer instincts and greater plasticity. His main task is to learn the answers that persons he will never see, persons long dead, have worked out. Once he has learned the formulas supplied by the culture of his group, most of his behavior becomes almost as automatic and unthinking as if it were instinctive. There is a tremendous amount of intelligence behind the making of a radio, but not much is required to learn to turn it on.

The members of all human societies face some of the same unavoidable dilemmas, posed by biology and other facts of the human situation. This is why the basic categories of all cultures are so similar. Human culture without languages is unthinkable. No culture fails to provide for aesthetic expression and aesthetic delight. Every culture supplies standardized orientations toward the deeper problems, such as death. Every culture is designed to perpetuate the group and its solidarity, to meet the demands of individuals for an orderly way of life and for satisfaction of biological needs.

However, the variations on these basic themes are numberless. Some languages are built up out of twenty basic sounds, others out of forty. Nose plugs were considered beautiful by the predynastic Egyptians but are not by the modern French. Puberty is a biological fact. But one culture ignores it, another prescribes informal instructions about sex but no ceremony, a third has impressive rites for girls only, a fourth for boys and girls. In this culture, the first menstruation is welcomed as a happy, natural event, in that culture the atmosphere is full of dread and supernatural threat. Each culture dissects nature according to its own system of categories. The Navaho Indians apply the same word to the color of a robin's egg and to that of grass. A psychologist once assumed that this meant a difference in the sense organs, that Navahos didn't have the physiological equipment to distinguish "green" from "blue." However, when he showed them objects of the two colors and asked them if they were exactly the same colors, they looked at him with astonishment. His dream of discovering a new type of color blindness was shattered.

Every culture must deal with the sexual instinct. Some, however, seek to deny all sexual expression before marriage, whereas a Polynesian adolescent who was not promiscuous would be distinctly abnormal. Some cultures enforce lifelong monogamy, others, like our own, tolerate serial monogamy; in still other cultures, two or more women may be joined to one man or several men to a single woman. Homosexuality has been a permitted pattern in the Greco-Roman world, in parts of Islam, and in various primitive tribes. Large portions of the population of Tibet, and of Christendom at some places and periods, have practiced complete celibacy. To us marriage is first and foremost an arrangement between two individuals. In many more societies marriage is merely one facet of a complicated set of reciprocities, economic and otherwise, between two families or two clans.

The essence of the cultural process is selectivity. The selection is only exceptionally conscious and rational. Cultures are like Topsy. They just grew. Once, however, a way of handling a situation becomes institutionalized, there is ordinarily great resistance to change or deviation. When we speak of "our sacred beliefs," we mean of course that they are beyond criticism and that the person who suggests modification or abandonment must be punished. No person is emotionally indifferent to his culture. Certain cultural premises may become totally out of accord with a new factual situation. Leaders may recognize this and reject the old ways in theory. Yet their emotional loyalty continues in the face of reason because of the intimate conditionings of early childhood.

A culture is learned by individuals as the result of belonging to some particular group, and it constitutes that part of learned behavior which is shared with others. It is our social legacy, as contrasted with our organic heredity. It is one of the important factors which permits us to live together in an organized society, giving us ready-made solutions to our problems, helping us to predict the behavior of others, and permitting others to know what to expect of us.

Culture regulates our lives at every turn. From the moment we are born until we die there is, whether we are conscious of it or not, constant pressure upon us to follow certain types of behavior that other men have created for us. Some paths we follow willingly, others we follow because we know no other way, still others we deviate from or go back to most unwillingly. Mothers of small children know how unnaturally most of this comes to us —how little regard we have, until we are "culturalized," for the "proper" place, time, and manner for certain acts such as eating, excreting, sleeping, getting dirty, and making loud noises.

But by more or less adhering to a system of related designs for carrying out all the acts of living, a group of men and women feel themselves linked together by a powerful chain of sentiments. Ruth Benedict gave an almost complete definition of the concept when she said, "Culture is that which binds men together."

It is true that any culture is a set of techniques for adjusting both to the external environment and to other men. However, cultures create problems as well as solve them. If the lore of a people states that frogs are dangerous creatures, or that it is not safe to go about at night because of witches or ghosts, threats are posed which do not arise out of the inexorable facts of the external world. Cultures produce needs as well as provide a means of fulfilling them. There exist for every group culturally defined, acquired drives that may be more powerful in ordinary daily life than the biologically inborn drives. Many Americans, for example, will work harder for "success' than they will for sexual satisfaction.

Most groups elaborate certain aspects of their culture far beyond maximum utility or survival value. In other words, not all culture promotes physical survival. At times, indeed, it does exactly the opposite. Aspects of culture which once were adaptive may persist long after they have ceased to be useful. An analysis of any culture will disclose many features which cannot possibly be construed as adaptations to the total environment in which the group now finds itself. However, it is altogether likely that these apparently useless features represent survivals, with modifications through time, of cultural forms once useful.

Any cultural practice must be functional or it will disappear before long. That is, it must somehow contribute to the survival of the society or to the adjustment of the individual. However, many cultural functions are not manifest but latent. A cowboy will walk three miles to catch a horse which he then rides one mile to the store. From the point of view of manifest function this is positively irrational. But the act has the latent function of maintaining the cowboy's prestige in the terms of his own subculture. One can instance the buttons on the sleeve of a man's coat, our absurd English spelling, the use of capital letters, and a host of other apparently nonfunctional customs. They serve mainly the latent function of assisting individuals to maintain their security by preserving continuity with the past and by making certain sectors of life familiar and predictable.

Every culture is a precipitate of history. In more than one

sense history is a sieve. Each culture embraces those aspects of the past which, usually in altered form and with altered meanings, live on in the present. Discoveries and inventions, both material and ideological, are constantly being made available to a group through its historical contacts with other peoples or being created by its own members. However, only those that fit the total immediate situation in meeting the group's needs for survival or in promoting the psychological adjustment of individuals will become part of the culture. The process of culture building may be regarded as an addition to man's innate biological capacities, an addition providing instruments which enlarge, or may even substitute for, biological functions, and to a degree compensating for biological limitations—as in ensuring that death does not always result in the loss to humanity of what the deceased has learned.

Culture is like a map. Just as a map isn't the territory but an abstract representation of a particular area, so also a culture is an abstract description of trends toward uniformity in the words, deeds, and artifacts of a human group. If a map is accurate and you can read it, you won't get lost; if you know a culture you will know your way around in the life of a society.

Many educated people have the notion that culture applies only to exotic ways of life or to societies where relative simplicity and relative homogeneity prevail. Some sophisticated missionaries, for example, will use the anthropological conception in discussing the special modes of living of South Sea Islanders, but seem amazed at the idea that it could be applied equally to inhabitants of New York City. And social workers in Boston will talk about the culture of a colorful and well-knit immigrant group but boggle at applying it to the behavior of staff members in the social service agency itself.

In the primitive society the correspondence between the habits of individuals and the customs of the community is ordinarily greater. There is probably some truth in what an old Indian once said, "In the old days there was no law; everybody did what was right." The primitive tends to find happiness in the fulfillment of intricately involuted cultural patterns; the modern more often tends to feel the pattern as repressive to his individuality. It is also true that in a complex stratified society there are numerous exceptions to generalizations made about the culture as a whole. It is necessary to study regional, class and occupational subcultures. Primitive cultures have greater stability than modern cultures; they change—but less rapidly.

However, modern men also are creators and carriers of culture. Only in some respects are they influenced differently from primitives by culture. Moreover, there are such wide variations in primitive cultures that any black-and-white contrast between the primitive and the civilized is altogether fictitious. The distinction which is most generally true lies in the field of conscious philosophy.

. . .

What good is the concept of culture so far as the contemporary world is concerned? What can you do with it?...

Its use lies first in the aid the concept gives to man's endless quest to understand himself and his own behavior. For example, this new idea turns into pseudo problems some of the questions asked by one of the most learned and acute thinkers of our age, Reinhold Niebuhr. In his . . . book *The Nature and Destiny of Man* Niebuhr argues that the universally human sense of guilt or shame and man's capacity for self-judgment necessitate the assumption of supernatural forces. These facts are susceptible of self-consistent and relatively simple explanation in purely naturalistic terms through the concept of culture. Social life among human beings never occurs without a system of conventional understandings which are transmitted more or less intact from generation to generation. Every individual is familiar with some of these and they constitute a set of standards against which he judges himself. To the extent that he fails to conform he experiences discomfort because his childhood training puts great pressure on him to follow the accepted pattern, and his now unconscious tendency is to associate deviation with punishment or withdrawal of love and protection. This and other issues which have puzzled philosophers and scientists for so long become understandable through this fresh concept.

The principal claim which can be made for the culture concept as an aid to useful action is that it helps us enormously toward predicting human behavior. One of the factors limiting the success of such prediction thus far has been the naive assumption of a minutely homogeneous "human nature." In the framework of this assumption all human thinking proceeds from the same premises; all human beings are motivated by the same needs and goals. In the cultural framework we see that, while the ultimate goal of all peoples may be the same (and thus communication and understanding are possible), the thought processes depart from radically different premises—especially unconscious or unstated premises. Those who have the cultural outlook are more likely to look beneath the surface and bring the culturally determined premises to the light of day. This may not bring about immediate agreement and harmony, but it will at least facilitate a *more* rational approach to the problem of international understanding and to diminishing friction between groups within a nation.

Knowledge of a culture makes it possible to predict a good many of the actions of any person who shares that culture. If the American Army was dropping paratroopers in Thailand in 1944, under what circumstances would they be knifed, under what circumstances would they be aided? If one knows how a given culture defines a certain situation, one can say that the betting odds are excellent that in a future comparable situation people will behave along certain lines and not along others. If we know a culture, we know what various classes of individuals within it expect from each other—and from outsiders of various categories. We know what types of activity are held to be inherently gratifying.

Many people in our society feel that the best way to get people to work harder is to increase their profits or their wages. They feel that it is just "human nature" to want to increase one's material possessions. This sort of dogma might well go unchallenged if we had no knowledge of other cultures. In certain societies, however, it has been found that the profit motive is not an effective incentive. After contact with whites the Trobriand Islanders in Melanesia could have become fabulously rich from pearl diving. They would, however, work only long enough to satisfy their immediate wants.

Administrators need to become conscious of the symbolic nature of many activities. American women will choose a job as hostess in a restaurant rather than one as waitress at a higher salary. In some societies the blacksmith is the most honored of individuals while in others only the lowest class of people are blacksmiths. White children in schools are motivated by grades; but children from some Indian tribes will work less hard under a system that singles the individual out from among his fellows.

Understanding of culture provides some detachment from the conscious and unconscious emotional values of one's own culture. The phrase, "some detachment," must be emphasized, however. An individual who viewed the designs for living of his group with complete detachment would be disoriented and unhappy. But I can prefer (i.e., feel affectively attached to) American manners while at the same time perceiving certain graces in English manners which are lacking or more grossly expressed in ours. Thus, while unwilling to forget that I am an American with no desire to ape English drawing-room behavior, I can still derive a lively pleasure from association with English people on social occasions. Whereas if I have no detachment, if I am utterly provincial, I am likely to regard English manners as utterly ridiculous, uncouth, perhaps even immoral. With that attitude I shall certainly not get on well with the English, and I am likely to resent bitterly any modification of our manners in the English or any other direction. Such attitudes clearly do not make for international understanding, friendship, and cooperation. They do, to the same extent, make for a too rigid social structure. Anthropological documents and anthropological teachings are valuable, therefore, in that they tend to emancipate individuals from a too strong allegiance to every item in the cultural inventory. The person who has been exposed to the anthropological perspective is more likely to live and let live both within his own society and in his dealing with members of other societies; and he will probably be more flexible in regard to needful changes in social organization to meet changed technology and changed economy.

Perhaps the most important implication of culture for action is the profound truth that you can never start with a clean slate so far as human beings are concerned. Every person is born into a world defined by already existing culture patterns. Just as an individual who has lost his memory is no longer normal so the idea of a society's becoming completely emancipated from its past culture is inconceivable. This is one source of the tragic failure of the Weimar constitution in Germany. In the abstract it was an admirable document. But it failed miserably in actual life partly because it provided for no continuity with existent designs for acting, feeling, and thinking.

Since every culture has organization as well as content, administrators and lawmakers should know that one cannot isolate a custom to abolish or modify it. The most obvious example of failure caused by neglect of this principle was the Eighteenth

Amendment. The legal sale of liquor was forbidden, but the repercussions in law enforcement, in family life, in politics, in the economy were staggering.

The concept of culture, like any other piece of knowledge, can be abused and misinterpreted. Some fear that the principle of cultural relativity will weaken morality. "If the Bugabuga do it why can't we? It's all relative anyway." But this is exactly what cultural relativity does *not* mean.

The principle of cultural relativity does not mean that because the members of some savage tribe are allowed to behave in a certain way this fact gives intellectual warrant for such behavior in all groups. Cultural relativity means, on the contrary, that the appropriateness of any positive or negative custom must be evaluated with regard to how this habit fits with other group habits. Having several wives makes economic sense among herders, not among hunters. While breeding a healthy skepticism as to the eternity of any value prized by a particular people, anthropology does not as a matter of theory deny the existence of moral absolutes. Rather, the use of the comparative method provides a scientific means of discovering such absolutes. If all surviving societies have found it necessary to impose some of the same restrictions upon behavior of their members, this makes a strong argument that these aspects of the moral code are indispensable.

Similarly, the fact that a Kwakiutl chief talks as if he had delusions of grandeur and of persecution does not mean that paranoia is not a real ailment in our cultural context. Anthropology has given a new perspective to the relativity of the normal that should bring greater tolerance and understanding of socially harmless deviations. But it has by no means destroyed standards or the useful tyranny of the normal. All cultures recognize some of the same forms of behavior as pathological. Where they differ in their distinctions, there is a relationship to the total framework of cultural life.

There is a legitimate objection to making culture explain too much. Lurking, however, in such criticism of the cultural point of view is often the ridiculous assumption that one must be loyal to a single master explanatory principle. On the contrary, there is no incompatibility between biological, environmental, cultural, historical, and economic approaches. All are necessary. The anthropologist feels that so much of history as is still a living force is embodied in the culture. He regards the economy as a specialized part of the culture. But he sees the value in having economists and historians, as specialists, abstract out their special aspects—so long as the complete context is not entirely lost to view. Take the problems of the American South, for example. The anthropologist would entirely agree that biological (social visibility of black skin, etc.), environmental (water power and other natural resources), historical (South settled by certain types of people, somewhat different governmental practices from the start, etc.) and narrowly cultural (original discrimination against Negroes as "heathen savages," etc.) issues are all inextricably involved. However, the cultural factor is involved in the actual working out of each influence—though culture is definitely not the whole of it. And to say that certain acts are culturally defined does not always and necessarily mean that they could be eliminated by changing the culture.

The needs and drives of biological man, and the physical environment to which he must adjust, provide the stuff of human life, but a given culture determines the way this stuff is handled—the tailoring. In the eighteenth century a Neapolitan philosopher, Vico, uttered a profundity which was new, violent—and unnoticed. This was simply the discovery that "the social world is surely the work of man." Two generations of anthropologists have compelled thinkers to face this fact. Nor are anthropologists willing to allow the Marxists or other cultural determinists to make of culture another absolute as autocratic as the God or Fate portrayed by some philosophies. Anthropological knowledge does not permit so easy an evasion of man's responsibility for his own destiny. To be sure, culture is a compulsive force to most of us most of the time. To some extent, as Leslie White says, "Culture has a life and laws of its own." Some cultural changes are also compelled by economic or physical circumstances. But most of an economy is itself a cultural artifact. And it is men who change their cultures, even if—during most of past history—they have been acting as instruments of cultural processes of which they were largely unaware. The record shows that, while situation limits the range of possibility, there is always more than one workable alternative. The essence of the cultural process is selectivity; men may often make a choice. Lawrence Frank probably overstates the case:

In the years to come it is possible that this discovery of the human origin and development of culture will be recognized as the greatest of all discoveries, since heretofore man has been helpless before these cultural and social formulations which generation after generation have perpetuated the same frustration and defeat of human values and aspirations. So long as he believed this was necessary and inevitable, he could not but accept this lot with resignation. Now man is beginning to realize that this culture and social organization are not unchanged cosmic processes, but are human creations which may be altered. For those who cherish the democratic faith this discovery means that they can, and must, undertake a continuing assay of our culture and our society in terms of its consequences for human life and human values. This is the historic origin and purpose of human culture, to create a human way of life. To our age falls the responsibility of utilizing the amazing new resources of science to meet these cultural tasks, to continue the great human tradition of man taking charge of his own destiny.

Nevertheless, to the extent that human beings discover the nature of the cultural process, they can anticipate, prepare, and —to at least a limited degree—control.

Americans are now at a period in history when they are faced with the facts of cultural differences more clearly than they can take with comfort. Recognition and tolerance of the deeper cultural assumptions of China, Russia, and Britain will require a difficult type of education. But the great lesson of culture is that the goals toward which men strive and fight and grope are not "given" in final form by biology nor yet entirely by the situation. If we understand our own culture and that of others, the political climate can be changed in a surprisingly short time in this narrow contemporary world providing men are wise enough and articulate enough and energetic enough. The concept of culture carries a legitimate note of hope to troubled men.

The Response of Education to Change in a Society

Margaret Mead

When we look realistically at the world in which we are living today and become aware of what the actual problems of learning are, our conception of education changes radically. Although the educational system remains basically unchanged, we are no longer dealing primarily with the *vertical* transmission of the tried and true by the old, mature, and experienced teacher to the young, immature, and inexperienced pupil. This was the system of education developed in a stable, slowly changing culture. In a world of rapid change, vertical transmission of knowledge alone no longer serves the purposes of education.

What is needed and what we are already moving toward is the inclusion of another whole dimension of learning: the *lateral* transmission, to every sentient member of society, of what has just been discovered, invented, created, manufactured, or marketed. This need for lateral transmission exists no less in a physics or genetics laboratory than it does on the assembly line with its working force of experienced and raw workmen. The man who teaches another individual the new mathematics or the use of a newly invented tool is not sharing knowledge he acquired years ago. He learned what was new yesterday, and his pupil must learn it today.

The whole teaching-and-learning continuum, which once was tied in an orderly and productive way to the passing of generations and the growth of the child into a man—this whole process has exploded in our faces. Yet even as we try to catch hold of and patch up the pieces, we fail to recognize what has happened.

Why should the businessman be concerned with this apparently academic issue? In our rapidly changing world, industry has taken the lead in practical consideration of problems of obsolescence and in many ways is capable of taking a position of leadership in the task of reorienting the training of people to live in this new world.

In order to understand the issues, let us begin by looking at some of the features and underlying assumptions of our American educational system as it is today. Even a brief examination of the picture we carry in our minds of "education" and of "students" will indicate the state of confusion at which we have arrived and the immediate need for creative leadership in working out a more realistic system of education.

We have moved into a period in which the break with the past provides an opportunity for creating a new framework for activity in almost every field—but in each field the fact that there has been a break must be rediscovered. In education there has been up to now no real recognition of the extent to which our present system is outmoded. Meanwhile, as the turmoil over our educational system grows, the various responsible groups in the United States are jockeying for position. But some of them, particularly those representing industry, have as yet hardly entered the field.

Historians point sagely to the last two educational crises—the first of which ended with the establishment of the universal high school—and with remarkable logic and lack of imagination they predict that the present crisis will follow the same pattern. (And what is history for if not to tell us exactly how to make the same mistakes as in the past!) According to such present predictions, the crisis [should have been over in] 1970, with the establishment of universal college education, accessible in principle to all young Americans.[1]

Implicit in this prediction is a series of other ideas, such as:

The assumption that our educational system has fallen behind in something (though it is not now clear what the "something" is—the work training of German apprentices,[2] or the technical training of young Soviets,[3] or the linguistic mastery of Netherlands students), and that it should therefore arrange to catch up.

The explanation that our difficulties are due to the "bulge"—the host of babies that tricked the statisticians peacefully extrapolating their population curves and bedeviled a people who had decided that orphan asylums could slowly be turned into homes for the aged and elementary schools into high schools as a population with a falling birth rate aged into maturity. (Only a few people followed out the simile to senility!)

The thinking of the people who are sure that the pendulum is swinging back to sense—to discipline and dunce caps, switches and multiplication tables, and the highly satisfactory forms of torture which somebody (they themselves or at least their grandfathers) once suffered in the cause of learning.

But in the midst of the incessant discussion and the search for scapegoats to take the blame for what everyone admits is a perilous state, extraordinarily little attention is paid to any basic issues. Everyone simply wants more of what we already have: more children in more schools for more hours studying more of something. The scientists want more students to be taught more mathematics, while the liberal arts advocates want more of their subject matter included in the curriculum. The planners want more school buildings built, and the educators want more teachers trained who have studied more hours and who will get more pay. Meanwhile, the child labor committees want more inspection and more attention to migratory children, and the youth boards want more social workers and more special schools and more clinics provided.

Likewise, extraordinarily little attention is paid to the fact that two great new educational agencies—the armed services and industry—have entered the field, and there is little awareness of the ways in which operations in these institutions are altering traditional education.[4] Recruitment programs of the armed services now include explicit statements of their role as educational institutions. For instance:

> The United States Armed Forces Institute . . . has enabled thousands upon thousands of young men to finish their high school education and begin college-level studies. A second Army program enables young men to attend courses at many civilian schools and colleges in off-duty hours . . . [A third program teaches soldiers— on their bases] such subjects as typing, stenography, foreign languages, literature, and many more.[5]

But most important, the pattern itself is hardly questioned. For we *think* we know what education is and what a good education ought to be; and however deficient we may be as a people, as taxpayers, or as educators, we may be actualizing our ideals. An occasional iconoclast can ask wistfully: "Wouldn't it be fine if we could scrap our whole school system and start anew?" But he gets no hearing because everyone knows that what he is saying is nonsense. Wishful dreams about starting all anew are obviously impractical, but this does not mean that someone should not ask these crucial questions:

Is our present historic idea of education suitable for people in the mid-twentieth century, who have a life expectancy of seventy years, and who live in a world of automation and global communication, ready to begin space exploration and aware of the possibility that we can bring about the suicide of the entire human species?

As all these present and pressing concerns of the human race are new, is it not possible that a system of education may be out of date which was designed for small societies that were connected by horse-drawn coaches and sailing ships, and where any war could threaten only small sections of the human species at any one time?

Is it not possible that the problem of the educational system's obsolescence goes beyond such issues as methods of teaching reading or physics, or the most desirable age for leaving school, or the payment of teachers, or the length of summer holidays, or the number of years best devoted to college, or even the comparative advantages of working while going to high school or college?

Is not the break between past and present— and so the whole problem of outdating in our educational system—related to a change in the rate of change? For change has become so rapid that adjustment cannot be left to the next generation; adults must—

not once, but continually—take in, adjust to, use, and make innovations in a steady stream of discovery and new conditions.

Our educational system, besides being the oldest system of universal free primary education in the world, bears the marks of its long history. But is it not possible to think that an educational system that was designed to teach what was known to little children and to a selected few young men (after which they could be regarded as "educated") may not fit a world in which the most important factors in everyone's life are those things that are not yet, but soon will be, known?

Is it not equally possible that our present definition of a pupil or a student is out of date when we define the learner as a child (or at best an immature person) who is entitled to those things to which a child is entitled—moral protection and a meager subsistence in a dependency position—and who is denied those things which are denied to a child—moral autonomy, sex and parenthood, alcoholic beverages, and exposure to hazards?

In the picture which we have of the student, we have muddled together *both* a conception of the young child who is unable to fend for himself or to protect himself against moral and physical hazards, and who is entitled to be fed and sheltered *and* our own historical conception of the scholar's role as one in which some few men could claim lifelong support provided they themselves accepted an economic dependency that was demeaning to other men and a type of life in which they were subject to supervision (and, until recently in Christian history, gave up sex and parenthood).

This composite picture is one into which we can fit the scholarly monk, the Cambridge don who was not permitted to marry, and the student who lives in college and whose degree depends on his sleeping there (a touchingly infantile method of attaining a degree). All of these match our conception of the learner as a dependent who is subject to supervision appropriate to a child and who must pay for his learning by abnegating some of the rewards of maturity.

Yet the combined ideas of the child and the monk do not complete our picture of the student; we have added still other things to it. With the industrial revolution there came new possibilities of exploiting human labor. Work, which through long ages had often been disliked by members of the upper classes and had been delegated to women, slaves, or serfs, became something different—more hazardous, more menacing. In this situation children were the most easily identifiable victims, and their fate was dramatized as a conflict between their right to an education and their subjection to dangerous and ruthless exploitation in the mines, in the factories, in dives, and in the street trades. The common school, born at a period in the United States when we were particularly concerned with extending the rights of the common man, was sponsored and fought for by labor groups. In this way the common school became doubly identified as the means of making all children literate and as the official enemy of child labor. A vote to raise the school-leaving age was a vote against child labor, and, like sin or cancer, child labor became something no one could be in favor of, officially.

So, as inevitably happens when different institutions in a culture become intertwined, raising the school-leaving age came to stand for several things: it was, on the one hand, a way of increasing the privileges of every child born in the United States and, on the other hand, a way of protecting children against the hazards of work to their health and morals.

That our picture of harmful labor is itself very complex can be seen even from a cursory examination of federal and state child labor laws.[6] Looking at these we find that work outdoors is better than work indoors, that work in small cities is better than work in large cities, that work in summer and during vacations is less harmful than work in winter or during school terms, that work done for parents does not count as work, and that there is one form of work in which all the rules can be broken about age, hours, places, hazards from the weather, weight of objects dealt with, being on the streets, going to strange places, and so forth— which, characteristically and in the best spirit of Horatio Alger, is delivering newspapers.

This one exception in our children's right to protection highlights the whole picture. In the American myth, men rise to success and greatness by working hard as children, and as we have progressively forbidden them this traditional preparation for greatness, we have left them the one symbolic activity of delivering newspapers. (Nowadays, however, it may be the father —bank president or chief justice—who actually delivers the papers because the son is in bed with a cold under the care of an expensive pediatrician.)

Slowly, as a society, we have codified both the rights and the disabilities of minors and also the conditions under which a minor may take on the privileges appropriate to adults because they require maturity. These are problems which are dealt with in the most primitive societies, though the way in which they are thought of may contrast with ours. What has happened in our contemporary society is that the codified rules, each intended to serve specific needs, fail to fit the contemporary situation—and the result is confusion.

The state of confusion that characterizes our attitudes toward maturity in students shows up in a variety of ways. For instance:

School regulations may forbid a married student to attend high school even though he or she may be below the age and the grade when it is legal to leave high school.

Even more quaintly, in one large city the schoolgirl who has an illegitimate child may go back to school after the child has been born, but the married girl who becomes a mother may not return.

In some school systems, not only expectant mothers but also expectant *fathers* are barred from the daytime high school.

The complexity of the total picture and the confusion about the relationship of being a child, a minor, a student, and a morally incapable individual are further increased when we include, as nowadays we must, the armed services. For in different degrees the armed services permit a boy to enlist who is too young to marry, to leave school, to buy cigarettes or to drink beer, to vote, to make a legal contract, to bequeath property, to change his citizenship, to work in a hazardous occupation or in other occupations between the hours of seven and seven, or to have contact with dangerous machinery. Yet by enlisting he is enabled to operate the complex instruments of death and to die for his country.

So, when we think about education and try to identify the student, we have in our minds—whether or not we are aware of it —an exceedingly complex picture, the elements of which are compounded and confused in their historic connections. Yet we must identify what they are if we are to remodel our educational system so that it is devoted to the kind of teaching and learning that is appropriate to the United States today. For this purpose a look at education in other societies will be helpful.

Education which is limited to small children is appropriate in a very primitive society like that of the Eskimo. The nine-year-old Eskimo child has learned, from father or from mother, the basic skills of a spoken language, the handling of tools and equipment, knowledge of the weather, relevant personal relations, and religious taboos. He must wait until he is physically mature before he can marry; as he grows older he will gain proficiency in hunting, in religious practices, in his knowledge of time, the seasons, and the landscape; and he may come to exercise leadership. But his education, in the sense of learning whatever adults could teach him directly, was over long before.[7]

In other societies, that are more complex, education may not be completed before adolescence, when some young people may elect, or may be chosen, to learn more complicated skills and may memorize the classics, master complex weaving skills, or become skilled craftsmen or leaders of ritual activities.

After the invention of writing and the development of mathematics and medicine, these did not become part of the whole tradition which had to be imparted to everyone. Like techniques of gold working or a knowledge of magical charms, they were taught by a few to a few in a long continuum of teaching and learning, in which the teacher responded as much to the pupil as the pupil did to the demands of the teacher, and both attempted not so much to add to the sum total of knowledge as to increase the skill of its manipulation.[8] Under these circumstances, new knowledge was added so gradually that the slow web of transmission of ancient skills was not torn.

Parallel to these developments was the special education given by specially chosen tutors and teachers to the children of the aristocracy; such an education was designed to ground the pupils well in many arts and graces and in a scholarship which they would not practice but would wear as an adornment or use for wise government.[9]

In a country governed by a conqueror or in a country to which large numbers of immigrants come, there are special problems of education as the government becomes responsible for people who speak a different language and have different customs. For, in these situations, the function—or at least one function— of the educational system is not the transmission to the next generation of something that all adults or that specialized groups of adults know, but rather the transmission of something the parents' generation does *not* know to children whom the authorities wish to have educated.[10]

So, looking at our educational system today, we can see that in various ways it combines these different functions:

The protection of the child against exploitation and the protection of society against precocity and inexperience.

The maintenance of learners in a state of moral and economic dependency.

Giving to all children the special, wider education once reserved for the children of privileged groups, in an attempt to form the citizen of a democracy as once the son of a noble house was formed.

The teaching of complex and specialized skills, which, under our complex system of division of labor, is too difficult and time-consuming for each set of parents to master or to hand on to their own children.

The transmission of something which the parents' generation does *not* know (in the case of immigrants with varied cultural and linguistic backgrounds) to children whom the authorities or the parents wish to have educated.

To these multiple functions of an educational system, which, in a slowly changing society, were variously performed, we have added slowly and reluctantly a quite new function: *education for rapid and self-conscious adaptation to a changing world.* Yet we hardly recognize how new this function of our educational system is. It is implicit in the demands of educators that schools develop flexibility, open-mindedness, and creativity; but such demands might equally well have been made 200 years ago, well before the rhythm of change had radically altered.

That we have as yet failed to recognize the new character of change is apparent in a thousand ways. Despite the fact that a subject taught to college freshmen may have altered basically by the time the same students are seniors, it is still said that colleges are able to give students "a good education"—finished, wrapped up, and sealed with a degree.

A student who is still in college can "go on" to a higher degree because he has not yet "completed" his education, i.e., the lump of the known which he has decided to bite off. But a student who has once let a year go by after he is "out of school" does not "go *on*," but rather "goes *back*" to school. And as we treat education as the right of a minor who has not yet completed high school (for the position of a boy who has completed high school at the age of fourteen is a different and anomalous one, in which he is exempt from most of the forms of protection accorded minors because a high school diploma is equated with physiological maturity, the capacity for parenthood, and the ability to resist the seductions of hostel and bowling-alley life), just so we equate marriage and parenthood with getting a diploma; both indicate that one's education is "finished."

Consistent with these ideas and with our conception of what a student is, our educational institutions are places where we keep "children" for a shorter or longer period. The length of time depends in part on their intelligence and motivation and in part on their parents' incomes and the immediately recognized national needs for particular skills or types of training—and as long as they are there, we treat them as minors.

Once they have left, we regard them as in some sense finished, neither capable of nor in need of further "education," for we still believe that education should come all in one piece, or rather, in a series of connected pieces, each presented as a whole at the elementary school, the high school, and the college level. All other behaviors are aberrant. So we speak of "interrupted" education— that is, education which has been broken into by sickness, delinquency, or military service—and we attempt to find means of repairing this interruption. Indeed, the whole GI bill, which in a magnificent way gave millions of young men a chance for a different kind of education than they would otherwise have got, was conceived of primarily as a means of compensating young men for unsought but unavoidable interruption.

Thus we avoid facing the most vivid truth of the new age: *no one will live all his life in the world into which he was born, and no one will die in the world in which he worked in his maturity.*

For those who work on the growing edge of science, technology, or the arts, contemporary life changes at even shorter intervals. Often, only a few months may elapse before something which previously was easily taken for granted must be unlearned or transformed to fit the new state of knowledge or practice.

In this world, no one can "complete an education." The students we need are not just children who are learning to walk and talk and to read and write plus older students, conceived of as minors, who are either "going on" with or "going back" to specialized education. Rather, we need children *and* adolescents *and* young *and* mature *and* "senior" adults, each of whom is learning at the appropriate pace and with all the special advantages and disadvantages of experience peculiar to his own age.

If we are to incorporate fully each new advance, we need simultaneously:

The wide-eyed freshness of the inquiring child.

The puzzlement of the near dunce who, if the system is to work, must still be a part of it.

The developing capacities of the adolescent for abstract thinking.

The interest of the young adult whose motives have been forged in the responsibilities of parenthood and first contacts with a job.

The special awareness of the mature man who has tempered experience, skepticism, and the power to implement whatever changes he regards as valuable.

The balance of the older man who has lived through cycles of change and can use this wisdom to place what is new.

Each and every one of these is a learner, not of something old and tried—the alphabet or multiplication tables or Latin declensions or French irregular verbs or the rules of rhetoric or the binomial theorem, all the paraphernalia of learning which children with different levels of aspiration must acquire—but of new, hardly tried theories and methods: pattern analysis, general system theory, space lattices, cybernetics, and so on.

Learning of this kind must go on not only at special times and in special places, but all through production and consumption— from the technician who must handle a new machine to the factory supervisor who must introduce its use, the union representative who must interpret it to the men, the foreman who must keep the men working, the salesman who must service a new device or find markets for it, the housewife who must understand how to care for a new material, the mother who must answer the questions of an observant four-year-old.

In this world the age of the teacher is no longer necessarily relevant. For instance, children teach grandparents how to manage TV, young expediters come into the factory along with the new equipment, and young men invent automatic programming for computers over which their seniors struggle because they, too, need it for their research.

This, then, is what we call the *lateral transmission* of knowledge. It is not an outpouring of knowledge from the "wise old teacher" into the minds of young pupils, as in vertical transmission. Rather, it is a sharing of knowledge by the informed with the uninformed, whatever their ages. The primary prerequisite is the desire to know.

Given this situation, which of the institutions that are concerned with the revision of our educational system is to take the initiative: the educational world, the government, the armed services, citizens' voluntary organizations, churches, or industry? Each has a stake in the outcome; each has power to influence what happens; each has its own peculiar strengths and weaknesses.

Industry, however, has the peculiar advantage of understanding the major evil from which our whole educational system is suffering—*obsolescence*. Modern ideas of obsolescence have come out of studies of industrial processes, and industrialists have made these ideas so much a part of their thinking that making allowance for the costs of obsolescence and supporting continuing research on problems of obsolescence are a normal part of their professional behavior. In any major effort to modernize our educational system, of course, it would be appropriate for all the institutions to have a voice. It would be well, for example:

For educators to watch out so that all they know would not be lost in the shuffle.

For government to guard the needs of the nation.

For church and synagogue to protect the religious values of the past.

For the armed services to concentrate on our defense needs.

For citizens to organize means of protecting the health, safety, and welfare (present and future) of their own and the community's children.

In these circumstances, would it not be most appropriate for industry to take the lead in highlighting the obsolescence of our present educational system? In the United States [a large number] of the civilian labor force are engaged in some kind of work in industry. Of the advances which account for obsolescence, a very large proportion have come out of industry. But, at the same time, much of the thinking that is holding up a real revision of our school system is based on an outmoded public image of industry as a monstrous and wicked institution which, if not restrained, would permit little boys to be sent down into coal mines or to work in conditions in which their lungs would be filled with powdered silicon.

In fact, industry has already taken the lead—within its own walls—in developing a new type of education that includes all levels of competence and training and that freely faces the need for education at the senior levels of management. . . . [If] industry, as represented by individual leaders from management and labor in many parts of the country, would come forward with plans which dramatized our dilemma, such plans would be heard.

What might these plans be? First, in regard to work performed by young people, industry could say to all those who believe that children should be kept in school primarily so that they will not be on the streets or at work under bad conditions: "We will agree that young people need more supervision than older workers—that someone should know where they are each day, that their health should be protected and checked, and that they should be protected from organized attempts to deprave them. We will undertake to train and supervise the young people who *at this time* cannot gain anything by remaining in school."

But this would not be enough. This offer would need to be accompanied by a second one: "As soon as *any* worker—of any age at any level—in our plant, office, or laboratory is ready to study again, we will facilitate his, or her, doing so."

This is, admittedly, a large order. But we cannot have one without the other. For as long as we continue to think that free and, when necessary, subsidized education is appropriate *only* when it is *preliminary* to work (though, exceptionally, it may be continued after some inevitable "interruption"), just so long the guardians of character, of political literacy, and of our store of talent that comes from all classes and in many cases shows itself only very slowly will argue for—and will get—longer and longer years of compulsory education and longer and longer years of free education.

Under these circumstances, the meaning of education and the

purpose of schools—especially for young people between the ages of fourteen and twenty—will only become more confused. On the one hand, the education that is absolutely necessary for those who, at an early age, are ready to go on to become scientists, statesmen, philosophers, and poets will be hamstrung by the presence of those others who, at the same age, do not want schooling; and on the other hand, the lives and characters of the temporary nonlearners will be ruined, and they will be incapacitated as potential later learners.

What we need to do, instead, is to separate primary and secondary education—in an entirely new way:

By *primary education* we would mean the stage of education in which all children are taught what they need to know in order to be fully human in the world in which they are growing up—including the basic skills of reading and writing and a basic knowledge of numbers, money, geography, transportation and communication, the law, and the nations of the world.

By *secondary education* we would mean an education that is based on primary education and that can be obtained *in any amount* and *at any period* during the individual's whole lifetime.

By so doing, we could begin to deal effectively with the vast new demands that are being made on us. The high schools would be relieved of the non-learners, among whom are found a large number of delinquents. But, more important, men and women, instead of preparing for a single career to which—for lack of any alternative—they must stick during their entire active lives, would realize that they might learn something else. The very knowledge that this was so would relieve much of the rigidity that now bedevils management. Women, after their children became older, could be educated for particular new tasks—instead of facing the rejection that today is related to fears about new learning that is acquired in middle age.

Whatever their age, those who were obtaining a secondary education at any level (high school, college, or even beyond) would be in school because they *wanted* to learn and *wanted* to be there —*then*. A comparison of GI and non-GI students has shown how great have been the achievements of students who have chosen to go to school.[11] Furthermore, the student—of whatever age—who was obtaining a secondary education would no longer be defined as someone without adult rights who must accept dependency and meager stipends and have a dedicated delight in poverty.

In an educational system of this kind we could give primary education and protection to actual children as well as protection and sensitive supervision to adolescents. We could back up to the hilt the potentiality of every human being—of whatever age—to learn at any level. And we could do this proudly.

The kind and amount of leadership that industry can best take in making individual plans for sending workers—*on pay*—to get more education, and the kind and amount of leadership that can best come from tax-supported activities is a problem that will have to be threshed out. In the United States, we usually depend upon private initiative to make the first experiments before tax-supported agencies pick up the check. So, too, we shall have to work out the problem of providing special work situations for adolescents and on this basis make our decisions as to whether tax-supported institutions—rather than individual industries—should become chiefly responsible for the employment of adolescents.

But we also need to recognize articulately that there are other routes to competence than the one route provided by the conventional school. Experimental cooperative-work plans in the public schools need to be supplemented by experiments in industry.[12] Such a plan is the one being conceptualized by Pylon, in which the sons of successful parents, who are financially able to continue their studies but find nothing rewarding in school work, are given a chance to learn under meaningful, money-making conditions.[13]

The right to obtain a secondary education when and where the individual could use it would include not only the right of access to existing conventional types of schools but also the right of access to types of work training not yet or only now being developed—new kinds of apprenticeship and also new kinds of work teams (such as the "Day Haul," which is helping to solve our seasonal labor needs [14]).

In thinking about an effective educational system we should recognize that the adolescent's need and right to work is as great as (perhaps greater than) his immediate need and right to study. And we must recognize that the adult's need and right to study more is as great as (perhaps greater than) his need and right to hold the same job until he is sixty-five years old. [Some] publications of the Department of Labor show that we are already beginning to recognize the importance of work for youth.[15]

Among the nations whose industrial capacities make them our competitors, the United States has a comparatively small total population. The more completely we are able to educate each individual man and woman, the greater will be our productive capacity. But we cannot accomplish the essential educational task merely by keeping children and young adults—whom we treat like children—in school longer. We can do it by creating an educational system in which all individuals will be assured of the secondary and higher education they want and can use any time throughout their lives.[16]

Are We Educating Our Children for the Wrong Future?

Robert Maynard Hutchins

The world is new and is getting newer every minute. Anything may happen, and what is most likely to happen may be what we least expect.

Almost every "fact" I was taught from the first grade through law school is no longer a fact. Almost every tendency that was proclaimed has failed to materialize. The "facts" and tendencies of today are those that nobody foresaw fifty years ago. I clearly remember the table of immutable elements and atomic weights that hung on the wall of the chemistry laboratory in 1916. I also recall my history professor's description at that date of the bright future of British rule in South Africa.

I am especially embarrassed by the facts and tendencies I proclaimed myself. I can only hope the students in the Yale Law School have forgotten what I taught them. The courts have overruled and the legislatures repealed most of what I knew.

Education, in the nature of the case, has to be concerned with the future. But if we ask ourselves what we positively know of the future, about all we can say is that it will not be like the present. The whole world is committed to the highest possible rate of technological change. The daily accomplishments of science are such as to convince us that we are eventually going to know how everything works. Then we shall be able to do anything, and anything can happen.

The first question about education we have to try to answer is: How can it prepare for a future so uncertain and contingent that the main outlines of it are, as Disraeli used to say, "shrouded in the dark shadows of dubiety"?

The second question results from one big, central, fundamental change we can foresee, and that is in man's relation to his work and in society's concern with production. This point requires some elaboration.

Ever since Adam and Eve were driven from Paradise and told to get to work, subsistence has been the primary preoccupation of men everywhere. Production has been regarded as so important that men were rewarded only if they produced. They were paid to work. If they did not work, they did not eat. Work and production were the means of individual and national strength, support, and salvation.

.   .   .

The Administration's [1] plan for bridging the widening gap between production and consumption is to cut taxes. The expectation is that this will stimulate demand, mop up surplus production, and lead to some reduction in unemployment.

But what if increasing production does not mean increasing employment? While production has been rising, unemployment has been holding steady. Although we are to have a tax cut of $11 billion, nobody expects unemployment to go below 4 percent. This is the new definition of an "acceptable" rate. It is twice the rate considered acceptable in Western Europe.

Meanwhile, in the advanced industrial countries of the West, the link between production and employment is being broken. Dr. Solomon Fabricant, the cautious director of research for the National Bureau of Economic Research, says: "Our immediate historical evidence indicates that there have been changes in basic materials and energy sources and tools and machines and in the relationship of the worker to his job. Eventually this will add up to a new industrial revolution."

What these somewhat opaque words mean is that automation and cybernetics are changing the world. They substitute the machine not only for muscles but also for minds. This is new, and no reassuring historical example, like the effect of the invention of the automobile on employment, is relevant.

W. Willard Wirtz, the Secretary of Labor, has said that machines can now do, on the average, whatever a high school graduate can do. If they can do that now, why should we expect them to stop there? They will go on until they can do whatever a college graduate can do, and perhaps more.

The effects on unskilled, or muscle labor are obvious. The disappearance of the muscular miner reflects a universal tendency. The importation of seasonal Mexican farm labor into California was discontinued because Americans wanted, or were said to want, the 60,000 jobs at stake. Now it seems unlikely that there will be any jobs. Machines are being developed to do the work.

The skilled worker is going, too. The managing director of Bahlsen's, the great automatic bakery in Western Germany, says, "Here the skill of the baker dies." The skilled baker is likely to be dangerous, because he may think (quite wrongly) that he can improve the product by interfering with the machine.

The *Wall Street Journal* has described the effects of automation on the skilled white-collar worker. White-collar employment in the financial concerns of Manhattan, for example, was lower in 1963 than in 1962. Employment in brokerage houses declined while the volume of trading increased. The New York Life Insurance Company tripled its business in ten years; but the number of its employees rose by only 300, or less than 10 percent.

These effects are now being felt by what is called "middle management." This is composed of highly skilled, white-collar people, mostly college graduates. Although they do not make important decisions on policy, they supply much of the information required for those decisions. They watch the flow of goods and money and see to it that both are in the right place at the right time. Computers can do better. They are quicker, more reliable, and, in the long run, cheaper. As they are improved and become still cheaper, they will drive the middle managers from the field.

The service trades seem a weak reed to lean on. Self-service and automatic vending machines are invading every department of retailing. The solemn and conservative magazine *U.S. News & World Report* says, "Food shopping at a supermarket will be automated. There'll be only one sample of every item on display, along with a punch card. Simply take a card for each item you want to buy, take the cards to the checkout counter. There, a machine will tally the cost. While you pay the clerk, all your purchases will be assembled, packed in a box or bag, and delivered to you as you leave the store."

Quoting "a top official of the General Electric Company," the article goes on to portray the automation of the home through computers that will make up your grocery list, remind you of appointments and anniversaries, take care of your finances, pay your bills, write your checks, figure out your income tax, and answer your telephone. Reproduction will be the only function performed by human labor.

The only possible conclusion is that the happy marriage between production and employment is being dissolved. The political, economic, social, cultural, and educational consequences cannot be overestimated.

What are we going to do with ourselves? Gerard Piel, publisher of *Scientific American,* has pointed out in a pamphlet written for the Center for the Study of Democratic Institutions that if we had continued with the sixty-hour week we would now have 27,000,000 unemployed. By reducing the hours of labor, we have spread work and leisure. Any proposal for the future must proceed along the same line. But I must emphasize that at the end of the line we shall find ourselves largely without work as we have understood work in the past.

Yet education has never been as job-oriented as it is today. This is a melancholy instance of the general truth that a doctrine seldom gains acceptance until it is obsolete.

The doctrine never was any good. In any country that has a highly mobile population and a rapidly changing technology, the more specifically education is directed to jobs, the more ineffective it is bound to be. Today such education is patently absurd. Everybody is aware that the official rate of unemployment among young people is double that among adults. The actual rate is undoubtedly higher, because many young people have thought it useless to apply for work. The general reaction to this situation borders on fantasy: it is to propose widespread extension of vocational training. In short, the cure for the disease of no jobs is training for them.

The archaic quality of such aspirations is sufficiently demonstrated by the case of key punch operators. They have now been superseded by machines and have been declared surplus by the California Employment Service. Today five vocational schools in Los Angeles advertise that they train key punch operators.

The matter goes deeper. [Some] years ago, a British group known as the Archbishop of Canterbury's Fifth Committee delivered itself of a statement that sums up the basic issue. It said:

> A nation which regards education primarily as a means of converting its members into more efficient instruments of production is likely not only to jeopardize its moral standards and educational ideals, but to discover that by such methods it cannot attain even the limited success at which it aims.

Our educational ideals these days are expressed in the phrase "marketable skills." But entirely apart from the inability of the educational system to keep up with the market and forecast what skills it will buy, and entirely apart from the inefficiency of vocational training in school as compared with that on the job, the idea of producing marketable skills is ignoble and degrading for an educational system. It is an ideal that seduces the system into doing what it cannot and should not do and that forces it to neglect what it can and should do.

What education can and should do is help people become human. The object of education is not manpower, but manhood. This object we are now able to attain. We can now make the transition from a working to a learning society.

We started with two questions: how to educate for an undecipherable future, and how to prepare for a world in which work has lost its significance. The answer to both questions turns out to be the same. The man who is truly educated, rather than narrowly trained, is ready for anything. He has developed his human powers and is able to use them and his understanding of the world to meet any new problem he has to face. He is prepared by his education to go on learning.

Hence he is prepared for the human use of his free time. This is, in fact, the purpose of education in childhood and youth. It is to inspire the desire for lifelong learning and to supply the training that will make it possible.

The democratic society is the learning society *par excellence.* The Constitution of the United States is intelligible only as a charter of learning. In the spirit of the Preamble, we are to learn together to govern ourselves. The law, the professions, the voluntary associations to which we belong, the political campaigns through which we suffer—all the institutions in our society should be regarded as teachers. Through them, as well as through the educational system, we can learn how to become human and how to organize a human society.

The special function of our educational institutions is to supply the intellectual tools, the intellectual discipline and the intellectual framework necessary to understand the new problems we shall face. Support for this position comes from an unexpected but highly practical source, the Chief of Police of Chicago. He remarked the other day that he wanted a "completely professionalized" force.

Then he went on to say, "But the professionalism must be based on a foundation of liberal arts. It's necessary to get a complete man who has an understanding of his society and its people—a sense of perspective that can only come from a knowledge of history and philosophy." One might almost say that now the most practical education is a theoretical one: the man with the theoretical framework will comprehend the new situation, whereas the man without it has no recourse but to muddle through.

For the educational system the transition from a working to a learning society means a drastic reorientation of schools, colleges, and universities away from jobs and toward intellectual power. It also means that the present miscellaneous, superficial, and inadequate programs offered under the head of adult education must be replaced by continuous opportunities for learning open to all inhabitants of the country all their lives. The obligation of our educational system to provide these opportunities is just as serious as their obligation to the young.

If we can readjust our prejudices, we can get started toward a learning society. I do not underestimate the difficulties of making the readjustment. We can understand why Lord Keynes, the famous British economist, looking forward to a workless West, said he viewed the prospect with a "certain dread." We were brought up on Horatio Alger and the doctrine of salvation by work. Our last formal declaration of public policy on this subject was the so-called Full Employment Act of 1946.

Horatio Alger will soon be as out of date as *The Arabian Nights*. If work is our salvation, we are lost indeed, and we are on the way from full employment to full unemployment. But if we will only recognize it, the great opportunity that men have always yearned for is ours at last.

Other nations have had affluence and leisure, or their ruling classes have had them. They have been destroyed, usually from within, and usually from causes associated with affluence and leisure. The experience of Athens was unique, and it was too limited and too brief to be reassuring.

Now one can seriously raise the question whether the American democracy will turn out, like the Athenian, to be a temporary flowering from an almost accidental combination of favorable circumstances. One can seriously ask whether in a country like this, in a world like this, democracy is any longer possible. I believe it is. But I believe it is only if we can achieve the learning society.

Social Change: Impact on the Adolescent

James S. Coleman

Adults have a special reason today to shake their heads and mutter, "the younger generation . . .," as adults are wont to do. For today's adults and today's teenagers have special problems of communication that make it more and more difficult for each to understand what the other is up to. These communication problems arise not because teenagers are in some strange new way different than ever before, but because of changes in the structure of our society. These changes have produced a number of special problems in education and in the whole process of growing up, of which the communication gap is only one. I would like to indicate what some of these structural changes are, and some of their consequences for adolescents.

Societal Changes and Family Cohesion

A number of changes have combined to make the family a less cohesive, less effective agent within which to raise children than ever before. One of these changes is the entry of large numbers of women into the labor force. Prior to World War II, in March 1940,

16.7 percent of married women held jobs outside the home. By March 1961, this had doubled to 34.0 percent. (In 1890, it was 4.5 percent.) This change need not, of course, make a given family less tightly knit, nor give adolescent children a less rich "psychological home," but it tends to do so, and the overall social impact must be in this direction.

Another change is the smaller and smaller number of families that have relatives—aunts, uncles, grandparents—living in the household. This means that the typical family of today in America is parents and children, with nothing more. Thus the family's strength depends far more on the parents than ever before. The relatives are not there to provide adults for the children to model themselves after, or adults in whom they can confide.

A third change, which reinforces the preceding one, is the greater geographic mobility of families, particularly since World War II. An urban or suburban family today does not have a homestead that passes from one generation to another; nor does it even have a stable place of residence for a single generation. More and more, the typical "life-cycle" of a family begins with a newly-married couple living in an apartment in the city; then with the first child comes a move to a suburb of families with young children; then later, as income and family grow, to a suburb of larger houses and older children; then, finally, after the children are gone, back to an apartment in the city.

Such moves mean that the adult neighborhood, which was once an extension of the household itself, is hardly so now. Children make neighborhood friends quickly, but their parents do not; and perhaps most important, the children have few contacts and even fewer stable relationships with other adults in the neighborhood.

Finally, a change that has been going on for a long time is the shift of the father's work from the home or the neighborhood (e.g., the farmer or merchant) to a distant office or factory. Thus, the son knows only abstractly what his father does; and he can never enter into the father's work.

Consequences of Change

The effects of these changes on the adolescent are many. One of the most interesting indicators is the recent large increase in "going steady" among adolescents. This phenomenon, virtually unknown in Europe, can be explained only in terms of overall changes that have taken place in the teenager's life. Looking closely at the practice of going steady indicates that it is not (as some adults fear) principally a license for sexual freedom. Instead, its basis is more nearly in the kind of psychological security it provides, a psychological closeness that today's adolescents seem to need. When we ask why they need it, the answer is clear: the family no longer provides the closeness and security it once did. Because of the structural changes indicated above, the family fails to provide the kind of close secure relationships that the adolescent had as a child and will once again have when he himself forms a family. His response comes by finding that close security in an attachment to another.

Going steady is only one of the consequences of these structural changes in society. Another is the greater and greater burden that falls on the school. The school was once a supplement to the activities of the family in making adults of its children. But the roles have reversed for today's adolescents: the home is more and more merely a supplement to the adolescent's life, which focuses more and more on the school. It may be, as some school administrators feel, that this places too great a responsibility on the school. Yet the condition exists, and many families, with their working parents, high mobility, and lack of other relatives in the household, are in no position to change the condition. The adolescents turn to one another, to the school, and to the entertainments of the larger society, for these are their only resources.

Another consequence of the family's weakness, one that stems from the same needs as does going steady, is the earlier age of dating and of interest in the opposite sex. The consequences of this for interest in schoolwork is particularly marked for girls. There is a sharp shift in early adolescence from a high evaluation of the bright girl to a much lower evaluation—for the girl who appears especially bright does not fare well in dates with boys. Among schools I studied a few years ago, this shift started slightly later in the rural schools than in the urban and suburban ones. In the former, the shift occurred during the ninth grade; in the latter, the shift had largely taken place before the ninth grade. In both sets of schools, the devaluation of brightness and the emphasis on good looks and popularity with boys was at its peak in middle adolescence. In the rural schools, it had sharply declined by the senior year in high school, while in the urban and suburban ones, the decline had already begun in the junior year.

It appears that the most intense focus of adolescent girls on problems of popularity and dating, and the greatest devaluation of schoolwork occurs when the rating and dating system is still unsettled, and the uncertainty of who will ask whom for a date is at its height. These years, among modern adolescents, are earlier than before—in junior high school and early high school. The consequence for schools may be a peculiar one: to make the junior high school years more difficult ones than in the past, for adolescents and for teachers and school administrators, and to make the senior high school years (in three-year high schools) less difficult.

The earlier age of interest in the opposite sex, and the consequent earlier shift of adolescent values in this direction derives only in part from weakened family ties. It derives in part from all the changes in society that bring about early social sophistication among adolescents. Partly urban and suburban living, partly television and other mass media (for example, both popular music and movies have come to be more and more oriented to teenagers), partly the money they now have to spend, partly their better-educated parents, and partly the school itself, have made adolescents more wise in the ways of the world.

The Desire for Sophistication

In the schools I studied recently, the sharpest difference I found in the adolescents of the most rural schools and those of the most middle-class urban and suburban ones, was in the sophistication of the latter. The rural ninth graders were still children, obedient to teachers, and the middle-class suburban pupils were already disdainful of the ways of childhood. Such sophistication, and desire for sophistication, is a double-edged sword. It means that adolescents are more ready for new ideas, new experiences, quicker to grasp things. But it also makes them far less easy to teach, less willing to remain in the role of a learner, impatient with teachers, less likely to look at the teacher as a model or an authority. It need not make them more interested in school, but perhaps even less so. For the world whose sophistication they are taking on is one outside the school. Schoolwork, with its daily assignments and homework, they associate with childhood. Many of these children learn only years later, in college or after, that hard work and carrying out of assignments, attention to the demands of the teacher, become more important, rather than less, the farther they go in school.

Of all the recent changes in adolescents, this early desire for sophistication poses perhaps the greatest problem and the greatest challenge for secondary schools. Teenagers are less willing to respond to the teacher just because he is a teacher; less willing to "be taught." But they are more responsive *if* their imagination is captured, more able and willing to respond to a real challenge. It makes the school's task more difficult, for it cannot take the adolescent's interest for granted; it must find new ways of capturing this interest and energy. It has no other alternative but to accept these more sophisticated adolescents, and turn their sophistication to the advantage of education.

Altogether, recent changes in society have had a sharp impact on our adolescents. They present now, and they will present even more in the future, both difficulty and opportunity to the schools.

The Affluent Delinquent

Gerald J. Pine

At one time or another nearly everyone has assumed the role of delinquency expert. Public and professional comment on juvenile delinquency seems never to die nor fade away. Like sex, religion, sports, politics, and the weather, delinquency can always provide a subject for discussion. One dimension of the delinquency problem which has been a good conversation piece of late is the occurrence of delinquent behavior in the middle and upper classes. Statistics released by the Federal Bureau of Investigation and other governmental agencies, the growing number of newspaper accounts describing the anti-social and aberrant behavior of privileged youth, and the frequency with which delinquency in suburbia is discussed during cocktail *tête-à-têtes* attest to an apparent rising incidence of affluent delinquency.

This [selection] examines the relationship between delinquent behavior and social class status. Its pivotal concerns are reflected in the following questions:

1. What is the extent of delinquent behavior in the middle and upper classes?

2. How is delinquent behavior treated in the middle and upper classes?

3. Are there any forms of delinquency which are more peculiar to one class than another?

4. What is the relationship between social class mobility and delinquency?

5. What are the factors which generate the affluent delinquent?

In attempting to answer these questions, I have expressed my notions in a series of propositions anchored so far as possible in research findings, in theory, and in my personal experience as a school counselor in an affluent suburban community.

Proposition 1. There is a significant relationship between an increase in a country's economic growth and a rise in delinquent behavior.

There is evidence that a significant increase in the gross national product of a nation is accompanied or followed by a significant increase in delinquent behavior. Teen-age crime, once little known in France, is up 400 percent over a decade ago. Prosperous West Germany is becoming concerned about crime by children, especially in the fourteen to eighteen age groups. Sweden, Denmark, Norway, Holland, and Switzerland all report increased teen-age criminality. Japan, which is enjoying the fastest rate of economic growth in the world, is also experiencing one of the most rapid escalations of delinquency.[1] Such trends offer a sharp contrast to the comparatively low rates of delinquency which appeared in the United States during the depression years.[2] An increase in economic growth triggers a great deal of social and spatial mobility. The by-products of mobility and their role in delinquent behavior will be discussed in the propositions to follow.

Proposition 2. There has always been a considerable amount of delinquency in the middle- and upper-class segments of our society.

Several investigations have attempted to ascertain the frequency and nature of delinquent behavior in the middle and upper classes by using samples vaguely defined as middle- and upper-class in terms such as "upper-income group," "children of the professional class," "college students," and "group from relatively more favored neighborhoods." In contrast to the evidence based on official records, these studies, notwithstanding the general definition of class, indicate delinquent behavior is more equally dispersed among the various social classes than the average American citizen realizes.

In 1946 Austin L. Porterfield [3] compared the offenses of 2,409 cases of alleged delinquents in the Fort Worth, Texas, area with the admitted conduct of several hundred students at three colleges of northern Texas. He found that many college students had committed one or more of the "delinquency offenses" but seldom had been so charged as in the case of their less fortunate counterparts.

Wallerstein and Wyle [4] distributed to an upper-income group a questionnaire listing forty-nine offenses under the penal code of the state of New York. All of the offenses were sufficiently serious to draw maximum sentences of not less than a year. Replies were received from 1,698 individuals. Ninety-nine percent of those questioned answered affirmatively to one or more of the offenses.

In response to a questionnaire which Bloch gave to 340 college juniors and seniors during the period from 1943-1948, approximately 91 percent admitted that they had knowingly committed offenses against the law, both misdemeanors and felonies. The groups sampled came from considerably better-than-average middle-class homes. Women students were as glaringly delinquent in this respect as men, although the volume of major offenses which they admitted to was somewhat smaller than that for men.[5]

In another study Clinard discovered that of forty-nine criminology students at a Midwestern university, 86 percent had committed thefts and about 50 percent had committed acts of vandalism.[6]

Exploring the implications of "white-collar criminality" in regard to delinquent behavior, Wattenberg and Balistrieri compared 230 white boys charged with automobile theft with 2,544 others in trouble with the Detroit police in 1948. They found the automobile theft group came from relatively more favored neighborhoods and had good peer relations.[7]

An investigation was conducted by Birkness and Johnson in which a group of delinquents was compared with a group of non-delinquents. Each group included twenty-five subjects. It was found that five times as many of the parents of delinquent children (in contrast with the non-delinquent children) were of the professional class. Almost twice as many parents of the non-delinquents were classified in the manual labor status in comparison with the parents of delinquents.[8]

A study carried out by Nye in the state of Washington revealed that there was no significant relationship between one's position in the social class structure and the frequency and severity of delinquent behavior, i.e., the middle- and upper-class adolescent was involved in as much norm-violating behavior as the lower-class adolescent.[9]

In summary, during the past twenty years there has been an accumulation of evidence to demonstrate that delinquency is not the exclusive property of the lower class; it appears to exist to a significant degree in all strata of our society. But if this is the case, why have we only now become so deeply concerned about the affluent delinquent? Certainly if we have been concerned we have not been "publicly" concerned to the degree that we are today. Perhaps the answer lies in the fact that within our social structure there is a protective shield which hides the affluent delinquent and which up to now has served as a curtain of silence making privileged delinquency socially invisible. [Thirty] years ago Warner and Lunt, in their classic work *The Social Life of a Modern Community,* observed that the disparity in number of lower- and upper-class arrests is not to be accounted for by the fact that criminal behavior is proportionately higher among lower-class juveniles or that there are more ethnic groups whose children have been imperfectly adapted to city life. It must be understood as a product of the amount of protection from outside interference that parents can give members of their families.

Proposition 3. Official delinquency data has been and is biased in favor of upper- and middle-class youth.

Delinquency is usually considered primarily as a lower-class problem. However, the research reporting significant relationships between delinquent behavior and lower socioeconomic status has been characterized by a built-in bias, i.e., the use of official delinquency statistics that do not reflect a considerable amount of upper- and middle-class delinquent behavior. Middle- and upper-class children are less likely to become official delinquency statistics, because their behavior is more frequently handled outside the sphere of formal legal institutions. The middle and upper classes control various means of preventing detection, influencing official authority, and generally "taking care of their own" through psychiatrists, clinics, and private institutions, thus avoiding the police and the courts—the official agencies.

In the following telling and graphic descriptions, Harrison Salisbury [10] describes the classic middle-class way of dealing with anti-social behavior:

> If sixteen-year old George and three of his friends "borrow" a nice-looking convertible from the country club parking lot and set off on a joyride and are caught speeding by the county police they are taken to the station house all right, but nothing goes on the blotter. The parents come down, there is much talk, the fathers bawl the daylights out of the kids, the boys promise to be good, the owners wouldn't think of making a charge, and by two o'clock in the morning everyone is back home, peacefully sleeping. There's no case, no records, no statistics, "no delinquency."
>
> When 17-year-old Joan gets pregnant after letting 18-year-old Dennis "fool around" at a beach party one summer night, she isn't sent to the Youth House. Nor is Dennis confronted with the dilemma of marrying the girl or facing a charge of statutory rape. There is an angry dispute between the two families. Joan's family blames Dennis. Dennis's family blames Joan. In the end Joan's father finds a doctor who takes care of Joan for $750. Joan is a month late starting school in the fall because, as her mother explains to the principal, she had a severe reaction from the anti-biotics they gave her at the camp up in New Hampshire where she went in August.

In addition to the built-in bias of official delinquency data, studies reporting on the relationship between social class status and delinquent behavior are characterized by another critical shortcoming: a paucity of empirical material on a significant dynamic of social class—social mobility.

Proposition 4. A significant factor related to delinquent behavior in the upper and middle classes is the dynamic of social mobility.

What bearing does movement from one social class to another class have on delinquent behavior? What are the implications of vertical movement between classes in regard to norm violations? The question of social mobility has an important place in the study of social class and its impact on delinquent behavior for two reasons:

1. Social mobility introduces a dynamic feature of possible change into a class system, and

2. it can alter the structure and patterns of class relationships as the consequence of mobility introduces changes into those close relationships.

Here I would like to share with you the results of a study designed to determine the significance of the relationships between social-class status, social-mobility status, and delinquent behavior.[11] The study was conducted to determine the significance of the relationships between social class, social mobility, and delinquent behavior. Data were collected from a population of 683 pupils (grades nine–twelve) attending an urban high school. Information regarding delinquency was gathered by using a 120-item anonymous "delinquency inventory." The chi-square technique was employed to analyze the data, which showed that, in general, there is no significant relationship between social-class status and delinquent behavior. A very strong relationship exists between social-mobility status and delinquent behavior. Adolescents moving downward in the social structure are more heavily involved in delinquency; adolescents moving upward are least involved.

The primary conclusion made in this study is that delinquent behavior is less a function of the class an individual is in at the moment and much more a function of the class to which he aspires or toward which he is moving. In examining the relationship between social class and delinquent behavior, it is not only important to know what class an individual is in but perhaps more important to know if he is securely located in the class, if he has just managed a toehold in the class, or if he has just moved down from a class.

The findings indicate delinquent behavior is not a lower-class phenomenon. However, one aspect of the question of class differential in delinquent behavior which invites further investigation is the relationship between value system and delinquency. Social-class status may be more accurately measured in terms of value systems than in terms of economic factors such as occupation, housing, residence, and income. The lower-class boy moving upward into the middle class may be guided in his behavior by a middle-class value system, and, therefore, might be more accurately described as a member of the middle class.

The behavior of the middle-class boy moving downward in the social structure may be influenced primarily by lower-class concerns, hence he might be more accurately described as lower class.

It is quite possible for a child to live in a lower-class neighborhood and in the midst of a lower-class culture and still be considered middle class.

An explanation of the strong relationship between downward mobility and delinquent behavior may be found in Reissman's hypothesis [12] regarding the psychological consequences of "downward mobility." He suggests that these consequences can be channeled away from the individual to avoid injury to self-conceptions and self-respect. The individual imputes to others the blame for his or his family's descent in the social structure. His frustration and his failure are poured into an explanation that implicates society or society's institutions as the cause of it all. Hostile and negative attitudes toward others and toward authority develop.

If the intensity of the psychological consequences of "mobility failure" is in proportion to the degree of failure, then it is not difficult to understand the strength of the relationship between downward mobility and delinquent behavior. Certainly, downward mobility represents the greatest failure in the mobility process. For, in a culture which highly esteems the success value, what constitutes a greater failure than the failure to at least maintain one's status quo in the social structure?

Proposition 5. Successful social mobility is a breeding ground for the development of delinquent behavior.

The research evidence presented in Proposition 3 indicates there is a statistically significant relationship between downward mobility of adolescents and delinquent behavior. Paradoxically, the downward movement of the adolescent may be the consequence of the successful mobility of his parents. Psychological tension and conflict often accompany successful movement in the social structure and may be expressed in delinquent behavior.

Successful mobility necessarily involves a major adjustment by the individual. He must reject the way of life of the group he has just left and assume the new way of life of the group he has just entered. It is a process of class "acculturation." Depending upon the change required, the reorientation of the individual can be enormous, depending upon the recency of the change, the reorientation can involve a great deal of insecurity.

Successful mobility places the individual, for some period of time, in a marginal social position. The individual's former friends and associates may find him threatening; his success is a mark of their failure. His newly created friends and associates produced by his successful move may find him too "different," too "raw," and too recent to be accepted as a bona fide member. The individual thus finds himself suspended in a "success limbo." The insecurity he feels may produce reactions the same as those exhibited by failure.[13]

Not only does the individual experience the results of success or failure but his family does also. Whyte [14] found that the individual's family must become implicated in his success just as they do in his failures.

On a larger scale, our society must experience the consequences for its emphasis upon social mobility, upon seeking and achieving success. Tumin [15] sets forth the following as by-products of the stress placed on social mobility in American society:

1. A "diffusion of insecurity" as more and more people become involved with trying to get ahead rather than developing any lasting and sure sense of the group and its needs. Traditional beliefs and values of society become threatened as behavior is more and more oriented toward "status acceptance and prestige ranking."

2. A "severe imbalance" of social institutions as a result of rapid mobility of the population as religion, education, and the family become tied to the struggle for economic success.

3. "Fragmentation of the social order" as more and more individuals become rivalrous with each other. Competition does not always lead to the greatest good for the greatest number.

4. "Denial of work" as the emphasis shifts from the importance of work and striving to the urgency of appearing to be successful. Preference is given to the open portrayal of *being* successful, as measured by the power and property which one openly consumes.

5. "Rapid social mobility" generates in the older portions of the population a cranky and bitter conservatism and worship of the past; and in the new mobile segments a vituperative contempt of traditions.

It is the accumulation and the complex interaction of these social by-products which fertilize the soil for the growth of affluent delinquency.

Proposition 6. The female-based household is a by-product of successful mobility and an important variable in the development of delinquent behavior.

Success and the striving for success in the middle and upper classes is frequently the incubator of the female-based household. A number of studies have identified the female-based household as a characteristic of lower-class society and as an influencing factor in the development of delinquent behavior. And yet anyone who has worked with middle- and upper-class youth is keenly aware of the large number of female-dominated families in suburbia. In order to insure and maintain his success, father often becomes a "weekend briefcase-toting visitor" who is either absent from the home or only sporadically present, or when present only minimally or inconsistently involved in the raising of the children. Mother becomes "chief cook and bottle washer," assuming both the maternal and paternal roles.

It is not too difficult to understand how female-centered families in the middle and upper class can produce delinquents, particularly in the male adolescent population.

Because of the inconsistent presence or involvement of an adequate masculine model in the home with whom the suburban boy can identify, many teen-age males develop uncertainties about their masculine identity at a time in their lives when identity is a crucial matter. For the adolescent male who feels insecure about his sex identification, delinquency represents a demonstrative vehicle for asserting his masculinity.

Proposition 7. The emphasis on success in our culture has led to the elongation of adolescence, a contributing factor in the development of delinquent behavior.

Another consequence of success in the middle and upper classes is the extension of adolescence as a period of growth and development. The emphasis on success in suburbia is epitomized in the pressures exerted on youth to get into college. For the vast numbers of young boys and girls who do go to college one fact is very clear: Adolescence doesn't end at eighteen or nineteen; it probably ends at twenty-one or twenty-two; and perhaps even later. Thus for a large number of our privileged youth at least four years have been tacked on to the process of growing up and four years can be a long time to wait to prove yourself—to demonstrate that you are a man or a woman. Four more years of that social limbo we call adolescence are very conducive to intensifying the already existing feelings of anxiety, tension, restlessness, and rebellion so common to high school youth. Adolescence is becoming an "existential vacuum," a social process lacking purpose and meaning. To the degree we elongate the process of adolescence without providing purpose for its existence, to that degree should we anticipate more frequent socially aberrant and rebellious behavior.

Proposition 8. A middle- and upper-class "sheepskin psychosis" nourishes norm-violating behavior.

In the middle and upper classes there is tremendous pressure placed upon youth to succeed. These pressures emanate from the dominating concern of parents for achieving and "getting ahead," and the feeling in youth of an ensuing sense of discrepancy between aspiration and achievement.

> This strong focus in the middle-class milieu may induce the whole perfectionist-compulsive syndrome, in which children have impossible ideas of what they should accomplish; the result for some individuals is a combination of neuroses built around the individual's inability to achieve internalized goals of various types, e.g., learning to read, being on the honor roll, or getting into the college of first choice. . . . The stresses imposed through the conflict over aspiration and achievement wake a wide variety of symptoms. One of these symptoms may take the form of norm-violating behavior.[16]

Proposition 9. Middle-class values which once served as behavior controls are weakening.

One of the identifying characteristics of the middle class is the tradition of deferring immediate gratifications for long-range goals. For years this tradition helped to instill in middle-class youngsters a capacity for self-denial and impulse control. However, there is mounting indication today that the strength of this tradition of focus on achievement, of directed work effort, and deferment of immediate pleasures is diminishing in a number of middle-class sectors. Impulse buying and installment plan financing are very representative of the "have-it-now" pattern of the lower-class culture. Concomitantly, compulsory education and a continuous promotion policy act to keep all youngsters in school regardless of effort, achievement, or future goal. These trends have tended to lessen the view of middle-class youth that success is achieved through deferred gratification, frustration tolerance, directed effort, and self-control. If delinquency is on the rise in the middle class, it may be attributable in part to a diminution in the classical middle-class tradition of "hard work today and rewards tomorrow."

Proposition 10. Middle-class youth behavior reflects lower-class values.

Currently, lower-class concerns and values are being sold to and bought by the middle-class consumer. Mass media and the advertising world have dipped deeply into the lower-class culture. Lower-class focal concerns such as force, duplicity, chance, excitement, trouble, autonomy, and "present pleasure" have been mined over and over again for use on the screen, the air waves, the picture tube, and the printed page. The effect of this cultural saturation has been the borrowing of lower-class concerns by middle-class youth. Adolescent fads, jargon, music, and behavior seem to mirror a number of lower-class behavior patterns. It would seem that the interaction of these recently assumed lower-class concerns with the other social and psychological by-products of social mobility constitute a powerful generative force in developing affluent delinquency.

Student Unrest

Edward Joseph Shoben, Jr.

For nearly two hundred years, a strongly shared set of values has shaped and given direction to the American dream. Inherited largely from the European Enlightenment and the traditions of Western liberalism, those values have been essentially the ones identified by Max Weber in his classic analysis of the Protestant ethic. At the core have been work, achievement, and security; playing more instrumental roles, self-control, an orientation toward the future, the supremacy of rationality over the impulses and emotions, and the potentially supportive and protective approval of society have all been vitally important. As the United States has grown, this central value-structure has provided room and reinforcement for individuality through frontier-related opportunities and through an enlarging multiplicity of forms, primarily occupational, over which the basic ethic could be effectively stretched.

Currently, the nation is subject to a panoply of forces that challenge that ancient pattern of dominant values. Among these powerful influences are the tempo and massiveness of contemporary social change, the technology of communication and its interaction with a highly literate population, the human crowding that results from population growth and urbanization, and the transformation of the economy from an industrial to what has been called a post-industrial base.¹ It is within this context that one can grasp some of the significance of student unrest and the dissidence of youth. What is crucial about these phenomena is not their greying of administrative heads or their interference with large-scale institutional machinery. Their importance lies, rather, in their strong suggestion of a sharp decline in the potency of traditional values to guide and animate American life.

Born to a time of jet travel and television, with little sense of either the Great Depression or the war against Hitler as much less remote than the Black Plague or the Thirty Years War, and aware from infancy of the near-genocidal weaponry that ironically defines modern man's most creative achievement, today's youth are, in the main, indeed, children of both affluence and anxiety. They are a part of what is most novel in our rapidly and radically changing age; and what is now most novel is what is least familiar to those with longer memories and more antique arteries.

It follows, then, that if there has always been a "generational gap" of some kind or other, the conditions for the gap's widening are presently particularly acute, and the magnitude of that gulf is lent special meaning by population projections. Almost half the American people are currently under twenty-five years of age. By 1972, a majority will be under twenty-one, and the median age of the American voter in that year should be about twenty-six. Beyond their increase in numbers, youth have attained a kind of solidarity by virtue of college attendance. Now enrolled in excess of six million on campuses across the country, students have been recognized as something roughly analogous to a social class. Selective Service deals with them on special terms; advertising identifies them as a distinctive and important "target public"; they are courted politically, and their mores are acknowledged, sometimes with acceptance and sometimes with retributive outrage, as different from those of older generations.

Numbers and a kind of corporate identity imply potential power. For potential power to become manifest, spokesmen are needed to give leadership and focus to size and membership; and spokesmen are now available among student activists who, even though they represent a minority of youth, still compose a considerable group. If only 3 percent of current college students can be called activists, they yet number in excess of 180,000, and they appear, in one way or another, to voice the sentiments of from one-fifth to one-third of their less directly involved peers.

Both intrinsically, therefore, and as the heirs apparent of American destiny, contemporary college students can hardly be ignored. And whatever one may say—and a good deal of importance *can* be said—about their style and manners, their primary concerns hardly merit neglect among thoughtful and goodwilled men.

In a complex fashion, four major themes have underlain student unrest as we have known it since 1960. One is civil justice. A second is the humanization and personalization of international relations, expressed basically in vigorous opposition to the American posture in Vietnam and in the endorsement of such person-to-person ventures as the Peace Corps. The third is the modernization of the university and its relationship to society. And the fourth, cutting across the other three, is an emphasis on individual freedom and self-determination, on the existential primacy of the present and of experience in contrast to the traditional dominance of the future or of either authority or the accumulated wisdom associated with guiding conventions.

In pressing for a hearing in the prosecution of these broad and humane interests, students have typically assumed a stance that is political and tactical, but their energizing convictions have been profoundly moral. Active and often risky involvement in the fight for civil rights, in opposition to the war in southeast Asia, and in battles for educational reform grow basically out of beliefs about the right way a man should live and commitments to the principle that individuals must contribute actively to the attainment of a more generous and decent world. Indeed, these involvements primarily reflect the social implementation of the ethic of individual freedom in the existential present: at their richest, freedom and authenticity of experience must be widely shared. Civil justice, peace, and more relevant forms of educational opportunity are, on the one hand, the conditions under which such a sharing can be most significantly achieved and enjoyed; on the other hand, the vigorous pursuit of these social goals makes possible the experience of meaningfulness and freedom that is the touchstone of the moral life.

Such an experiential and existential touchstone contrasts sharply with the traditional moral criterion of how well behavior accords with conventions or time-established rules. It has little to do with work and earned security as our civilization has enshrined them, and it often flies in the face of a prudent self-control or cultivation of social approval. When applied to such

affairs as sexual conduct, the use of marijuana, and personal appearance, the existential test can too readily be misunderstood as
a legitimizing of license, an escape from the harsh realities that
a truly moral man faces, and an unsocialized sloppiness. Although
the way of wisdom with respect to sex, drugs, and dress is more
than merely moot, and although one need not be at all convinced
that the advocates of the New Left or of the hippie mode are
within gunshot of newly persuasive and genuinely humane insights, the basic issues here are very different. They concern such
matters as the right of privacy in an era when that right is subject to subtle but enormous and debilitating erosion. They concern the question of the extent to which pharmacological agents
can be employed for the improvement of the human condition and
for the enlargement of personal experience in a time when psycho-
active drugs have become commonplace in the adult community—
witness the huge annual bills paid for caffeine, nicotine, alcohol,
and a startling variety of tranquilizers by the most stable and
conventionally contributive members of our middle class. They
concern the question of the degree to which contemporary life
has come to focus on traditional forms and the externals of social
interchange as against the experience of pleasure and the real
substance of personal relationships. Such matters have always
been of moment to civilized men, and history has consistently
recorded the indebtedness of cultures to those who, by searching
out the elements of hypocrisy and decadence and self-delusion in
them, have helped to revitalize them.

But the thoroughly appropriate debates that can be held about
the specific positions of activist students on particular problems is
not our business here. The present thesis is a twofold one: First,
the confrontation that has been shaping up between the student
sector and traditional society is an authentically moral one,
fundamental and serious in tone and implications, generative of a
healthy rethinking of ethical ideas and the ways in which they
can be made manifest in social policy, and a decided aid in helping America gear itself to the pace and pattern of the changes
that are the hallmark of the age. Second, insofar as it has accepted the slogan of "from dissent to resistance," the moral force
of student activism has become corrupt and subject to decay.

It is not that the escalation of criticism and protest to disobedience and disruption is hard to understand. . . . Conscious of
their numbers and their college-based corporate solidarity, informed and concerned students are unlikely to be put off for very

long by silence, a figurative pat on the head, or mere access to a patient but inattentive ear of authority. The point holds in spite of the discourtesy, disrespect, and deliberately provocative style of which students have frequently been guilty in their search for a proper forum in which to make their case. Youthful bad manners have often been not only tactically stupid; they have contravened the argument for increased humanization that has been the main and most convincing tenet in their pressure for reform in both the university and the larger society. Nevertheless, their sins have sometimes been less objectionable—on the grounds, by the way, of quite traditional concepts of civility and wisdom— than the neglectful, patronizing, or intransigent reaction from responsible and established seats of power.

If, however, this state of affairs helps to explain, it in no way justifies the move from dissent to resistance, from a vigorous competition among moral ideas and ethical models to a clash in which raw might is the only determiner of the outcome. Almost by definition, this shift in the character of the confrontation removes it from the moral domain. When contending parties attempt to settle their differences by weapons alone, one side always considers the other to be illegitimate, unredeemable in its villainy, and inaccessible to either reason or moral suasion. It is for this reason that war is so typically callousing to the human spirit. Because of the imperfections that so mark man's condition, resorts to warfare may be comprehensible, but they give no warrant to anyone to engage in organized violence in the name of an unsullied morality.

Clarifying this position in the context of student unrest today requires an examination of the notion of civil disobedience with respect both to violating the law and the deliberate breaking of institutional rules. The flouting of duly adopted social regulations is dangerous, of course, on two scores. On the one hand, it rends the fabric of community, opening the doors to anarchy and disorder. On the other hand, because the basic reason for laws in the traditions of the West is to protect society against the tyranny of men, civil disobedience always carries with it the risk of the rise to power of a charismatic dictator or an authoritarian junta; the restoration of social stability and the achievement of some regularity in the community's operations have often provided the road over which a Führer has traveled to prominence. At the same time, experience suggests certain circumstances under which the systematic and planned violation of social rules may be looked upon as acceptable, justified, and beneficial:

1. The existence of a societal state of affairs so inhumane and indefensible as to demand extreme corrective measures. This condition is adequately fulfilled only when (a) no mode of appropriate redress is available through law or the usual political machinery and (b) the moral or political principles by which the existing state of affairs is judged intolerable are articulate, explicitly formulated, and supported on behalf of the *total* community.

2. Techniques of civil disobedience that entail minimal or no risk of injury to others.

3. Minimal or no infringement of the legal rights of others, including those against whose interests the disobedience is aimed.

4. The avoidance of violence.

5. The acceptance of the consequences of civil disobedience. By definition, civil disobedience involves not opposition to law but breaking a particular and offensive law in support of a "higher" moral or social principle. Attempts to escape the penalties imply both that no offensive law has been broken and that the higher principle is not worth the sacrifice.

6. Clear support of the justifying principle by a substantial minority of the population subject to the rule which has been attacked. Because the violation of regulations is a community affair, it cannot properly and on principle be acted out unless both the basic grievances and the justifying principle have a base in significant community endorsement.

7. Some probability that disobedience will achieve a remedy to the ill that initiated it.

Unless these conditions are met, civil disobedience can readily degenerate into indiscriminate rioting, a technique for serving selfish interests, and a route to one brand or another of fascism. Despite the strength of the instigations and the desperation that may lie at the roots of civil resistance, the resistance movement itself is likely to prove, in such a case, self-defeating. Social action not infrequently has consequences unforeseen by those committed to it, and totalitarian outcomes are rarely the aim of civil disobedience. In any event, without full regard for the justifying circumstances, civil disobedience can lose its moral base and slide rapidly into mob violence, the venting of miscellaneous frustrations, and the ugly expression of a variety of doubtfully relevant hostilities.

In any context, then, a progression from dissent and protest to resistance and disobedience must prove its moral validity by adherence to the conditions set out here. In a university, this kind of proof is particularly difficult to attain. Among its central functions, the university must give a high place to serving as a forum for the exploration and debating of significant ideas. The processes of exploration and debate can be abridged or stifled in many ways, and this kind of interference is no less objectionable when students are responsible for it then when a legislature or an administrative officer is at fault.

To provide a meaningful forum, a college campus must be thoroughly open,[2] offering hospitality to speakers who attempt to recruit minds and to officials from government and business who attempt to recruit talents. To demonstrate against the ideas and practices that an agent of the Department of Defense or the Dow Chemical Company may represent is quite legitimate; to capture him, to prevent his doing his lawful job, and to interfere with access to him on the part of other possibly interested students— such activities have too much in common with a ban on speakers, the censorship of the college newspaper, or restrictions on the circulation of "dangerous" library books. In all these instances, a fundamental purpose of the university is subverted, and the morality of the subversion is hard to find and harder still to justify.

There is another ground on which the dissent-to-resistance notion seems questionable. Any morality, including an ethic of immediate experience, gives some attention to the consequences of acts and to the future entailments of conduct. In the case of contemporary student activism—particularly those aspects of it concerned with Black Power, nihilistic efforts to overthrow the entire educational and social system, and some of the most extreme protestations against the war in Vietnam—it seems probable that the advocates of disobedience are breeding a backlash that could make the McCarthyism of the early 1950's seem tame and generous. John Fischer [3] has recently pointed out this very real danger:

> . . . Some members of the New Left . . . have openly proclaimed their allegiance to Mao or Castro . . . and their hopes of destroying or at least "dislocating" American society. Others have engaged in what now can be excused as idealistic gestures—burning draft cards, assaults on induction centers, blocking of troop trains, mobbing Cabinet officers. Tomorrow, in the hot glare of a Senate investigating chamber, a skillful demagogue could easily make such behavior look like giving aid and comfort to the enemy.
>
> Moreover, the New Leftists are busily undermining their own best defense: the American traditions of free speech and tolerance. Increasingly, they are taking the position: "I'm right. You are wrong. Therefore, I cannot permit you to be heard." So, in the name of morality, they are stoning and howling down anyone who might disagree with them. . .
>
> The saddest prospect is that the coming reaction will fall not only on these [New Leftists] but also on . . . a good many students of the kind described by Nan Robertson of the *New York Times* as "intellectual hobbits—warm, lovable, and a little furry-minded." Among them, too . . . will be people like Mr. Rovere [4] and myself, who still believe in the old-fashioned virtues of free speech and fair trial—and who will feel compelled, therefore, to oppose the new crop of witch-hunters as we opposed McCarthy. . . .

Unless there is evidence of some appropriate concern for this disturbing possibility, it seems only accurate to read the morality of student radicalism, recently so promising and so vital, as decaying at its center and as far less humane than many of us would prefer to believe.

Finally, there is another problem that must be considered in evaluating the new morality that has found its voice in youth—particularly college youth. Throughout the history of man, his communities have had to steer between the Scylla of ossification through too much discipline and too slavish a reverence for tradition and convention and the Charybdis of dissolution or conquest because of an efflorescence of individualism and privatism that makes cooperation impossible. Many civilizations have failed, foundering on the rocks of either overorganization or anarchy. Because extremes tend to beget extremes, and because ours is an age in which the bureaucratization, systematization, rationalization, and routinization of life proceed at a subtle but startling pace, it may be well to remember that the correctives, deeply desirable as they may be, hold their dangers, too. The existentialist, highly personal moral stance of many contemporary young people, despite its considerable virtues, recalls Bertrand Russell's observation [5] that "with subjectivism in philosophy, anarchism in politics goes hand in hand." If we are to achieve both authentic personhood and a genuine sense of community in the modern world, and if the university is to play its significant part in the quest for that achievement, then the emerging power of contemporary youth must be disciplined by an awareness of the moral vulnerability common to all men. That vulnerability is currently italicized by the attractiveness of the dissent-to-resistance slogan, and a major question before us all is whether students will display the sensitivity of the genuinely educated in responding to it.

The Educational Impact of Present American Foreign Policy

Charles Frankel

A number of years ago I addressed the American Association for Higher Education on the subject, "The Happy Crisis in Higher Education." The theme of my remarks was that higher education was full of problems. But I expressed the view that these problems might have a good side to them. They might wake us up. They might give us the provocation to examine the premises of our activities and to do some intellectual housecleaning that was long overdue.

There is still a crisis in higher education. Added to the old one, in fact, there is a new one. Since I am somewhat older, perhaps it is simply the changes in my metabolism that lead me to take a less cheerful view of our current situation than I did of the situation we faced some years back. But I don't really think that the grim picture I see before me is merely the reflection of my advancing years. It would be odd if any thinking man were to pronounce anything but a severe judgment on the present condition of higher education in our country.

Let us get the qualifications out of the way first. Almost a hundred and fifty years ago, a Mrs. Trollope, a British visitor to these shores, remarked: "In conversing with Americans I have constantly found that if I alluded to anything which they thought I considered as uncouth, they would assure me it was local, and not national; the accidental peculiarity of a very small part, and by no means a specimen of the whole. 'That is because you know so little of America,' is a phrase I have listened to a thousand times, and in nearly as many different places." Well, the lady was right, and so were her critics. Even before leveling my criticisms I could hear the defensive words in people's throats. I confess I could hear them in my own. Obviously, no generalization that says disagreeable things about our country could possibly apply to it without qualifications.

It is true that no nation has ever before undertaken to educate so large a proportion of its people between the ages of seventeen and twenty-two. It is true that our nation, along with others like the Soviet Union and Japan, has turned higher education into a powerful instrument for reducing class barriers. It is true that during the last ten years, and particularly during the life of the present national Administration, the public funds spent on higher education represent a new and ambitious national commitment. And it is true that American scholarship has added immensely to its luster during the last generation. In its methods, in the talent available to it, in its achievements, it is a major resource for the entire international community.

But it is precisely these truths that compel one to take a jaundiced view of American higher education's present performance. The capacities of American higher education are considerable. It is in those terms that it is not doing well. In terms of what we have in this country, in terms of what, at the beginning of the sixties, we knew that we would have to do, we are performing badly.

The problems that existed at the beginning of the sixties are worse now than they were then. We knew then that, in too many places, undergraduate education had become unacceptably impersonal. That situation makes more trouble, not less, today. We knew at the beginning of the sixties that, for all our achievements in scholarship, something was missing. What was it? A quality of skepticism that turns back on the conventions of each discipline and questions them? A quality of commitment that would make the practitioners of each discipline eager to teach it to the young, because they would regard it as an instrument for civilizing the mind? No matter. People who find such questions not truly scholarly are still in command of most of our fields of learning. And we knew at the beginning of the sixties that something systematic would have to be done to guard the university's sovereignty. Yet the universities today are engaged more extensively than before in research and teaching that represent concessions to the highest bidder, and not expressions of any considered decision about what is intrinsically best for the progress of education and learning.

I hope I shall not be misunderstood. I don't think that people in colleges and universities are so preternaturally wise that they can make the right decisions without ever being presented with alternative ideas from the outside. And I think it is a caricature of the truth to say, as some do, that the colleges and universities of this country have been turned into servile instruments of something known as "the military-industrial complex." Nothing more is needed to refute that proposition than the fact that most of those who say it are inhabitants of college and university campuses.

Equally, it is fatuous to speak as though every dollar received from a federal source had something tainted and threatening about it, something inherently corrupting of honesty and courage. Undeniably, there are congressmen who haven't read the Constitution of the United States with full attention, and who therefore become confused when professors who receive federal funds go right on acting as though they enjoyed full freedom of expression. And undoubtedly, there are bureaucrats who tremble when these solons squeak. But the fact remains that the federal government's support of higher educational enterprises has almost invariably been accompanied by an understanding of the conditions of academic work and by respect for the rights of the educational community. Its record, surely, is at least as good as that of most state legislatures or alumni organizations.

The erosion of educational sovereignty of which I speak has not come from censorship. It has come from the pattern of ad hoc research contracts and short-term commitments for support that reduce colleges and universities to the status of intellectual handymen selling their services from door to door. It has come from the diversification of energies, the buying up of talent, the loss of a consistent sense of priorities. And in this process the federal government has played a considerable role, though, of course, not the only role.

It is at this point that I come to the central subject of my paper: the educational impact of foreign policy, the consequences for education of the foreign policies that we follow. If the policies are short term, then educational resources will be devoted to short-term purposes. If these policies are subject to uncertainties, then an element of uncertainty is introduced into the educational community. And that has happened. It is the first and simplest effect of our foreign policies on our educational affairs.

Undoubtedly, the short-term, contractual relationships between the federal government and higher educational institutions have also had a good effect. They have permitted much good research and interesting teaching to take place that might not otherwise have occurred. But these arrangements have also meant the depletion of the educational community's limited resources. Very often, too, they have meant that the university must undertake long-range commitments even though the federal government itself offers no assurance of continued federal support.

The situation is not a good one. Efforts have been made to repair it, through changes in AID (Agency for International Development) legislation, through proposals that Senator George McGovern has put before his colleagues, and through the International Education Act, which was passed in 1966. But all these efforts have been abortive. Although some changes have taken place, we are substantially where we were five or six years ago. In fact, in certain respects we have slipped backward. Allow me a brief discussion of principles to make plain what I mean.

The colleges and universities still preserve the major portion of their sovereignty, despite the problems that I have just mentioned. They do so because most of them have firm sources of support apart from short-term contracts. But if these institutions are to realize their full potentialities as independent centers for research, criticism, and social leadership, the federal government is going to have to play a large role in keeping them properly financed.

The support that the federal government gives should be support that is cut loose from short-term requirements or emergencies. It should have the characteristics of regularity and predictability. It should permit institutions of learning considerable discretion with regard to the use of the funds they receive. And it should be support aimed not at this or that quick result, but at the strengthening of education in its long-range purposes. Such federal support, needless to say, should not be the only kind of support available to higher educational institutions. Other sources of support are also indispensable. In unity there may be strength, but, as far as educational financing goes, in plurality there is freedom.

It is in these terms, I think, that we are now worse off than we were. A few years ago the federal government seemed to be moving with confidence and imagination toward putting the principles I have just described into practice. Now, although these principles still receive official declarations of loyalty, the government has turned back on itself, and is moving in the opposite direction. There have been substantial cutbacks in support to education, scientific research, and international exchange. Even more tragic have been the cutbacks in the hopes the American people were permitted and encouraged to entertain even as recently [in 1968] as thirty months ago.

Federal support to the arts and the humanities remains scandalously low, and is in peril of extinction. The International Education Act has received not a dollar with which to be implemented. The statements of intention of this Administration with regard to the initiation of a worldwide program of educational advancement are still merely statements of intention.

To be sure, you may think that it was wrong for the federal government ever to get into the business of supporting higher education; but whatever you think on that subject, you cannot think that it is good for the federal government to follow a policy of now-you-see-it-now-you-don't. It is possible to show that some things have been done; it is possible to play with figures. But it is not possible to play with people's expectations and to imagine that there will be no consequences. It is not possible to stir their expectations one year and to leave them in the lurch the next without doing damage. Much is said these days about the importance of keeping our commitments. I think that is a commendable idea. It is a principle of sound government at home as well as abroad.

I do not want to ask who is responsible for what has happened —the President, or the Congress, or perhaps Ho Chi Minh. I think, however, that there can be no argument about *what* is responsible. The major cause of these events is our foreign policy, and, most immediately, our policy in Vietnam. This does not in itself prove, needless to say, that this policy is wrong. But it does indicate part of the price we pay for it.

Yet so far I have mentioned only the less important consequences of foreign policy. Our foreign policy is also the reason for our selective service system. That system has changed the relation of students to their teachers, to grades, to their educational experience in general. It affects the outlook, the choices, the frame of mind, probably of every student in the country, women as well as men. It subjects many of the most sensitive of them to cruel dilemmas and choices. It has contributed, as we all know, to fractiousness, indiscipline, and suspicion on a very large number of the campuses in this country. That does not prove, I would admit again, that either the selective service system or the foreign policy that requires it are wrong. It is merely another price that we are willing to pay.

But as we add up these prices, it would be natural to ask at some point, I presume, what the worth of a foreign policy is. We live in a period of cost-benefit analysis. Have we applied this method of analysis to our foreign policy? Even to ask the question is a kind of oddity. The normal approach to these matters is to determine foreign policy goals and then to ask whether we have the wherewithal to reach them. It is not often asked, if ever, what these goals are worth, or what other goals will be sacrificed. And the reason it is not often asked, of course, is that one does not ask such questions where something called "the national interest" is at stake.

And so I come to my ultimate question. What is the relation of education to "the national interest"? What do we mean by that solemn phrase anyway, which need only be introduced into a discussion to silence everyone but the man who has spoken it?

I would like you to think about a fact that is perfectly obvious when you stop to think about it: The largest single external influence on the shape and focus, the atmosphere and health, of American higher education is exerted by American foreign policy. The major decisions made in government affecting higher education are made by people who usually aren't thinking about higher education at all.

This raises a question that is the reverse of the one usually asked, but still I think it is reasonable to ask it. The fact that it is unusual to ask this question indicates how oddly we view foreign policy, how much we insulate it as an artificial thing, how much we set it aside and apply assumptions and value judgments to it that are separated from the normal business of our lives.

The question that is raised, it seems to me, is a straightforward one. What is the impact of our foreign policy on the education of the American people? It is common to ask what contributions higher education can make to the fulfillment of this country's purposes in the international arena. And it is, of course, perfectly proper to ask such a question. But the reverse question is at least as urgent. It is astonishing, indeed, that it is not commonly asked. Indeed, this in itself is a symptom of the power of foreign policy to mesmerize us and at times to turn normal modes of thought upside down.

Am I suggesting, then, that a test of American foreign policy should be its impact on education? Yes. Not the only test, but a test. Am I saying that what is good for education, and particularly higher education, is good for the foreign policy of the country? I believe I am. And that what is bad for higher education is bad for the foreign policy of the country? Not invariably, but generally, yes. Well, then, am I not guilty of the same sort of confusion about means and ends that gained a one-time president of General Motors undying fame? No. With all respect for automobiles, there is a difference between the functions of General Motors and the functions of a college or university. There is a difference between things and people.

The essence of the conviction that separated the Greeks from those they called the barbarians was that a society is, as we now say without thinking about what the word means, a *culture:* it is a soil, a setting, in which people grow, in which the character of the individual is formed. Everything about it, therefore, has an educational meaning. Everything about it can be judged by the kind of educational impact that is exerted. The heart of liberal civilization lies in the idea that you measure the worth of a society by the quality of the human beings it produces. And crucial to a society's achievement, therefore, are its formal institutions of education.

This is the background of the Greek view that their freedom, by which they meant participation in the affairs of the commonwealth, was the first and greatest of their possessions. They liked democracy (when they did) because they thought it educational. They liked it, among other reasons, because they thought it offered the right setting and orientation for formal institutions of education. And when the Athenians looked down on the Spartans it was because the Spartans, as the Athenians thought, had reversed the proper order of things. They educated men to be warriors. They did not realize that the function of education was to make good men, and that good men would be good warriors when they had to be.

All this indicates, I think, that it is not insane to ask about a foreign policy: what is its educational impact? And I suspect that if we asked this question more insistently, we might come to assess our foreign policies with clearer eyes and a sterner intelligence.

Consider, for example, our arguments about foreign assistance. What is the case for foreign assistance in Africa or in India? Is it really because we fear the power of the people of these areas if they turn against us? Is it because they have material resources we absolutely need? Are our economic or strategic interests seriously involved? It seems to me that a hard and honest look at the facts would yield a negative answer to all these questions. We give ourselves practical reasons not because these are reasons that stand up but because they are the only sorts of reasons we are supposed to admit publicly. We give ourselves these reasons, if I may suggest it, because they are the kinds of reasons which convention tells us are practical.

But being practical, after all, merely consists, as I understand it, in doing something for a good and urgent reason rather than for a frivolous one; it consists, beyond that, in choosing one's ends so that they fit one's means and capacities. So there does seem to me to be an entirely practical reason for foreign assistance. It is a far better reason, I think, than those that are usually given.

It is simply that we do not want our children to grow up in a world in which, on one side, we Americans sit back in indifference, while on the other side, large portions of mankind will be prey to famine, epidemic, and despair. We do not want such a world because it would be possible to live in it only on one of two conditions. Either we would be ashamed, but would do nothing about it; or we would have lost our sense of shame. In neither case would we have a good environment in this country in which to bring up children. In such a world there would be a quality of retreat and indifference in higher education, a separation of conscience from learning, that would make a college or university campus an unhealthy and grossly disagreeable place to be.

I know of no better argument against isolationism. I know of no other argument that we need. It is not, I confess, a very difficult argument to follow. It doesn't measure up at all to the subtle and intricate arguments, ranging from the domino theory to the theory of games, on which our foreign policy is so often alleged to be based. Still, it does not seem to me to be beneath consideration for this reason. Indeed, it is an argument that helps me to know what I am talking about when I use the phrase "the national interest." And that is a reassuring feeling.

The educational test for foreign policy has even more utility, I think, when we ask about the impact of foreign policy not only on education in the United States, but on education elsewhere. There are some purposes which, as educators know (and, I suspect, as a great many ordinary men know), simply cannot be achieved by force. There are some purposes which are destroyed when force is used. The most important and long-distance purposes of the United States in the international arena are of this sort. Education has a chance to achieve them. And a foreign policy that makes it difficult to turn to education is a mistaken foreign policy.

Moreover, a foreign policy that is based on the presumption that it is we who shall educate others is also, on these tests, a grievously mistaken policy. It is a disturbingly innocent policy. There are some things that people cannot learn unless they learn them for themselves. There are many things they simply will not learn if others are trying to teach them. And there are also a good many things that we Americans do not know. We don't know the answers in our own country, much less the answers for others. It is the recognition of this, I suspect, that explains much of the restiveness and cynicism now on our campuses.

I do not mean to say that our present foreign policies rest entirely on these innocent presumptions. There are more sensible impulses in them as well. But these simple-minded and self-congratulatory impulses are there too, and they are the ones that get us into trouble. We are not invariably harmful, we are not even invariably useless when we go overseas. On the contrary. But our usefulness to others is proportionate, I suspect, to our recognition that there is a need to educate ourselves. The important consequence to us of a foreign policy that made education a major concern is that our own intellectual and emotional resources would be greater. Our colleges and universities would be better. They would be more cosmopolitan; more aware of alternatives; more sober; more sensitive to the sound that the American voice makes in other people's ears.

This is not the moment to spell out the ways in which the

colleges and universities of this country might play their part in an educationally oriented foreign policy. That is something for the future—I hope for the not too distant future. The present moment is one in which we must ask ourselves, more simply, to contemplate two large tendencies in foreign policy. For two general possibilities have long been present on the American scene, and are before us now. They ought to be compared from the point of view of their educational significance.

On one side, we have the tendency to make foreign policy decisions in isolation from their educational impact at home or abroad. This, it is commonly thought, is realism in foreign policy. Foreign policy, according to these conventions, is not philanthropy; it cannot go in for frills. And because this presumably realistic approach takes a narrow approach to the business of foreign policy, it deprives itself of a variety of instruments that might be available. The natural consequence is that it drifts increasingly into reliance on force. It finds itself seeking to accomplish purposes through the employment of means that are not designed to achieve such purposes and that are disproportionate to the value of any of the ends that are sought.

Most immediately relevant to our present discussion, such a policy is educationally disruptive. Is it surprising that there is stress on the American campus when the increasingly dominant tendency in American foreign policy is to employ instrumentalities which Americans have been taught all their lives to condemn and abhor? Is it surprising that there is stress on the university campus when our foreign policy, if we wish to support it, requires us every day to go in for extensive rationalization and excuse giving?

I do not want to oversimplify the issue. It is a complex one. I do not think that any government can live by the standards of morality that are appropriate to the behavior of individuals. I do not mean to say that we must expect governments to be immoral. I mean to say only that the standards of morality and responsible behavior that apply to individuals are different from the standards applicable to governments—not better or worse, but different. No less a philosopher and moralist than Spinoza[1] held this view, so I do not think that I am entirely a cynic in adhering to it.

There is, however, an important qualification that has to be added. It is a qualification that applies particularly to governments that derive their legitimacy from the consent of the governed, and to a country that took its conception in the phrase "a decent respect to the opinions of mankind." The government of such a country does not have to abide by standards that are absolutely identical with those appropriate to the individual and his private life. But these standards cannot be so different that the country's most sensitive citizens, and particularly its young people, are left stunned or bewildered. This difference in standards does immeasurable social damage. It erodes the basis of authority on which a government of this sort depends. And it produces a foreign policy too grossly out of character to be successful.

There is an alternative. There has always been one. It is to have a foreign policy that conceives the important purposes of foreign policy in educational terms. I do not assume that, overnight, we can dispense with armies or with disagreements that verge on violence. I do not suppose that that will be possible in any reasonably foreseeable future. I assume only that we cannot use violence intelligently without measuring its educational impact and asking the price.

But one can speak in more positive terms. Looking at Vietnam, looking beyond Vietnam, what are our sensible purposes in foreign policy? It is a purpose of American foreign policy, I think, to reduce the tensions between the poor and the rich countries; this requires, above all, the better distribution of information and ideas, the better distribution of educational opportunity, and underlying all the rest, the better education of Americans in the facts of international life. A crucial instrument for such a purpose is the American college and university.

And it is a purpose of American foreign policy, I think, to move toward a system of habitual negotiation and accommodation between nations and between different social systems; in this respect again, the problem we confront is essentially educational. To deal with it requires the development of partnerships that cross the borders, the building of practical interests that hold people together and give them an interest in resisting together the divisive tendencies of political rivalries and ideological superstitions. No institutions offer more promise with respect to the building of such partnerships and interests than American colleges and universities.

I cannot help but think that there is more realism in this path than in the paths that are conventionally called realistic. Such a conception of the function of American colleges and universities would enable them to do their jobs better. It would ennoble them, and it would move to the center of this nation's relations with other nations those aspects of our national life that carry the most hope for us and for the rest of mankind.

Notes

CULTURE AS A FORCE: MIRRORING MODERN MAN/KLUCKHOHN

1 *Editors' Note:* in World War II.
2 *Editors' Note:* in America during, again, the second World War.

THE RESPONSE OF EDUCATION TO A CHANGE IN SOCIETY/MEAD

1 See the resolution in favor of free education through college passed by the National Education Association, *New York Times,* July 6, 1958, Section 4.
2 See, for instance, David Whitlock, "The Number of Apprentices Needed and How to Reach This Goal," an address presented at the 49th Annual Convention of the American Vocational Association, San Francisco, December 3, 1954.
3 U.S. Office of Education, Division of International Education, *Education in the USSR,* Bulletin No. 14, 1957.
4 U.S. Army Recruitment Service, "Pathway to Maturity: A U.S. Army Booklet for Parents." See also U.S. Army Recruitment Service, "The Army and Your Education" and "Reserved for You: Technical Training Opportunities in the U.S. Army for High School Graduates"; Harold F. Clark and Harold S. Sloan, *Classrooms in the Factories: An Account of Educational Activities Conducted by American Industries* (Rutherford, New Jersey, Institute of Research, Fairleigh-Dickinson College, 1958).
5 "Pathway to Maturity," op. cit.
6 U.S. Department of Labor, Wage and Hour and Public Contracts Divisions, "A Guide to Child-Labor Provisions of the Fair Labor Standards Act (The Federal Wage and Hour Law)," *Child-Labor Bulletin,* No. 101 (Revised), June, 1957.
7 Franz Boas, "The Central Eskimo," *Sixth Annual Report of the Bureau of American Ethnology* (Washington, 1888), p. 399.
8 Margaret Mead, "Our Educational Emphases in Primitive Perspective," in *Education and the Cultural Process,* edited by Charles S. Johnson (Nashville, Fisk University, 1943,) pp. 5–12.
9 Thomas Woody, *Life and Education in Early Societies* (New York: The Macmillan Company, 1949).
10 Margaret Mead, *The School in American Culture* (Cambridge, Harvard University Press, 1951).
11 Norman Frederiksen and W. B. Schrader, "The Academic Achievement of Veteran and Nonveteran Students," *Psychological Monographs,* Volume 66, No. 15.
12 See Board of Education, City of New York, High School Division, "Our Public Schools: Cooperative Education," Part IV, *Report of the Superintendent of Schools* 1954–1955; and U.S. Office of Education, *Work Experience Programs in American Secondary Schools,* Bulletin, 1957, No. 5.
13 Don A. Luscombe, *Pylon: A New Concept and a New Institution* (a nonprofit organization chartered under the Laws of Pennsylvania), (Gwynedd, Pennsylvania, no date).
14 "What Goes on Here," *Woman's Day,* June, 1958.
15 See District of Columbia Department of School Attendance and Work Permits, *You May Employ Youth: A Guide to the Application of Child Labor Standards in the District of Columbia* (1957); U.S. Bureau of Labor Standards, *Employment Certificates—Help You Help Youth,* Bulletin No. 183, 1955; and U.S. Bureau of Labor Standards, *You CAN Hire Teenagers: Here's How* (Washington, September, 1957).

[16] Margaret Mead, "Closing the Gap Between the Scientists and the Others," *Daedalus* (American Academy of Arts and Sciences), Volume 88, No. 1 (Winter, 1959), pp. 139–146.

ARE WE EDUCATING OUR CHILDREN FOR THE WRONG FUTURE?/HUTCHINS

[1] *Editors' Note:* the Johnson Administration.

THE AFFLUENT DELINQUENT/PINE

[1] *Boston Sunday Globe* (UPI), August 22, 1964, p. 53.
[2] Negley K. Teeters and David Matza, "The Extent of Delinquency in the United States," *Journal of Negro Education*, Summer, 1959, pp. 200–213.
[3] Austin L. Porterfield, *Youth in Trouble.* Texas: Leo Potishman Foundation, 1946.
[4] James S. Wallerstein and G. J. Wyle, "Our Law-abiding Lawbreakers," in *Probation*, 1946, pp. 107–112.
[5] Herbert A. Bloch and Frank T. Flynn, *Delinquency: The Juvenile Offender in America Today.* New York: Random House, 1956, p. 11.
[6] Marshall B. Clinard, *Sociology of Deviant Behavior.* New York: Holt, Rinehart and Winston, 1957, p. 165.
[7] W. W. Wattenberg and J. Balistrieri, "Automobile Theft: A Favored Group Delinquency," *The American Journal of Sociology*, May, 1952, pp. 575–79.
[8] V. Birkness and H. C. Johnson, "Comparative Study of Delinquent and Non-delinquent Adolescents," *Journal of Educational Research*, April, 1949, pp. 561–72.
[9] F. Ivan Nye, *Family Relationships and Delinquent Behavior.* New York: John Wiley and Sons, 1959.
[10] Harrison E. Salisbury, *The Shook-up Generation.* New York: Harper & Bros., 1958, pp. 107–109.
[11] Gerald J. Pine, "Social Class, Social Mobility, and Delinquent Behavior," *Personnel and Guidance Journal*, April, 1965, pp. 770–74. See also: Pine's "Occupational and Educational Aspirations and Delinquent Behavior," *The Vocational Guidance Quarterly*, Winter Issue, 1964–65.
[12] Leonard Reissman, *Class in American Society.* Glencoe, Ill.: The Free Press, 1959, p. 369.
[13] *Ibid.*, pp. 371–72.
[14] W. H. Whyte, "The Wives of Management," *Fortune*, October, 1951; and "The Corporation and the Wife," *Fortune*, November, 1951.
[15] Melvin C. Tumin, "Some Unapplauded Consequences of Social Mobility in a Mass Society," *Social Forces*, October, 1957, pp. 32–37.
[16] William C. Kvaraceus and Walter Miller, *Delinquent Behavior: Culture and the Individual.* Washington, D. C.: National Education Association, 1959, pp. 99–100.

STUDENT UNREST/SHOBEN

[1] Daniel Bell, "Notes on the Post-Industrial Society," *Public Interest* (Winter 1967), pp. 24–35; (Spring 1967), pp. 102–118.
[2] See the memorandum of October 1967, by President Martin Meyerson to all members of the academic community at SUNY-Buffalo. The statement was drafted immediately after an episode of interference with the activity of a Dow Chemical recruiter.
[3] John Fischer, "The Consequences of Peace," *Harper's Magazine* (February 1968), p. 18.

[4] *Editors' Note:* Richard Rovere, currently a staff writer on political affairs for the *New Yorker*, has written frequently on political issues and figures, among them the late Senator Joseph McCarthy.
[5] In *A History of Western Philosophy* (New York: Simon and Schuster, 1945), p. xi.

THE EDUCATIONAL IMPACT OF PRESENT AMERICAN FOREIGN POLICY/FRANKEL

[1] *Editors' Note:* the seventeenth century Dutch philosopher who expounded the view that God, or an Infinite Substance, pervades all aspects of the world.

Further Reading

In addition to references cited by authors in this Part the following texts may be useful.

Callahan, Raymond E. *An Introduction to Education in American Society.* New York, N.Y.: Alfred A. Knopf, 1965.

The student is referred especially to Chapter 14 which deals effectively with the topics of philosophy, education, and intellectual values.

Gezi, Kalil I., and James E. Myers (eds.). *Teaching in American Culture.* New York, N.Y.: Holt, Rinehart and Winston, Inc., 1968.

Pages 188–233 provide a pertinent discussion of foreign school systems.

Havighurst, Robert J., and Bernice L. Newgarten. *Society and Education,* 3rd Ed. Boston, Mass.: Allyn & Bacon, 1967.

Part III, "The School in the Community" treats comprehensively the role of the school in the wider social setting.

Kneller, George F. *Foundations of Education.* New York, N.Y.: John Wiley and Sons, Inc., 1967.

One of the outstanding recent works in sociology of education, this text provides meaningful insights in a wide range of related areas. Pages 298–331 dealing with culture and education are especially thought provoking.

Pounds, Ralph L., and James R. Brynner. *The School in American Society,* 2nd Ed. New York, N.Y.: The Macmillan Co., 1967.

Among most comprehensive of recent works in educational sociology, the text is especially instructive on problems of American family life (Chapter 6) and on problems of crime and juvenile delinquency (Chapter 8).

Films of Related Interest

"Automation—Part I" McGraw-Hill, 34 min.

Discusses the problem of automation in a modern industrial society.

"Uptown" McGraw Hill, 30 min.

Portrays life in the South Bronx of New York City.

"Valley Town" New York University, 27 min.

Emphasizes changing American life patterns as influenced by technology and machines.

Part III

Teaching and Learning: Processes, Skills, and Values

What a man thinks, that does he become.

—Veda
Hindu sacred writings

Among the strongest cross currents in American educational thought in recent years has been the debate about whether, and to what extent, education ought to concern itself with the encouragement of humanistic values in a society that seems increasingly bent on technocratic scientism, or whether it should concentrate its primary efforts on the most efficient means of putting the learner in touch with specific factual and methodological information and skills. Both views have occupied a respected place in the developing thought of educational psychology and educational philosophy. Like any complex inquiry, the question defies easy summarization, but we might rephrase it in terms of whether we are interested, in effect, in producing "good" men before "competent" men, or the reverse.

As so often happens with questions touching on the goals of education, the extremists on each side of this issue, once so clearly demarcated, now seem to be retreating, while concerned thinkers of both persuasions appear to be coming together somewhat to explore this fundamental question further. The result is today's intensive focus on "learning"— what it is, how it occurs, what forms it can take, how it can be perpetuated and increased. The inquiry gives promise of adding considerably to the canon of educational knowledge.

Much of the relatively recent thrust in educational research has served to point up, on the one hand, how shockingly little of what is done in classrooms year after year has much retentive value, and, on the other hand, how many seemingly difficult instructional objectives can be accomplished when certain generally accepted characteristics of the learning process are used as organizing concepts in instruction. The ensuing reevaluation of learning and instruction is carving out new fields of disciplined inquiry into areas such as the "teaching" of values and the optimal arrangements for various types of learning (large-group, small-group, individual, computer-assisted, problem-centered, student-centered).

Which leaders of educational and psychological thought seem to have exerted the greatest effect on education in America?

What is learning theory, and how has it been put into practice in American schools?

What are some appropriate roles the school can play in teaching values?

To what extent is a young person's individual religious outlook a concern of the schools?

In what ways does learning in a group situation differ from learning in a purely individual setting in which the learner interacts with a tutor of one kind or another (a book, a teacher, a computer)?

What is meant by an "unmotivated student?" What are some solutions to this problem, according to modern learning theory?

Leaders of Educational Thought: A Review

Lloyd E. Robison

Disciplines develop through the acquisition of a body of knowledge consisting of closely related components. The acquisition of knowledge which formulates a discipline has normally been attributed to the work of or the influence of individuals who are recognized leaders in their particular field. The study of human growth and development had its beginnings in philosophical disputation and physiological investigation. Only in the twentieth century has this particular field emerged as a full-blown discipline. The emergence and continual growth of the discipline has been fostered by many individuals including the following representatives.

Seventeenth Century

John Amos Comenius (1592–1670) In 1657 Comenius published *Orbus Pictus,* which in English means *the world in pictures.* This publication was the first recognized attempt to develop a picture book designed specifically for children. In his work as a teacher, Comenius gave recognition to the theory

177

that children are cognizant of objective facts before they grasp the meanings of abstract terms. He made the initial attempt to educate the child on the basis of ability because he recognized that each child is an individual who is unique and who does not have the characteristics of a miniature adult. These concepts were not new but ones which Comenius attempted to practice and to effectively publicize.

John Locke (1632–1704)   Locke became prominent in the field of human understanding in the latter part of the seventeenth century. He had the good fortune of attracting the interest and the support of the thinkers of his time. Man's fitness to live in a free society in a humane and enlightened manner was a favorite topic of his time and he was its primary spokesman. Locke made an outstanding contribution in providing the rational basis for the school of association.

Summary

The seventeenth century was not void in its attempts at giving the individual a position of status. A realization that each man must be of some importance and that each man differs from his fellow being began to receive some recognition, but little was done to further general acceptance of these concepts which are essential for the advancement of the study of human growth and development.

Eighteenth and Nineteenth Centuries

Johann Heinrich Pestalozzi (1746–1827)   Pestalozzi believed that children learn through their observation of what is happening around them. Because of this belief, he promoted the beginning of the concept that children learn through experience, and that teaching should evolve around the natural phenomena observed through the senses. Learning through the memorization of information is unrealistic in its approach, according to Pestalozzi, and the way to help a child learn is through developing his skills of observation.

Johann Friedrich Herbart (1776–1841) One of the greatest contributions ever made to the study of human growth and development grew from Herbart's presentation of a theory of *readiness*. Readiness simply implies that the individual is physically, emotionally, intellectually, and experientially ready to learn. Herbart advocated that a child could not learn that which has had no relationship to his past experience. Here, for the first time, was recognition that learning proceeds in a logical systematic pattern from that which is familiar to the learner, to that which is unfamiliar but closely related. Teaching began to materialize as a science requiring disciplined study through observation and experimentation. Herbart attempted to develop exact means of measuring psychological phenomena, especially learning, with little success. He did wield, however, great influence in presenting psychology as an empirical science (by discovering evidence through observation and experimentation.)

Friedrich W. A. Froebel (1782–1852)   A close follower and promoter of the concepts of Pestalozzi, Froebel reasserted the necessity of experience as a teacher by providing children with attractive stimuli (colored blocks, toys, shapes, etc.) in the classroom. Because of his devoted interest in young children and his work with them, Froebel is credited with founding the kindergarten movement. He was convinced that play was of tremendous educational value to the young child.

Summary

The eighteenth and the beginning of the nineteenth centuries provided a continued impetus in the study of individual differences with special emphasis upon the attempt to understand how learning occurs. The fundamentals of experiment and observation began to be established and the first attempts were made to develop exact quantitative measurements of learning. There was a realization that children learned when they had had previous experiences which could be related to new experiences. This concept may be one which seems relatively obvious today, but in the early nineteenth century it was revolutionary in character. Until that time, it had been considered enough to provide the learner with unrelated pieces of information which he would digest and recall when necessary, and it was firmly believed that the mind could be disciplined by subject matter and through severe punishment. Little, if any, consideration was given to individual differences.

Later Nineteenth Century

Charles Robert Darwin (1809–1882) Every high school graduate has been exposed to the theory of evolution ac-
credited to the work of Charles Darwin. A study of
the history of evolution soon discloses that Darwin's theory was
by no means original. His own father, among many others, had
previously proposed such a theory, but Darwin received the
recognition because of the mass of evidence which he presented
in its support.

The study of human growth and development, as it exists
today, undoubtedly owes as much to the work of Darwin as to any
single person who has ever lived. The seemingly conclusive evidence of man's descent from the lower animals erased the gulf
that had been created between the human element and the
animal kingdom. Recognition of the feasibility of studying animal
behavior to gain information concerning human behavior introduced innumerable avenues of exploration for the psychologist
and physiologist. The concept of environmental influences affecting man's growth and development draws the bulk of its defense
from the basic hypothesis supporting change through evolution.

Wilhelm Preyer (1841–1897) Many consider Preyer to be the
"father of child psychology." He did make some of the initial attempts to study human growth and development under
partially controlled laboratory conditions. He recorded daily
observations of his son from birth to three years of age
while simultaneously studying the development of chicks,
rabbits, and guinea pigs, thus demonstrating that animals and
humans show similar trends in the acquisition of skills involving muscle control. The contributions made through this
comparative study paved the way for future development of
many experimental techniques.

Sir Francis Galton (1822–1911) Sir Francis Galton was greatly
influenced by the work of Darwin and did much to further
the understanding of the influence of inherent characteristics
which are passed from a man to his children. He was the
first to indicate that intelligence may be inherited. Galton
was important also because he was the first to establish
a standard procedure for showing the degree to which
two variables are related. To illustrate: men differ in

height (variable X), some being tall, some short, and some in between; while they also differ in weight (variable Y), some being fat, some thin, etc. The question then is, how likely is it that a tall man will be heavier than his shorter brother? Galton developed a means of predicting the answer to such questions through a basic graphic technique which was the basis of a mathematical formula referred to today as "the coefficient of correlation." Although Galton was responsible for the graphic technique and theory of correlation coefficient, it was his student, Karl Pearson, who developed the mathematical formula so frequently used in studies of human growth and development.

Wilhelm Wundt (1832–1920) Wilhelm Wundt was the founder of the first laboratory of experimental psychology responsible for giving the field of psychology an identification of its own. Interest in the complexities of human beings had been present for some years but this interest was merely an adjunct to the study of philosophy, biology, theology, or other related areas. The establishment of Wundt's laboratory marked the end of an era in the study of human growth and development and the beginning of the science of the mind and behavior of man.

Summary

There are many other names that could be included as influential in advancing the study of human growth and development but these should be sufficient to provide a basic synthesis of the circumstances existing at the beginning of the twentieth century.

At that time, the following observations could have summarized the status of man's thought concerning his growth and development:

1. Man's learning proceeds from concrete experiences to abstract meanings. (A child counts his fingers to build a concept of the symbol "five.") [Comenius]

2. Man is capable of self-government and therefore is capable of self-motivation. [Locke]

3. Man learns through experience and it is necessary to structure somehow the experiences in terms of desired learning outcomes. (This is the basis of current curriculum patterns.) [Pestalozzi]

4. Learning does not occur through meaningless memorization but through observation. [Pestalozzi]

5. There is an identifiable set of principles applicable to the art of pedagogy (teaching). [Herbart]

6. Play is necessary for the advancement of learning in young children. [Froebel]

7. Learning occurs only when the individual has reached a state of readiness for learning. [Herbart]

8. It is possible to learn about the development of man through the study of the development of lower animals. [Preyer]

9. Experimental techniques can be established for the study of man's growth and development. [Galton]

10. Methods can be developed for the quantitative measures of an individual's pattern of difference from his fellow man. [Galton]

11. A new science has come into its own!

The foundation for advancement was established in the nineteenth century and many of the taboos and physical barriers blocking the scientific study of man were beginning to crumble. The movement toward the recognition of each man as a unique individual was well under way. This recognition was especially true on the new frontiers of the western world where there was a need to increase population in both quantity and quality.

Twentieth Century

It has been stated previously that the study of human growth and development is a new field of investigation. It is as new as the industrial revolution and to a great extent has been highly correlated with man's mastery of the machine. The more the machine has released man from his labors the more time has been made available for him to become concerned with what he is and how he can improve his state. The more complicated the machine has become the greater the demand has been upon man's intellect to master the machine and further improve upon it which, in turn, has created the necessity of understanding how the increased demand for learning may be accomplished more efficiently. This demand places a great premium upon knowledge of how man grows and develops. Man must be prepared to react when the machine makes an error.

We have discussed many of the major personalities involved in preparing the stage for the advancements which are occurring in this century. If all major contributors who have advanced our knowledge of the field since the beginning of the twentieth century were discussed in a similar fashion, this text would be too large to carry. There is, however, a nucleus of names which finds general acceptance among contemporary writers in the fields related to the study of man's development. Any discussion of such personalities invariably begins with Granville Stanley Hall. There is no reason to digress from established practice.

Granville Stanley Hall (1846–1924) Wilhelm Preyer is normally credited with being the first to experiment with children in a laboratory setting, but Hall retains the unofficial title of "father of child psychology." His most important contribution is not to be found in the many studies conducted in his laboratory, but rather in the tremendous influence he had in generating interest in the child study movement. Hall was an incessant writer, promoter of periodicals, and developer of child study organizations. His writings attempted to relate processes of development to the theory of evolution or organic changes within the body. The recognition gained by Hall is probably based more upon negative reaction to his theories than to the contribution they made to understanding the child. The recapitulation theory may serve as an example.

Hall assumed from his study of Darwin's works that an individual recapitulates (relives, repeats, goes over the same ground) the historical development of his race. Children climb because they are repeating the performance of earlier primates who were members of their family tree. Very early in development, prior to birth, there is a series of folds present along the general area of the neck, which, according to the recapitulation theory, is the remnant of gill structures used by man's ancestors when they roamed through the salty waters of the earth.

Regardless of varying opinions concerning such a theory, Hall must be recognized for the total impact he had upon the study of man's growth and development. Probably no individual has enjoyed a greater personal influence in the development of an area of study.

William James (1842–1910) William James has no challenger for the role of leader of the American psychology movement, if for no other reason than he was the educator of so many students who became prominent scholars because of his influence upon them. This personal influence was somewhat unique and perhaps amazing. The only readily identifiable contribution he made to contemporary studies was in a readjustment of attitude toward what comprises the area of psychology. Psychology was progressing readily toward becoming a science of mechanistic gadgets and laboratory sterility when James injected the influence of philosophy.

He was a primary influence in developing recognition that the *exception* deserved at least the same diligent study as the *expected* in the analysis of psychological data. This interest in the exception may have been the precursor of an emphasis upon individual psychology.

James was an idea man; a genius of creative thought, a divergent thinker, a source of motivation for other men. It would be extremely difficult, if not completely impossible, to identify the innumerable subtle influences which may be attributed to his efforts.

Ivan Petrovich Pavlov (1849–1936) A Nobel prize for studies of the digestive process provided the world's introduction to Ivan Pavlov, but his dominant role in the field of human psychology began as an incidental observation of reactions of dogs used in his experiments. This incidental observation of reactions became the core of Pavlov's future work. He identified his discoveries as "conditioned reflexes" and did much experimentation to discover how his dogs reacted to a signal which meant that food was on the way. He became interested in the ability of the dogs to discriminate between one signal and another and opened many avenues for experimentation in psychology. One of the last people to accept the importance of this contribution was Pavlov himself.

Pavlov continually worked to influence his students to avoid psychological problems. Regardless of his efforts, however, his original experiments became the fundamental basis of "classical conditioning." A number of psychologists continue to advocate that all learning is the result of "conditioned" response or the belief that a man learns because he realizes that a specific kind of behavior will result in his receiving reward or punishment.

It has been found that if a specific stimulus elicits the desired response and this response is always rewarded, eventually the stimulus will elicit the desired response even though the reward is not present. A massive collection of studies has been conducted in the attempt to prove that intellectual development is or is not the result of conditioning. The basis of teaching machines and programmed learning may be traced directly to Pavlov's original incidental observation of the reactions of his dogs.

Sigmund Freud (1856–1939) There is little question that more words have been written by and about Freud than any other contributor to the field of human understanding. It may be sufficient to say that the school of psychoanalysis and theories pertaining to the role of the unconscious in man's behavior are two of the significant contributions with which we should concern ourselves. Space does not allow elaboration on these points but the reader is encouraged to explore the work of Freud as time and inclinations allow.

Any study of Freud would be incomplete if it did not include an investigation of the work of Carl Jung (1875–1961), Alfred Adler (1870–1937), Eric Fromm (b. 1900), and Karen Danielson Horney (1885–1952).

Alfred Binet (1857–1911) Binet manifested an inveterate interest in individual differences which culminated in his studies of thought processes. Under the appointment of the French Minister of Public Instruction and in collaboration with Theodore Simon, Binet developed the idea of identifying and testing intelligence. His test provided a score, *mental age,* which today is commonly converted into an *intelligence quotient.*

Binet was continually concerned with the question of what should be included in the quality of intelligence and suggested many definitions, but it is doubtful that he was ever completely satisfied with any of them. Basically, he recognized that human beings must be able to follow instructions, concentrate on problems for a length of time sufficient for finding solutions, and have the capability of recognizing and correcting their own errors.

The reader may wish to investigate the work of Louis M. Terman and Maud A. Merrill for further elucidation on Binet and an understanding of the intelligence quotient.[1]

John Dewey (1859–1952)   John Dewey enters the field of human growth and development through education and philosophy. His academic training had been in philosophy but much of his interest centered on education. The thesis of his philosophy was "experience" and he saw a channel in the schools that would provide the experience for participation in a democratic society.

He felt that man should be scientifically studied in his social surroundings with the same degree of precision that is applied to the study of his physical surroundings and devoted much of his early work to the discovery of how the organism adjusts to its environment. This provided the impetus for his emphasis upon the individualization of education through the so-called "progressive education" movement.

Dewey has been praised, maligned, and adulated for practically every change, good or bad, which has occurred in American education during the twentieth century. Perhaps his efforts are too recent for us to truly appreciate or evaluate his total contribution to the understanding of man.

James McKeen Cattell (1862–1944)   Cattell devoted much of his life to investigating how long it would take to react to a stimulus (specifically, words and symbols) and analyzing what actually happened *physiologically* to cause the reaction. He became quite interested in what occurred when a person reads letters or words and provided the basis for a multitude of experiments concerning the problems of reading.

In his many projects and research ventures, Cattell was continually impressed with the variability among humans. He became involved in a constant effort to mathematically quantify the differences he observed which provided additional avenues for future research.

Edward L. Thorndike (1874–1944)   The principles of learning were the primary concern of Thorndike. He was the first psychologist to investigate the effect of giving rewards for the completion of a learning task. It is true that Pavlov and other physiologists had begun previous investigations of this principle, but they did not comprehend the implications of how their findings related to human understanding. In fact, they made a concerted effort to keep their results out of the realm of psychology.

From the very extensive work accomplished by Thorndike, there arose further propagation of three basic principles of learning which were not purely original, but which were strongly supported by his research. Very briefly they are:

1. *The principle of readiness.* If the opportunity to accomplish a task is provided at the right time, the time of readiness, the act of accomplishment will be very satisfying. If the opportunity is not provided and action cannot take place, the subject will become disturbed.

2. *The principle of exercise.* Those things which we learn will stay with us if we use them, but they tend to dissipate if they are not used. Everyone reading this text has at some time learned to find the square root of a number. Can you do it now?

3. *The principle of effect.* Learning is most effective when it is rewarded or produces a pleasant result. Lack of reward or punishment will retard learning.

The full implication of these principles will become more evident in the discussion of the various schools of thought and in the discussion of the principles of human growth and development.

Arnold Lucius Gesell (1880–1961)   Through his work at the Yale Clinic, Arnold Gesell developed a wealth of information and elaborate schedules of development for normal children. Through comparison of these schedules, the developmental age in weeks, months, and years may be established for a given child. The true importance of the schedules lies in the contribution they make in developing a more thorough understanding of patterns of development.

Kurt Lewin (1890–1947)   At the time Lewin, a physicist and mathematician, became interested in psychology, the forces of the world were being defined in terms of "fields of force" that interacted with each other. It was assumed that if one could identify the forces that were interacting, a mathematical prediction could be made of the interacting relationship. Lewinian forces are loosely classified as drives, barriers, and threats. Drives have a positive or attracting valence ($+$) which pull an individual toward a mode of behavior. Barriers may be present between the individual and the goal, mode of behavior, which he seeks. Barriers are said to have no valence (O). A third factor is the threat which is present in any situation involving a decision. These threats have a negative valence (−) which will affect the resulting behavior.

A highly simplified illustration is the child who prefers watching television over the task of doing his homework. Watching television is the drive (+). Homework is the barrier (O). Accomplishing the homework or not accomplishing it is of very little importance to the child. The threat (−) is an irate parent and possible disciplinary action. This, then, is the child's "field" of forces. He has a number of options for resolving the conflict present in this field and much depends upon the strength of the competing forces. If the threat is great enough, he may remove himself from the field entirely by retiring to his homework where daydreaming will easily circumvent the threat presented by his parents.

Lewin and his followers place great emphasis upon the importance of the immediate field of forces affecting a person's behavior. "It is a simple fact, but still not sufficiently recognized in psychology and sociology, that the behavior of an individual depends above all upon his momentary position." [2]

Jean Piaget (b. 1896)   Jean Piaget is a Swiss psychologist who has recently been catapulted into the foreground as a leading influence in the field of developmental psychology. Piaget began his academic career as a biologist and holds a Ph.D. in that field, but because of his interest in epistemology (the study of the limits and validity of knowledge and the nature of how it is acquired) he has devoted his energies to the field of psychology for a large portion of his professional career.

He has concentrated his efforts on discerning how knowledge and thought evolve in the young child up to the stage of adolescence. He has given his work the label of "genetic epistemology."

In contrast to Gesell, Piaget has insisted upon observing the child in his natural surroundings—at play, in conversation with peers, etc. He has asked hundreds of children questions concerning how they perceive the world around them and has accomplished the amazing feat of recording their exact responses. He made voluminous notes about his own child on the basis of observations every hour during the early stages of development to determine how children discover and respond to the physical world.

A primary thesis of Piaget states that intellectual capabilities develop through utilization and the greater the perceptual opportunity the greater the enhancement of mental development.[3] He also contends that in early stages of development the child is unaware of himself as an entity and it is only later that he becomes aware of himself as a participating member of the universe.[4]

The total impact of Piaget's work upon the field of developmental psychology remains to be determined. His writing is extremely difficult to interpret, and this has severely hampered the rapid spread and assimilation of his ideas. The concepts discussed here are a small representation of the total work of Piaget. They should indicate, however, how important his work may prove to be for educators and developmental psychologists of the future.

Margaret Mead (b. 1901) Much of the current concern and recognition of the effect of cultural deprivation upon human development may no doubt be traced directly to Margaret Mead, an anthropologist, who has devoted her life to making comparative studies of differing culture patterns. She also has been influential in changing attitudes toward the much-beleaguered adolescent period of development and has pointed out many errors commonly committed in training children to live in a highly complex society.

Dr. Mead has conducted extensive research by studying adolescent sexual development and society in the primitive cultures of Samoa, New Guinea, and Bali. From her findings she developed many new insights into the nature of the adolescent in the Western World in general and the United States in particular. Her writings have been influential in modifying G. Stanley Hall's concept that adolescence must of necessity be a period of "storm and stress." She has been a primary force in the general advocacy of cultural environment as a determining factor in the individual's developmental pattern.

Summary

The listing here is incomplete but indicates the scope of progress made in human understanding during the twentieth century. In summary, we may glean the following statements from this discussion of these representatives of contemporary schools of thought.

1. It has been well established that man can be studied scientifically and much can be learned about man's behavior through observing the behavior of lower animals in scientifically controlled situations. [Pavlov]

2. Man's behavior can be stated in easily interpreted quantitative terms. [Binet, Cattell]

3. The study of man cannot be completely mechanistic but must be based upon and supported by philosophical precepts. [Lewin, James]

4. Man reacts or responds to a given set of stimuli for the purpose of attaining a goal and will respond correctly more often if the attainment of the goal proves to be rewarding. [Thorndike]

5. Man's reaction to the simplest kind of stimulus is an extremely complicated pattern of interaction, but the patterns in the interaction are identifiable and can be measured. [Binet]

6. Man's innate ability to learn can be measured. (We have yet to truly identify all the characteristics of learning ability or to predict how well an individual will succeed because of his ability.) [Binet]

7. Every man is an individual whose differences from other men are as important to understand as are his similarities to other men. [James]

8. The social culture to which a man is exposed will affect his pattern of development. [Mead]

9. The research techniques which can be applied to man are limitless. [Cattell]

10. Many disciplines are involved in painting the total picture of man's growth and development. [Lewin]

Luella Cole, Arthur T. Jersild, Elizabeth B. Hurlock, Ruth Strang, and scores of other individuals have devoted their professional lives to advancing our knowledge of man's developmental turmoils and rewards. Each has had an impact of significant and lasting importance. We may say that the twentieth century has truly been the century of the discovery of man. All of the answers have not been found, but the questions are beginning to be more clearly identified. No answer can be found until the questions are understood.

Learning and Thinking: A Contemporary Viewpoint

Jerome S. Bruner

I have been engaged, these last few years, in research on what makes it possible for organisms—human and subhuman alike—to take advantage of past learning in attempting to deal with and master new problems before them now. It is a problem with a deceptively simple ring to it. In pursuit of it, my colleagues and I have found ourselves observing children in schoolrooms, watching them learning. It has been a revealing experience.

I

We have come to recognize in this work that one of the principal objectives of learning is to save us from subsequent learning. This seems a paradox, but it is not. Another way of putting the matter is to say that when we learn something, the objective is to learn it in such a way that we get a maximum of travel out of what we have learned. A homely example is provided by the relationship in arithmetic between addition and multiplication. If the principle of addition has been grasped in its deeper sense, in its generic sense, then it is unnecessary to learn multiplication. For, in principle, multiplication is only repeated addition. It is not, as we would say in our curricula, another "unit."

Learning something in a generic way is like leaping over a barrier. On the other side of the barrier is thinking. When the generic has been grasped, it is then that we are able to recognize the new problems we encounter as exemplars of old principles we have mastered. Once over the barrier, we are able to benefit from what William James long ago called "the electric sense of analogy."

There are two interesting features in generic learning—in the kind of learning that permits us to cross the barrier into thinking. One of them is *organization;* the other is *manipulation.* If we are to use our past learning, we must organize it in such a way that it is no longer bound to the specific situation in which the learning occurred. Let me give an example from the history of science. It would have been possible for Galileo to have published a handbook of the distances traversed per unit time by falling bodies. School boys for centuries thereafter could easily have been tortured by the task of having to remember the Galilean tables. Such tables, cumbersome though they might have been, would have contained all the necessary information for dealing with free-falling bodies. Instead, Galileo had the inspiration to reorganize this welter of information into a highly simplified form. You recall the compact expression $S = \frac{1}{2}gt^2$: it not only summarizes all possible handbooks but organizes their knowledge in a way that makes manipulation possible. Not only do we know the distances fallen, but we can use the knowledge for bodies that fall anywhere, in any gravitational field—not just our own.

One of the most notable things about the human mind is its limited capacity for dealing at any one moment with diverse arrays of information. It has been known for a long time that we can deal only with about seven independent items of information at once; beyond that point we exceed our "channel capacity," to use our current jargon. We simply cannot manipulate large masses of information. Because of these limits, we must condense and recode. The seven things we deal with must be worth their weight. A simple formula that can regenerate the distance fallen by any free body, past or future, is under these conditions highly nutritious for its weight. Good organization achieves the kind of economical representation of facts that makes it possible

taught in a school. So too with algebra. Algebra is not a set of rules for manipulating numbers and letters except in a trivial sense. It is a way of thinking, a way of coping with the drama of the unknown. Lincoln Steffens, in his *Autobiography,* complains upon his graduation from the University of California that his teachers had taught him only of the known, how to commit it to mind, and had done little to instruct him in the art of approaching the unknown, the art of posing questions. How does one ask questions about the unknown? Well, algebra is one technique, the technique for arranging the known in such a way that one is enabled to discern the value of an unknown quantity. It is an enriching strategy, algebra, but only if it is grasped as an extended instance of common sense.

Once I did see a teacher specifically encourage a class to organize and use minimal information to draw a maximum number of inferences. The teacher modeled his technique, I suppose, on the tried method of the storyteller. He presented the beginnings of the Whiskey Rebellion and said to his pupils, much in the manner of Ellery Queen speaking to his readers, "You now have enough to reconstruct the rest of the story. Let's see if we can do it." He was urging them to cross the barrier from learning into thinking. It is unhappily true that this is a rare exception in our schools.

So knowledge-getting becomes passive. Thinking is the reward for learning, and we may be systematically depriving our students of this reward as far as school learning is concerned.

One experiment which I can report provides encouragement. It was devised and carried out by the research group with which I am associated at Harvard in collaboration with teachers in the fifth grade of a good public school. It is on the unpromising topic of the geography of the North Central States and is currently [in 1959] in progress so that I cannot give all of the results. We hit upon the happy idea of presenting this chunk of geography not as a set of knowns, but as a set of unknowns. One class was presented blank maps, containing only tracings of the rivers and lakes of the area as well as the natural resources. They were asked as a first exercise to indicate where the principal cities would be located, where the railroads, and where the main highways. Books and maps were not permitted and "looking up the facts" was cast in a sinful light. Upon completing the exercise, class discussion was begun in which the children attempted to justify why the major city would be here, a large city there, a railroad on this line, etc.

The discussion was a hot one. After an hour, and much plead-
ing, permission was given to consult the rolled up wall map. I
will never forget one young student, as he pointed his finger at
the foot of Lake Michigan, shouting, "Yipee, *Chicago* is at the end
of the pointing-down lake." And another replying, "Well, OK:
but Chicago's no good for the rivers and it should be here where
there is a big city (St. Louis)." These children were thinking,
and learning was an instrument for checking and improving the
process. To at least a half dozen children in the class it is not a
matter of indifference that no big city is to be found at the junc-
tion of Lake Huron, Lake Michigan, and Lake Ontario. They were
slightly shaken up transportation theorists when the facts were
in.

The children in another class, taught conventionally, got their
facts all right, sitting down, benchbound. And that was that. We
will see in six months which group remembers more. But which-
ever does, one thing I will predict. One group learned geography
as a set of rational acts of induction—that cities spring up where
there is water, where there are natural resources, where there are
things to be processed and shipped. The other group learned pas-
sively that there are arbitrary cities at arbitrary places by arbitrary bodies of water and arbitrary sources of supply. One learned
geography as a form of activity. The other stored some names
and positions as a passive form of registration.

The Episodic Curriculum

In a social studies class of an elementary school in a well-to-do
suburb of one of our great eastern cities, I saw groups of twelve-
year-old children doing a "project" on the southeastern states.
Each team was gathering facts that might eventually end up on a
map or a chart or some other graphic device. The fact-gathering
was atomized and episodic. Here were the industrial products of
North Carolina. There was the list of the five principal cities of
Georgia. I asked the children of one team what life would be like
and what people would worry about in a place where the principal
products were peanuts, cotton, and peaches. The question was
greeted as "unfair." They were gathering facts.

It is not just the schools. The informational environment of
America seems increasingly to be going through such an atomiza-
tion. Entertainment is in fifteen minute episodes on TV, to be
taken while sitting down. The school curriculum is built of epi-

sodic units, each a task to itself: "We have now finished addition. Let us now move to multiplication." Even in our humor the "gag" threatens to replace the shrewd observer of the human comedy. I have seen an elementary school play fashioned entirely on a parody of radio commercials. It was a brave effort to tie the 10-second atoms together.

I do not wish to make it seem as if our present state of education is a decline from some previous Golden Age. For I do not think there has even been a Golden Age in American public education. The difference now is that we can afford dross less well than ever before. The volume of positive knowledge increases at a rapid rate. Atomizing it into facts-to-be-filed is not likely to produce the kind of broad grasp that will be needed in the world of the next quarter century. And it is certainly no training for the higher education that more and more of our children will be getting.

I have not meant the above as a plea for the "central subject" or the "project" method of teaching. It is, rather, a plea for the recognition of the continuity of knowledge. One hears professional educators speak of "coverage," that certain topics must be covered. There are indeed many things that must be covered, but they are not unconnected things. The object of learning is to gain facts in a context of connectivity that permits the facts to be used generatively. The larger the number of isolated facts, the more staggering the number of connections between them—unless one can reduce them to some deeper order. Not all of them can. Yet it is an ideal worth striving for, be it in the fifth grade or in graduate school. As Robert Oppenheimer put it in a recent address before the American Academy, "Everything cannot be connected with everything in the world we live in. Everything can be connected with anything."

The Embarrassment of Passion

I should like to consider now the guiding myth. Let me begin with a summary of the young Christopher Columbus as he is presented in a popular social studies textbook. Young Chris is walking along the water front in his home town and gets to wondering where all those ships go. Eventually he comes back to his brother's cobbler shop and exclaims, "Gee, Bart, I wonder where all those ships go, whether maybe if they just kept going they wouldn't come back because the world is round." Bart replies with pleasant brotherly encouragement. Chris is a well-adjusted kid. Bart is a nice big brother. And where is the passion that drove this obsessed man across uncharted oceans? What impelled this Columbus with such force that he finally enlisted the aid of Ferdinand and Isabella over the protest of their advisors? Everything is there in the story except the essential truth—the fanatical urge to explore in an age of exploration, the sense of an expanding world. Columbus did not have a schoolboy's whim, nor was he the well-adjusted grownup of this account. He was a man driven to explore, to control. The justification for the pablum that makes up such textbooks is that such accounts as these touch more directly on the life of the child.

What is this "life of the child" as seen by text writers and publishers? It is an image created out of an ideal of adjustment. The ideal of adjustment has little place for the driven man, the mythic hero, the idiosyncratic style. Its ideal is mediocentrism, reasonableness above all, being nice. Such an ideal does not touch closely the deeper life of the child. It does not appeal to the dark but energizing forces that lie close beneath the surface. The Old Testament, the Greek Myths, the Norse legends—these are the embarrassing chronicles of men of passion. They were devised to catch and preserve the power and tragedy of the human condition —and its ambiguity, too. In their place, we have substituted the noncontroversial and the banal.

Here a special word is needed about the concept of "expressing yourself," which is our conception of how one may engage the deeper impulses of the child. I have seen a book review class in a public school in which the children had the choice of reporting on any book they wished to choose, in or out of the school library, and where the discussion by the other children had to do entirely with the manner in which the reciting child presented his material. Nothing was said about the book in the discussion. The emphasis was on nice presentation, and whether the book sounded interesting. I have no quarrel with rewarding self-expression. I wonder simply whether it is not perhaps desirable, too, to make known the canons of excellence. The children in this class were learning to be seductive in their recounting; they were not concerned with an honest accounting of the human condition. The books they had read were cute, there was no excitement in them, none to be extracted. Increasingly the children in American elementary schools grow out of touch with the guiding myths. Self-expression is not a substitute. Adjustment is a worthy ideal, if not an ennobling one. But when we strive to attain it by shutting our eyes to the turmoils of human life, we will not get adjustment, but a niggling fear of the unusual and the excellent.

The Quality of Teachers

I do not wish to mince words. The educational and cultural level of the majority of American teachers is not impressive. On the whole they do not have a good grasp of the subject matter that they are teaching; courses on method will not replace the absent subject matter. In time and with teaching experience this deficiency is often remedied. But in so many cases there is no time: the turnover in the teaching profession as we all know is enormous; the median number of years of teaching before departure for marriage or motherhood is around three.

This leaves us with a small core of experienced teachers. Do we use them to teach the new teachers on the job? No. The organization of the school with respect to utilization of talent is something short of imaginative. It consists of a principal on top and a group of discrete teachers beneath her, and that is all. In large metropolitan high schools this is sometimes supplemented by having departments at the head of which is an experienced teacher. The communication that goes on between teachers is usually at a highly informal level and can scarcely be called comprehensive. It is usually about problem-children, not about social studies or mathematics or how to bring literature alive.

I would urge, and I believe that educators have taken steps in this direction, that we use more experienced teachers for on-the-job training of less experienced new teachers. I would also urge that there be established some means whereby the substantive topics taught in our elementary and high schools be included in some kind of special extension program provided by our eighteen hundred colleges and universities in the United States for the benefit of teachers. I am not speaking only of teachers colleges, but rather of all institutions of higher learning. Institutions of higher learning have a responsibility to the lower schools, and it can be exercised by arranging for continuous contact between those, for example, who teach history at the college level and those who are teaching history or social studies at the lower levels. And so, too, with literature or mathematics, or languages. To assume that somehow a teacher can be "prepared" simply by going through teacher training and then by taking courses on methods in summer school is, I think, fallacious. Often it is the case that the teacher, like her students, has not learned the material well enough to cross the barrier from learning to thinking.

III

It is quite plain, I think, that the task of improving the American Schools is not simply one of technique—however comforting it would be to some professional educators to think so. What is at issue, rather, is a deeper problem, one that is more philosophical than psychological or technological in scope. Let me put it in all innocence. What do we conceive to be the end product of our educational effort? I cannot help but feel that this rather overly simplified question has become obscured in cant. There is such an official din in support of the view that we are "training well-rounded human beings to be responsible citizens" that one hesitates to raise the question whether such an objective is a meaningful guide to what one does in classroom teaching. Surely the objective is worthy, and it has influenced the techniques of education in America, not always happily. For much of what we have called the embarrassment of passion can, I think, be traced to this objective, and so too the blandness of the social studies curriculum. The ideal, sadly, has also led to the standardization of mediocrity by a failure of the schools to challenge the full capacity of the talented student.

Since the war, there has been a perceptible shift in the problems being faced by schools and parents alike. It is the New Competition. Will Johnny and Sally be able to get into the college of their first choice, or, indeed, into any college at all? The origins of the concern are obvious enough—the "baby bulge" has made itself felt. The results are not all bad, I would urge, or need not be. There are, to be sure, severe problems of overcrowding that exacerbate the difficulties already inherent in public education. And it is true that parental pressures for grades and production are increasing the proportion of children with "learning blocks" being referred to child guidance clinics.

But the pressures and the competition are also rekindling our awareness of excellence and how it may be nurtured. The shake-up of our smugness by the evident technical thrust of the Soviet Union has added to this awareness. Let me urge that it is this new awareness that requires shaping of expression in the form of a new set of ideals. Grades, admission to college, followed by admission to graduate school—these are surely not the ideals but, rather, the external signs.

Perhaps the fitting ideal is precisely as we have described it earlier in these pages, the active pragmatic ideal of leaping the barrier from learning into thinking. It matters not *what* we have learned. What we can *do* with what we have learned: this is the issue. The pragmatic argument has long been elaborated on extrinsic grounds, that the higher one has gone in the educational system the greater the economic gain. Indeed, at least one eminent economist has proposed that parents finance college education for their children by long-term loans to be repaid by the children on the almost certain knowledge that higher earning results from such education. All of this is the case, and it is indeed admirable that educational progress and economic success are so intimately linked in our society. I would only suggest that the pragmatic ideal be applied also to the intrinsic aspects of education. Let us not judge our students simply on *what* they know. That is the philosophy of the quiz program. Rather, let them be judged on what they can generate from what they know —how well they can leap the barrier from learning to thinking.

Problem Solving as an Approach to Learning

Richard E. Gross and Frederick J. McDonald

Down through the centuries master teachers have liberally interspersed the learning experiences of their students with problem resolution. Despite the virtues claimed for this educational approach, there has been comparatively little application of the process in the schools of the nation. This holds true even in lessons and courses in mathematics and science where one would expect to find the most meaningful use of effective thinking procedures. Forward-looking science educators have decried the mistaken notion held by so many teachers in all curricular fields that problem-solving abilities are merely by-products of the memorization of the lesson or result almost automatically from learning a set of facts. Such conditions have continued to plague science instruction in spite of the fact that every "major report in the field of science education for the past quarter of a century has emphasized the importance of the problem-solving objective."

What accounts for the continuing sparsity of problem-centered teaching? In addition to nine reasons for these conditions which have been outlined recently, two basic causes may be cited. In the first place, no psychological area has been subjected to less diligent and thorough research and, while considerable research at the laboratory level has been conducted, many studies have limited application in the schoolroom. In 1941 when Glaser was preparing his own research on critical thinking, out of some 340 studies which he reviewed he found fewer than thirty holding any practical application for teacher use in the classroom. A review of experimental findings in the decade following Glaser's study reveals much the same situation. A prime, continuing need is for more controlled experimentation and well-planned action research in school situations which may help develop proof for the theoretical claims made for the problems approach.

Secondly, much of the psychological research which does not hold implication and meaning at the instructional level has not been made readily available or understandable for the practitioner. The average teacher can gain little from the intricate, specialized reports, and few psychologists or educators have attempted to state results in forms useful for the teacher in the lower schools. Two yearbooks of the National Society for the Study of Education have devoted a number of chapters to problem solving wherein some of the contributing authors did attempt to translate some of the technical research into useful terms. Much more of this is needed.

Another difficulty in this area is the differing conceptions as to just what is involved in and meant by problem solving, and this is true among both psychologists and educators. Some teachers, for example, hold to the belief that studying *about* a problem, generally as a topic, is problem solving. Others are satisfied with the student analysis of a remote problem drawn from some aspect of subject matter. A third group of teachers feels that pupil consideration of problems which are essentially adult and of a social nature fulfills the process. Still other teachers will only accept direct pupil involvement and action concerning immediate personal and social problems of real moment for the students as providing a full experience in problem solving. Just what is problem solving?

From Finding Rules to Formal Reasoning

One of the major difficulties in psychological research on problem solving has been to clarify the characteristics of the phenomenon under study. There is at present no common agreement on what is meant by "problem-solving behavior," and, as a consequence, there is considerable diversity in the kinds of behavior that have been investigated as well as in the methods of investigation. In terms of the operations used in research, problem solving has been described on some kind of a continuum which includes behavior varying from finding exceptions to rules to formal reasoning of a complex nature. Included among these definitions are descriptions of problem solving as reorganization, as integration, and as "insight." This diversity of meaning should alert the reader of research in this area to the intimate connection between what has been found about problem solving and how the process is defined. The diversity further suggests that it is probably more meaningful to think of problem solving as a complex of many functions rather than as some singly unitary function.

Dewey Gave Us Logical Analysis

Essentially, psychological research is oriented to determine how people go about solving problems. Dewey's conception of the stages in the problem-solving process has dominated thinking about this process, but what is too frequently overlooked is that Dewey's description is a logical analysis rather than a description of how people in fact do go about solving problems. A number of investigations have been concerned specifically with this problem: that is, given a problem, what is the method of attack used by the problem solver? The results of these investigations suggest that any problem-solving process involves three essential functions: (a) an orienting function; (b) an elaborative and analytical function; (c) a critical function. The first of these aspects is an information-gathering function, the second, a hypothesis-formation function, and the third, a hypothesis-testing function. These processes, while they can be identified in problem-solving situations, are not necessarily sequential in character in each individual, nor is there any reason to believe at the present that they necessarily depend on each other. The problem of psychological investigation is to determine how these aspects of the process vary with the problem to be solved and in relation to the characteristics of the solver. While investigation of these problems is far from complete, a considerable body of evidence has been developed that gives us some insight into the factors involved in problem solving.

The influence of the problem on the process has been investigated in terms of the kind and complexity of the problem. The more complex the problem, the more apparent the differences in the problem-solving processes utilized by problem-solvers. Subjects who solve easy problems seem to depend largely upon immediate and obvious cues, whereas subjects who are capable of solving more complex problems appear to be capable of formulating a variety of hypotheses and to be able to ferret out less obvious cues.

Of particular interest to the educators are investigations dealing with the life-likeness of the problem. A common assumption is that problems solved by students must be as "life-like" as possible. Do "life-like" problems in effect lead to "better" problem solving? At least one series of investigations suggests that the realism of the problem does not necessarily produce qualitatively superior solutions to problems. When problems are presented to subjects on a realistic to unrealistic dimension, that is, when the problem permits the solver to deal immediately with the materials of the problem versus the situation in which the problem-solver merely thinks about the problem, expected differences in the kinds of solutions evoked do not appear. As a matter of fact, when laboratory problems with varying degrees of realism are used, or when laboratory problems and field problems are compared, subjects in general generate the same kinds of solutions, and do not appear to benefit from the greater reality of some problems than of others. In solving field problems as against solving laboratory problems, new elements do appear in the solutions but these do not apparently change the general character of the solution. One difference that does emerge is that a greater amount of time appears to be necessary for the solution of laboratory problems than for field problems. This may suggest a greater degree of involvement in a field type problem which motivates quicker solutions, or it may suggest that clues which are available are more quickly grasped in the field situation than they are in the laboratory situation.

"Life-Like" Problems?

It should be noted that this research does not suggest that "life-like" problems should not be used, but that their use does not appear to evoke superior solutions. This kind of a problem may in fact have other values, such as transfer values, potentiality for arousing interest, task involvement, and changing attitudes that would recommend their inclusion in curricular experiences, though these questions themselves should be investigated.

A major theoretical question and one that is of great practical importance to the educator concerns the amount of information and guidance that is necessary in the problem-solving process. The question has been formulated most frequently in the form, "Should the method or principle be taught?" A recent investigation has provided some answers to this particular vexing question. The general conclusions in this respect are: (a) that the amount of information used in guiding problem-solving activities must be appropriate to the task set for the student; (b) that some appropriate guidance is beneficial, but that failure to provide it will delay rather than prevent the solution; (c) that the effectiveness of guidance does not depend solely on the amount of information imparted; (d) that more explicit instruction may be just as effective as more directive guidance for the less able students. The less able students appear to profit little from knowledge of the principle of solution and tend to be more effective when a method is available.

Problem-Solvers Use Many Methods

When the focus of interest in investigation has been on the general methodology of the problem-solver, it has been consistently found that subjects tend to use a variety of general methodologies. These can be roughly grouped into three categories: (a) trial and error behavior; (b) sudden insights; and (c) gradual analysis. These three methods are not necessarily qualitatively different but may be arranged on a continuum, and subjects in investigations shift from one general method to another during the problem-solving process. It is probably unduly confusing to refer to these approaches as methods, particularly since it is not known under what conditions these various kinds of approaches are evoked or can be evoked.

Considerable research has been done on the characteristics of problem-solvers and the relationship of these characteristics to the correctness, the quality, and the speed of solution of problems. More recent investigations have concentrated on the anxiety level of learners, and the general conclusion of these investigations has been that high anxiety tends to produce a rigidity of set which interferes with learning and with problem solving.

The problem of "set" in problem solving has been one of the more fruitful areas of investigation. It has been demonstrated repeatedly that inflexibility of set interferes with problem solving. The theoretical problem is to determine what personality characteristics of the solver tend to produce inflexible sets and what elements in the problem-solving situation are likely to evoke "sets." Luchins has outlined the factors which appear to maximize and reduce sets. Among the factors maximizing set are: (a) an increase in the number of set-inducing problems; (b) creation of a "stress" atmosphere; (c) giving instructions to generalize a method of solution; (d) presenting tasks as "isolated drill." Among factors tending to reduce set are: (a) increasing the number of problems requiring a direct solution as distinct from problems for which a method is available; (b) interspersing problems solvable by a method and those solvable by a direct attack; (c) increasing the complexity of detail in the problems; (d) offering clarification of the nature of sets and their possible deleterious effects. Other research suggests that set varies with the complexity of the task, and that there is some tendency for set to persist the more complex the task.

A persistent problem and one of concern to educators is the relationship between group and individual problem-solving processes. Studies in this area have suggested that group solutions of problems tend to be superior on many dimensions to individual solutions. However, this conclusion is somewhat suspect because the studies in this area have not been rigorously controlled. One explanation for the differences that have been found is that group activity maximizes the amount of information available for the solution of a problem, introduces more hypotheses for solution. and permits the greater exercise of the critical function. However, what is not known is whether in establishing groups for problem solving the process of building groups automatically insures in some way finding a problem solver in each group who is essentially responsible for the group's superior success in this respect. While a wide variety of problems have been used in these studies, it is still not known whether group problem solving is uniformly better than individual problem solving for all kinds of problems. Most studies have also shown that while the group is superior there are frequently individuals within the groups who have solutions which in effect are better than the groups' solution, either qualitatively or in terms of such factors as the speed of solution and the like. Again it should be noted that group approaches to problems may have other values which recommend this approach to educators. But present evidence certainly does not permit the conclusion that a group is superior to individuals simply because it is a group, and it is important therefore for educators to clarify what they expect to be achieved by using group methods.

Surveying the diversity of literature in this field shows that there is general agreement on what is involved in the problem-solving process. The process appears to involve the following elements: (a) an awareness of a problem which is personal in character; that is, the problem-solver is disturbed by a given situation; (b) a data-gathering phase, in which the solver familiarizes himself with the task and the materials available for solution; (c) a hypothesis-formation stage in which the solver formulates solutions; and (d) a hypothesis-testing phase in which solutions are tested. The educational process can contribute to the development of competence in several aspects of this total process. Thus it is the curriculum which can provide problems which evoke the problem-solving behavior. Furthermore, curricular experiences can develop competency in data-gathering techniques and methods for hypothesis-testing.

What are the implications for educators in this research on problem solving? The present state of the research does not provide immediate, usable answers to many particular questions. The research does suggest certain lines of inquiry that educators can fruitfully pursue. The major problem for the educational process is to determine the character of problems to which students will be exposed in the course of their educational experience. What range and kinds of problems will have maximum utility in developing problem-solving abilities and at the same time will have the greatest transfer value for out-of-school activities? Probably the curriculum should contain a wide variety of problems so that students will be exposed to as many different kinds of problems as possible. In any event, it seems necessary to keep distinct, when planning curricular activities, two aspects of the function of problems in the curriculum, namely their utility in developing problem-solving ability and their utility for transfer to out-of-school activities.

How Can Curriculum Help?

A second implication from psychological research would be that problem solving should not be thought of as a single, simple unitary process, but as an extraordinarily complex process which has many different aspects. The problem for the school is to determine what aspects of the problem-solving process can be effected by curricular experiences. It seems obvious that the school can improve the information-gathering abilities of students and likely influence the hypothesis-forming abilities of students, though the range of individual differences in this respect will probably affect what the schools can do. Finally, the schools can certainly develop methods of testing hypotheses which can be communicated to students.

The question of group versus individual problem solving needs to be pursued in educational settings. A considerable emphasis on group methods may be wasteful in terms of developing competent problem-solvers. On the other hand, the group method may have values which strongly recommended it. In any case, this question of appropriate methodology needs to be more thoroughly explored than it has tó date.

We Must Apply Psychological Research

What seems most important for the practical application of psychological research to education is that educators themselves become concerned with experimentation in this area. Such factors as the influence of set upon problem solving are important factors that must be analyzed in terms of what it is in the learning situation which tends to produce inflexible kinds of sets. Variables such as the method of instruction, the mode of presentation, previous experiences in problem solving, and so on, are undoubtedly all important factors. Bloom, for example, found lack of reading ability to be a key factor in failures to solve problems at the college level. What are other sources of inadequacy? Is certain content or are particular courses more efficacious for the process? Furthermore, problems such as the developmental characteristics of problem-solving abilities need to be investigated. For example, do younger children approach problems differently from adolescents or adults? Are there significant sex differences in problem-solving competency? Still another important unknown is the relationship between concept formation and problem solving.

Williams, in his recent survey of problem solving, concludes that educators need: (a) to identify the types of problem situations which offer the best opportunities to develop effective thinkers; (b) to build awareness in the students of multi-factored, non-academic problem situations and just what they demand; (c) to help students understand the factors which affect problems and problem solving such as personal attitudes, physical and environmental conditions, and motivation; and (d) to provide deliberate and repeated problem-solving situations and practice.

It is impossible in a brief article to review school level research on the problems approach in all curricular areas. Selections from the field research in the area of social education will now be cited to reveal what has been done and to point out gaps and opportunities open to interested investigators.

Many stimulating reports on problem-solving experiences at all grade levels are available, but commonly these represent a teacher's after-view of a new but essentially uncontrolled situation. While such expositions may lead readers to launch their own trials with effective thinking procedures, they provide very limited evidence as to the value of the problems approach as measured against other means of instruction and curricular organization.

Cook and Koeninger experimented with different methods and varying course organization for college sociology classes. They attempted to measure increases in factual knowledge, in the skills of critical thinking, and in changed attitudes. Students working in groups via the problems approach gained as much in knowledge of content as those in classes otherwise organized and at the same time improved much more in attitudinal tendencies and critical-thinking ability. Glaser in the study mentioned earlier pitted four control classes against four classes given guidance in the principles and processes of problem solving via special units. After evaluation with instruments he himself developed he concluded that the four experimental classes had made significantly greater progress in developing critical-thinking ability and that pupils' attitudes toward rational problem-solving procedure are susceptible to educational improvement. He pointed up the fact that group problem-solving experiences are especially valuable because children learn thereby the essential democratic means of cooperating with their fellows.

How Teach Social Studies?

A significant experiment in this area was the Stanford Social Education Investigation. Most of the important findings of this five-year study, which involved ten teachers in five school systems, have been reported in *Education for Social Competence*. The staff attempted to contrast the relative effectiveness of the chronological, topical, and problems methods in social studies classes at the senior high-school level. Although many results, such as improved skills and attitudes, favored the problems groups, Quillen and Hanna were restrained in their concluding recommendations. Differences between classes often were very narrow and students in the chronologically-organized classes did make the most significant gains in the amount of information learned about American history and, perhaps surprisingly, in research techniques. These results are not compatible with certain statements of other investigators who claim students always learn more facts as well as varied social studies skills when using the problems method, no matter what the course may be. Students in topically-organized classes generally made the least significant progress in a number of areas. This is important to note, since so many texts are organized in this fashion, at least in part, and especially since the type of "problems approach" applied by many instructors is merely a topical study of problems stated in the form of a question. The all-important role of the teacher, regardless of the form of curricular organization, was clearly evidenced in the results of this investigation.

Curriculum Presentation Recommendations

A more recent study by Kight and Mickelson attempted to investigate the related effects of problem- and subject-centered types of presentation upon learning facts, learning rules of action, the ratio of rules of action learned to factual information, and the connecting of specific facts with their corresponding rules of action. In attempting to circumvent one of the difficulties related to the influence of teaching personnel revealed in the Stanford study, twenty-nine teachers taught problem- and subject-centered units in rotation to 1,450 students in English, science, and social studies classes. In terms of total combined results, pupils learned more factual information in problem-centered units; however, differences were not great in a number of cases and social studies groups gained fewer facts than rules of action as a result of their problem-centered units. The problem presentation showed marked superiority in helping pupils learn rules of action in all areas. There was a high positive correlation between learning facts and rules of action by problem solving, as compared with a low correlation in the subject-matter approach units. Four recommendations for curriculum organization made by the investigators are:

1. Organize each instructional unit around a clearly stated, genuine pupil problem.

2. Elaborate the major pupil problem into its sub-problems.

3. State and present the problem and sub-problems in each instructional unit as something to do rather than something to know.

4. Focus all factual information presented directly on the solution of the pupils' problems.

Five further recommendations for classroom presentation follow:

1. Make every effort to show the pupils that the problems stated in the instructional units are their own personal problems.

2. Make doing rather than knowing primary in the presentation of all pupils' problems.

3. Focus all factual information presented indirectly on the solution of the pupils' problems.

4. State clearly and teach specifically the rules of action necessary to the solution of the problems.

5. Point out the factual information which serves as reasons for rules of action taught.

Kight and Mickelson found the problems method superior for children of both low and high I.Q. Two other teachers working with slow learners have likewise claimed that the problems approach and group planning and discussion increase the ability of students to distinguish between fact and opinion and enable them to recognize various sources of information as holding effective solutions for the problems under consideration. They maintain that generally the skills of critical thinking are much better learned in the pursuit of meaningful problems than when taught as abstract exercises.

In the Philadelphia Open-Mindedness Study, an attempt was made to find out what problems are important to elementary school children and to help them deal with complex problems by checking on availability of facts and opportunity for solution. These simple steps were formulated to guide them: (1) know the problem, (2) get the facts, (3) put the facts in order, and (4) reach a conclusion. Results indicated that pupils recognized the importance of facts in relation to the problem concerned; that they were stimulated to acquire information by the problems approach. Russell has recently gathered much of the research concerning problem-solving abilities and applications appropriate for elementary school children.

Skill With Technique Slow to Develop

Bayles has reported on six studies with "reflective thinking" which he directed. Basically all were concerned with how well do members of classes taught in a problem-solving manner compare with those taught conventionally in regard to what is covered in typical, standardized examinations. He reports that without qualification, even where the conventionally taught students were coached for the tests, the pupils in the experimental classes did significantly better. An important observation coming from these studies concerns the point that improvement in problem-solving teaching is slow. Gains grow considerably after a teacher has had several years with the approach.

At the secondary school level, problem-centered teaching has found its strongest support in recent years from those educators who have been promoting the core movement. Much more research, however, is needed with core courses. These classes, which cut across subject-centered divisions and wherein teachers and pupils plan out units based upon problems of real concern to the young people, need to be compared in many ways with more conventionally organized courses. Teachers and administrators who favor the "guidance approach" in educational programs have also done much to promote problem solving in the schools. Writers in this area have uncovered some amazing opinions about the true problems of normal adolescents as well as those of delinquents; these pose provoking challenges to those who seek a functional, general education for youth.

Peterson's study of the historical development of the problem-solving method in education isolated ten basic postulates which form the philosophical basis of the problem-solving approach. His conclusions underscore the points and recommendations made in this article. Research to date on problem solving and on the problems approach indicates primarily the need for much more and more carefully planned and integrated research in this area which is indigenous to and so important in American education.

Learning in Groups

Alexander Frazier

To most of us, continuous attention given to how best to group children is warranted because we see the group as much more than a center of instruction. How groups are composed, how they are staffed, how their time is scheduled, and how they are expected to operate—we see all these as more than simply details for the school administrator to work out. But what do we think really matters in grouping pupils? Let us look at some points currently being considered.

What Groups Are Good For

Community . . . is the being no longer side by side *with* one another of a multitude of persons. And this multitude, though it also moves toward one goal, yet experiences everywhere a turning to, a dynamic facing of, the other, a flowing from *I* to *Thou*. Community is where community happens.[1]

A group of pupils is potentially much more than simply a roomful of children for instruction, though it is that, too. A group can be many things:

1. A resource for learning, which provides an opportunity for its members to learn from one another—new information, new values, and new ways of behaving.

2. A testing ground where pupils learn about all kinds of subjects, including themselves.

3. A creator of "common learnings" (the general knowledge and skills that all citizens need) through interaction, consensus, and continuous extension of ideas and deepening of insight and understanding.

4. A context for learning, which depends upon relationships continuing in time so that pupils may learn to plan together, to lead others, and to work toward common ends.

5. A kind of culture, a community rather than merely a "collectivity" which Buber defines as "not a binding but a bundling together."

New Ideas that Affect Our Thinking About Groups

With team teaching, Billy can look forward to new acquaintances in each room.[2]

Behind many of the current proposals for better ways of grouping pupils and scheduling their time for learning are new fears, new convictions, and new ideas that we need to understand. In the proposals themselves these ideas may sometimes be hard to see because we cannot accept the immediate purposes they present or the context in which the proposals appear. I refer to such fears and ideas as these:

1. The fear that the individual may get lost in the multitude, that emphasis on the same information and skills for all may lead to conformity.

2. The fear that emphasis on group instruction may have crowded out opportunities for independent study and research that pupils need if they are to become self-directing and to develop their talents.

3. A new sense of urgency for making sure that some pupils are not held back by slower pupils.

4. A belief that a single teacher is incapable of dealing with all of a pupil's needs for knowledge and that, with less to teach, a teacher could become more highly specialized and thus more

useful; that with multiple teachers, even for a single course or class, a pupil would learn more.

5. A new conviction that some needs of elementary school pupils are not met when they are grouped with pupils their own age, that they need to be in groups with other pupils, possibly both younger and older.

6. A contention that the size of the group has little or no effect on pupils' learning.

7. A contention that less time than we thought necessary should be provided for pupils to have experiences in small groups, that only enough time for essential interaction is necessary, and that more time should be provided for some study in large groups—in getting information, for example—and for study outside the group.

8. A contention that better ways of teaching than by oral instruction can be found, that the drudgery can be removed from teaching, and that the teacher can become counselor and stimulator of learning.

9. A contention that master teachers (there are not now and perhaps never will be many), using such devices as large classes and television, can greatly improve instruction.

Doubts To Be Expressed

"No," said the priest, "it is not necessary to accept everything as true, one must only accept it as necessary." "A melancholy conclusion," said K. "It turns lying into a universal principle." [3]

As professional educators, we view many of the proposals for different ways of grouping and scheduling as uninformed, if not injurious. We suspect both the breadth of the background in education and the motives of some of the sponsors. We should bring our doubts out into the open and look at them directly. We may, for example, think that some sponsors of these ideas are interested in only some kinds of learning, only in the bright pupils and master teachers; that they are contemptuous of most teachers and slow and needy pupils; that they do not understand the great variety of individual differences, and the facts that the teacher must continuously try to provide for differences, that children learn from one another, that there is value in pupils learning social customs and standards of behavior and that both individual and the group can learn in a group setting. We may think that other sponsors merely desire to save money or to accommodate to rising enrollments and the threat of a teacher shortage, or that they are preoccupied with gadgetry and materials and have no well-developed conception of learning as discovery and the place of materials in such a conception. Some of us may think that sponsors are more interested in indoctrinating than in educating pupils.

Conviction To Be Retested

Courage does not need the safety of an unquestionable conviction. It includes the risk without which no creative life is possible.[4]

It must now be clear to all of us that our beliefs about what groups are good for have been challenged on almost every count. And it must be just as clear that we need to state as well as we can the values we see in group experience so that we can not only identify the essentials to be held to but also ask whether there are new ways to realize these values. Let us look at and retest our own convictions, among them these:

1. Pupils of most ages need knowledge of social behavior and customs which they can acquire only by interaction with others of the same age.

2. Many kinds of learning are possible only in a group in which members have time enough together to get to know each other well.

3. A teacher has to be with the same group of pupils for a considerable length of time in order to find out the needs of the individuals in it and to plan for them to have opportunities for suitable experiences.

4. Enduring relationships between a teacher and a member of a group of pupils and among the pupils themselves are basic to their successful learning; if such relationships are to develop, the group and the teacher must spend most of each day together.

5. Pupils learn to live democratically, to create a sense of community, and to acquire the many skills they need only in the daily give and take of their home group, and such experience is worth the teacher's continuous attention.

6. Almost all the kinds of learning we most value in school cannot take place unless pupils and teacher have opportunity for continuous interaction.

Issues To Be Explored

Some time ago a woman, believing me to be in sympathy with all scientific innovations concerning the school, showed me with evident satisfaction a corset or brace for pupils. She had invented this and felt that it would complete the work of the bench. . . . All this is the logical consequence of a material application of the methods of science to the decadent school. Evidently the rational method of combating spinal curvature in the pupils is to change the form of their work—so that they shall no longer be obliged to remain for so many hours a day in a harmful position. It is a conquest of liberty which the school needs, not the mechanism of a bench.[5]

With all our feelings out in the open, we may need to take the new ideas seriously and put our convictions earnestly to the test. The rash of lay or semi-professional proposals may be attempts to answer the wrong questions, but they could also be symptoms of something wrong; they could also mean that something remains to be done in addition to what we ourselves recognize.

Can we identify some issues that interest us and that we feel we can afford to explore professionally? Let me suggest a few for a start:

1. Are we bringing pupils enough richness from adults in our communities? Could we find ways to provide for more professional assistants in elementary schools? Science consultants, for example?

2. Are we doing all we can to help children gain the knowledge that can come from their association with children of different ages? What knowledge comes from such association and how much do we value it? Can we organize pupils of different ages into classes that would be in keeping with our convictions?

3. Do we need to think through again possible uses of teaching large groups? Are there values that a pupil can gain from experiences as part of an audience that we are not now recognizing in our programs? Can a mass medium be used in large groups on its own terms; that is, can it be used as a medium carrying messages which are valuable in themselves rather than as instruction or aids to instruction?

4. Are we offering pupils maximum opportunity to learn through interaction in most of our classrooms? Do our pupils get the values we think they do from small groups and enduring relationships? Could we do better?

5. Do we need to reexamine provisions for independent learning in our programs? Do we plan to create new programs with room for different interests and abilities? Do we use school time wisely in independent studies? Do all children have time to study independently?

6. Could we think more deeply about the problem of simultaneously insuring group learning and fostering individual creativity? Can we be more inventive by varying our routes? Do we waste time in letting pupils learn too little too well? Do we value pupils' differences and try to develop them?

7. What is the minimal time a child needs with one teacher to acquire a feeling of security? Could we try out new combinations of pupils without endangering the home base?

8. Has our concern for meeting group standards of achievement impeded pupils' progress? Have grade standards and too-tight confinement to study materials interfered with pupils' learning? Can we loosen up the situation within grades as an alternative to cross-grade achievement grouping?

9. Is it possible that we could learn to do a better job of instruction if we depended less on oral teaching? Do we waste time in trying to provide too much group instruction? Could we use some closely programed materials on our own terms or develop some of our own?

10. If we tried, could we ourselves become more inventive in proposing and testing better bases for setting up group and individual relationships that might meet newly recognized needs on a truly professional basis? What might such better bases be?

The Limitations of Subject Matter

Robert E. Bills

Have we ever really shown concern for the individual learner or is he a thorn in our sides? Has not our concern been for learning rather than learners, teaching rather than teachers, administration rather than administrators, and achievement rather than achievers? I believe you will agree that these are bold questions and that they probably require some clarification.

What I am asking is this: Have we ever really been concerned with individual differences, and doesn't the question of grouping, whether homogeneous or heterogeneous, indicate that we have not yet concerned ourselves with the individuality of the learner?

Let me elaborate. The psychology of individual differences, as it is taught in most colleges, is usually a course in normative statistics. Such courses deal with averages and deviations from the averages. When we look at a pupil's score we describe him in terms of how much he deviates from the average of the group. Usually we compare a pupil's deviation with some measure of group variability to see how he stands in relation to his group. We ignore his own uniqueness and see his importance only in comparisons with a group. Although we try to ignore him, the individual remains as the basic unit in educational work, and one individual cannot be added to another without destroying the individuality of both.

Granted my statements are extreme, but so are our practices. We move more and more toward the group, toward such things as helping the individual accept his role in society, toward helping him learn the things which we believe he needs to know in order to function in society, and toward the use of measuring instruments that ignore his individuality and bind him to his past instead of freeing him for his becoming. We hear over and over that we must engage ourselves in mass education because of the mass of children facing us. Let me suggest that we may be asking the wrong question. Instead of asking, "How can we engage ourselves in mass education?" we should be asking, "How can we educate the many who present themselves at our doors?"

When we ask, "Should we use homogeneous or heterogeneous grouping?" we are probably trying to reach a better basis for individualizing instruction. I suggest, however, that none of these methods is anything more than an administrative device to cope with the large numbers of children we are supposed to teach and the task of taking these large numbers of children in the directions we believe they should go.

Most studies of grouping try to answer the question, "Will children learn more when they are grouped in a particular way?" And we seem to mean, "Will children learn more subject matter or skill or something else if we organize them in groups in a particular way?" Our concern, although fairly nonspecific and nonspecified, seems to remain with teaching children what we believe is important, and most people remain unconcerned with helping children develop in ways which children see as important or in helping them move in self-determined directions. We use such terms as "enhancing," "modifying," and "maximizing" capacity or potential, but what do these terms really mean to us? We use them when what we are trying to do is to help a person increase his ability to be intelligent in his behavior. This goal requires us to be concerned with a multitude of factors all operating at the same time. This is difficult to manage.

But it is also difficult for us to ignore this multitude of factors when we know they are important in human behavior and human welfare. As an afterthought many studies ask, "What happens to those other things such as attitudes, values, self-concepts, etc. ?"

Few directors of studies have tried to devise learning situations in which they could try to change the multitude of variables important to human welfare, human well-being, and human behavior.

I see homogeneous groups, not as an effort to get beyond subject matter and skills, but as a device for ignoring human variability and for reducing our need to concern ourselves with individual pupils. Once children are homogenously grouped, we assume that the differences are no longer matters of concern. Nor do I see heterogeneous grouping as a deliberate effort to do any more than to teach subject matter and skills. We often hear that homogeneous grouping has harmful effects on pupils' personality and that these can be avoided in heterogeneous grouping, and that youngsters of diverse talents can learn better from each other in heterogeneous groups, and so forth. But please note: What we are saying is that if we group heterogeneously we do not have to pay attention to these variables because they will take care of themselves.

We have not tried to change the multitude of variables because we have not really seen them as of primary importance in human behavior or as primary results of education. We say, "Oh, yes, these are nice results, but are they our primary goals?" "Is not our primary goal the teaching of the skills, techniques, and knowledge required for proficiency in reading, arithmetic, and for the other skills which our children will need?" Most of us would agree that elementary schools exist primarily to teach reading skills, etc., but I imagine many of us would also agree that reading, for example, is not just a matter of practice, skill vocabulary, and technique, but a complex behavioral task which is an expression of the total person.

But it is not always easy to convince ourselves, parents, and other adults of this. It is easier to believe that our world is rational and knowable, that the extent to which we can deal rationally with the world and have knowledge about it, to this extent we can cope with it and can become successful.

I believe, however, that we live in an unknowable world which man can use in many ways and that man imposes himself on his world and seeks to know it by means of the framework he has constructed. In contrast, though, education often takes as its task the communication of agreements which seem necessary to cause other people to see the world as we now see it or have agreed it is.

But each of us lives his life in his own individual world which does not resemble the world of any other person. Each person has experience, and the raw data of his experience differ from those of any other person. Furthermore a person is "set" to interpret his experience according to his own world.

We need to make sense of our individual world. In it we must discover consistency, and if we cannot discover it, we must impose it on ourselves through stereotypes and generalizations. And here we begin to encounter difficulty. Since generalizations are abstractions from data, they can never truly represent the data and thus never exactly fit a situation. However, if we did not abstract and generalize to arrive at some form of consistency, we would be left in a buzzing confusion of facts and would constantly receive sensory data devoid of any meaning.

Consistency of perception is necessary to existence. Our interpretations of our past experience provide this consistency and serve as a screen through which we receive new experience. Thus present experience tends to be interpreted as identical with past experience. Interpretation is more or less structure bound by the past.

One way of avoiding making our own generalizations is to attempt to adopt what we think are other people's generalizations. And one way of achieving security is to have other people accept our generalizations as meaningful to them. We see many teachers trying to have children accept their perceptions and children who are more than willing to accept the teacher's perceptions as the easy way out. We have children trying to avoid conflict by acting as if someone else's perceptions were their own, which, incidentally, may be the quickest way to develop a personality conflict.

But some children cannot accept someone else's perceptions; they must make sense of their own world. Such children often present discipline problems, leave school early, are under-achievers, or appear to be poorly motivated. Too often, they are the best potential the world possesses.

To accept another person's goal as suitable for our behavior means that we must deny our own experience and attempt to act as if the other person's experience were our own. Since we cannot experience as another does, we are left without experience on which to base our behavior. It is therefore not only difficult and at times impossible to change a person's behavior by force, manipulation, persuasion, or other means, but also usually harmful, for it causes him to deny his own experience and thus to have less experience on which to base his behavior.

If we desire to change human behavior by means of education, we must seek other means than force—either subtle or obvious. Suppose we approach the problem by asking, "What causes human behavior?"

Perceptual theory holds that what a person does is consistent with the structure of his perceptual field *at the instant of action;* that is, as a person sees, so he behaves. Man's basic drive is the need to maintain or to enhance his status. In other words, man's behavior is directed toward maintaining or enhancing his present status. When man has a choice of action he chooses to do that which offers him what he sees as the greatest possibility for raising his status. To put this more strongly, man *must* do what seems to him to be best for him at that instant.

The perceptual field of the healthy person is an ever-changing pattern, and it is doubtful that the structure at any one instant will ever again be repeated in its entirety. Thus what our perceptions and behavior are at any one instant will not be repeated exactly at any other.

To change behavior through education we must know what determines the structure of the perceptual field and why it is that the behavior of some people tends toward rigid consistency.

The key to the structure of the perceptual field is experience. And the key to intelligent behavior is a broad background of experience readily available to the behaver, without distortion or denial. Experience can be divided into a number of areas of belief. I cannot go into these areas here except to say that they may be divided into beliefs about facts, faith, superstition, values, attitudes, self-concepts, and others. The main point is that a person interprets his experience, and these interpretations are his beliefs. Although his beliefs may bear little resemblance to the beliefs of another person, they determine the structure of his perceptual field.

Once the field is structured, the structure itself begins to determine future structure. Since no one type of belief has primacy in determining behavior, behavior cannot be significantly altered by changing only one type of belief. This raises a serious question about the almost exclusive emphasis some teachers and some schools place on subject matter. It is obvious that *significant changes in behavior cannot be accomplished by subject matter alone. Intelligent behavior is dependent on the breadth of experience which is available to a person without distortion or denial at the instant of his action and on his ability to be open to new experience so that he can modify his past behavior.*

A variety of factors can cause experience not to be available or not to be available without distortion or denial. Several have particular relevance to teaching. An incomplete or damaged organism and an impaired or inadequately developed central nervous system cannot receive the experience necessary for intelligent behavior. Physiological malfunctioning resulting from disease, malnutrition, toxic poisons, and the like can also prevent the complete and undistorted reception of experience. Some of these can be treated in school, others outside the school. But here we are concerned with factors amenable to control in the classroom.

The primary factor in denial and distortion of experience is called threat. Attempts to force a person to change his perceptions usually cause him to deny and to distort his experience. If he acquires experience in ways that mean little to him, he will find little personal meaning in it and consequently ignore it. To force him to accept experience as meaningful when it is not is threatening and thus distorting.

When threatened, a person begins to defend and protect himself. He begins to deny or distort his experience, to make it what he wants it to be or thinks it should be. The greater the threat, the more he is closed to the meaning his experience had for his organism at the time he had it. The most important factor in determining a person's openness to experience is a threat.

Given this information about behavior and behavior change, we can say that the task of education is to provide a person with opportunity to acquire a breadth of experience that will be personally meaningful and readily available to him when he needs it. In addition, education must enable a person to remain open to experience and to seek new experience, and thus continue to learn to behave more intelligently.

Obviously this goal cannot be attained through teaching which emphasizes only a textbook approach to mastery of subject matter. Few teachers would disagree with this, but it seems necessary to say it here in the light of the criticism being leveled at education and the reaction of many educators to the criticism. Such criticism has led to what are called strengthened curricular requirements, to requirements of mastery in a great number of subject fields, and to greater concentration on formal subject matter in the elementary school. But can we effectively educate boys and girls through these emphases alone, even though we group them homogeneously, heterogeneously, or for individualized instruction? How we organize will be of little consequence as long as our goals and emphases remain unchanged.

The Schools and Religion: The Historical Present

Robert Ulich

In view of the centuries-old interpenetration between government, religion and education, the First Amendment (1791) represents an astonishing act of legislation. Its far-reaching character has never before been so evident and at the same time so confusing as today, certainly much more confusing than the founding fathers ever anticipated. The Amendment says that

> Congress shall make no law respecting an establishment of religion, or prohibiting the free exercise thereof.

To be sure, the First Amendment was never intended to drive religion and prayer out of the school. Rather it wanted to guarantee the right of the states to regulate their religious affairs independent of federal control. And, as Professor William H. Marnell has shown in his book *The First Amendment*, the advocates of disestablishment [1] did not act out of personal animosity against religion as such, whatever their personal opinions in this matter. They simply saw themselves confronted with the growth of rival sects, the Presbyterians against the Anglicans in the

South, and the Baptists, Methodists, Unitarians, Catholics and other denominations against the Calvinists in the North. As a matter of fact, at several places disestablishment existed before the Bill of Rights, either out of convenience or out of respect for religious liberty or out of both.

It is also certain that our early legislators did not consciously aim at founding a "Christian nation," as so often has been said. Rather they considered the Constitution a political document to be kept free from the strife of religionists as much as possible. Nor is it correct to assume that the people of North America of the eighteenth century were altogether church-devoted folks. In his book *From State Church to Pluralism,* Franklin H. Littell, Professor of Church History at Chicago Theological Seminary, has proved the contrary. If the statistics (which I have to take on faith) reflect reality, not more than 5 percent of the population belonged to any church in 1776. The fact that at present the majority of the American citizens are church-affiliated is largely due to later immigration and the changes in the cultural climate during the second half of the nineteenth and during the twentieth century.

However, whether the population of the early United States was more or less religious or secular (and we all know that church membership is no clear indication), the curricula and the textbooks of the time prove that religion was taught wherever there was a formally established public school. State establishments, according to Professor Paul A. Freund, continued in New England until the 1830's. Even Horace Mann, a liberal who so valiantly fought the educational backwardness of the Boston ministers and teachers, nevertheless wanted to save religion in school by reading the Bible without note and comment.

Nor did the majority of the teachers of the time of Horace Mann and even later object to religious instruction. Rather it was the intolerance of the clergy in regard to different interpretations of the Gospel that made it difficult and well-nigh impossible for the schools to transmit the religious heritage to their pupils without creating denominational protests. At the same time the growing number of immigrants of different faiths, some of them not Christian, aggravated the situation, while the growth of humanism, of atheism, of relativistic philosophies and of new scientific theories such as Darwinism created a widespread indifference, erosion and even hostility in regard to the Christian tradition of this country. Now nothing, I believe, besides communism could more persuade the average American citizen that, whatever the past, he belongs to a "Christian nation"—so-called —than the belligerent attitude of Mrs. Murray who forced upon the Supreme Court its decision concerning religious ceremonies in the public schools.

The Present Situation

As is well known, legal decisions do not easily change the minds of people who believe in their defending a rightful cause. So it is also with the just-mentioned interpretation of the First Amendment by the Supreme Court. Thus one cannot be surprised that there is now a movement to secure a constitutional amendment that would permit voluntary prayers in public schools. According to my information, nearly 150 proposed amendments have been submitted to the House Committee on the Judiciary. There is certainly a profound irony in the fact that a part of the Constitution, originally designed to allow the States the necessary freedom in matters religious, has now become not only a restriction upon their autonomy, but also on the religious freedom of local school boards and parents. Was it, so many people ask, logically cogent and historically wise on the part of the highest judges to go all the way they went? Indeed, the formal logic of law is not always the logic of history, especially when the experts disagree about the first.

Naturally, educators as well as parents are confused by the ambiguous language of the Supreme Court. Judging from my own inquiries from the East to the West of this country, prayers are still offered in a number of schools, and grace is said before luncheon. The argument that as a consequence of the pluralistic composition of the school population some pupils might be offended or at least embarrassed by religious exercises, did convince some, but not others who pointed at the chance given to dissidents to abstain from prayer or to leave the school room. Nor were these teachers impressed by the possible uneasiness of a child who has to display his nonconformism (or better, that of his parents) before his critical coevals. However, the school principals who attended a seminar I conducted at a Western university felt no desire for becoming religious martyrs themselves. They just continued the custom of prayer because they hesitated to offend the majority of the parents in their community. They would have preferred not to be bothered.

Interestingly enough, those who unequivocally supported the Supreme Court came from two opposite camps: the strict secularists on the one side, and the honestly religious believers on the other, the latter protesting that school prayers had often degenerated into a mere formality skirting on blasphemy. On the whole, it seemed the teachers were less excited about "the great debate" than certain parent groups to which the prayer decision offers a welcome change for righteous indignation and for quarreling with neighbors and schools.

But let us talk about the serious among the opponents. They are aroused by the fear of taxation of religious institutions and by the threat of an unhistorical disruption of national customs and symbols (which today have more of a patriotic and aesthetic appeal, anyway, than a deeply-felt religious one). But there are even profounder, though sometimes unconscious, reasons for the anxiety of many people. These reasons became clear to me when I read the book by the novelist Herman Wouk, *This is My God*. The author rightly believes that the Jewish people could not have survived the long era of persecutions without their faithful adherence to its rituals, festivals and prayers. May then the loss of the Christian past not jeopardize the future of *this* nation, just as the desertion from the Covenant would have jeopardized the survival of the Jews? Nations as well as men, though living on bread, do not live on bread alone.

Indeed, such concerns about the conditions of deeper cultural survival cannot simply be brushed aside as superstitious. For every historian knows that rituals, religious as well as secular, help men, families and whole communities to preserve their identity. Even a superficially understood ceremony may keep warm the ember so that it bursts into flames when survival is threatened. Many a German Jew who had rarely been in a synagogue became proud and spiritually supported by his awakening faith under Hitler's persecutions. The same happened, *mutatis mutandis*, with many Christians. And if rituals were merely a sort of decorative superstructure over the life of a body politic, why then would all revolutionary leaders of the past and the present have been so eager to replace the old symbols of allegiance by new ones to which they would like to attach a strongly emotional, almost religious, appeal?

Nor is the problem solved by the remark of the late President Kennedy that the home should take care of the child's religious education. How many do? And if they do, should home and school be divided?

Finally, the proponents of religious education are afraid that with the banishment of prayer (a merely negative act that they consider indicative of the abandonment of religion as a whole) the public school will devote itself entirely to instructional drill devoid of deeper meaning, to sport and other surface activities. Thus, as its enemies already assert, it will become more and more a "godless" institution. Patriotism, symbolized by the daily salute of the flag and the oath of allegiance, will then be the only gesture that points toward trans-individual values. But all forms of national incorporation of the individual (even those under democratic auspices) need, besides the horizontal line of collectivization, the vertical line that makes man conscious of his obligation to universal human values. No nation can decently survive unless it develops, together with the sense of national self-preservation, the moral urge to help the whole of mankind in its struggle for ever higher achievements. Only that political education which reminds youth of this fact is good education. Without this transcendent urge every institution will sooner or later become totalitarian.

As an answer to these predicaments, more and more parents will send their children to private and denominational schools. Indeed, several articles have already appeared in public and scholarly journals that predict that the growth of nonpublic schools, enhanced by the religious issue, may sooner or later force the public schools into the role of a minority.

I personally do not in the least deny that a comprehensive understanding of the sciences may help a person to transcend his ego and the boundaries of national interest just as much as religion, and that a deep understanding of idealistic, humanistic and existentialist philosophies can achieve the same result—certainly a better one than mere religious conventions. And so much have the established churches connived at, and enhanced, divisive and aggressive tendencies among men and nations that one may sometimes ask, "How much have they really contributed to the progress of mankind?" However, the modern national states have not behaved better. Humility and a mighty bad conscience are needed with regard to both the ecclesiastical and the secular powers.

The Morality Issue

Then the question arises whether the future of the public school in the United States will be completely separated from the nation's religious heritage. The answer will be "yes," and Jefferson's famous metaphor about the wall of separation between church and state will apply to our public schools, if by religion is meant allegiance to a particular creed. But the answer will be "no," if the term "religion" connotes an attitude or a sentiment that expresses a person's reverential feeling concerning the cosmic powers that surround him, that nourish and sustain him and on which he depends in birth, life and death. Under this aspect, how can any sensitive person avoid religion, and how can any good form of education remain completely aloof from it? And let us assume that, as a consequence of a radically secular education, such aloofness be achieved, would not that also be a kind of indoctrination in regard to the metaphysical aspects of humanity?

Therefore, the Court's legal decisions concerning prayer ceremonies in no way relieve the American public school from its responsibilities for the whole and wholesome development of the student's personality. And no legal decision should be or can be a complete answer to the question concerning the inner relation between education and religion. Rather, after the liberation of the public school from denominational pressure, the conscientious educator should feel like a strategist who after a serious battle has moved his army into an advanced position, but knows that he will not be able to hold it unless he prepares his troops with a new spirit of initiative. Or, in order to phrase it differently, I personally regard the end of interference of political or ecclesiastical powers with religious convictions as one of the greatest, though not yet fully accomplished, achievements of the modern mind. For, among other similar events, I cannot easily forget that as late as 1732—less than two decades before the birth of Goethe—the archbishop Firmian of Salzburg, a graduate from the Jesuit college of Rome, dared expel more than twenty-two thousand Protestants from his realm. But I would also be afraid of an atmosphere in our schools where freedom from religious indoctrination becomes an excuse for comfortable laziness with respect to the spiritual tradition of humanity. If education fails in this realistic appraisal of the situation, the victory over sectarianism will be a Pyrrhic victory, an impending defeat rather than a success.

However, so many people will argue, in raising the issue of religion in our schools, we raise at the same time the issue of moral education. For schools are not merely centers of learning. They should also be moral institutions as, so many parents will contend, true morality needs the support of religious convictions, just as the philosophical discipline of ethics, according to their opinion, requires the assumption of a metaphysical order. I have no intention to discuss this problem which is as old as systematic philosophy. However, in this context we cannot avoid the question of whether the school can discharge its moral obligations unless it moors its teaching to a religious ground.

Now, we all know that nonreligious or even anti-religious persons have been virtuous people and have educated their children accordingly, whereas many saints have arrived at sainthood after a rather wild youth, being, as it were, disgusted with themselves. To confess it frankly, sometimes the suspicion has crept on me that some people might be so concerned with religion because they suffered from such severe conflicts as self-alienation that they lost the courage necessary for a normal and natural life as, e.g., that most influential modern theologian Sören Kierkegaard.[2] Subjectively, of course, these people are right and just as justified in defending and systematizing their inner experiences as their opponents. No doubt they have contributed decidedly to the deepening of man's self-understanding. But are they right objectively?

Furthermore, when I read about the moral conduct of certain pious folks, confessedly unable to imagine a school without prayer, against the atheist fighter Mrs. Murray (resembling the conduct of other pious whites against Negroes), then I have difficulty in discovering any positive interrelation between the public display of religion on the one hand, and moral behavior on the other. Or can anyone prove that French morals have suffered after the introduction of *morale laïque* in their public schools?

Finally, modern anthropological and psychological investigations concur increasingly with the old human experience that the only sound basis of personal development is provided not by ideological factors but by the example of the parents, the right mixture of love and discipline on their parts (especially that of the mother), and the natural relation of the child to his playmates.

Thus, rather than get violently aroused about religion inside or outside the school, should a nation not be grateful if it has a public school that teaches honesty, cooperativeness, truthfulness and the other virtues in the code of civilized societies? Why then add the religious issue to its many difficulties? And if the public school, as we hope, conveys to our youth a sound moral conscience, does it then not also provide a firm underpinning for a productive religious life? For even though religion transcends morality, what else is it but an aesthetic and vacuous sentiment unless it expresses itself also in moral action and commitment?

Nevertheless, religious people will always remain convinced that there is no first and second. Either religion and morality are jointly interwoven by early forms of education and indoctrination, or neither one will yield the full human harvest. And about this proposition one can and will argue endlessly. Neither party will convince the other.

The Future

Must we then leave the educational scene of the United States with a feeling of unresolved and insoluble conflict? No doubt the rivalry between secularism and transcendentalism will persist with all its intellectual ferment, but also with its dangers for the spiritual unity of this nation and of other nations too, for our whole modern culture reflects a split mentality.

However, are the defenders of the so-called "secular" public school entirely defenseless against the reproaches of the religious critic? In answering this question, I may refer here to an earlier statement where I said that, whatever the decision of the Supreme Court, it will never be able to divorce the religious from the educational spheres in our educational system. Somehow, the two will always encroach upon each other, simply because a good life refuses to squeeze the imminent and the transcendent into watertight compartments. The human soul is a whole; it cannot be bisected.

It will, then, depend on our teachers whether they want to be paid merely as "instructors" of a number of skills and knowledges, go home and leave the inner life of their charges to the chances of the environment, or whether they think that their pupils, while learning the so-called subjects of the curriculum, should at the same time learn about the meaning of these subjects within the larger meaning of human existence. There is a world of difference between the gladly forgotten drillmaster, on the one hand, and the teacher whom his pupils will later remember as a source of personal enrichment because he has shown them that the special areas of knowledge are not merely isolated islands on the *globus intellectualis,* but appear to the searching mind as integral parts of a "cosmos" or a "universe," instead of a "chaos" or "multiverse." If our teachers conceive of their mission in such a comprehensive way, they will educate free minds who, on the one hand, appreciate the depth in man's religious tradition, but to whom, on the other hand, the old denominational and dualistic conflicts appear secondary, if not inhibitive to, the formation of a unifying world outlook, or a *Weltanschauung*.

If a teacher who possesses such an understanding of human existence and would like to convey it also to his pupils, if such a teacher is in charge of mathematics, he will make it clear to his pupils that mathematics is not merely a series of tricks, but the language of measure. He will show them that it was the discovery of measures and proportions existing in the world as we see it that made curious astronomers out of the Babylonian and Mexican priests and caused a Pythagoras [3] to marvel at the relation between numerical ratios and certain regularities in the physical world. Most great mathematicians were philosophers of a kind, sometimes very great ones, and many, if not most, of the great philosophers were mathematicians. Also music and mathematics have always been akin. Johann Sebastian Bach, so I have been told, wrote mathematical formulae on the margins of his compositions. And if you study the minds of the great mathematicians who originated the scientific revolution in the seventeenth century, you will see that they did not merely wish to produce new empirical data, but that they were inspired by the desire to discover the deep inner harmony in the multifarious events of the universe. Constantly, their search bordered on both, the religious and the aesthetic.

And if mathematics and the sciences, imaginatively taught, can help the student to see the world in a mood of philosophical curiosity, how could it be possible for a teacher of literature to conceal from his students the intimate kinship between a country's poetry and its religion? Similarly, a teacher of history must be mentally blind who fails to explain to his students the interrelation between religion and the great landmarks of culture—between the rise of Christianity and the decay of the spiritual and social foundations of the Roman Empire, between the disintegration of medieval Christianity and the emergence of the Renaissance and the Reformation, between the corruption of churches and the growth of liberalism during the eighteenth century, or between the retardedness of Russian orthodoxy and the victories of communism in our time. No doubt, such a historical perspective would create exciting discussions about our present when our old national states are confronted with the idea of mankind, and our old religious denominations with the idea of world religion.

To the Teacher

But will we have the teachers who can combine the sincere desire for objectivity (more we cannot demand) with the capacity for creative inspiration?

The answer will depend on the spirit of the institutions entrusted with the professional preparation of our teachers. There is now a tendency even among schools of education to relegate the teaching of the broad cultural subjects to departments in the university at large. Indeed, that is necessary. For what, after all, does the liberal arts college exist? The first pamphlet that I published in this country, with the title "On the Reform of Educational Research," resulted more or less from my disappointment in the lack of cooperation between the schools of education and the university as a whole. If the latter does not feel the obligation to widen the cultural horizon of the future teacher, the departments of education will work against insurmountable odds.

But I also know that mere scholarly knowledge of a subject does not yet make a good teacher. Necessary as it is, it is not enough. Just as important is the teacher's capacity for getting intellectual materials out of the academic storehouses where they have accumulated in the course of centuries of specialization, and rendering them vital and meaningful to the young learner. Only in very rare cases can this process of transformation be taught by the typical academic courses in the sciences and the humanities. It is even not their purpose. Nor can it be their purpose to relate their instruction to the functions and responsibilities that the teacher will have to discharge in his community. Our society expects from him more than the instructing of children; rather, it wants his advice concerning the guidance of the young, the resolutions of parent councils and the educational policy of the town. If a community considers the teacher merely a person hired for cramming and giving grades, then it is the fault of the teaching profession itself. It has submitted too willingly to the American prejudice that the teacher should not mingle in public affairs and should leave the "pioneer spirit" to other citizens.

For these and other reasons the task of the schools of education, especially those on the graduate level, will become greater and greater every year.

There has now emerged an increasing number of people I may call "efficiency experts," concerned with the improvement of teaching and teacher education. We should be grateful for their advice as far as it can help the schools of education and the public schools to achieve better results in the various subjects of the curriculum. But in their aversion to the discussion of the broader human goals of education, these experts seem to forget that efficiency in learning, just as elsewhere, can be used for evil as well as for good purposes. It is used for the good only if it helps the maturing person to understanding the truth in Socrates' famous statement that the morally unexamined life is not worth living.

This continued self-examination that should be required from every educated person will confront our teachers with problems that reach far beyond the immediate utility of this or that subject of learning. What, after all, is the purpose of learning? Merely to provide a "union card" for this or that vocation or profession, now generally called a "job," or also for the formation of a full and meaningful life? Sometimes it seems to me that the confessed atheist and the agnostic are more interested in these eternal problems of humanity than the conventional Christian and the satisfied and well-paid specialist.

If our departments of education fail to understand their task of providing the competent, and at the same time searching, teacher, they will increase the dangers of modern mechanization, conformism and other depersonalizing trends in our modern civilization. If, on the other hand, they succeed in making the teacher conscious of his broad cultural mission, they will help our nation to survive both physically and spiritually and raise even the religious life of modern man to that stage of maturity where at the present, despite millennia of history, it is not, but where, for mankind's sake, it should be.

Education in 1985

Kimball Wiles

Although it *is* possible that schools in 1985 will be used as instruments of thought control and social classification, the writer, nevertheless, is optimistic enough to believe there will continue to be a social commitment to freedom, creativity and equality of opportunity. With this basic assumption, an attempt is made in the following statement to project the changes that technological advances and social problems will produce.

Purposes and Program—1985

Planners of the education for adolescents hope that each pupil will: (a) develop a set of values that will guide his behavior; (b) acquire the skills necessary to participate effectively in the culture; (c) gain understanding of the social, economic, political and scientific heritage; and (d) become able to make a specialized contribution to the society.

The program of the school is designed to promote these goals and is divided into four phases: (a) analysis of experiences and values; (b) acquisition of fundamental skills; (c) exploration of the cultural heritage; and (d) specialization and creativity.

240

Analysis of Experiences and Values

In the school each pupil spends six hours a week in an Analysis Group. With ten other pupils of his own age and a skilled teacher-counselor he discusses any problem of ethics, social concern, out-of-school experience, or implication of knowledge encountered in another class he or any student brings to the group. No curriculum is established in advance. The exploration of questions, ideas or values advanced by group members constitutes the primary type of experience.

The purpose of the Analysis Group is to help each pupil discover meaning, to develop increased commitment to a set of values and viewpoints held by members of the society.

The membership of an Analysis Group is carefully selected to provide persons of relatively equal intellectual ability but varied social and economic values. The group remains as a unit throughout its high school program. Changes are made only when deep emotional conflict develops between students or between a student and the teacher-counselor.

The teachers of Analysis Groups are emotionally mature people. They were selected early in their teacher education program because they displayed a high degree of empathy and were warm, outgoing personalities that other people liked. They were given special training in counseling, communication and value analysis. Each has been taught to see his role as helping others feel more secure, clarify their values, and communicate more effectively with their colleagues. If a teacher of an Analysis Group attempts to sell his viewpoint, he is considered unsuccessful and is replaced.

Each Analysis Group teacher meets three groups, or thirty-three students, during the week. His time beyond the eighteen hours in the discussion groups is for individual counseling with the thirty-three pupils and their parents.

The Analysis Group is considered the basic element of the educational program. In the sixties it was recognized that unless citizens had values they accepted, understood and could apply, the social structure would begin to disintegrate unless authoritarian controls were applied. To counter the danger of collapse of a democratic way of life, the school was assigned the task of making as sure that each child develop a set of values as that he could read. The Analysis Group evolved as the best means of performing the values development function.

Acquisition of Fundamental Skills

Citizens in 1985 must have fundamental skills far superior to those [now] necessary to be considered literate.

In the home and in the elementary school, children learn to read, spell and compute at their own rate of learning by the use of teaching machines. In the school for adolescents, mathematics, foreign languages and many scientific processes and formulas are taught by machines supervised by librarians and a staff of technicians.

It has been proven that the machines can teach basic skills as effectively and efficiently as a human. The work of Skinner and of persons working with foreign language laboratories in the late fifties paved the way for this development. All the activities needed for teaching all fundamental skills have been programed.

Each student planning a high school program is told the skills he must master. He works through the needed program as rapidly as he can. When he wants to work on a skill, he goes to the librarian, schedules a machine and a program and goes to work.

Certain skills are needed by all citizens, and each adolescent's program includes the requirement that these skills be acquired. Other skills are considered vocational in nature and are added to a student's program if he indicates he has college entrance or a specific vocation as a goal.

Some students complete their basic skills work early in their high school program. Others work on them until they leave the high school.

Two librarians, one to issue programs and the other to help on request, and a staff of mechanical technicians supervise the work of 200 students. Disorder is at a minimum because each person works on his own level and on his purposes. Moreover, each student works in his own soundproofed cubicle.

The teaching machines laboratories for the various subject matter areas, mathematics, languages, grammar, are an integral part of the Materials Center of the school.

Exploration of the Cultural Heritage

The explosion of available knowledge in the first three quarters of the twentieth century confronts educators with the need for selecting, synthesizing, interpreting and seeking better methods of transmitting it. The things that an effective citizen needs to know in 1985 are a multiple of the knowledge necessary in 1960. Textbooks with less than master teachers are not enough, and ways of bringing each student into a working relationship with the best teachers available have been sought. Basic knowledge from the essential fields is prepared in the most easily understood media and presented as dramatically and forcefully as possible. This knowledge from the humanities, the social sciences, and the physical and biological sciences is considered the Cultural Heritage.

Roughly a third of the program of each high school student is designed to help him acquire the basic knowledge of his culture. By exposure to the experiences, ideas, and discoveries of the past, it is hoped that the individual will become literate enough about the basic ideas of his culture to participate in discussions of them or to understand reference to them. It is further hoped that the experience in the Cultural Heritage portion of the program will develop a desire to further enhance the values on which the society is based.

Classes in the Cultural Heritage program are large. Sometimes as many as 500 or 1000 are in a single section.

Teaching is by television, films or a highly skilled lecturer. No provision is made for discussion because ideas that produce a response can be discussed in the Analysis Groups.

Only one teacher and an assistant are needed in each subject matter field in each school. The teacher lectures or presents the material by an appropriate medium. The assistant prepares quizzes and examinations and records the marks made on the machine scored tests.

The high pupil-teacher ratio in the Cultural Heritage area, one teacher for each 500 to 1500 students, makes possible the low ratio, one to thirty-three, for Analysis Groups and highly individual instruction for the exceptional student.

Teachers for the Cultural Heritage program are selected early in their teacher education program. They speak well, like to be before an audience, have a sense for the dramatic and are attractive persons. In addition to intensive work in their field, they are given work in speech, dramatics, logic, and mass media.

Specialization and Creativity

The Analysis Groups, the Cultural Heritage Courses, and the Fundamental Skills work constitute the program required of all.

But, in addition, each student is encouraged to develop a specialization. It is not required, but the opportunity is presented.

Shops, studios and working laboratories are available for specialized activities. All students who wish are encouraged to engage in some creative activities since the Cultural Heritage phase of the program is essentially a passive reception.

Writing laboratories are staffed to help students who want to develop creative writing ability. School newspapers, magazines and telecasts are written in the laboratories.

Other students select work experience in various industries and businesses in the community. These students have decided they will not seek higher education and are using their specialized program to insure a smooth transition to regular employment.

Special opportunities are available for the persons who qualify in terms of ability and intensity of purpose.

Seminars in the various content fields, and some of an interdisciplinary nature, are available for those who can qualify. Students must have displayed unusual ability and show evidence of a desire for individual investigation in a field before they are permitted to enroll.

Seminars are limited to fifteen students. They meet for two two-hour periods per week and the remainder of the time the students conduct independent research in the library or laboratories.

Small laboratories are kept open for full time use by the individual researchers from the seminars. In fact, students who are not expected to become scientists or technicians in an area do not use laboratory facilities. Laboratory experience was abandoned as a general education procedure in the mid-sixties.

In the specialized fields the pupil-teacher ratio is low, one to forty or fifty pupils. Teachers give individualized supervision and plan with the Analysis Group teachers the experiences individuals should have.

No longer do the colleges blame the secondary schools for inadequate preparation. Graduation days have been eliminated. Students continue to work in the secondary school until they pass their college entrance examinations or move to a job. Most students enter the secondary school at thirteen, but some leave at fifteen and others at twenty. A student's decision to leave the program is conditioned by his completion of the Cultural Heritage experiences, his acquisition of fundamental skills, and his individual purposes.

The School Plant   The school plant has many different sized rooms. Analysis groups, specialized education classrooms, studios and laboratories are small. Cultural Heritage courses are held in large halls equipped for lectures and mass media programs. Libraries and studios and shops are large. Areas where individuals work with teaching machines to perfect basic skills are divided into small work cubicles. Buildings with uniform size classrooms are obsolete.

Basis of Support   The program described above is paid for from federal funds. It was recognized in the late sixties that, with a population as mobile as ours, neither local communities nor the national government could afford to allow the great differences in educational opportunity to continue. No community was immune to poor education in another and the national government was thus neglecting a large percentage of its human resources.

Evolution of the Program

The program was not achieved without some difficult struggles. Many voices arose in the late fifties and early sixties clamoring for a copying of a European educational system. Some wanted to use tests and allocate the pupil to a specialized curriculum as early as ten years of age and give him the required courses the experts deemed suitable for him. They proposed restricting the curriculum of the secondary school to the intellectual pursuit of information in certain areas of knowledge. Values and social development were to be left to the home and church.

However, increasing juvenile delinquency, more homes with both parents working, increasing mental and emotional disturbance could not be ignored. The secondary school program had to be made broad enough to deal with values, human relations, fundamental skills in communication, the cultural heritage, as well as work in a student's special field.

Notes

LEADERS OF EDUCATIONAL THOUGHT: A REVIEW/ROBISON

[1] Lewis M. Terman and Maud A. Merrill, *Measuring Intelligence: A Guide to the Administration of the New Revised Stanford-Binet Tests of Intelligence.* (Boston: Houghton-Mifflin Company, 1937), pp. 3–71.
[2] Kurt Lewin, "Field Theory and Experiment in Social Psychology," *American Journal of Sociology,* 1939, p. 874.
[3] Jean Piaget, *The Origins of Intelligence in Children* (New York: International Universities Press, Inc., 1952).
[4] Jean Piaget, *The Construction of Reality in the Child* (New York: Basic Books, Inc., Publishers, 1954), p. 352.

LEARNING IN GROUPS/FRAZIER

[1] Martin Buber, "Dialogue," in *Between Man and Man.*
[2] Arthur D. Morse, *Schools of Tomorrow—Today!*
[3] Franz Kafka, *The Trial.*
[4] Paul Tillich, *Dynamics of Faith.*
[5] Maria Montessori, *The Montessori Method.*

THE SCHOOLS AND RELIGION: THE HISTORICAL PRESENT/ ULICH

[1] *Editors' Note: Disestablishment* is the term commonly used to refer to the separation of church and state in this country. To disestablish, in this sense, is to deprive an institution (the church) of any official connection with the government.
[2] *Editors' Note:* Danish philosopher (1813–1855) who first articulated several of the tenets of modern Existentialism.
[3] *Editors' Note:* the Greek philosopher and mathematician of the sixth century, B.C., who formulated certain key principles in the development of modern mathematics.

Further Reading

In addition to references cited by authors in this Part the following texts may be useful.

Bruner, Jerome S. *The Process of Education.* New York, N.Y.: Vintage Books, 1960.

One of the best works by an author whose writings have influenced curriculum and the learning process in modern American schools.

Lindgren, Henry Clay. *Educational Psychology in the Classroom.* New York, N.Y.: John Wiley and Sons, Inc., 1967.

This text provides up-to-date material on the application of psychological findings in the classroom situation. The student is referred especially to Chapter 5, dealing with the learner and his group.

Reichart, Sandford. *Change and the Teacher*. New York, N.Y.: Thomas Y. Crowell Co., 1969.

This book is an effective treatment of the effects of change upon American schools today.

Robison, Lloyd E. *Human Growth and Development*. Columbus, Ohio: Charles E. Merrill Publishing Co., 1968.

Chapter 3 provides a useful summary of the work of a number of important personages in the field of education.

Winder, Alvin E., and David L. Angus (eds.). *Adolescence: Contemporary Studies*. New York, N.Y.: Van Nostrand Reinhold Co., 1968.

In this collection dealing with a much neglected subject in American education and psychology, the student is referred especially to pages 189–216, dealing with the adolescent peer group.

Films of Related Interest

"Jimmy" National Education Association, 29 min.

The story of a dropout and his decision to return to school.

"Operation Head Start" Bailey Films, 16 min.

Depicts a Head Start program in operation in California. Narrated by Burt Lancaster.

"Our Changing Family Life" McGraw-Hill, 23 min.

Portrays the change from farm living to urban living patterns in the United States (1880–1965).

Part IV

Students on the Threshold: Culturally Different Youth

We come then to the question presented:
Does segregation of children in public
schools solely on the basis of race, even
though the physical facilities and other
"tangible" factors may be equal, deprive
the children of the minority group of
equal educational opportunities? We believe
that it does.

Chief Justice Earl Warren
from Brown v. Board of Education, Topeka, Kansas,
May 17, 1954

It is difficult to discuss education at all today without introducing the issue of the so-called disadvantaged or culturally different school-age children and youth. The term seems to become more inclusive as our awareness of those who exhibit unique cultural heritages expands. It now includes such diverse elements as Indian children who have never seen the inside of a city, black children who have never been outside the city, Spanish-speaking children of Puerto Rican parents whose heritage is largely that of another part of the world, and the youth of the Appalachian mountains region, many of whose ancestors came to this country earlier than those of most readers—and authors—of this book.

Cultural diversity is not a new challenge for American education, as we have seen from the historical and sociological selections earlier in this volume. Why then the current attention to cultural differences in education—at a time when the country seems in many respects more homogeneous than ever before, through the uniting effects of a common communications network which brings the same television programs, the same news, into every home; when our cities, suburbs, and even our countryside, our forms of dress, our food, appear to become more and more similar as time passes? America's schools have a long history of acting as the filter through which generations of ethnic minorities have passed into the mainstream of society. Italians, Jews, Greeks, and dozens of other immigrant groups have achieved upward mobility—and concomitant aspirations—which they acquired in American schools. Why then do today's "culturally different" young people seem to pose a new challenge?

Some have speculated that the non-mainstream youth of today constitute more than just another challenge—that they constitute, in effect, a threat —to the educational system. Others have gone so far as to suggest that a significant number of mainstream youth are beginning to respond to the schools in a manner that is not very dissimilar from that of their counterparts who have not enjoyed the usual American advantages.

The question is complex. If we were to try to formulate some tentative generalized answer, however, it would probably revolve around the idea that the group of young people we call "disadvantaged" are, first and foremost, those who **do not learn** according to the established content and methods of our schools. But once we make a statement like this, a flood of questions arises.

Are the content and methods of contemporary schools obsolescent?

Is it that these "disadvantaged" students do not learn because they cannot, or because they do not wish to?

What is society's responsibility to young people who mount attacks on the schools, who wish to change them to fit their own wishes?

How is it possible to accommodate both mainstream and non-mainstream students in the same educational system?

What educational problems exist for the following special groups among our citizens: Blacks, the Urban Poor, Migrants, American Indians?

To what extent is it the responsibility of education to facilitate upward mobility among disadvantaged groups in our fast-moving, technological age?

What would you estimate to be the minimum education an individual needs in order to support himself in our society?

What is happening to traditional concepts of "work" in our society? To the concepts of "professional," "skilled," "unskilled"? What kinds of work do today's youth want to do? How can the schools respond?

"Relevance" has been among the most widely used terms in the rhetoric about contemporary education. What are some of the things it signifies? Are they relatively new to American education, or is "relevance" just a new term for an old problem?

Are the concerns and needs of "disadvantaged" youth entirely dissimilar, in your opinion, from those of mainstream youth?

How effectively has integration been implemented in American schools since the Supreme Court decision of 1954?

Can We Categorize the Children of the Poor?

Robert J. Fisher

One of the curious by-products of the awakening interest in the educational fate of the children of the . . . poor is the inappropriateness of vocabulary in current usage. Every few years a new term is coined, but none of the terms is quite satisfactory. Who are these children and how shall we describe them? How can we counteract stereotypes, avoid a patronizing point of view, and keep from offending the people themselves? If these children are *culturally-deprived*, who deprived them of their culture? If they are *underprivileged*, what privileges have been taken away? If they are *educationally-handicapped*, what evidence do we have to support this? If they are *lower-class*, why won't they admit it?

If we cannot find a word or a concept to encompass adequately what we want to say, could it be that we really are not clear about what we are trying to describe? We are trying to reduce a complicated convergence of forces, problems, conflicts, and social dislocation involving a multitude of people into simplified descriptive terms. We are currently seeking answers to failures we have long recognized: our inability to provide adequate educational opportunities for the children of the urban poor. Within the older sections of our larger cities the most pressing problems of our nation converge and baffle us. As usual, our society looks to education for long-range social solutions. But we have difficulty even trying to describe the people who live in our cities. Sometimes, we assume that if we give them a name we will create a reality with which we can then deal as if it were something tangible and capable of descriptive analysis.

Taking five of the current terms in common usage, we can ask: How adequately do they really describe reality?

1. *Culturally-Deprived Children* Anyone who is deprived of a culture must certainly be in a bad way. We get visions of illiterate children grunting incomprehensibly at each other, living in barren rooms, stricken by the debilitating influences of poverty, neglect, and cultural disorganization. In actuality, no children can exist deprived of a culture. Children who grow up in the inner city have an influential, meaningful, even rich and varied culture which often teaches them more quickly and forcefully how to cope with the demands of the environment than the culture of suburbia teaches suburban children.

The cultural demands of the big city may be neither pleasant nor enhancing. There is nothing romantic about poverty. But children learn to cope with demands, meet crises, and survive challenges. They just do not learn much of this in school rooms; they learn more on the streets and in overcrowded living quarters. Some facets of the subculture stimulate the fears, angers, and disapproval of many middle-class educators, but in some respects this is because educators themselves are "deprived" of an understanding and appreciation of the culture in which these children function.

What people really mean to say when they use the term "culturally-deprived" is that these children do not have the advantages of a culturally-rich environment with a capital "C." These children do not have books and magazines in the home, stereophonic records, well-furnished rooms, green grass, and frame houses. Their parents do not use a rich and varied vocabulary, buy their offspring educational toys or children's books or records, nor indoctrinate them with the niceties of acceptable manners and morals.

Instead, culturally-deprived children are viewed as functionally illiterate for school achievement, unable to communicate, with limited experience, flattened by an impoverished environment. Pre-school programs which attempt to foster communication skills, build experiential backgrounds, and release potentials of creativity are noteworthy attempts to enrich the "impoverished culture." Such programs may improve falsely-depressed intelligence test scores and stimulate initial success in reading, that over-riding criterion of school adequacy.

But what is overlooked in any assessment of cultural deprivation are the cultural opportunities and cultural challenges which the neighborhood environment does provide. After all, have not people been living in cities for hundreds of years and learning much that is significant from the streets and alleys, store fronts and city playgrounds, schools and churches, and crowded living quarters?

2. *Underprivileged Children* What privileges have poor children in the city been denied? Do we assume that to be denied the opportunity to grow up in the suburbs to the hum of power lawnmowers, the smell of backyard barbecues, and the ting-a-ling of the Good Humor man's truck is debilitating? We dislike the hustling traffic of the city streets. We reject the noises, smells, dangers, and disorganization of crowded living conditions. We flee, if we are able, to the suburbs and create family patterns, recreational patterns, and housing facilities that symbolically serve to ward off the unpleasant reminders of our harried existence.

We assume that city children are denied the good life by not partaking of the joys which relative economic security and relatively stable family patterns provide. This may be true enough, but there are still large numbers of tense and anxious children living in suburbia. On the other hand, even though the children of the urban poor lack many economic and cultural privileges and may even have to endure hunger and neglect, they may not be suffering as much from lack of privilege as is sometimes assumed. The handicaps of the underprivileged are relative. How hurtful is the lack of privacy? What is the consequence of a diet which lacks food from the Basic Seven? The absence of a father figure is a more serious deprivation, but are there not other male models in the neighborhood who are available to the children of a fatherless home? Often overlooked in descriptions of the instability of the urban family are the available sources of love and support and even encouragement from parents, siblings, neighbors, and members of the extended family.

No useful purpose is served by either deploring, on the one hand, or disregarding, on the other, the difficulties of overcrowded urban living. It is tough to grow up without the privileges which a stable family life and relative economic security can provide. But it is a mistake to categorize the central city and the suburb as two opposing poles on the happiness-misery continuum. The city and the suburb are simply different locales where people struggle, with not much more success in one place than another, to meet a host of challenging demands. There are "underprivileged" children trying under serious handicaps to mature in both kinds of settings. There are "privileged" children who are being given help and support in both settings as well. Needless to say, the significant privileges may well be the more intangible factors involved in loving relationships than those resulting from material surroundings.

3. *Educationally-Handicapped Children* A large number of children in the central cities suffer educational handicaps. They may be receiving an inappropriate education at an inadequately supported school in an out-dated building staffed by personnel who have considerable difficulty identifying with their culture, motivation, behavior, and moral code. But this term is not used, as a rule, to describe the handicaps encountered by these children in their attempt to make sense out of the education provided for them. Instead it usually is used to *describe the children* who do not seem to succeed in large enough numbers in meeting the extrinsic demands of the school system.

Existence of educational handicaps is simple to document. When compared to children in more favored sections of the city or in the suburbs, the mean scores of central-city children on standardized achievement tests are lower. The children start out with lower mean achievement scores in the first grade, and, as the children progress through the grades, the mean achievement scores become somewhat lower yet than those of their counterparts in more well-to-do neighborhoods. Later the young people drop out of school in larger numbers, attend college in smaller numbers, get into trouble in larger numbers, and are a credit to their teachers in smaller numbers.

Various explanations are given. Seldom do we now hear that this lower educational achievement is the result of biological or cultural inferiority. Instead the surroundings are blamed. The parents, the neighborhoods, the peer groups, the crowded conditions, and all the results of cultural deprivation and poverty are deplored. Programs to modify the culture and to enrich the environment in order to stimulate higher achievement test results have been given considerable publicity.

And yet just what do standardized test results reveal? What

do they measure? How does the reporting of mean scores obscure differences? What kinds of comparisons are being made between groups and how valid are such comparisons?

In the first place, standardized achievement tests are ill suited to measure even the present achievement and certainly not the potential achievement of children whose culture deviates from the norm. The educational profession has already accepted this limitation of standardized intelligence tests. But achievement test scores with their seemingly self-evident grade-level norms need to be as rigorously challenged.

In the second place, standardized achievement tests in wide use today measure only a small segment of the curriculum. They may not even measure the important objectives in the skill subjects; they usually pay scant attention to the content fields in science and social studies; and they certainly do little to measure such objectives as problem-solving, creative thinking, artistic expression, skills of group living, independent judgment, and physical strength or dexterity.

In the third place, it is likely that achievement tests ignore the motivation, the thinking patterns, and even the environment and vocabulary of children in the central cities. If this is true of standardized intelligence tests, why would it not be equally true of standardized achievement tests? What if children lack understanding about what they are asked to do? What if children are not challenged to "do their best" on a seemingly meaningless task with no rewards that make any sense to them?

But with all the weaknesses of achievement tests—and there are many others—the startling surprise is that a large number of poor children do "pass" the tests. To report test results in terms of mean scores always obscures the great variability within any given sample. Many children in the most impoverished neighborhoods score at or above grade level on even the most inappropriate instruments.

The term "educationally handicapped" when based upon test results has the weakness of reducing that which is used to judge adequacy of performance to that which is currently being measured. One of the greatest educational handicaps many children suffer results from the attempt to assess achievement and potential by inappropriate instruments and from the unwarranted generalizations made on the basis of such inadequate evidence.

4. *Lower-Class Children* So far in this discussion, the term "lower-class" has been deliberately avoided. It is a useful term, a

sociological construct, commonly employed to describe behavior and conditions which can be contrasted with another sociological construct, the middle-class. In using these constructs we need to recognize that they are abstractions which obscure or ignore more differences than they describe.

Of course, the term "lower-class" or that more precise descriptive category the "lower-lower class" tends to be offensive to the people described. Educators have shied away from these terms and have been searching for a euphemism which seems less offensive. At times the terms "working-class" or "blue-collar class" have been used, but these two concepts are not interchangeable with the "lower-lower class" category.

None of the class-associated terms has been successful in communicating with teachers. They tend to create stereotyped images which block effective communication. They also make people who are not sociologists uncomfortable. Indeed, much of the effort to find a term to describe poor people and their children is the search for an inoffensive, non-judgmental term which will communicate accurately. None of the terms thus far discussed seems adequate.

5. *Children of the Urban Poor* This is a concept which is seldom applied in the current literature, perhaps because it is largely an economic rather than a cultural or a sociological term. In one sense, it may well be that which most of the people discussed do have (or lack) in common. Poor people do not have enough money. With few exceptions they exist at a standard of living which is inadequate. The children of the poor are very different from each other, but the children and their parents have poverty in common.

As a profession we have recently become more concerned about the education of children in congested urban areas. We are concerned about poor children. We are talking about large numbers of fairly recent migrants to the city as well as the long-term urban poor who have been trapped in deteriorating sections while others have escaped to the outer rings of the city or the suburbs. We are talking about the Negro poor, the Puerto Rican poor, the Appalachian white poor, and the second and third generation poor of earlier immigrant families. We are talking about poor people, but we have difficulty understanding that most poor people retain a sense of dignity and purpose in life and that they subscribe to positive cultural values.

There are sub-cultural differences among ethnic segments of

the poor, and there are cultural differences between the poor and those with adequate incomes in our society. There is plenty of evidence of cultural disorganization in the so-called "slums." But in popularized articles, at least, this cultural disorganization is often overdramatized. Conditions in the congested urban areas are bad enough, but there are patterns of life available which can and do provide children with psychologically healthy means for learning to accommodate to cultural demands.

The trouble is that once we have agreed that poor people have poverty in common, we have not said very much. Poor people have many children, and these children are very different from each other. They grow up in an environment which confronts them with untold hazards but which also offers a larger degree of release from parental pressures, more freedom to move about and explore, and more ready access to immediate sources of pleasure and satisfaction than the more supervised play of more economically favored neighborhoods. Schools just do not happen to be one of the sources of pleasure and satisfaction for many of the children of the urban poor.

The schools which these children attend will need to build upon the sounds and smells, the voices and vocabulary, the motives and the problems which the city culture provides. One move in this direction will be a readiness on the part of educators to accept cultural differences in the infinite variety in which they are found on the big city streets and to stop trying to reduce this variety by use of terms that tend to obscure reality.

In summary, each of the terms in current usage has unfortunate connotations, since each encourages stereotypes, is based on faulty conceptualization, and detracts from the potential of the surrounding environment for learning. The most accurate and the least offensive concept is poverty, particularly if poverty is conceived as an objective economic condition. Current federal poverty legislation is designed to improve economic opportunities. This is probably what the poor need most of all—the opportunity to take their place within the mainstream of American culture through better available economic opportunities. Educational opportunity is increasingly the door to economic opportunity. The poor need not always be with us. With adequate educational provisions, the children of the poor are still our greatest untapped resource.

Cultural Deprivation as a Factor in School Learning[1]

Hilda Taba

The term "culturally deprived child" suggests only a variation on a theme. It denotes a group of children who previously were called problem children, retarded, slow learners, underprivileged, and under-achievers. It is hoped that this new appellation is more than just another euphemism, that it indicates both a new statement of the problem we are facing and a new approach to it. The previous designations described only the difficulties of such a group in school. "Cultural deprivation" points to a possible cause of the phenomenon.

For some sort of a theoretical orientation, four questions need to be asked about this theme: (1) What is the situation? (2) What are the social and psychological factors which account for it? (3) What is the educational problem? (4) What is the task of the schools?

The Situation

Two developments seem to be responsible for the present interest in cultural deprivation as a factor in school learning. One, curiously enough, is a consequence of our success in achieving an educational goal dictated by the democratic ideal. The fact that school attendance approaches the 100 percent limit of the school-age group represents a fulfillment of this ideal of providing education for all the children of all of the American people. But this attainment also creates another phenomenon with which our schools seemingly are not prepared to cope. As the percentages of the age groups attending school increase, school also draws increasingly from the "bottom of the pile." The able, the adjusted, and the motivated, the upper 30 percent in ability, have always been in school. Extension of school attendance can only add students from the lower end of the span: the emotionally and the physically handicapped, the less willing and able, and the less motivated, those less able to cope with the school culture and its expectations, or even hostile to what school represents. The result is that the school population becomes more heterogeneous in practically every conceivable respect.

The second development is the increasing migration from the rural areas into the great industrial cities. These large centers draw people both from the rural areas of the United States and from other countries: Negroes and Puerto Ricans in the East; Spanish-Americans, Mexicans, and Indians in the Southwest; and marginal farmers and hillbillies everywhere (Jenks, 1962). The 1950 U.S. census figures indicate that of this population 25 percent have either themselves migrated from foreign countries or have foreign-born parents. (Bureau of Census, 1956).

Many of these people are actually making a jump from the Eighteenth to the Twentieth century in one generation. This transition involves a difficult adaptation, for it represents not only a shift from a simpler culture into a more complex one but also into a society which is mechanized, anonymous, and alienated. Recently the debilitating effect of unemployment or the threat of it has been added. In this culture individuals and families are cut off from familiar contact; there are few sources for advice and support for what one is, and little reinforcement for the values these groups brought with them. In addition, in urban centers, these migrants are hemmed in in encapsulated environments which prevent opportunities to learn the larger culture in which they exist. Instead the city surrounds them with the hedonism of slum life, and with a dangerous freedom born of anonymity which permits license without teaching the limits and controls.

These conditions create the problems facing the schools in the great cities: an increasing heterogeneity and an increasing social distance between the school culture and that of the home and the neighborhood. The greater the social distance, the greater also the difficulty in using the means of learning that the school provides, the likelihood of hostility to school, and the resistance to what it teaches.

Among the children from such conditions the usual difficulties that plague the public school in large cities are magnified. They show generally poor performance. They have a high proportion of failure, of drop-outs, of reading and learning disabilities, and innumerable life-adjustment problems. Sexton's tables of correlations between income and education show that the lower income groups show a consistently lower performance on practically every index: they have lower I.Q.'s, achievement, and grades; poorer health; and are beset with deficiencies in reading and language, the two chief tools on which success in school depends. The yield of merit scholars by professions and income levels dramatizes this discrepancy. In producing merit scholars the professors' families are at the top, and especially so the sons and daughters of librarians. This group produces 234 merit scholars per 12,672 families. At the lowest end are the laborers. They produce one merit scholar per 3,581,370 families (Sexton, 1961). Since it seems reasonable to assume that potentiality is distributed much more evenly than the incidence of merit scholarships suggests, one must look for some other factors at work.

Meanwhile, quantitatively, the problem is increasing. According to Reissman (1962) in 1950 fourteen large cities had one culturally deprived child in ten; in 1960 there was one in three; and the prediction is that in 1970 there will be one in two. Fifty percent of the children in schools in these cities will come from environments that can be described as culturally deprived. Deutsch (1962) suggests, in addition, that at least in elementary schools anywhere from 40 to 70 percent of the students will be from minority groups.

These conditions also indicate the new proportions of the problem which confronts the public schools: the task of providing adequate and equal educational opportunities not only for the few exceptions from the rule, but for masses of students who do not or cannot respond to its curriculum and instruction. This means that a large proportion of future citizens will grow up not only poorly equipped academically, but that the effectiveness of the school as a socializing agent is diminished also. Social distance between the school culture and the home culture results in the inability to use the means of learning that the school provides, generates hostility to school, and resistance to what it teaches.

This is not news. In 1950, Allison Davis made a dramatic impact on the audience at the White House Conference on Education by declaring that 40 percent of children go through school untouched by it, except for acquiring a meager literacy. As characters, as persons, as possessors of academic competency, they might just as well not have been in school. From this population we get disproportionate contributions to delinquency, particularly among the brighter ones because their genius and energy turns to organizing delinquent activities in order to express their antisocial feelings.

The Psychological Meaning of Cultural Deprivation

It is one thing to recognize the difficulties. It is another matter to build a theoretical understanding of the causes of these difficulties and the psychological dynamics which underlie them. A sound theoretical basis for educational programs must be based on the understanding of the culture of the groups that feel the critical impact of cultural deprivation.

The relationship between cultural background and school learning is not simple and not too well understood. More or less adequate research is available on social-class differences in values, behavior patterns, and aspirations. We know, for example, that the homes of these children have a limited educational tradition and, hence, also little "know-how" about the school and its expectation. Not only are the parents themselves uneducated, they also have a meager understanding of the requirements for success in school. Therefore, they cannot help their children with academic content, skills in conduct, or in kindling aspiration for continued education.

Generally, also, the parents of these children have low ambitions for the educational careers of their children. And what ambitions they have, they cannot communicate for lack of proper models or because they are in the dark about the operational steps or means necessary for preparing the child to take advantage of the available learning opportunities. Negro boys, for example, tend to have no model of a successful male. Consequently, they have no psychological framework which suggests that effort can result at least in the possibility of achievement (Deutsch, 1962).

This phenomenon has been described in numerous studies. Kahl (1953), for example, compared the college aspirations of the "common man's" sons with sufficient ability to qualify for college work, with boys from the middle or upper-middle class families on the same ability level. Scarcely any of the parents in the "common man" group perceived a college education as an objective for their sons. Those who had aspirations did not know what was needed to realize them. The author observed a similar phenomenon in an all-white, lower-class eighth grade in an eastern industrial city. While the parents who were interviewed about their ambitions for their children indicated interest in college, these ambitions were vague and planless (Taba, 1955). These facts, probably, still hold in spite of the recent rise in the level of aspirations, especially among the Negroes.

Culturally disadvantaged children also lack the skills and the habits necessary for meeting the expectations of conduct in school. The author has observed first-grade classrooms where the children did not even distinguish one piece of paper from another one. They might tear out a page from one book to make a marker for another, then cherish a piece of toilet paper. They had had no training in disciplined group behavior, such as the middle-class child gets around the dinner table, because they seldom had dinner as a family group. Consequently, they lacked the habits and skills necessary for reading in groups. The teacher reported her bafflement at the fact that these children sat down obediently enough, but soon would go each about his own business.

The stories these children dictated about their families provided the clues. There were recurring examples of such behavior, especially when facing a conflict. When father gets mad he "goes away and stays all night"; when brother gets mad "he goes to a baseball game"; when mother gets mad she "takes us to the movies and doesn't bring us back".

Similar observations abound about difficulties with speaking or being spoken to in groups, and such virtues cherished in school as cleanliness, punctuality, and orderliness. Instead of being perceived by teachers as functional habits learned at home and in the neighborhood, such behavior is treated as malicious conduct to be corrected by appropriate punishment.

Another series of difficulties result from lack of readiness for the learning tasks in school. Children from such homes and neighborhoods may be potentially able, but developmentally retarded so far as learning to read and to master the content of school subjects is concerned.

Since schools can measure only the functioning capacity, individual potentiality is a vague quality about which we know little. It is obvious that individual potentiality is an unmarketable commodity if the child has no means of developing it, or if there are no ways of identifying it. Our instruments identify only a particular limited kind of potentiality, namely, the capacity to manipulate verbal symbols and abstractions. These are precisely the accomplishments which are the least stimulated in the culturally deprived environment.

Recently some observations have emerged regarding the role of stimulus deprivation in intelligence and learning. Studies of intelligence point out that intelligence is a product of a transaction between an individual and the environmental stimulation. For example, Miner (1957) describes intellectual stimulation as a product of the interrelationship of three factors: individual potential, motivation, and environmental stimulation. Individual potential is presumably evenly distributed among all groups of people and is probably greater than we have as yet learned how to release. Environmental stimulation involves more than the degree, complexity, and variation of the environment. It also involves motivation, or the extent to which the environment affects the individual's responses. Different individuals respond to different cues in the same environment. The variations in these responses are generated in part by the individual's motivation and in part by the availability of adult mediation in facilitating conceptualization. A potentially rich environment may therefore be functionally unstimulating and, in reverse, a limited environment may be highly stimulating if it is exploited to the fullest. Variety in stimulation combined with mediation tends to sharpen and to force the accommodating modification in the mental structure.

Deutsch (1962) points out that the greater the variety of stimulation and the number of situations which challenge modification of conceptualization, the more mobile and differentiated the mental structure becomes. In other words, the more the child hears, sees, and interprets, or is being helped to interpret, the more likely he will want to see and hear, and the more he will get from what he sees and hears. The greater the variety of reality situations with which the child has coped the greater his ability to cope (Deutsch, 1962). Any of these conditions—limited environment, a lack of systematic and ordered interpretation and mediation, or a limited motivation (or a combination of them)— may bring about stimulus deprivation and with it a deficiency in the development of intelligence.

Some researchers suggest that the conditions of life in slums tend to be meager in all these respects. Deutsch points out that slum life provides a minimum range of stimulation and of opportunity to manipulate objects or to experiment with them in an orderly manner. Restriction in the range of the variety of input limits the output in expression, and reduces precision and the ability to perceive relationships or other abstract qualities, such as size, shape, distance, and time (Deutsch, 1962).

The lack of mediation, in addition, reduces the opportunities to link experience with interpretation of it, i.e., with the ability to convert objects and events to verbal symbols, to explore casual relationships, and to form abstractions.

Examination of the diary materials of lower-class children in city slums confirms this. These diaries describe the typical day, characterized by a rapid shift from one activity to another one, by lack of attention to one thing. One is impressed with the meagerness of experiences with abstraction. For example, dinner-time, which is the only time when parents and children are together, tends to be spent on two things: to mete out the punishments for infractions committed the day before, and to allocate the chores to be done. In one group of twenty-five eighth graders, only one family used dinner-time to describe what happened to them as persons during the day (Taba, 1955). Bernstein (1960) points out, further, that the lower-class conversations are limited to the immediate instant and generally do not include time sequences, relationships between concepts, logical sequences, or causal relationships.

Thus, the problem of deficiency is not limited to non-verbality or bi-lingualism. It includes also the level of cognitive skills and of relationships expressed in whatever language is used. This combination of non-verbal orientation and an absence of conceptualization alone may very well account for what we call low intelligence.

Recently the possibility has been suggested that early stimulation may be crucial in laying the psychological foundation for the capacity to process information. If this should be true, early stimulus deprivation may create a lifelong handicap in response capacity and in the assimilating and manipulating of facts and ideas (Hebb, 1949; Hunt, 1961).

The factors and conditions described above create deficiencies in the skills and the mental equipment necessary for success in school tasks: the ability to distinguish the meaning of one word from that of another; the capacity to handle the abstractions which organize the physical, geographical, and geometric characteristics of the environment; and the capacity for sustained attention.

Cognitive deficiencies alone, no matter how serious, might be easier to correct, if it were not for the additional complications of emotional characteristics and attitudes. The psychologists describe a syndrome of feelings and attitudes which the majority of culturally deprived children tend to share as follows: both the family climate and experience tend to induce a feeling of alienation; their self concept is low; they question their own worth, fear being challenged, have a desire to cling to the familiar, and have many feelings of guilt and shame; there is a limited trust in adults, they tend to respond with trigger-like reactions, are hyperactive, and have generally a low standard of conduct; and they usually show apathy and lack of responsiveness. It is difficult for them to form meaningful relationships (Krogman, 1956).

These tendencies translate themselves into an attitudinal orientation which is difficult for teachers to understand: a negative attitude toward school, teachers, and achievement; the tendency to seek immediate gratification over and above any long-range purposes; the freer use of violence in solving conflicts than is permissible in a school setting. Some of this conduct, such as fighting, plays havoc in school and is therefore a great cause for disciplinary action and misinterpretation. Haystack, a seventh grader, stated the difference between the teacher's perception and that of a slum child rather neatly when he said: "Teachers are funny, they are so afraid of a leetle beet of fighting." What Haystack described as a "little bit of fighting" was a regular gang war.

Discrepancies exist also between the motivating devices used in school and the motivational patterns. Achievement as a means of making further education possible is relatively little understood. Getting by rather than getting ahead is, therefore, the rule. Hence, grades, promotions, and all other external similar incentives used by the schools will not work nearly as well as expected.

Factors in School Experience

The experience in school adds to the difficulties described above. Variations in background naturally create a discrepancy between the cognitive, perceptual, and emotional development of the child and the school expectations and curriculum. The differences in the meanings involved in the content of the curriculum and the meanings which the children from a deviate background attach to the verbal cues of that content is one example of this discrepancy and, therefore, also one factor in the deficiency in academic performance. This discrepancy is more than a deficit in skills. It is a discontinuity between the conceptual scheme developed and meanings acquired in previous experience and that employed or implied in the curriculum and teaching. The description of one fourth-grader of what a policeman means to him is a vivid illustration of this discontinuity (Taba, 1955).

> To tell the truth, I don't like policemen, because one day I was walking on Broad Street and I saw a police car on Western Avenue. There were no police there. I waited for a while. Soon the police came out of the house. They had a man and a girl with them. The man and the girl were put in the police car, and taken away to the jail. I don't know what they had done, but the reason I don't like cops is because they are so rough when they arrest people. They didn't have to push the girl down when they put her in the car.
>
> Yes, I would have run home if a cop had stopped me fighting in the street, because I am afraid of a cop. I did run away once and hid in my house. I was playing on the roofs of some houses with some other boys and the ball went through a skylight and broke it. The cops heard us and chased us. I ran home, but some boys must have told him, for he came to my home. He said that if I didn't let him in he was going to come in through the window and get me. I knew I had to open the door then. He said, "Why'd you break that skylight for?" "I ain't been out. I been right here like my father told me." He said, "You are lying, boy, because I saw you run." I kept right on lying and he left. I was afraid, just shaking, and I felt like bursting out crying, but the cop didn't know that. He thought I was tough.

The above image of the "cop" is very different from the one which the teacher was using in talking about policemen as "community helpers."

Similar discontinuities exist in the meanings of such terms as cooperation and control. A considerable proportion of material which describes family life, homes, human relations, or the work of the world consists of content which is alien to the experience of these children. For example, when a teacher in a semi-rural, lower-class area showed the pictures of the homes in primers and asked whether they knew these homes, a loud "No" arose in response. Yet, when asked to describe the homes they knew, the descriptions were both sensible and differentiated. They talked of large families who had to live in small houses, and the problems that this situation created. They could describe adequately a variety of homes, including trailers and shacks. They were just not acquainted with white houses with green shutters, in front of which stood a smiling mother with a starched white apron welcoming a father returning home carrying a briefcase. Naturally, such alien content makes the mastery of reading skills vastly more difficult.

The differences between the social learning of the children from culturally deviate backgrounds and the schools create also severe acculturation problems, which further affect their academic performance. It is difficult for any person to span two cultures. For the first-grader from a culturally deviate environment, the spanning of two cultures represents a difficult enough task to be described as culture shock. The psychological consequences of this shock could be mild or severe, depending on the distance between his particular culture, his expectations, his level of understanding, and those of the school. If the discontinuities in the demands of the two contending cultures are mild they may only impede the socialization power of the school. If they are severe they may lead to disorganization or neurotic behavior (Allinsmith and Goethals, 1956).

The problem of acculturation is still more difficult for the minority children, for in their case the problems of isolation, language, conduct and the difficulties with academic content converge. Elam (1960) describes cases resulting in a total incapacity to respond. Writing about the Puerto Rican children in New York, he describes the consequences of the acculturation shock which causes them to cease responding altogether. They evade responsibility because to function is to fail. The safest thing is not to respond at all. Milder cases are observed in which children "tune out" when directions are given.

School often adds to the difficulty by failing to recognize the problem, to diagnose the gaps, and by demanding too abrupt a transition, by paying too little attention to the role school life plays in facilitating acculturation.

Finally, there is the problem of the hidden I.Q., which is

created by the nature of the tests used for diagnosing ability, for grouping, and for setting expectations. Since it is well known that generally the children from culturally deprived areas earn lower I.Q.'s, and since it seems difficult to believe that the potential ability is distributed according to economic or social privilege, the appropriateness of the measures of ability has been questioned. Guilford (1956) has attacked the concept of I.Q. as a single ability and points out that intelligence tests results do not reflect either cultural or personal variations, because they are compounded of too narrow a range of abilities. Sigel (1963) says that such tests have limited usefulness, because the "rightness" of the response is determined by the cultural conventions assumed by the testmaker. This imposition of a cultural convention is the case when Mexican children with no experience with saucers pair the cup with the table, instead of with the saucer, and are marked wrong—even though the pairing is perfectly logical in the light of their experience. Thus the culturally biased choice of the test content, together with the limitation in the mental systems represented in the performance required, produces the phenomenon of a hidden I.Q. and undiscovered potential. As Eells and Haggard suggest, the I.Q. may be described as the cement which fixes the individual to the class of his birth (Eells, 1953; Haggard, 1954).

These deficiencies in the background and the problems encountered in the school compound themselves into a vicious circle. Culturally deprived children come to school with acculturation problems, an ill-developed capacity to differentiate and to conceptualize experience, and less well-developed verbal articulation than the school work requires. This results in lower performance on ability tests, which leads to designating them as slow learners or low achievers. This reduces the already low self-esteem and self-expectation. Meanwhile, these children are required to learn the most crucial skill—reading—at a point at which the acculturation problems are at their peak. The first-graders from culturally deprived homes thus carry a double load in their first school year: that of mastering a new skill, while handicapped with problems of acculturation and lack of readiness for reading. Naturally, it is impossible for them to master either task adequately.

Moreover, the "socialization" process is carried on in the school in a manner which induces conflict between the child and his home. In effect, this process requires him to deprecate both himself and his parents, his way of life and the values which he has invested with feelings and emotional identification, and on which, therefore, his self-esteem rests.

The net result is that these students are labelled uneducable and treated as such. Little is expected of them and little is offered. The students, in turn, expect little and get little. Comparatively speaking, such students "get dumber" as they grow older. By the fifth grade they are three years behind. This, in turn, adds to lowering of self-expectation and generates hostility to school, teachers, and the whole business of learning. This is probably the dynamics which turns those children who in kindergarten are described as curious, cute, affectionate, warm, independently dependent, and mischievous, into the ones described in the fourth grade as alienated, withdrawn, angry, passive, and apathetic (Deutsch, 1962). Something is happening in this three-year interval for which the school itself is responsible.

The Task of the School

The contemplation of the above facts redefines the task of the school. First and foremost is the task of developing a better understanding of the implications of the social and psychological dynamics of cultural deprivation, and the translation of this understanding into educational programs: the training of teachers and administrators, and the planning of curriculum and instruction.

Another important requirement is to recognize the complexity and seriousness of the problem. One is distressed to observe the repeated efforts to effect a "cure" by crash programs which depend on some simple single device, such as remedial reading, counseling, visits to the opera, or reciting poetry in old English. If there is a principle governing the program-building for these children, it is that no single device will suffice for a complexity of factors has produced the problem.

Educators also need to realize that the lack of success in school for certain groups of children suggests a two-way cause: the factors residing in the backgrounds of the children and the factors residing in the school program. Usually, the efforts to diagnose the problems have overemphasized the first and overlooked the second. Somehow, the fact has escaped our attention that the basic features of our curriculum and instructional methods were formulated when only the most able and willing constituted the school populations. Therefore, the programs tend to stress remedial measures ahead of the possibility of revising the fundamental approach to curriculum and teaching in order to effect prevention.

A careful diagnosis of the emotional dynamics and the cognitive styles of deviate children is necessary for effective program building in many different ways, irrespective of whether or not we regard the objective to be to enable these children to adopt the middle-class ways. Sufficient knowledge of the cognitive styles is needed to provide optimum opportunities for learning. The understanding of the emotional dynamics is indispensible for treating these children as individuals, and as human beings with positive qualities, instead of as so many minuses and gaps. This knowledge also is essential to finding proper ways for eliminating the blocks to learning. These are tasks that should have priority over the remedial programs to correct disabilities in skills.

If the double burden of dealing simultaneously with acculturation problems and learning is to be avoided, supplementary experience in early education seems almost a necessity. Administratively, this possibility may be implemented by an ungraded sequence in the first few years, by an addition of a pre-school year devoted to the task of filling the gaps in experience, or by postponing the learning of reading. Such an addition stands a chance of preventing the formation of a negative attitude towards learning, and a lowering of self-esteem. It is possible, moreover, that the separation of these tasks would do more to improve the level of achievement than any single measure.

Unlocking the hidden potentiality requires a more radical change in the program. Both the materials and the methods of teaching need to be brought into line with the psychological realities of these children. At least in the primary grades, the content of curriculum needs to be in tune with their out-of-school experience or else derived from experiences provided by the school. Producing reading material in school in the form of stories written about some gripping and exciting experiences is not beyond possibility, as demonstrated by one first grade which produced enough stories on one trip to San Francisco harbor to last for an entire year. The stories were, in fact, well written, beautifully illustrated, included poetry, and used a precise as well as a beautiful vocabulary. Evidently, the use of this material eliminated the problem of motivation to read: children were observed coming to school and reading the stories (covering three walls) before they even removed their coats (Landis, n.d.).

Research on the cognitive style and language patterns cited above suggests also the need to capitalize on materials and tasks using operational and concrete, rather than verbal, stimuli. To cultivate mental activity without the hindrance of poor language development indicates the value of using audio-visual materials developed with the purpose of providing for concrete thought operations through manipulation and experimentation with objects and processes. In effect, this would amount to providing a greater variety of modes of learning. In addition to learning from books, provisions are needed for examining objects and processes and emphasizing analysis, comparison, and precision in verbal description to cultivate the mental structures with which to turn later to books.

A considerable shift may be needed in the motivational devices also. The research on motivational patterns suggests the futility of emphasis on external rewards and the need for stressing the kindling of curiosity, the opportunities for experiencing one's power over the materials, and other intrinsic motivating devices.

It is surprising to note that in spite of considerable evidence of the efficacy of "belonging" in school life as a factor in enhancing learning and staying power, so little has been done in the current programs for the culturally deprived toward creating fuller participation in school life and forms of grouping and of learning which enhance interaction and a sense of belonging. Opportunities for interaction which are present within a sufficient heterogeneity in cultural background and ability would permit some learning of the culture across the shoulder, so to say. The learning of the common culture is too often made difficult when this learning has to be accomplished across the social distance, from verbal exhortations, and not from models and examples. Wisely designed cultural heterogeneity in classrooms probably would do much to reduce the cultural deprivation by providing models for motivation, conduct, ways of thinking, and aspirations—as well as for language patterns.

All this adds up to a conception of education as a countervailing agent. In today's climate, which emphasizes excellence and "no-nonsense" disciplined learning, the idea that school be a countervailing force may not be too popular. It is much easier to assume that if Moore at Yale can teach the three-year-olds to read, early training in reading for all children is not only possible but also desirable. Yet, for culturally deprived children, school must be supplementary and counteract their social learning if they are to have an equal opportunity to learn. School must fill the gaps left by social learning at home and mend the conflict between the culture of the home and of the school.

The Overlooked Positives of Disadvantaged Groups

Frank Riessman

I have been interested in the problems of lower socio-economic groups for about [twenty] years, during most of which time there has been a lack of concern for educational problems of children from low-income families. In the last [ten] years, however, this attitude has changed markedly. There is now an enormous interest on the part of practitioners and academic people in this problem. I think we are on the point of a major breakthrough in terms of dealing with this question.

After appraising a good deal of the recent work that has been done on the education of disadvantaged children, I feel that there is a considerable agreement regarding many of the recommendations for dealing with the problem, although there are some very different emphases. What is missing, however, is a theoretic rationale to give meaning and direction to the action suggestions. I should like to attempt to provide the beginnings of such a rationale.

I think that a basic theoretic approach here has to be based on the culture of lower socio-economic groups and more particularly the elements of strength, the positives in this culture. The terms "deprived," "handicapped," "underprivileged," "disadvan-

274

taged," unfortunately emphasize environmental limitations and ignore the positive efforts of low-income individuals to cope with their environment. Most approaches concerned with educating the disadvantaged child either overlook the positives entirely, or merely mention in passing that there are positive features in the culture of low socio-economic groups that middle-class groups might learn from, but they do not spell out what these strengths are, and they build educational programs almost exclusively around the weaknesses or deficits.

I want to call attention to the positive features in the culture and the psychology of low income individuals. In particular, I should like to look at the cognitive style, the mental style or way of thinking characteristic of these people. One major dimension of this style is slowness.

Slow vs. Dull

Most disadvantaged children are relatively slow in performing intellectual tasks. This slowness is an important feature of their mental style and it needs to be carefully evaluated. In considering the question of the slowness of the deprived child, we would do well to recognize that in our culture there has probably been far too much emphasis on speed. We reward speed. We think of the fast child as the smart child and the slow child as the dull child. I think this is a basically false idea. I think there are many weaknesses in speed and many strengths in slowness.

The teacher can be motivated to develop techniques for rewarding slow pupils if she has an appreciation of some of the positive attributes of a slow style of learning. The teacher should know that pupils may be slow for other reasons than because they are stupid.

A pupil may be slow because he is extremely careful, meticulous or cautious. He may be slow because he refuses to generalize easily. He may be slow because he can't understand a concept unless he does something physically, e.g., with his hands, in connection with the idea he is trying to grasp.

The disadvantaged child is typically a physical learner and the physical learner is generally a slower learner. Incidentally, the physical style of learning is another important characteristic of the deprived individual and, it, too, has many positive features hitherto overlooked.

A child may be slow because he learns in what I have called a one-track way. That is, he persists in one line of thought and is not flexible or broad. He does not easily adopt other frames of reference, such as the teacher's, and consequently he may appear slow and dull.

Very often this single-minded individual has considerable creative potential, much of which goes unrealized because of lack of reinforcement in the educational system.

Analysis of the many reasons for slowness leads to the conclusion that slowness should not be equated with stupidity. In fact, there is no reason to assume that there are not a great many slow, gifted children.

The school in general does not pay too much attention to the slow gifted child but rather is alert to discover fast gifted children. Excellence comes in many packages and we must begin to search for it among the slow learners as well as among the faster individuals.

My own understanding of some of the merits of the slow style came through teaching at Bard College, where there is an enrollment of about 350 students. There I had the opportunity of getting to know quite well about forty students over a period of four years. I could really see what happened to them during this time. Very often the students I thought were slow and dull in their freshman year achieved a great deal by the time they became seniors. These are not the overall bright people who are typically selected by colleges, but in some area, in a one-track way, these students did some marvelous creative work. It was too outstanding to be ignored. I discovered in talking with students that most of them had spent five or six years in order to complete college. They had failed courses and made them up in summer school. Some had dropped out of college for a period of time and taken courses in night school. These students are slow learners, often one-track learners, but very persistent about something when they develop an interest in it. They have a fear of being overpowered by teachers in situations where they don't accept the teacher's point of view, but they stick to their own particular way of seeing the problem. They don't have a fast pace, they don't catch on quickly, and they very often fail subjects.

At the present time, when there is a measure of public excitement for reducing the four-year college to three years, I would submit that many potentially excellent students need a five or six year span to complete a college education.

The assumption that the slow pupil is not bright functions, I think, as a self-fulfilling prophecy. If the teachers act toward these pupils as if they were dull, the pupils will frequently come to function in this way. Of course, there are pupils who are very well developed at an early age and no teacher can stop them. But in the average development of the young person, even at the college level, there is need for reinforcement. The teacher must pick up what he says, appeal to him, and pitch examples to him. Typically this does not occur with the slow child. I find in examining my own classroom teaching that I easily fall into the habit of rewarding pupils whose faces light up when I talk, who are quick to respond to me and I respond back to them. The things they say in class become absorbed in the repertoire of what I say. I remember what they say and I use it in providing examples, etc. I don't pick up and select the slower pupil and I don't respond to him. He has to make it on his own.

In the teacher training program future teachers should be taught to guard against the almost unconscious and automatic tendency of the teacher to respond to the pupil who responds to him.

Hidden Verbal Ability

A great deal has been said about the language or verbal deficit supposedly characteristic of disadvantaged children. Everybody in the school system, at one time or another, has heard that these children are inarticulate, non-verbal, etc. But is not this too simple a generalization? Aren't these children quite verbal in out-of-school situations? For example, that the educationally deprived child can be quite articulate in conversation with his peers is well illustrated by the whole language developed by urban Negro groups, some of which is absorbed into the main culture via the Beatnik and the musician, if you dig what I mean.

Many questions about the verbal potential of disadvantaged children must be answered by research. Under what conditions are they verbal? What kind of stimuli do they respond to verbally? With whom are they verbal? What do they talk about? What parts of speech do they use? Martin Deutsch of New York Medical College is doing some very significant research trying to specify these factors and I surveyed some of his findings in my book, *The Culturally Deprived Child.* I think Deutsch is getting at some very interesting things. One technique he uses is a clown that lights up when the children say something. "Inarticulate" children can be very verbal and expressive in this situation.

Disadvantaged children are often surprisingly articulate in role-playing situations. One day when I was with a group of these youngsters, sometimes mistaken for a "gang," I asked them, "Why are you sore at the teachers?" Even though I was on good terms with them, I could not get much of a response. Most of them answered in highly abbreviated sentences. However, after I held a role-playing session in which some of the youngsters acted out the part of the teachers while others acted out the parts of the pupils, these "inarticulate" youngsters changed sharply. Within a half-hour they were bubbling over with very verbal and very sensitive answers to the questions I had asked earlier. They were telling me about the expressions on the teachers' faces that they did not like. They reported that they knew the minute they entered the room that the teacher did not like them and that she did not think they were going to do well in school. Their analyses were specific and remarkably verbal.

However, the quality of language employed has its limitations and I think herein lies the deficit. As Basil Bernstein indicates, the difference is between formal language and public language, between a language in a written book and the informal, everyday language. There is no question in my mind that there is a deficit in formal language. Since this deficit is fairly clear, the question might be asked, why make such an issue of the positive verbal ability to these children.

The reason is that it is easy to believe, that too many people have come to believe, that this formal deficit in language means that deprived people are characteristically non-verbal.

On the other hand, if the schools have the idea that these pupils are basically very good verbally, teachers might approach them in a different manner. Teachers might look for additional techniques to bring out the verbal facility. They might abandon the prediction that deprived children will not go very far in the education system and predict instead that they can go very far indeed because they have very good ability at the verbal level. In other words, an awareness of the positive verbal ability—not merely potential—will lead to demanding more of the disadvantaged child and expecting more of him.

Education vs. The School

There is a good deal of evidence that deprived children and their parents have a much more positive attitude towards education than is generally believed. One factor that obscures the recognition of this attitude is that while deprived individuals value education, they dislike the school. They are alienated from the school and they resent the teachers. For the sake of clarity, their attitude toward education and toward the school must be considered separately.

In a survey conducted a few years ago, people were asked, "What did you miss most in life that you would like your children to have?" Over 70 percent of the lower, socio-economic groups answered, "Education." The answer was supplied by the respondents, not checked on a list. They could have answered "money," "happiness," "health," or a number of things. And I think this is quite significant. Middle-class people answer "education" less frequently because they had an education and do not miss it as much.

A nation-wide poll conducted by Roper after World War II asked, "If you had a son or daughter graduating from high school, would you prefer to have him or her go on to college, do something else, wouldn't care?" The affirmative response to the college choice was given by 68 percent of the "poor," and 91 percent for the more prosperous. The difference is significant, but 68 percent of the poorer people is a large, absolute figure and indicates that a large number of these people are interested in a college education for their children.

Why then do these people who have a positive attitude towards education hold a negative attitude towards the school? These youngsters and their parents recognize that they are second-class citizens in the school and they are angry about it. From the classroom to the PTA they discover that the school does not like them, does not respond to them, does not appreciate their culture, and does not think they can learn.

Also, these children and their parents want education for different reasons than those presented by the school. They do not easily accept the ideas of expressing yourself, developing yourself, or knowledge for its own sake. They want education much more for vocational ends. But underneath there is a very positive attitude towards education and I think this is predominant in the lower socio-economic Negro groups. In the Higher Horizons program in New York City the parents have participated eagerly once they have seen that the school system is concerned about their children. One of the tremendously positive features about this program and the Great Cities programs is the concern for disadvantaged children and the interest in them. This the deprived have not experienced before and even if the programs did nothing else, I believe that the parents and the children would be responsive and would become involved in the school, because of the demonstrated concern for them.

Some Weaknesses

A basic weakness of deprived youngsters which the school can deal with is the problem of "know-how." Included here is the academic "know-how" of the school culture as well as the "know-how" of the middle class generally. Knowing how to get a job, how to appear for an interview, how to fill out a form, how to take tests, how to answer questions and how to listen.

The last is of particular importance. The whole style of learning of the deprived is not set to respond to oral or written stimuli. These children respond much more readily to visual kinesthetic signals. We should remodel the schools to suit the styles and meet the needs of these children. But no matter how much we change the school to suit their needs, we nevertheless have to change these children in certain ways; namely, reading, formal language, test taking and general "know-how."

These weaknesses represent deficiencies in skills and techniques. However, there is one basic limitation at the value level, namely the anti-intellectual attitudes of deprived groups. It is the only value of lower socio-economic groups which I would fight in the school. I want to make it very clear that I am very opposed to the school spending a lot of time teaching values to these kids. I am much more concerned—and in this I am traditional—that the schools impart skills, techniques and knowledge rather than training the disadvantaged to become good middle-class children.

However, I think there is one area indigenous to the school which has to be fought out at some point with these youngsters; that is their attitude toward intellectuals, towards knowledge for its own sake, and similar issues.

These children and their parents are pretty much anti-intellectual at all levels. They do not like "eggheads." They think talk is a lot of bull. I would consciously oppose this attitude in the school. I would make the issue explicit. There would be nothing subtle or covert about it. I would at some point state clearly that on this question the school does not agree with them and is prepared to argue about the views they hold.

Other Positive Dimensions

In my book, *The Culturally Deprived Child*, and in various speeches, I have elaborated more fully on these and other positive dimensions of the culture and style of educationally deprived people. A brief list would include the following: cooperativeness and mutual aid that mark the extended family; the avoidance of the strain accompanying competitiveness and individualism; the equalitarianism, in informality and humor; the freedom from self-blame and parental over-protection; the children's enjoyment of each other's company and lessened sibling rivalry, the security found in the extended family and a traditional outlook; the enjoyment of music, games, sports and cards; the ability to express anger; the freedom from being word-bound; an externally oriented rather than an introspective outlook; a spatial rather than temporal perspective; an expressive orientation in contrast to an instrumental one; content-centered not a form-centered mental style; a problem-centered rather than an abstract-centered approach; and finally, the use of physical and visual style in learning.

Summary and Implications

I have attempted to reinterpret some of the supposedly negative aspects—e.g., slowness—that characterize the cognitive style of disadvantaged individuals. I have given particular attention to the untapped verbal ability of these individuals and have indicated the basic weaknesses of the disadvantaged child which the school must overcome, such as the lack of school know-how, anti-intellectualism, and limited experience with formal language. Others which should be noted here are poor auditory attention, poor time perspective, inefficient test-taking skills, and limited reading ability.

The school must recognize these deficiencies and work assiduously to combat them. They are by no means irreversible, but even more important, because neglected, the positive elements in the culture and style of lower socio-economic groups should become the guide lines for new school programs and new educational techniques for teaching these children.

There are a number of reasons why it is important to emphasize the positive:

1. It will encourage the school to develop approaches and techniques, including possibly special teaching machines, appropriate for the cognitive style of deprived children.

2. It will enable children of low income backgrounds to be educated without middle-classifying them.

3. It will stimulate teachers to aim high, to expect more and work for more from these youngsters. Thus, it will constrain against patronization and condescension, and determinate, double-track systems where the deprived child never arrives on the main track.

4. It will function against the current tendency of over-emphasizing both vocational and non-academic education for children of low-income background.

5. It will provide an exciting challenge for teachers if they realize that they need not simply aim to "bring these children up to grade level," but rather can actually develop new kinds of creativity.

6. It will make the school far more pluralistic and democratic because different cultures and styles will exist and interact side by side. Thus, each can learn from the other and the empty phrase that the teacher has much to learn from deprived children will take on real meaning. General cultural interaction between equal cultures can become the hallmark of the school.

7. It will enable the teacher to see that when techniques such as role-playing and visual aids are used with deprived children, it is because these techniques are useful for eliciting the special cognitive style and creative potential of these children. All too often these techniques have been employed with the implicit assumption that they are useful with children who have inadequate learning ability.

8. It will lead to real appreciation of slowness, one-track learning and physical learning as potential strengths which require

careful nurturing. The teacher will have to receive special training in how to respond to these styles, how to listen carefully to the one-track person, how to reward the slow learner, etc. Special classes for slow learners will not culminate in the removal of these youngsters from the mainstream of the educational process on a permanent second track, and longer periods of time in school and college can be planned for these students without invidious connotations.

Dr. Irving Taylor, who has been concerned with various types of creativity in our American society, has observed that the mental style of the socially and economically disadvantaged learners resembles the mental style of one type of highly creative persons. Our schools should provide for the development of these unique, untapped national sources of creativity.

A Talk to Teachers

James Baldwin

Let's begin by saying that we are living through a very dangerous time. Everyone in this room is in one way or another aware of that. We are in a revolutionary situation, no matter how unpopular that word has become in this country. The society in which we live is desperately menaced, not by Khrushchev, but from within. So any citizen of this country who figures himself as responsible—and particularly those of you who deal with the minds and hearts of young people—must be prepared to "go for broke." Or to put it another way, you must understand that in the attempt to correct so many generations of bad faith and cruelty, when it is operating not only in the classroom but in society, you will meet the most fantastic, the most brutal, and the most determined resistance. There is no point in pretending that this won't happen.

Now, since I am talking to schoolteachers and I am not a teacher myself, and in some ways am fairly easily intimidated, I beg you to let me leave that and go back to what I think to be the entire purpose of education in the first place. It would seem to me that when a child is born, if I'm the child's parent, it is my obligation and my high duty to civilize that child. Man is a social animal. He cannot exist without a society. A society, in turn, depends on certain things which everyone within that society takes for granted. Now, the crucial paradox which confronts us here is that the whole process of education occurs within a social framework and is designed to perpetuate the aims of society. Thus, for example, the boys and girls who were born during the era of the Third Reich, when educated to the purposes of the Third Reich, became barbarians. The paradox of education is precisely this—that as one begins to become conscious one begins to examine the society in which he is being educated. The purpose of education, finally, is to create in a person the ability to look at the world for himself, to make his own decisions, to say to himself this is black or this is white, to decide for himself whether there is a God in heaven or not. To ask questions of the universe, and then learn to live with those questions, is the way he achieves his own identity. But no society is really anxious to have that kind of person around. What societies really, ideally, want is a citizenry which will simply obey the rules of society. If a society succeeds in this, that society is about to perish. The obligation of anyone who thinks of himself as responsible is to examine society and try to change it and to fight it—at no matter what risk. This is the only hope society has. This is the only way societies change.

Now, if what I have tried to sketch has any validity, it becomes thoroughly clear, at least to me, that any Negro who is born in this country and undergoes the American educational system runs the risk of becoming schizophrenic. On the one hand he is born in the shadow of the stars and stripes and he is assured it represents a nation which has never lost a war. He pledges allegiance to that flag which guarantees "liberty and justice for all." He is part of a country in which anyone can become President, and so forth. But on the other hand, he is also assured by his country and his countrymen that he has never contributed anything to civilization —that his past is nothing more than a record of humiliations gladly endured. He is assured by the republic that he, his father, his mother, and his ancestors were happy, shiftless, watermelon-eating darkies who loved Mr. Charlie and Miss Ann, that the value he has as a black man is proven by one thing only—his devotion to white people. If you think I am exaggerating, examine the myths which proliferate in this country about Negroes.

Now all this enters the child's consciousness much sooner than we adults would like to think it does. As adults, we are easily fooled because we are so anxious to be fooled. But children are very different. Children, not yet aware that it is dangerous to look too deeply at anything, look at everything, look at each other, and draw their own conclusions. They don't have the vocabulary to express what they see, and we, their elders, know how to intimidate them very easily and very soon. But a black child, looking at the world around him, though he cannot know quite what to make of it, is aware that there is a reason why his mother works so hard, why his father is always on edge. He is aware that there is some reason why, if he sits down in the front of the bus, his father or mother slaps him and drags him to the back of the bus. He is aware that there is some terrible weight on his parents' shoulders which menaces him. And it isn't long—in fact it begins when he is in school—before he discovers the shape of his oppression.

Let us say that the child is seven years old and I am his father, and I decide to take him to the zoo, or to Madison Square Garden, or the U. N. Building, or to any of the tremendous monuments we find all over New York. We get into a bus and we go from where I live on 131st Street and Seventh Avenue downtown through the park and we get into New York City, which is not Harlem. Now where the boy lives—even if it is a housing project—is in an undesirable neighborhood. If he lives in one of those housing projects of which everyone in New York City is so proud, he has at the front door, if not closer, the pimps, the whores, the junkies —in a word, the danger of life in the ghetto. And the child knows this, though he doesn't know why.

I still remember my first sight of New York. It was really another city when I was born—where I was born. We looked down over the Park Avenue streetcar tracks. It was Park Avenue, but I didn't know that Park Avenue meant *downtown*. The Park Avenue I grew up on, which is still standing, is dark and dirty. No one would dream of opening a Tiffany's on that Park Avenue, and when you go downtown you discover that you are literally in the white world. It is rich—or at least it looks rich. It is clean— because they collect garbage downtown. There are doormen. People walk about as though they owned where they were—and indeed they do. And it's a great shock. It's very hard to relate yourself to this. You don't know what it means. You know—you know instinctively—that none of this is for you. You know this before you are told. And who is it for and who is paying for it? And why isn't it for you?

Later on when you become a grocery boy or messenger and you try to enter one of those buildings a man says, "Go to the back door." Still later, if you happen by some odd chance to have a friend in one of those buildings, the man says, "Where's your package?" Now this by no means is the core of the matter. What I'm trying to get at is that by this time the Negro child has had, effectively, almost all the doors of opportunity slammed in his face, and there are very few things he can do about it. He can more or less accept it with an absolutely inarticulate and danger- ous rage inside—all the more dangerous because it is never expressed. It is precisely those silent people whom white people see every day of their lives—I mean your porter and your maid, who never say anything more than "Yes Sir" and "No Ma'am." They will tell you it's raining if that is what you want to hear, and they will tell you the sun is shining if *that* is what you want to hear. They really hate you—really hate you because in their eyes (and they're right) you stand between them and life. I want to come back to that in a moment. It is the most sinister of the facts, I think, which we now face.

There is something else the Negro child can do, too. Every street boy—and I was a street boy, so I know—looking at the society which has produced him, looking at the standards of that society which are not honored by anybody, looking at your churches and the government and the politicians, understands that this structure is operated for someone else's benefit—not for his. And there's no room in it for him. If he is really cunning, really ruthless, really strong—and many of us are—he becomes a kind of criminal. He becomes a kind of criminal because that's the only way he can live. Harlem and every ghetto in this city— every ghetto in this country—is full of people who live outside the law. They wouldn't dream of calling a policeman. They wouldn't, for a moment, listen to any of those professions of which we are so proud on the Fourth of July. They have turned away from this country forever and totally. They live by their wits and really long to see the day when the entire structure comes down.

The point of all this is that black men were brought here as a source of cheap labor. They were indispensable to the economy. In order to justify the fact that men were treated as though they were animals, the white republic had to brainwash itself into believing that they were, indeed, animals and *deserved* to be treated like animals. Therefore it is almost impossible for any Negro child to discover anything about his actual history. The reason is that this "animal," once he suspects his own worth, once he starts believing that he is a man, has begun to attack the entire power structure. This is why America has spent such a long time keeping the Negro in his place. What I am trying to suggest to you is that it was not an accident, it was not an act of God, it was not done by well-meaning people muddling into something which they didn't understand. It was a deliberate policy hammered into place in order to make money from black flesh. And now, in 1963, because we have never faced this fact, we are in intolerable trouble.

The Reconstruction, as I read the evidence, was a bargain between the North and South to this effect: "We've liberated them from the land—and delivered them to the bosses." When we left Mississippi to come North we did not come to freedom. We came to the bottom of the labor market, and we are still there. Even the Depression of the 1930s failed to make a dent in Negroes' relationship to white workers in the labor unions. Even today, so brainwashed is this republic that people seriously ask in what they suppose to be good faith, "What does the Negro want?" I've heard a great many asinine questions in my life, but that is perhaps the most asinine and perhaps the most insulting. But the point here is that people who ask that question, thinking that they ask it in good faith, are really the victims of this conspiracy to make Negroes believe they are less than human.

In order for me to live, I decided very early that some mistake had been made somewhere. I was not a "nigger" even though you called me one. But if I was a "nigger" in your eyes, there was something about *you*—there was something *you* needed. I had to realize when I was very young that I was none of those things I was told I was. I was not, for example, happy. I never touched a watermelon for all kinds of reasons. I had been invented by white people, and I knew enough about life by this time to understand that whatever you invent, whatever you project, is you! So where we are now is that a whole country of people believe I'm a "nigger," and I *don't,* and the battle's on! Because if I am not what I've been told I am, then it means that *you're* not what you thought *you* were *either*! And that is the crisis.

It is not really a "Negro revolution" that is upsetting this country. What is upsetting the country is a sense of its own identity. If, for example, one managed to change the curriculum in all the schools so that Negroes learned more about themselves and their real contributions to this culture, you would be liberating not only Negroes, you'd be liberating white people who know nothing about their own history. And the reason is that if you are compelled to lie about one aspect of anybody's history, you must lie about it all. If you have to lie about my real role here, if you have to pretend that I hoed all that cotton just because I loved you, then you have done something to yourself. You are mad.

Now let's go back a minute. I talked earlier about those silent people—the porter and the maid—who, as I said, don't look up at the sky if you ask them if it is raining, but look into your face. My ancestors and I were very well trained. We understood very early that this was not a Christian nation. It didn't matter what you said or how often you went to church. My father and my mother and my grandfather and my grandmother knew that Christians didn't act this way. It was as simple as that. And if that was so there was no point in dealing with white people in terms of their own moral professions, for they were not going to honor them. What one did was to turn away, smiling all the time, and tell white people what they wanted to hear. But people always accuse you of reckless talk when you say this.

All this means that there are in this country tremendous reservoirs of bitterness which have never been able to find an outlet, but may find an outlet soon. It means that well-meaning white liberals place themselves in great danger when they try to deal with Negroes as though they were missionaries. It means, in brief, that a great price is demanded to liberate all those silent people so that they can breathe for the first time and *tell* you what they think of you. And a price is demanded to liberate all those white children—some of them nearly forty—who have never grown up, and who never will grow up, because they have no sense of their identity.

What passes for identity in America is a series of myths about one's heroic ancestors. It's astounding to me, for example, that so many people really appear to believe that the country was founded by a band of heroes who wanted to be free. That happens not to be true. What happened was that some people left Europe because they couldn't stay there any longer and had to go someplace else to make it. That's all. They were hungry, they were poor, they were convicts. Those who were making it in England, for example, did not get on the *Mayflower*. That's how the country was settled. Not by Gary Cooper. Yet we have a whole race of people, a whole republic, who believe the myths to the point where even today they select political representatives, as far as I can tell, by how closely they resemble Gary Cooper. Now this is dangerously infantile, and it shows in every level of national life.

When I was living in Europe, for example, one of the worst revelations to me was the way Americans walked around Europe buying this and buying that and insulting everybody—not even out of malice, just because they didn't know any better. Well, that is the way they have always treated me. They weren't cruel, they just didn't know you were alive. They didn't know you had any feelings.

What I am trying to suggest here is that in the doing of all this for 100 years or more, it is the American white man who has long since lost his grip on reality. In some peculiar way, having created this myth about Negroes, and the myth about his own history, he created myths about the world so that, for example, he was astounded that some people could prefer Castro, astounded that there are people in the world who don't go into hiding when they hear the word "Communism," astounded that Communism is one of the realities of the twentieth century which we will not overcome by pretending that it does not exist. The political level in this country now, on the part of people who should know better, is abysmal.

The Bible says somewhere that where there is no vision the people perish. I don't think anyone can doubt that in this country today we are menaced—intolerably menaced—by a lack of vision.

It is inconceivable that a sovereign people should continue, as we do so abjectly, to say, "I can't do anything about it. It's the government." The government is the creation of the people. It is responsible to the people. And the people are responsible for it. No American has the right to allow the present government to say, when Negro children are being bombed and hosed and shot and beaten all over the deep South, that there is nothing we can do about it. There must have been a day in this country's life when the bombing of four children in Sunday School would have created a public uproar and endangered the life of a Governor Wallace. It happened here and there was no public uproar.

I began by saying that one of the paradoxes of education was that precisely at the point when you begin to develop a conscience, you must find yourself at war with your society. It is your responsibility to change society if you think of yourself as an educated person. And on the basis of the evidence—the moral and political evidence—one is compelled to say that this is a backward society. Now if I were a teacher in this school, or any Negro school, and I was dealing with Negro children, who were in my care only a few hours of every day and would then return to their homes and to the streets, children who have an apprehension of their future which with every hour grows grimmer and darker, I would try to teach them—I would try to make them know—that those streets, those houses, those dangers, those agonies by which they are surrounded, are criminal. I would try to make each child know that these things are the results of a criminal conspiracy to destroy him. I would teach him that if he intends to get to be a man, he must at once decide that he is stronger than this conspiracy and that he must never make his peace with it. And that one of his weapons for refusing to make his peace with it and for destroying it depends on what he decides he is worth. I would teach him that there are currently very few standards in this country which are worth a man's respect. That it is up to him to begin to change these standards for the sake of the life and the health of the country. I would suggest to him that the popular culture—as represented, for example, on television and in comic books and in movies—is based on fantasies created by very ill people, and he must be aware that these are fantasies that have nothing to do with reality. I would teach him that the press he reads is not as free as it says it is—and that he can do something about that, too. I would try to make him know that just as American history is longer, larger, more various, more beautiful, and more terrible than anything anyone has ever said about it, so is the world larger, more daring, more beautiful and more terrible, but principally larger—and that it belongs to him. I would teach him that he doesn't have to be bound by the experiences of any given Administration, any given policy, any given time—that he has the right and the necessity to examine everything. I would try to show him that one has not learned anything about Castro when one says, "He is a Communist." This is a way of *not* learning something about Castro, something about Cuba, something, in fact, about the world. I would suggest to him that he is living, at the moment, in an enormous province. America is not the world and if America is going to become a nation, she must find a way—and this child must help her to find a way—to use the tremendous potential and tremendous energy which this child represents. If this country does not find a way to use that energy, it will be destroyed by that energy.

Negroes and Poverty

Alan Batchelder

Presumably, a Negro family receiving $2,400 annually would experience, because of such low income, discomfort identical with that experienced by a white family in exactly the same circumstances. Why then a special paper on Negro poverty? Because, in America, the white and Negro situations are never identical. Surely, because of discrimination, poor Negroes are psychologically more discomfited than poor white. But economists do not investigate such discomfiture. Why, then, a special economics paper on Negro poverty?

Because at least five economic considerations distinguish Negro from white poverty. As Wordsworth observed of the echo, "Like, —but oh how different."

First, $1,000 buys less for a poor Negro than for a poor white.

Second, the demographic cross-section of the Negro poor is unlike that of the white poor.

Third, poor Negroes suffer though the general weal benefits from secular changes in urban renewal, education medians, agriculture, manufacturing location, technology, and social minimum wages.

Fourth, the effect of government transfer payments is different for poor Negroes than for poor whites.

Fifth, discrimination operates against Negroes to restrict access to education and to the jobs that can provide an escape from poverty.

These considerations will be discussed in turn.

Some Historical Perspective

When considering American Negro affairs, one must remember that social and economic conditions of Negroes are most responsive to unemployment rates. In 1900, 90 percent of American Negroes lived in the South, most on farms. The few urban Negroes were totally excluded from manufacturing and from all but menial and laborious jobs. The situation changed to the Negro's advantage only during German nationalism's wars. Wartime labor shortages induced managers of large manufacturing corporations to admit Negroes to the production jobs that permitted Negroes to make relative income gains.

During peacetime, the Negro position remained the same or deteriorated. When labor markets softened between 1949 and 1959, the income position of Negro men relative to that of white men fell in every section of the country. [1] Rising productivity cut the number of whites and Negroes living in poverty, but the incidence of poverty among Negroes rose between 1950 and 1962 from 2 to 2½ times the white rate [26, p. 339].

The past decade's many admonitions and laws opposing discrimination could not raise the Negro's relative economic position in the face of rising unemployment. If Negroes are to approach economic and civil equality in the future, unemployment rates must fall.

Full employment affects all Negroes. Attention now turns to the characteristics distinguishing poor Negro from poor white Americans.

The Negro Dollar: Second-Class Money

When citing statistics of poverty, the portion of Negro families receiving incomes below a particular figure, e.g., $3,000, is often compared with the portion of white families receiving incomes below $3,000. Such comparisons implicitly assume the Negro's $3,000 buys as much as the white's $3,000. It does not.

American cities have two housing markets: the city-wide white market and the circumscribed Negro market. Because supply is restricted, Negroes [*33, p. 36*] "receive less housing value for their dollars spent than do whites. . . . Census statistics indicate that . . . non-white renters and home owners obtain fewer standard quality dwellings and frequently less space than do whites paying the same amounts." A Chicago welfare department study found [*18, p. 13*] "housing defects significantly greater for Negro than for white families, despite the fact that rents for Negro families are 28 percent a month higher than for white private dwellings."

Landlords are sometimes judged greedy extortionists for charging Negro tenants higher rents than whites. But they are operating in a market of restricted supply; high Negro rents reflect supply and demand relationships, not conspiratorial landlord greed. Since 15 percent of the consumption expenditures of urban Negro families is for shelter [*27*], real income is significantly reduced by relatively high rents.

Poor urban Negroes also pay more than whites for identical consumer durables bought on credit [*3, pp. 12–20*]. (Negroes pay more than whites for residential financing, too [*31, p. 344*].) The difference may be due to white reluctance to sell to Negroes (Becker's discrimination [*2*]), to Negro immobility, or to the sellers' assumption that poor Negroes are poorer risks than poor whites. Whatever the cause, real income suffers.

Poor Negro families average a half-person larger than poor white families [*11, p. 10*]. Consequently, per capita real income of poor Negroes is even farther below per capita real income of poor whites.

If, then, $3,000 in Negro money buys only as much as $2,800 or even $2,500 in white money and is distributed over more people, one should keep in mind appropriate reservations when comparing percentage of whites with percentage of Negroes below some income level.

Differences in Demographic Characteristics

The Negro poor differ from the white poor in demographic characteristics. Remembering that Negro numbers will be understated, uniform dollar incomes can be used to identify nonwhite (not Negro) and white poor. Defining as poor, families with incomes under $3,000 and individuals living independently with incomes under $1,500 in 1959, four social-economic variables distinguish the nonwhite from the white poor.

First, the nonwhite poor are concentrated in the South. In 1960, 72 percent (52 percent)* of poor nonwhite families; only four of ten (27 percent) poor white families lived in the South (unless otherwise noted, all statistics in this section are from reference [25]). The 32 point difference in southern concentration resulted because, in 1960, the proportion of nonwhites was double the proportion of whites living in the South.

Second, low income is more of a rural phenomenon for whites than for nonwhites; eighteen of every 100 (4 percent) poor white families, twelve of every 100 (3 percent) poor nonwhite families lived on farms in 1960. Fully 84 percent (79 percent) of nonwhite, only 44 percent (63 percent) of white farm families were poor in 1959, but nonwhites have withdrawn from farming more completely than have whites.

Third, the aging of husbands is a much more important cause of white than of nonwhite poverty. Other forces are important in causing nonwhite poverty. In 1959, 29 percent of poor white families but only 13 percent of poor nonwhite families were headed by a man older than sixty-four years. Among unrelated individuals, 40 percent of the white poor, only 26 percent of the nonwhite poor were past sixty-four.

Fourth, nonwhite poverty, far more than white, is associated with families headed by women. American Negro women have always borne exceptionally heavy family responsibility. In 1910 there were twenty gainfully employed white women for every 100 employed Negro men [20, pp. 66–67]. Even in 1959, only 8 percent of white families but 21 percent of nonwhite families were headed by women. Three-fourths of these nonwhite families were poor in 1959. Consequently, 32 percent of all poor nonwhite families, only 19 percent of all poor white families, were headed by women in 1959.

Urban Renewal, Shrinking the Supply of Dwellings

A lilting song of World War I charged

> It's the same the whole world over,
> It's the poor wot gets the blame,
> It's the rich wot gets the pleasure,
> Ain't it all a blooming shame.

* The figures in parentheses refer to individuals living independently.

Forces afoot today give the affluent society and even poor whites the pleasure while injuring poor Negroes. One of these forces is urban renewal. It replaces slums with aesthetically attractive, commercially profitable structures, some of which provide low-income housing superior to that which the private market could provide.

Yet urban renewal seems to effect a net reduction in housing supply for poor Negroes. L. K. Northwood found [32, pp. 107–08] "the supply of housing has been reduced in areas formerly occupied by Negro families. . . . 115,000 housing units were . . . planned to replace 190,500 . . . a net loss of 75,000." Because many urban Negroes live in slums, 60 percent of the persons dispossessed by urban renewal demolition have been Negroes [31, p. 348].

The long-run tendency to reduce the supply of low-cost housing is aggravated in the short run because time must elapse between demolition of old and dedication of new buildings. During short runs as long as five years [8, pp. 132–33] urban renewal reduces housing supply by demolition uncompensated by new construction.

Poor whites may move elsewhere; poor Negroes must face reduced supply. Reduced supply should raise prices, and there is evidence that Negroes displaced by urban renewal pay rent 10 percent higher after relocation than before [14, pp. 72 and 82].

Until President Kennedy's November, 1962, executive order, the supply-restriction effect was even greater, for no federal rule prohibited urban developers from practicing racial discrimination [30, p. 441]. The 1962 order alleviated the problem but could not end the irony that poor Negroes suffer from programs designed to promote urban welfare.

Education: The Illiterate Fall Farther Behind

E. F. Denison estimates [4, p. 73] that from 1929 to 1957 improved education "contributed 42 percent of the 1.60 percentage point growth rate in product per person employed." Improved education is manifested in rising median school years completed. The 1950 Negro medians for men and for women, past age twenty-four, lagged [behind] white medians by 2.8 years. By 1960, Negro medians had pushed up a year and a third. So had white medians [26, p. 113]. Average Negroes remained in the same relative position, but rising educational medians increased the comparative disadvantage of the 2,265,000 nonwhite functional illiterates (less than five years of school) making up 23.5 percent of the 1960 nonwhite population past age twenty-four [*23, pp. 420–21*].

Many poor whites are illiterate, but figures on school years completed understate the number of illiterate Negroes and the size of their educational disadvantage. Understatements result for Negroes because so many attended inefficient segregated southern schools. Testing poor Negro literacy, Illinois departments of public aid recently sampled able-bodied Negroes aged sixteen— sixty–four receiving public assistance (not a random sample of all Negroes). Each person was asked his school attainment; each took the *New Stanford Reading Test*. Of persons educated in Illinois, 3 percent were functionally illiterate; 35 percent tested as illiterate. Of persons educated in Mississippi, 23 percent were functionally illiterate; 81 percent, four of five adults, tested as illiterate [*17, p. 118*].

Of nonwhites living North or West in 1960, 41 percent had been born in the South [*24, p. 2*]. These educationally deprived poor southern Negroes are increasingly disadvantaged in regions where the median education of the local labor force and the quality of local schools rise each year.

Poor Negro boys are especially disadvantaged because of parental limitations and because their homes and the larger society offer so few successful men inspiring academic emulation. Special counseling and educational arrangements can offset those conditions and send slum boys to college [*13, pp. 275–76*], but society devotes few resources to such arrangements.

Left ever farther behind rising national educational norms, poor Negro families are ever less qualified to compete for jobs or to help their children acquire the education required to escape poverty.

Agriculture: End of an Exodus

Since 1945, the mechanization of cotton culture has revolutionized southern agriculture [*16*]. There has also been persistent change in crops grown and livestock raised [*15*]. These changes raised agricultural productivity and expelled hand labor from southern farms. In 1930, there were 882,000 Negro farms (with

4,680,500 residents). In 1950, there were 559,000 (with 3,167,-000 residents) ; in 1959 only 265,000 (with 1,482,000 residents) [*26, p. 618*] [*21, p. 599*] [*23, pp. 359–60*].

The economy benefits as productivity rises. The effect on Negroes is less favorable. As whites left, the white farms that averaged 130 acres in 1930 grew to average 249 acres in 1959. But Negro farms showed little growth. They averaged forty-three acres in 1930 and fifty-two acres in 1960 [*34, p. 1035*].

Change has not resulted in larger, more prosperous Negro farms. Change has expelled from southern farms the most ill-educated Americans.

Looking ahead, the Negro reservoir is nearly exhausted. The number of rural farm Negroes in 1960 was only 47 percent the number in 1950 [*23, pp. 359–60*]. The Negro exodus can never again approach the scale reached during the 1950's. Poor Negroes are already committed to the city.

Manufacturing Migration: Jobs Out of Reach

Since 1950, southern manufacturing has expanded more rapidly than northern. From 1950 to 1960, the number of manufacturing jobs grew 28 percent in the South, only 12 percent in the North [*22, pp. 407–11*] [*23, pp. 730–32*]. Because most poor Negroes live in the South and because Negroes' wartime income gains were based on accession of Negroes to production jobs in manufacturing, Negroes are particularly affected by shifts in manufacturing employment.

Manufacturing's southern migration to new markets and new sources of raw material [*15, pp. 46–47*] has distributed American resources more efficiently. It has taken jobs to poor whites but not to poor Negro men. Between 1950 and 1960, the number of jobs in southern manufacturing rose by 944,000. Of these 944,000 jobs, 12,000 went to Negro women (proportionately fewer than to white women) ; none went to Negro men [*22, p. 410*] [*23, pp. 728–29*].

Manufacturing: Technological Change Clocks the Exits

During wartime, rural southern Negroes proved themselves in manufacturing and developed vested interests in the growth of unskilled and semiskilled manufacturing jobs.

Today, technological change benefits all by raising productivity. It also changes America's occupational cross-section. In 1880 textile mechanization replaced skilled workers with unskilled rural immigrants [6, p. 63]. Negroes would prefer such changes today, but in 1964 skilled workers replaced unskilled.

In recent years, the occupations that during war gave Negroes a chance to get ahead have not grown as rapidly as the number of Negroes seeking work. Between 1947 and 1964, as male employment rose 10 percent, the number of manufacturing production jobs rose only 5½ percent [19, p. 3] [28, p. 14]. Between 1950 and 1960, male employment rose 6.9 percent; the number of semiskilled jobs in manufacturing rose only 4.1 percent [23, pp. 528–31].

Most unfavorable for aspiring unskilled poor Negroes, the number of men's laboring jobs in manufacturing fell 20 percent (by 200,000) between 1950 and 1960 [23, p. 533].

These changes in America's occupational cross-section result from technological developments that raise society's affluence; but, as present trends continue, manufacturing will offer fewer exits from poverty for Negroes handicapped by rural southern origins.

The Rising Social Minimum Wage and the Able-Bodied Unemployed

Two centuries ago, when sheep began gobbling up the people of England's countryside, the victims were deposited in cities in much the same condition as the untrained Negro migrants of today. The bold English peasantry, dispossessed from Sweet Auburn, could say of the city, "Thou found'st me poor at first and keep'st me so," but they were employed—though oppressively and irregularly.

Many Negroes transplanted to cities are unable to obtain steady work. Long's argument that America's social minimum wage rises above the marginal revenue product of society's least productive members [7, p. 16] applies especially to urban Negroes with rural southern antecedents. Law and respectable custom press upward on the social minimum wage. The general welfare benefits as many low-income persons receive more money and employers increase efficiency to offset higher costs [29, pp. 1139–40]. But the first increase in the minimum causes the discharge of the least able persons employed. Successive increases cause the discharge of successively more able persons among the less able employed [*29, p. 1141*].

It is the function of the market to choose technology appropriate to available resources as reflected in flexible resource prices. But the market does not operate below the social minimum. Weighed down with their heritage from the Southern Way of Life, able-bodied Negroes with marginal revenue products below the social minimum wage must either find employers paying below the minimum or depend on transfers.

So much for forces benefiting the general public but hurting poor Negroes.

Transfer Payments: Paternal Substitute and Golden Age Equalizer

For fifteen years, Negro unemployment rates have been double white rates [*26, pp. 216–18*]. This distinguishes Negro from white need for transfers, but does not distinguish poor Negroes from poor whites.

Respecting government transfers, poor Negroes do differ from poor whites because proportionately more Negro households have feminine heads and proportionately more Negroes are past sixty-four.

Relatively few Negroes receive OASDI (old age, survivors, and disability insurance). In 1962, 6.7 percent of the 12,500,000 recipients were nonwhite. This low figure was due to the nonwhite's shorter age span and the dissimilar work histories that led 73 percent of elderly whites but only 58 percent of elderly nonwhites to qualify [*10, pp. 5 and 9*]. In contrast, old age assistance goes to 38 percent of elderly nonwhites, 12 percent of elderly whites [*10, p. 11*].

OASDI brings elderly Negroes and whites close to income equality. For all persons, Negro income averages half of white income [*1*]. Yet the average income of nonwhites runs 80 percent the average total income of whites receiving OASDI [*10, p. 5*]. This happens because many Negroes continue in poverty while many whites sink into poverty after retiring.

Because Negro fathers so often decamp, Negro children receive a disproportionate share of ADC (aid to families with dependent children). Of 900,000 families (with 2,800,000 children) receiving ADC in 1963, 44 percent were Negro [*9, pp. 3–4*].

Per capita, ADC pays much less than retirement programs. Old age assistance meets 94 percent of the needs of the elderly; ADC supplies 58 percent of children's needs [12, p. 7]. Playing surrogate to absent fathers of poor Negro families, ADC never raises incomes or aspirations above levels at which the mothers' and absent fathers' "only legacy to their children is the same one of poverty and deprivation that they received from their own parents" [11, p. 12].

"The legacy of poverty" is a foreboding term. Seeking auspicious signs, at what points is Negro poverty most vulnerable to forces of improvement?

Prospects

Since poor Negroes pay more than poor whites for housing, any laws, changes of white hearts, or construction serving to increase the supply of housing open to Negroes will especially benefit the Negro poor.

Lengthening Negro men's lives, strengthening wedding bonds, and, most important, improving job opportunities for Negro men will strengthen the poor Negro family. This will immediately add a male income earner to the family and will eventually induce male youth to look more ambitiously toward futures in the market economy.

During the 1950's, the numbers of men and of women of working age grew equally, but the number of jobs for women grew 34.5 percent, the number for men only 7.3 percent [23, pp. 528–31]. This was especially important for Negro women whose income rose relative to that of white women and Negro men [1, pp. 531–33]. The trend continues; between 1960 and 1964, the number of jobs for women grew fourteen times as fast as the number of jobs for men [26, p. 216].

Because half of southern Negro mothers of preschool children work [5, p. 9], mothers and children would benefit from preschool nurseries freeing the mothers for work and preparing the children for school. Because many receive ADC, higher payments or training schools for ADC mothers would particularly benefit poor Negroes.

Since poor Negro mothers are least informed regarding birth control [8, pp. 153–66], their education in this regard would permit great improvements in Negro health, real per capita incomes, and family manageableness.

Each year Negroes have less interest in programs aiding poor farmers, for farmers become more nearly all white each year. Contemplating old age, poor Negroes will benefit as urban migration and extension of coverage bring more under OASDI.

As social minimum wages rise, perhaps engineers will be able to provide employers with machinery that will combine profitably with the unskills of rurally educated southern Negroes. If not, they must depend upon transfers.

Finally, since southern segregated Negro schools have placed poor Negroes at a greater disadvantage than poor whites, since racial discrimination keeps qualified Negroes from demanding jobs, since weak labor markets remove the inducement that historically has been most important in helping Negroes score economic gains, the position of poor Negroes will improve dramatically in response to appropriate pressures at these three points.

Peroration

Because of discrimination in education and employment, there is one last important difference between the Negro and white poor. Logic rather than statistics suggests its existence. To begin, assume the innate ability distribution of Negroes is identical with that of whites. Next assume the inexorable winnowing out of those least able to earn is the dominant cause of white poverty, but is only a partial cause of Negro poverty. It follows that poor whites are the least able whites, but that poor Negroes include those least able as well as many of middling to superior ability. These able Negroes are poor because of racial discrimination; society denied them access to the channels in which their earning ability could be developed and used.

The economist then concludes that the marginal efficiency of social capital invested in educating and finding work for the Negro poor could be much higher than the marginal efficiency of social capital similarly invested in the white poor. However, we know that the conversion of the poor Negro's potential into dollar product is very difficult in American society. The potential return is latent in the Negro poor. Able innovators are required if that potential is to be realized.

Physical Integration Is Not Enough

Nathaniel Hickerson

In 1910, 10 percent of America's Negro population lived in the North. Today, more than half of the Negro people in our country live above the Mason-Dixon line. The majority of the Northern Negroes live in the large metropolitan areas. New York City has more than a million Negroes, while Chicago has in excess of 500,000. Almost half the population of Newark, New Jersey, is Negro. Hundreds of thousands of Negroes live in Philadelphia, Detroit and Cleveland. In California, Los Angeles County and the San Francisco Bay area are centers of Negro population.

For the most part, the Negro people in the major cities live in clearly defined and contained sections of the community. Usually these ghettos are found in the oldest, or least desirable parts of town. Only in recent years has a small fraction of the Negro population been able to break out of its ghetto into former all-white neighborhoods. More often than not this spreading out was made imperative by the need for more housing, and was accomplished against strong opposition of white residents and their allies, the real estate interests, in the affected area. With the appearance of a Negro family in a white neighborhood, the white residents often moved elsewhere and soon another ghetto was created.

New York City has Harlem, the traditional home of the Negroes in that city, and now there is Little Harlem, the new Negro and Puerto Rican ghetto lower down on the west side of Manhattan. As recently as 1950, the area now called Little Harlem was predominantly white. Today this neighborhood is almost entirely black. In San Francisco, Negroes first lived in the western addition and Fillmore districts. In time, like Harlem, these became ghetto areas. Today the Ingleside section, five miles from downtown San Francisco, is becoming a Negro ghetto where ten years ago practically no Negro families could be found.

Among other reasons, two primary causes for the growth of these ghettos are basic. First, since the average income of Negro families is markedly lower than for the whites, many Negroes find it impossible to live in any but the poorest and most neglected and dilapidated sections of a city. Second is the tacit understanding among many real estate interests that living quarters in certain sections of every Northern city are not to be sold or rented to Negroes—even to those who can afford them, though restrictive covenants are declared illegal in property documents in many Northern cities.

The concentration of Negroes in specific sections of our Northern cities has led to the development of ghetto schools. The old honored American tradition of sending children to the neighborhood school has suddenly developed ramifications never before considered. Today in many Northern cities neighborhood schools mean *de facto* segregated schools. Even among those who may have no desire to segregate Negroes, the tradition of sending children to the closest school is so strong as to influence them to place the value of neighborhood schools above the value of school integration. It is not unusual to find an elementary school in one of our Northern cities with a 90 percent Negro attendance, while not more than a mile away, another elementary school has less than 5 percent Negro enrollment. In city after city, boundary lines for each school are fixed either (perhaps) by accident or possibly by design so that Negroes and whites are often forced into separation. (This is not to say that there are no physically integrated schools in Northern cities. Needless to point out, hundreds of thousands of American children, both Negro and white, attend school together. However, there are still many schools not integrated in states where segregation has long been a violation of the state educational code.) In these *de facto* segregated schools, one might find no Negroes or a handful in a student body of hundreds or thousands of students or conversely, none or a few whites in a student body of hundreds or thousands of Negroes. Feelings against the neighborhood school and its concomitant segregation are running high and have reached startling proportions. Picket lines have appeared protesting extra-legal segregation; strikes have been held by Negro parents and white supporters demanding that the local school be integrated, or that their children be sent elsewhere; law suits have been filed to force boards of education to integrate ghetto schools, or to close them altogether.

Some of these protests against the neighborhood *de facto* segregated school have culminated in positive action. In New Rochelle, New York, for example, children may now attend any school in the city. New York City Negro children are bussed to previously all-white neighborhood schools and whites to predominately Negro schools. In Oakland, California, a citizen's committee has been appointed by the Board of Education to study *de facto* segregation in the public schools there. In San Francisco a newly-designated junior high school was not opened in September, 1962, as scheduled as a result of the protest raised by Negro and white parents that this new junior high school would be at least 60 percent Negro. The children who would have had to go to this school are now being transported to other parts of the city to attend other junior high schools.

The arguments against *de facto* segregation, advanced by the NAACP and other groups interested in the education of Negro children, center around four principal points:

1. Segregation, whether *de facto* or legal, diminishes the opportunity for all members of the community of different races to have adequate contact with each other. Consequently, Negro and white children living in segregated neighborhoods and attending segregated neighborhood schools, have little chance to come to know each other at first hand and to learn to act together as citizens of a common community, sharing mutual interests. School segregation can only help to keep alive the distrust and enmity that has characterized Negro-white relations and make it difficult to destroy the artificial image of the racial stereotype so common in American culture.

2. Segregation, *de facto* or not, tends to reinforce feelings of rejection by members of a minority group. If Negro children

grow up with only minimal contact with white children, the isolation is bound to intensify these feelings. Conversely, if the white children have little or no contact with Negro children, rejection of the minority by whites is endlessly perpetuated. Negro children learn that to be a Negro is more important than to be a citizen, and white children learn that to be white is a blessed relief. The Negro child learns that his life is separate and remote from the world of the dominant white. What is left for him is withdrawal and feelings of inferiority. So aware are some Negro leaders of this, that organizations such as the Afro-American Association have established a program to teach Negro children about their ancestors, the contribution of Africans to world culture, and the value and worth of Negro people in the world today.

3. Schools with large numbers of Negro students tend to be staffed by inferior faculties. In many school districts where transfer of teachers within the system is possible upon request, better teachers often ask to be transferred out of ghetto schools to schools with "nicer" and "more easily educable" children. The principals in the schools outside of the Negro ghetto are glad to get these superior teachers. The poorer or less favorably regarded instructors are unable to secure transfers and remain in the ghetto schools, often against their will.

4. It is suggested that all of these factors: separation and isolation, feelings of rejection, and inferior teachers lead to denigration of the school and its values by the Negro. If the school stands as an institution reinforcing the present reality of Negro second-class citizenship, then why should Negro parents and students feel loyalty to the institution? The *de facto* segregated school and its values are enemies of the Negro, implementing what Negroes know to be the unacceptable focus of American race culture. The Negro child, like his parents, is ghetto-wise and each day of his school life as he faces hostile and impatient whites, he knows that he is neither understood nor considered of much value as an individual. (This is not to say that there are no Negro teachers in predominantly Negro schools in the North. To be sure, more Negro teachers are being hired each year. But they are still a minority and in some Northern cities so scarce as to be almost non-existent. Further, let it be understood that there are fine, devoted non-Negro teachers in ghetto schools whose excellent work has produced results indicative of what Negro children can do when given opportunity and encourage-

ment. Generally, however, the ghetto school is regarded with suspicion and hostility by Negro children and parents alike.)

The rejection by the Negro of the *de facto* segregated school as a tool of present American race culture has manifest and unfortunate ramifications. Negro students as a whole do poorly in their work, care little about "studies," and "going to college," and treat the school experience (particularly from the 4th and 5th grades on) as an unnecessary evil. Why should the Negro student work hard in a "white man's school" when that school confirms what he knows to be true about the white man and his race culture. As one bright Negro high school student remarked when admonished by his well-meaning white counselor for not doing well in high school work and having no plans for college: "Why should I go to college? I don't want to be the best educated steel worker in the plant." We may argue with his logic but not with his realistic appraisal of what life in all probability holds for him. Most Negroes will be isolated and rejected by whites as adults, as they are now isolated and rejected as children. Most Negroes will face hostile whites as adults, as they now face hostile whites as children. As Negro adults are bitter and contemptuous of the white world "downtown," so do the children become bitter and contemptuous of the white teacher in the school around the corner. Our *de facto* segregated schools teach Negro children their lessons well as they prepare these children for admission to what is at present American race culture.

From the sociological, psychological, and educational point of view, then, leaders in the movement to raise Negroes to the position of first class citizenship in America are protesting against *de facto* segregation in the public schools. These schools, they say, perpetuate existing separation of the races and isolation of the Negroes; tend to reinforce feelings of rejection common among our Negro people; and further strengthen the myth that Negroes are unable to absorb academic learning and to compete with whites. Negro and white leaders striving for improved Negro education insist that physical integration of schools must take place if the Negro is to avoid the evils inherent in *de facto* segregated schools. With this the writer wholeheartedly agrees. However, the question arises whether or not Negro students in the North who do attend physically well-integrated public schools as they are now constituted profit by the experience. Does it follow that, because the number of Negro and white children who enter the same school building each morning are in realistic proportion to the community's racial population, education for the Negro at present is better in such a school than it is in a *de facto* segregated school? I think not. I believe that there is no evidence to show that in Northern cities Negro children improve their attitudes toward school, suffer less from feelings of rejection or isolation, work harder or do better in their studies because they attend a physically integrated school.

What I have just said is not to be construed as a defense of *de facto,* or any other kind of segregation. Public school integration is an essential step if we Americans are to do something about our frightening racial difficulties. Distinctions made among peoples because of race, religion, ethnic background, or any other artificial criteria are abhorrent and indefensible; they are illogical and mark anyone who makes such distinctions an irrational human being.

My questioning of the fight against *de facto* segregation is based rather on assumptions made that mere physical integration of schools in Northern cities is the solution to the educational problems of Negro children. Physical integration in Northern schools if not accompanied by an increase in the quality of schooling for Negro children may turn out to be of little value at all.

At present Negroes in physically integrated schools in the North are denied equal opportunity; they are discriminated against by bigoted and race-minded school officials; they are channeled out of academic courses by counselors who have not one bit of training for dealing with minority group children; they are evaluated as slow learners and herded into slow learning groups as early as the first grade, on the basis of observation by teachers who themselves may be filled with prejudice or sympathy for the "poor little things." They are declared slow learners on the basis of so-called intelligence and achievement tests, the validity of which have been challenged over and over again by educators and psychologists who claim that these tests reflect middle-class values and thinking more than intelligence or ability; they are saddled with teachers and counselors who haven't the foggiest notion of Negro culture or conditioning; they are isolated from social activities of the school (particularly in junior high and high schools); they are defeated so long, so often and so continuously by the integrated American race-culture-perpetuating public school, that for the most part they reject education as a waste of time and effort. (In the few isolated cases where real effort has been made by the Negro, or Negro and white teachers together, to improve the quality of education for Negroes in either nearly all-Negro or integrated schools, the results have been noteworthy enough to indicate that anyone who attributes the Negro's poor achievement in school to inherent inferiority is taking an indefensible position. For one to assume the superior intelligence of one race as opposed to another in light of modern anthropological, psychological and biological information is to assume something which is scientifically unsound and unsupportable.) Typical of what takes place in a physically-integrated public high school in the North is the case of a school located in the Bay Area of California which was recently studied by the author. The results are shown in Table I.

Perhaps the few Negroes enrolled in the college prep program could be explained by the fact that almost all of the fathers of the Negro students in the school were employed as unskilled, semi-skilled or skilled factory workers or craftsmen while many of the fathers of the white students were professional and semi-professional people. However, further investigation of this high school indicated that even when the students were matched up according to father's occupations as skilled, semi-skilled and unskilled workers almost identical percentages resulted. Thus, the white children whose fathers were employed as factory workers or craftsmen were enrolled in a college prep program four times as often as Negro pupils whose fathers were similarly employed. Only one or two Negro graduates out of hundreds in this high school has ever completed college. There are no Negro teachers, counselors or administrators in this high school; one of forty-four Negro seniors was enrolled in college preparatory last year, while sixty-five of 160 whites were so enrolled. Although

Table I Percent of Students In College Preparatory Classes In a California Bay Area School, According to Ethnic Groups

Ethnic Group	% of Students	% of Ethnic Group in College Prep Classes
Caucasian	62	45
Mexican-American	13	31
Filipino	6	45
Negro	19	11

many of the school's athletes were Negroes, there were no Negro cheerleaders or pom-pom girls. Of the 130 or so girls in the Pep Club, only seven were Negro.

I believe that this is a typical story and that a study of most physically-integrated Northern public schools would show that Negro children are so universally denied educational opportunities, so discouraged by their experiences in the integrated school, and consequently so often tend to become uninterested in school and its values that integrated schools do not serve the purpose of improving Negro education or relations between whites and Negroes simply because they are integrated.

If *de facto* segregated schools are evil, then so are many physically integrated schools as we know them today. Physical integration, for the sake solely of integration, does not get to the heart of the matter. The question of real importance is, when will our Negro children be given the opportunity to fulfill their potentialities as white children are encouraged to do, and when will our Negro children see reason for working hard in school and accepting the school's values as having significance for them?

Of course, it cannot be expected that the public school alone can develop all the conditions in American society which will give Negroes reason for expending maximum effort. The school can do little, for example, to change the minds of adult bigots; nor can the school suddenly and by some magic, convince employers that Negroes should be allowed to compete with whites for better jobs. Neither is it likely that the public school will tomorrow convince residents of all-white neighborhoods that the enlightened thing to do is to welcome Negroes into their neighborhoods as worthwhile additions. There are things, however, the schools can do, and do promptly. They can encourage Negro children and their parents to look upon the school as an ally and not a foe. There are ways to start the ball rolling and to begin to build the momentum that can carry the concept of equality of the races on into the society beyond our schools.

If we reject *de facto* segregation as inimical to American democracy, then we must reject mere physical integration of Negroes and whites in schools as inimical to the best interests of Negro children. If we decide that we are going to integrate the *de facto* segregated schools in the North, as we should, then we must decide that this integration is to be more than placing of Negro and white children in the same school building. This kind of integration can be meaningless. In the Northern schools already integrated, and in those which we are attempting to integrate, we must carefully consider certain steps which should be taken to encourage Negro children to use the school as a means toward gaining first class citizenship. At the same time, as the Negro identifies more and more with the school and improves in his academic work, the distorted image that white children have of the Negro, all too often encouraged by race-minded parents and teachers, may be sharply altered.

There are, I believe, nine basic steps to be taken to improve the education of Negro students in integrated schools in the North and to guide these children to look upon such schools as allies rather than enemies.

1. A realistic proportion of Negro teachers, counselors, and administrators should serve in the public schools, particularly integrated schools.

2. Teachers, both white and Negro, with special interests and training in education of minority groups should be employed whenever possible in integrated schools.

3. Teacher training institutions must offer courses in minority-group education, and should sanction for employment in schools with an integrated student body only those teachers who have successfully completed these courses.

4. Race-minded and bigoted faculty members, employed in integrated schools, should be identified and ruthlessly removed whenever possible. Perhaps expressions of racial hostility could be grounds for immediate dismissal as a violation of policy of the board of education. Administrators in integrated schools must, as a group, be on the lookout for and ready to identify such teachers whose general attitudes toward Negro children indicate hostility. If this is a difficult task which may depend upon subjective determinations, one need only consider the alternative of allowing hate-minded people to continue to deal with Negro children on a teacher-student level.

5. All schools, but particularly those that are integrated, must place emphasis upon the historical contributions of Negroes to the development of man's culture and American institutions. Most history textbooks today ignore Negro history in America except for a line mentioning Nat Turner and a

paragraph describing how Dred Scott was considered a piece of property and not a man.

6. Business, professional, union, civic and sport leaders, both white and Negro, should be encouraged to come to the school in the community to discuss with students the kinds of employment opportunities available for those who do well in school and who plan to continue in advanced training of one kind or another. The presence of Negro professionals, union and civic officials, businessmen, and sport figures may not only do a great deal to encourage Negro students to feel that there is opportunity for them, but may as well open the eyes of a few white children concerning the role and the worth of the Negro in American society.

7. Schools, through home visits by faculty personnel, should encourage Negro parents to attend school functions and to become identified with the school and its problems.

8. Negro students (together with white) in junior high and high schools should be sent as missionaries into the lower grades of the elementary schools to talk with the children and impress upon white and black alike the necessity of treating school seriously. Again, the presence of Negro upperclassmen in an elementary classroom talking intelligently to small children about school and its value may not only encourage Negro children to consider school as worthwhile, but may impress upon white children that Negroes are worth looking up to.

9. Special programs such as Compensatory Education and Operation Head Start should be used always by school districts in integrated situations.

It is not to be suggested that this is all we need to do in America to eradicate race-mindedness from our society. Schools, as mentioned before, can only directly influence children. This influence, however, may become a powerful factor, particularly when it is accompanied by ever-increasing demands for equality in law, housing, employment, and social conditions for our Negro citizens.

If we do not begin today to extend to our Negro children the opportunity to receive equal education we may sorely wish tomorrow that we had.

American Indians: The Most Oppressed Group in the United States

Joseph S. Roucek

The 400,000 American Indians living today on reservations constitute "the most oppressed minority group in the United States," according to then Senator Hubert Humphrey, who pointed this out at the beginning of May, 1964, at a national conference in Washington on improvements in education, housing, and health for the underprivileged citizens. He stressed also that the average family income is low, and that their unemployment rate was "seven or eight times" the national average. "Poverty is the everyday life of the American Indian. No other group in American Life is so victimized," he said.

Another example of the fate of the Indians is provided by the current treatment of the Seneca Indians. They are being driven from their homes by the rising waters of the Kinzua Dam in Western Pennsylvania, although in 1794 the United States signed a treaty with the Seneca Indian nation granting it a reservation along the banks of the Allegheny River in Western New York which the Senecas were to enjoy undisturbed "forever" or, at least, "as long as the grass grew green."

Obviously, government, like young suitors, should not be taken seriously when they use words like "forever," for the Indians are being dispossessed, because most of their land will be submerged under water when the Kinzua Dam flood control project twenty-seven miles downstream will have been completed.

The Indians may, in their wisdom, understand that the living cannot always be bound by the promises of the dead. In 1794, the America west of the Atlantic coast was a great wilderness that Thomas Jefferson thought would take a thousand years to settle, and no one could foresee that the United States population would multiply forty-five times in 170 years. No man dreamed of the mechanization, the rapid transportation, and all the other things that created a larger human gap between 1964 and 1794 than existed between the infant United States and the Roman Empire.

One thing, however, the Indians cannot understand is why it should take so long for them to be paid for their land. A twenty million dollar reparations and rehabilitation bill, passed by the House (and cut down to $9.1 million by a Senate sub-Committee), lay in limbo sidetracked by apparently more pressing business, although some 140 Indian families had to find new homes by October 1. They no longer refer to the President as "the Great White Father," and as far as they can tell, the white man still speaks with a forked tongue.

[The] War on Poverty

Yet, the problems of the Indian have not been entirely forgotten in Washington. . . . For, ironically, the Indian in the United States has been the subject of such concern by the federal government for a longer time than any other group in the nation. In fact, the special character of the Indian problem is attested by the foundation of the Indian service as a branch of the federal government with no counterpart in all the other American minority situations—although the problem of the American Red Man concerns directly less than one-half of 1 percent of the total American population.

[Most would] agree that a major problem involved in fighting Indian poverty—and no one denies it is some of the worst poverty in the nation—centers on the reservations. Should the aim be to end the reservation system and force the Indian abruptly to enter the "mainstream" of American life? Or should it be to strengthen the reservation, to cause the Indian to turn more toward his own culture and its ways of solving problems?

These two approaches represent the two extremes. The former was the policy of the New Deal under which Indian Commissioner John Collier sometimes set up schools to teach Indians their own language. The latter was the policy of the Eisenhower administration which sought to "terminate" Indian tribes, to bring to an end the special relationships they had had with the federal government.[1]

Nevertheless, neither approach appears to have brought the Indian very far up from poverty. All evidence shows that the "terminated" or otherwise "landless" Indians have frequently ended up in Indian slums, such as can be found in Rapid City, S. D., or in Billings and Great Falls, Montana. The responsibility for the care of them has been simply shifted from the federal to local governments. On the other hand, the Indian living on a reservation has realized a strong sense of identification with it, often becoming completely dependent on a paternalistic federal government, refusing to be budged into any movement toward self-sufficiency.

Using as a guide a report prepared by a task force headed by Commissioner Nash, [recent] administrations have tried to find a middle way and, at the same time, [to stress] less a "way" than a pragmatic approach to each problem, an approach geared to the general belief that self-sufficiency is needed.

"There are many encouraging signs of success," claim some Indian leaders.[2] But these leaders also emphasize that these programs have been scratching only the surface, and that they must be greatly expanded before they make a significant and permanent dent in Indian problems.

The Role of Education

Most of the Indian leaders agree that training or educating young Indians so that a large percentage can live away from the reservation is an important goal. They add, however, that many Indians will remain on the reservation, and that general welfare programs, housing sanitation, and education there must be improved.

The whole history of the efforts of the federal government to "educate" the Indians is rather sordid, since the Federal Bureau of Indian Affairs has often failed to interest the Indians in education and self-improvement and has come to be looked upon as a "father figure" which would solve the Indians' problems. Thus, the Indians have declined in a "welfare culture" basically alien to them. In fact, this is one of the most pitiful stories of the misguided educational efforts in American educational history in regard to America's original "minority."

The historical background is quite interesting in this respect. The original colonies were little interested in Indian education, although several colleges, including Dartmouth and Harvard, made provisions for tuition-free admissions of the Red Man, and the Continental Congress employed, in 1775, a schoolmaster for the Delawares.[3] The Revolution stopped educational efforts on behalf of the Indian, and until 1819 Indian education was left entirely to a few missionary societies; from that year to 1873 ten thousand dollars was appropriated annually for the work, and most of it was turned over to the missions.[4]

In 1871, Congress decreed that no Indian tribe shall be acknowledged or recognized as an independent nation, tribe or power, with whom the United States may contract by treaty,[5] thus marking the beginning of a definitely new phase in Indian-white relations. The Indians became wards of the federal government, a unique status for any minority group in the United States. The policy of the Indian Office from that time on aimed at weakening the tribal organization of the Indians, destroying their culture, and forcing their assimilation as individuals into the normative American way of life.

One phase of forced assimilation concerned the educational program. Indian children of school age were taken out of their tribal homes and placed in boarding schools, where the use of Indian languages and the practice of Indian folkways and mores, such as dress and hair styles, were prohibited. The curricula there were largely those of the white schools, without any consideration as to the particular needs of the Indians. Whatever practical training the Indian children secured either for making a living or making better homes was gained from the labor they performed to help to support the schools; thus a mediocre school system tried to prepare Indian children to live like white people, when in fact most of them would return home to live as Indians.[6]

It is true that the appropriations by the federal government were increased regularly after 1873; but until 1929 Indian education had been a hodge-podge. Most Indians attended public schools—and this is still true—while large numbers went to mission schools. Many attended boarding schools, both on and off the reservations, established late in the last century on the theory that Indian education needed the removal of the children from their parents and home life, so that they could be "civilized." Force was often used to take them from their homes, and the schools were characterized by a rigid discipline and a standardized outmoded course of study. Half of the time was devoted to school work, the other half to doing routine institutional tasks such as laundering, cleaning, wood-chopping and food preparation. Since the work was hard, physically, and required many hours a day, this often affected the health of the pupils. Conditions were worsened by insufficient operating funds, resulting in dangerously low standards of living. Forbidden to speak their own language in school, out of touch with family and tribal life, denied the normal experience and education needed to prepare them for life as Indians, the children would return home from school dissatisfied misfits, unable to readapt themselves to reservation life and equally unable to find a place in a white community. They had learned to read and write, but they were unfamiliar with the customs and language of their own people, and found their schooling of little use in making a living. . . .[7]

The New Deal policy replaced this first phase of the Indian reservation policy in 1934. Yet, even the new ideology has hardly made any dent in the overall problem of Indian education. Economically, the American Indian was pauperized, and the education of the younger Indians had made them marginal individuals *par excellence,* not ready to take their place in the white American world, and unsettled for Indian life. This policy of "acculturation" had failed simply because the forms of Indian culture patterns still were more divergent from the dominant WASP (White-Anglo-Saxon-Protestant) culture pattern than that of any other American minority. A complicating element was introduced by the record of low standards of personnel of the Indian service.[8]

The Indian Program Since World War II

It is true that World War II did much to have the American Indian accepted into the American stream of life, yet, in September 1951, John R. Ride, Winnebago Indian killed in action in Korea, could not be buried in a cemetery in Sioux City, Iowa, because he was not of the "Caucasian race." It was only because of the direct intervention by President Truman that he was buried with military honors in the Arlington National Cemetery.[9]

Furthermore, in spite of the hopes to liquidate the government's responsibility to the Indians by the policy of "relocation" and "termination," the United States has been unable to convert the American original natives to the "American way of life."

In 1952 the Bureau of Indian Affairs scheduled the Voluntary Relocation Program under which reservation Indians, as individuals or as families, were granted financial and other help to move to industrial centers for permanent employment and settlement. The Bureau put the proportion of relocated Indians who by 1955 had returned at about 24 percent. This program hardly influenced the more basic problem of helping the reservation Indians to develop viable economies, working out their own problems, and being able to decide how much of the traditional Indian heritage they might want to retain.

On August 1, 1953, Congress passed the "termination" program, aiming to have tribes request termination of their relations to the federal government. But this meant also in many cases dissolution of tribal organizations and division of tribal assets among the members, with the resulting demoralization and pauperization of many tribes.

Perennial Educational Problems

Noteworthy in the present situation are the difficulties faced by the Indians of school age.

The Indian youngster, even today, lives in a continuous state of conflict. This is especially true in regions where the color line is not sharply drawn, and where there are no absolute prescriptions marking off the role shared by all other citizens and the role of Americans shared only by those with colored skin. Under such circumstances, the Indian can never be certain of his status or sure of his welcome. While restricting casteways are undoubtedly detrimental under any conditions, they are bound to be more traumatic to the individual when they are not an integral, inevitable, and therefore impersonal part of the social structure. School segregation in former days also had a most unfavorable effect on the Indian pupils, seriously interfering, in extreme cases, with both their work and play. Confused by the failure of the authorities to offer a rational explanation for it, such children sometimes reached the conclusion that it must be a form of punishment for being "red." Many, therefore, on the basis of surface impressions, developed defenses against their anxiety by repressions, substitutions, overcompensations, and anti-social behavior.

This, therefore, presents the perennial problem of American education when confronted by the existence of "minorities": how to relate the concepts of cultural pluralism to total assimilation. Should young Indians be integrated into American society as Indians, or should they be encouraged to acculturate as rapidly as possible to the typical "American way of life," although this might lead to complete estrangement of their families' background?

Obviously, the integration of Indian children into schools off their reservation has been a mixed blessing. The Indian child's clothes, languages, and social customs set him apart psychologically, and the situation was complicated by his inability to participate financially in most extracurricular and social activities on equal terms with his white classmates. This feeling of being different accounts in large measure for the 60 percent drop-out rate among Indian high school children.[10]

Then there are the conflicts in the educational goals. While the typical American educational system favors individualism and competition, the Indians are group-minded. For the Navaho Indian, for instance, to take initiative in any obvious manner has the psychological effect of separating him from his own social group. By training and experience he works best as a "member of a familial group where authority is diffuse, informal, and shared, and where adequate performance is enforced by the subtle action of 'shaming.' " [11] In fact, most American Indians see no value in competition. To strive to excel in games or compete in school work is to them quite impolite, to say the least. For instance, some Hopi school children evidenced embarrassment and resisted the injunction to turn around from the blackboard just as soon as they finished a problem. Distinction of this sort was not a part of their culture.[12]

The "deculturalization" of the Indian child has, in turn, produced quite an abyss between the world of their families and of the school, reaching the point where the federal government once withdrew rations on an Indian reservation to force Indian parents to send their children to school.[13]

Underlying all these factors has been the persistent race consciousness of dominant-status Americans, evaluating often Indians as "colored" peoples and hence, as inferior.

The contemporary goal of governmental policy toward the American Indian is that he should attain economic self-sufficiency and develop skills in retaining his lands and natural resources. The assumption is that this will make them no more vulnerable than other Americans and enable them to compete with the rest of the world. The goal is also to have the Indian assume full responsibilities for citizenship, including payment of taxes on land now held in trust for him by the government. (In the opinion of most specialists this is not likely to be reached any earlier than the year 2,000.) In fact, some critics stress that there is still no firm, definite program to reach such goals, and no rigorous timetable to achieve it. Nor, they claim, is there even a real trend of policy or a vigorous drive among officials to head for it. Indeed, the Bureau of Indian Affairs has been accused of arbitrary methods that inadvertently reverse the advance of the Indians toward "complete self-reliance and delay the end of their paternalistic supervision by the government." [14]

The Views of the Indians

So far, we have been viewing the problem of the American Indian from the "American" point of view. Little is actually known about the social attitudes of the Indians, especially of the youngsters. In this respect, two pieces of research on Indian attitudes—from a relatively small sample—by Spindler using the Rorschach technique lead to some interesting conclusions.

The Spindlers describe a rather remarkable group of Indians "who had attained occupational and social positions equivalent to those of high status in the nearby white towns," and had undergone a psychological transformation toward the middle-class American value system; in the other case, the Indians who have appeared acculturated gave evidence of a corroded psychological structure, in which such shifts as had taken place were "regressive and disintegrative." [15]

The conclusion of the Spindlers is that there are some older Indians still holding to the ancient values of their people with conviction, but that the great majority of adults stand between the old and the new in various degrees of confusion and society. But all are "insecure." [16]

About half of the American Indians are under the age of twenty, and we can only guess how much regression and disintegration found by the Spindlers among older Indians exists among them. We do know, however, that the young Indians tend to leave school earlier than white children. While the average number of years of schooling for adults over twenty-five in the general population is over ten years, for Indians on reservations it is between five and six.[71] The proportion of Indian children who graduate from high school is less than two-thirds of whites.[18]

An analysis of the hopes of the young Indians is offered by Hoyt who studied 582 essays on "My Hopes for My Life in Leaving School" from Indian children fifteen to seventeen years of age in all types of schools (boarding and day, federal public integrated and public exclusively, Indian, missionary, vocational and nonvocational institutions) in the Southwest. He then secured 207 essays from white children of the same ages for purposes of comparison.[19]

Hoyt's report is that reference to the old values of Indians "was entirely negative. This is the more striking since the essays were from the Southwest. There was incidental reference to values learned in school, values some children wanted to carry back to their people." But nearly one third of all these children featured love or concern for their parents, family or tribe, "reference to family being about twice as common as references to tribe, and especially common among the children of the least sophisticated of the schools. No white child of native parentage spoke of love for parents or family, but a few white children spoke of love for humanity or desire to serve it." [20]

Regarding the material aspects of the standard of living, one-third of the Indian children wanted to own something of their own, "car" being most frequently noted. But white children favored cars, too, although "less frequently, no doubt taking them for granted." Thus, "in general the frequency of expression of interest in material things to be owned was similar among Indian children and white children."

Most interest was shown in a job by the Indian children: 91 percent wanted a regular job, and most wanted it off the reservation. Nearly the same percentage of white children wanted a job, but mentioned nothing steady or regular about it "which was no doubt taken for granted."

"The concentration of interests in jobs and the remarks relating to achievement—and possible frustration"—were the most striking thing about these essays. The mention of "steady" and "regular" was particularly interesting in view of the fact that

Indians have the reputation for being interested primarily in casual or seasonable labor, tasks which require a major but temporary concentration of effort.

But these children knew hardly anything about the jobs available to them or what was needed as preparation for them. The uncertainty of Indian children seemed primarily to be uncertainty as to what possible jobs there might be; the uncertainty of white children seemed to rise from knowledge of too many jobs, from which they could not choose.

In general, "Indian children in integrated schools knew somewhat more about jobs than the other Indians; these schools were in urban communities and the Indian children were rubbing shoulders with other children whose fathers had a variety of jobs." And the second "most striking thing about the essays was the psychological insecurity some children expressed. They had much more humility of ambition and much more lack of confidence than the white children." In fact they had "various fears that they might not 'make the grade,' even for low-level jobs. Many were concerned for their family and tribe should they have to leave them for jobs. While the older and embittered Indians ascribe Indian failures to the prejudices of whites, these children felt no bitterness about this."

It is obvious that formulating an approach to the war on poverty among Indians is immensely complex, and that much confusion exists. Undoubtedly this is true of the war on poverty in general, and Indian leaders and federal officials hope that the Indian experience will produce some useful knowledge which can be applied to similar situations.

The Migrant: Exploited Man of the Year

John A. Palmer

Previous articles have discussed those members of our society who have not enjoyed many of the presumed advantages of the American mainstream—individuals whose children come to the public schools with attitudes, achievements, and aspirations considerably different from those of the dominant group. In practically every case, the author has sketched in the physical milieu of the group being discussed, so that the reader has been able to visualize the crowded tenements of Harlem and "Spanish Harlem" in New York City, the gutted storefronts in Newark's central ward, the line of rickety cabins leading out of Jackson or Mobile or Birmingham, the tenements of Detroit, Denver's barrio, Seattle's decaying waterfront, or the sharply stratified neighborhoods of East Los Angeles. Or any ghetto that you may happen to know better than those above.

In each case there has been an indigenous setting in which the vicious cycle of poverty, discrimination, illiteracy, and exploitation is played out—a neighborhood of some sort in which a child could grow up within certain primary and secondary groups: his immediate family plus the extended family of grandparents, cousins, and the like; and then his immediate environment, in which a nucleus of neighbors, store operators, everyone from area clergymen to nearby hustlers was known to him and knew him. The assortment may be an unorthodox one: no father, perhaps, or a group of illegitimate siblings, or adult models who might be considered inappropriate by some. Nevertheless, there is a "community," and it provides a reasonably predictable environment over which the individual eventually achieves some degree of mastery.

Even this relatively stable part of life, however, is often the subject of attack, today, by an impersonal society-at-large. Large-scale urban renewal projects which demolish whole neighborhoods in a matter of weeks, plus the effective liquidation of certain geographically associated occupations such as coal-mining in West Virginia, are making staggering inroads against the sense of home and community. (In the case of the miners, or pockets of elderly people caught in a city neighborhood which has become the center of a new and unfamiliar ethnic minority group, however, it appears that many, if given the choice, would rather remain where they are—amidst the familiar—even if it means a loss of livelihood. In the case of urban demolition, of course, no such choice is possible.) In general, the feeling of community is strong among individuals who lack the financial and professional mobility which could take them away from their birthplace.

There is one segment of our population, however, whose lives are characterized by extreme mobility—who have, in fact, no permanent home or, at best, several homes. They are the migratory workers who follow the crops, going where labor is needed. For the most part they work for wages considerably below those the proprietors would have to pay local residents to do the same work, and they tolerate conditions that other workers would find intolerable. Their story is a shameful chapter in American history. The neglect of their children by the American educational system is equally appalling in a society dedicated to universal education.

With the advent of efficient mechanical equipment as a result of the Industrial Revolution, small farmers could not compete with the giant farming combines. Due to advancing technology, therefore, many small farm owners in the Northeast left their land. They tended to move into the city, although some took up the life of a migrant worker because they understood only farming. In the South the Negro and Anglo families who were forced to migrate had never known anything but poverty. Marginal farm owners, displaced tenant farmers, or simple sharecroppers, they were unable to compete with a growing mechanized agriculture. Uneducated beyond the farm and unskilled in other pursuits, they had no option but to join the migratory stream. In the West, a similar demand for cheap labor encouraged the migration of Mexicans, Chinese, Japanese, Filipinos, Hindustani, itinerant whites and blacks, and, today, Hawaiians.

Among the first migratory routes in America was one that crisscrossed the incredible "Miller Empire" in the Southwest. Founded by an enterprising German immigrant, Henry Miller, who landed in America in 1847 with only a few dollars in his pocket and subsequently developed a large estate, this early labor camp set the tone for much of the subsequent treatment of migrants in this country. Miller actively solicited itinerant individuals, encouraging them to pass through his vast estate during harvest time so that he could give them a job. The stream in which they traveled to and from Miller's land became known as the "Dirty Plate Route"—named because Miller's foremen gave the workers their one meal a day after the foremen had eaten, so that the workers could eat from the foremen's unwashed plates. Miller expressed the view that feeding the workers more frequently would encourage them to stay on after they had fulfilled their tasks.

The major migrant streams as we know them today flow from Florida up the East Coast, or across to Texas, and from Texas up the western part of the United States. This pattern began to take shape in 1920, when rich farm lands were developed in the Florida Everglades.

Florida's subtropical climate can harvest three or four crops a season, enabling the migrant to work winters in Florida, then move up the Middle Atlantic States during the early summer, finishing in the North during the summer and early fall. Alternately, he can move into Texas and from Texas on up the West Coast. This pattern was solidified in 1950 when a new variety of tomato was developed in Florida, intensifying the demand for cheap seasonal labor. Solidification of the migrant stream gave rise to the "crew leader" who has become an important entity in the life of the migrant worker.

It is the crew leader who wields real power over many migrants, for he is the liaison man between migrant and grower. It is he who contacts the farmer, does the hiring of migrants, and in most cases arranges for transport of migrants from farm to farm. His mode of conveyance may be a dilapidated bus or a ramshackle truck loaded to the brim with migrants. The crew leader also controls the purse of the migrant worker. If he is honest the migrant will go "home" (his base is usually in Florida or Texas) with savings earned from his harvesting. If the leader is dishonest, he will contrive to drain the migrant of all or most of his money before he leaves the area—either by subsidizing the migrant and then charging him exorbitant prices for food, drink, lodging, and transportation, or by making a deal with the local storekeeper to up the prices of goods and then taking a percentage of the receipts himself. There are approximately 8,000 crew leaders in the U.S. migratory stream.

Some migrants fend for themselves, traveling in rundown trucks, buses or jalopies. No better off than those who travel with a crew leader, they may, in fact, be subjected to even greater prejudicial treatment by the foremen.

What does the migrant worker find when he lands at a farming camp? Actually, he has a high degree of what might be called autonomy, for, although the camp is owned by the grower, the grower allows the migrant to operate it—up to a point. In essence, this means that no one picks up the garbage and no one collects the debris which builds up in the area. Repairs on the chicken coop hovels or tin shacks are nonexistent. Paint is unknown. The floors, if they exist, sag badly. The roofs leak. The walls are cracked and uninsulated. Doors and windows lack screens and, in many instances, window panes. The average size of these "holiday homes," as they have been called, is about eight feet by sixteen feet. Illumination usually consists of one bare, glaring light bulb, although some may actually have an antique kerosene lamp. If the arriving migrant comes upon the kerosene fixture, he realizes he is in trouble, for this sets the tone for the basic conditions of the camp. In all probability there will be an unvented kerosene stove for cooking. Beds will have vermin filled mattresses. Adding to the impoverishment, these "homes" usually do not have any running water, so that privies, frequently "four seaters" located behind the "homes," are necessary.

In recent years "motel" types of camps have been constructed in response to demands from the British and Mexican governments that improved living standards be provided for West Indian and Mexican workers. Such camps are less objectionable, in that everything is constructed of concrete: walls, chairs, tables, the floors, even the beds. A number of these camps have hot and cold running water. Compared to the standard American migrant camps, they are palaces. Although migrant camps in general have shown some improvement in recent years, however, most remain almost as they were thirty years ago.

The irony of this situation is that the ill-used migrant must pay rent for sub-standard accommodations forced upon him. Growers or crew chiefs charge these people as much as $2.00 to $3.50 rent per week. Migrants must also pay for utilities used. The flagrant abuse this can involve is illustrated by a case in western New York in which a worker paid $8.55 for electricity for one month, $2.78 for stove gas, and $9.06 for one week's supply of kerosene for his cabin heater. Payment of these bills must come out of the worker's meager wages, which range from fifty cents an hour to $1.25 an hour.

Food in the community store (provided the migrant can get to the store) is usually priced 30 to 40 percent higher than food sold to year-round customers. Liquor is almost impossible to obtain. One migrant worker in western New York paid a dollar for a pint of wine, and $2.75 for a half pint of cheap whiskey obtained through the crew leader. As might be expected, the crew leader may also traffic in drugs and in prostitution.

It would seem that these itinerant workers do not have adequate assistance in obtaining their basic rights within our society —despite the fact that the Teamsters Union has maintained it was working for their advancement. In their quest for justice, these indigents, from the grape pickers in California to the migrants of Long Island, have taken special encouragement in recent months from the United Farm Workers Organizing Committee headed by a Mexican-American, Cesar Chavez.

For five years Chavez has fought tenaciously for better working conditions and more equitable pay for migrant workers. His main objective in California, currently his home state, have been the growers of table grapes. After three years of turmoil in California, which yielded no tangible results, he was able to organize a surprisingly effective national boycott of table grapes. Picket lines against the purchase of California table grapes were set up in most of the large cities in the United States.

Equally important to his cause was Chavez's charismatic personality. His dynamism and persistence attracted the attention of the nation at large, above and beyond the college students who worked for him and well-known personages like Charlotte Ford and the late Senator Robert Kennedy. Chavez's tireless efforts were finally rewarded on July 30, 1970, when he and his followers signed a viable working agreement with 75 percent of California's grape growers.

Even though there has been some success of this kind in gaining a foothold for the migrant, however, many communities still remain totally aloof to the plight of the itinerant worker.

The communities in which these people labor are not always directly involved in their exploitation, yet they must undoubtedly be declared guilty in the last analysis, if only because they tend to look askance at the indigents, regarding them perhaps as a necessary evil to be tolerated until the harvest is over. For the most part, the local community tends to view them as indolents who want only to drink, eat, sleep, and do as little work as possible. Without doubt, it would be painful to open their eyes to the needs and desires of this neglected group.

This is especially true for the migrant children. Born in a broken-down hut or, at best, in the emergency room of a local hospital which he will probably never visit again, the child adopts the field for his nursery and the artifacts of the camp area for his toys. He grows up in an environment of the most rustic type, ignorant of anything beyond his immediate surroundings. He may stay at a camp as long as three days or three months. As he moves from place to place, he is unable to develop a traditional concept of a home.

The migrant child's mobility also curtails his chances for an education. At the very best, statistically, he will achieve a fourth grade level of competence. Compulsory education laws require that all such children attend the local school wherever they are, but incomplete records make enforcement difficult and some communities would prefer to close one eye to truancy rather than disrupt the ongoing school system. As soon as he is old enough, the child is under great pressure to enter the fields in order to supplement parental income.

Lacking any informed perspective on his situation, the child is likely to fall prey to an endless cycle of migrant thinking which will consume his energy. The victim of a poor diet, he will be prone to certain sicknesses—although he may ultimately be stronger than many of his non-transient counterparts.

These here-today-and-gone-tomorrow children, it seems fair to say, are clearly "deprived" of much that makes childhood a rich and exploratory period of life. Exposed early—often exclusively—to the potentially satisfying experience of working with the natural environment, they are nevertheless denied not only the rewards of the harvest but even the opportunity to witness the complete cycle of planting, growing, reaping.

It cannot but be acknowledged that community shortcomings do mitigate against better treatment for the migrant child. Rural communities which require seasonal work do lack funds to provide for migrant children. They do lack teachers to respond to the particular needs of the migrant child. There *are* placement problems for migrant children in community schools, and there *is* overcrowding when migrants enter a community. A number of communities, however, knowing the provision for migrant children is an important part of their educational mandate, have seemingly gone "overboard" on their plans for migrants' instruction, in a way that separated these children from their contemporaries. In his important book, *La Raza*, the story of the Mexican Americans, for example, Stan Steiner cites a sample migrant school curriculum from the "master migrant plan" of the state of California, which includes:

Physical education-English cultural games and activities. . .
Creative arts and crafts-Introduction to English culture, music and song. . .
Arithmetic-Concrete objects, English concept of arithmetic. . .
Social Studies-Developing knowledge of characteristics of English culture. . .[1]

Steiner points out, of course, the conspicuous absense of studies on the Indian, Spanish, or Mexican cultures of the Southwest. He might well also mention the lack of attention to West Indian or Puerto Rican history. The point is clear, that, whatever the advantages of setting up special schooling for migrant children who cannot attend one school regularly, the advantages appear outweighed by what seem to be concerted efforts to "English-ize" these children, despite the fact that their life style and life work will tend to be grounded much more fully in the subculture to which they belong than to the Anglo society which would school them. Until we recognize that primary group and extended-family loyalties may well be stronger than ties to the mother country, this dichotomy of educational objectives will probably persist.

John Steinbeck wrote, many years ago:

. . . in the eyes of the hungry there is a growing wrath. In the souls of the people the grapes of wrath are filling and growing heavy, growing heavy for the vintage. . . .

The Dropout: Family Affect and Effect

Robert D. Strom

"The most vivid truth of our age," Margaret Mead has suggested, "is that no one will live all his life in the world into which he was born, and no one will die in the world in which he worked during his maturity." Rapid change appears to be the mode for our time with all facets of community life subject to adaptation. Serving to lessen or undermine the cohesion of society's primary unit, the family, has been a passing of home industry, the frequent employment of both parents, the invention of the automobile, and the development of commercial amusements.

In spite of universal exposure to these changes, our society today is comprised of more divergent family types than ever before. Differing by section of the country, communities within cities, ethnic and religious groups, economic and social classes, and vocations, families vary according to life cycle, number and role of family members, locus of authority, and life style. Both in apparent variety and essential unity, the American family needs to be viewed in a perspective of ongoing transition from an old rural institution form to a democratic companionship type of relation geared to an urban environment with a shift of emphasis from rigid stability to adaptability.

Juxtaposition of Dropout Effect—1900–1963

Just as family operation has altered during recent times, so too has the changed effect of school dropout on families. Early in this century, when a youngster quit school his decision had a negligible effect on the home. Indeed, in some cases the family encouraged such a decision. Because 90 percent of the working population were persons whose secondary education was incomplete, there was no stigma attached to leaving school before graduation.

Nor was a dropout's family held in disdain by neighbors, for they viewed a youngster's preference of work to school not as a shameful choice but as a legitimate alternative. Moreover, there was no public cause for concern about whether a dropout would constitute a social liability as the transition from education to employment was a smooth one with over half the available jobs requiring few if any skills and little or no academic preparation.

However, drastic changes in the economy and occupational structure have served to diminish job prospects for today's dropout. No longer are a third of our people employed on farms, as was true in 1900. Today only 10 percent are so employed and it is predicted the ratio will decline to 5 percent by 1970. No longer are most available jobs for the unskilled. Today these jobs constitute only 17 percent of the positions in our labor market, and it is predicted this percentage, too, will decline to 5 percent by 1970. Indeed, the number of unskilled jobs in our economy is less today than it was 15 years ago despite the fact that the work force has increased by several millions in that period.

The problem is not that there are more dropouts today but that there is a smaller demand for them than ever before. There no longer is the absorptive quality in the work force to take care of mistakes made in the educational system.

No Room at the Bottom

Accompanying the decrease in job opportunity for less-educated persons is an unprecedented growth in the number of young people entering the labor market. During [1960–1970] the number of workers under age twenty-five [was expected to] increase by at least 45 percent. Since most of this influx is comprised of men and women who have twelve or more years of formal schooling, it is understandable that the approximately

700,000 dropouts each year are last in line to secure an ever-diminishing number of low-level jobs for which they might be suited. For the first time, there is "no room at the bottom."

At this juncture, communal concern becomes more than just a regard for wasted talent. The dropout's problem makes him a public liability; his lack of funds becomes a public debt rendering a severe financial burden upon the community in which he resides.

For example, some 270,000 persons are on public assistance in Cook County, Illinois. Fifty percent of the Chicago area reliefers cannot read at the eighth-grade level; over half of them are under thirty-two years of age. Because of their youth the latter group may be expected to reproduce young who will, in turn, drop out. According to Raymond M. Hilliard, director of public aid for Cook County, grants totaling approximately $15 million a month are made to these people. . . .

The Culture of Poverty

It would appear that leaving school before graduation has a deleterious effect on the dropout and his family, for without economic efficiency he lacks a vital requisite for community respect. It follows that parents of dropouts may view their youngsters' decisions with disappointment, distress, or anger. None of these emotional reactions are exclusive to a particular stratum of society. It is not always the middle-class parent who is disappointed nor is it always the lower class parent who doesn't seem to care. Because this is true it would profit us to examine the reciprocal of dropout effect on the family and concern ourselves with the family affect on dropout.

In considering the lower class, one finds that novelists and urban sociologists have been preoccupied with an image of the slum as a place where the violent contrasts of city life find their sharpest expression. Slums are seen both as urban jungles in which lawlessness prevails and, because of their association with tight little immigrant colonies, as the last stronghold of traditional, intimate social life in the impersonal city. These two images—the slum as jungle and the slum as ghetto—still dominate both the sociological and literary approaches to this subcommunity. Which approach is more correct is subject for conjecture.

Conditions May Foster Dropout

One can say with certainty, however, that within the neighborhood where the so-called "culture of poverty" exists, there are familial tendencies which induce conditions that foster dropout.

Here one finds a high proportion of disrupted and broken homes where the father often is absent and in which a distance of parental relationship results in dilution of affection for the young. Ten to 15 percent of the fathers in white slum families are seldom home evenings while 50 percent among the Negro fathers are seldom home. Where no father is present in the evening, there is usually no organized meal, no organized opportunity for language exchange, no real interaction. The common result is a cumulative deficit in the language component of a youngster's development. This becomes most obvious by the eighth grade, where in the area of reading such children are usually two years behind.

Then, too, there is a dearth of family activity outside the home. In the case of many youngsters this means they have never been to the country, to another city, or even out of their neighborhood.

Recognizing the inadequacy of the life space in which such children function, some educators have attempted to compensate for cultural deprivation by initiating preschool or early-school enrichment programs designed to include a dimension of experiences which are comparable to the background usually brought to school by children from middle-class families. Ostensibly this exposure will allow the child from a poor neighborhood a more adequate chance to compete in school.

Strengths Emerge from Slums

If, in fact, competition is a virtue of school programing, it is unfortunate that we eliminate the competitive potential of youngsters from slum areas. We do this by failing to recognize certain strengths emerging from their background. When these strengths are declared off limits they become non-functional and the child is forced to compete at a disadvantage by using strengths characteristic of the middle class. For example, youngsters of poverty often have a richness of language expression which is unacceptable in the classroom. Though high in verbal output, such a child usually has poor command of syntax and verb form so that he is unable to say what he would like to say inasmuch as class rules demand that proper expression be used.

Students from slums have a remarkable degree of independence and seldom need continued adult approval for their actions. As a result they might well be given responsibilities in the classroom; but under the current system anyone with poor grades is denied such an opportunity.

Studies in New York City have shown some pupils from poor areas to be more co-operative than their peers from better neighborhoods; for having always been at the bottom, they less often seek a scapegoat.

It also has been shown these children have a lengthy interest span for that which is familiar to them. Lamentably, most of the materials in texts do not represent the type of life to which they have been exposed; so, their attention span is considered, unfairly, as shorter than that of middle-class youngsters. It is hoped that some of the strengths of children from the culture of poverty may become functional in the school if our aim to encourage and enhance self-esteem is to be realized.

Teachers Expect Little

Finally, parents in the culture of poverty have an adverse effect on the schooling of their young as a result of the social image they represent to the community. A recent statement by John Neimeyer, president of Bank Street College, New York, asserts that a major reason for low achievement among children in poor neighborhoods is the low expectation held by the teachers as to their learning capacity. Instructors often perceive a youngster in this element who misunderstands directions as one who is challenging school authority. An inadequate tax base assures the schools in low-income districts of substandard teacher salaries so that, for the most part, tired or inexperienced teachers are attracted.

In fairness, one should say that the parents in low-income areas may be naive but they do have deep hope that, through the school, their children will achieve a better life than they themselves have had, even though these parents may not know how to give the support which is the logical concomitant of this attitude. In terms of fundamental motivation which can serve to aid learning, what more can a school ask?

Middle-Class Affect

The magnitude of problems in the culture of poverty ought not to prompt one to assume that the desired parent-student relationship exists in the middle class. Looking at the social structure of the common suburb one finds a paradox. On the one hand, it arranges matters so that the daily life of the individual, no matter what his age or sex, is divided into many compelling tasks that leave little or no time for freely chosen activities. Like modern industrial employment, which it fundamentally resembles, the suburb is fanatically devoted to the rhythm of keeping busy with even the playtime of children subject to routine. Many families find that the separate schedules of the various members leave no time for intimate moments with one another.

On the other hand, while people are so desperately busy, they do not know or have forgotten how to perform some of the most elemental tasks. Most glaring evidence of this is the crisis over child-rearing, where anxious mothers, uncertain how to raise their children, turn to scientific experts to find out whether their children are normal or, even more important, what the standards of normality might be.

For many parents in this middle-class segment of society who live through their children as extensions of themselves, somehow hoping to accomplish through their progeny what was not possible in their own lives, the concept of preparation for college becomes a paramount concern from the day the child enters kindergarten to the senior prom.

Realizing that promotions, honors, awards, and scholarships are contingent upon marks, many parents early choose grades rather than growth as a goal for their child in school. The student, if successfully indoctrinated, relocates his interest from subject to grade. That this occurs is obvious to any who have taught in middle-class neighborhoods where report cards are used by parents as status symbols. A premium is put on marks; parents often bribe, cajole, or threaten a child to obtain them.

Underlying the pressure imposed on the child is an assumption that most, if not all, can have high grades if they just work hard enough. In many cases this results in a student's making lower marks than his industry would normally permit him to make, simply because his concern impedes effective concentration. Some pupils whose school work has become grade-oriented are unduly disappointed as they perceive failure to get a grade as complete failure and hence lose even that which is within their reach. Although one cannot accurately assess the degree to which preoccupation with grades retards learning, few psychologists would deny the amount as influential.

All of us should be acquainted with the unnecessary anxiety, disappointment, and parental disfavor accompanying report time for some youngsters. By the nature of grading systems, the weaker student is forced to endure failure over and over again. Aside from the questionable desirability of such negative motivation, the blighting effects of constant frustration upon personality development should be a matter of grave concern.

The School As Parent Surrogate

Attention has been given to the affect of low- and middle-class families on dropout. But what of the family with which we are most familiar—the school? As parent surrogate operating under *in loco parentis*—in place of parents as agents or substitutes—how does it affect the dropout? In some ways the affect has been to stimulate enrichment and remedial programs but by and large it has been negligible or negative.

Before the potential dropout can realize his appropriate educational opportunity, certain views must undergo alteration. Popular acceptance is needed for a concept which allows quality to occur within a framework of quantity. Presently quality is viewed solely as academic rigor and as such necessarily is confined to those whose intellectual prowess has been demonstrated. Adherence to this limited view of quality finds expression in schools around the country which perpetuate a restricted, formalized curriculum that was appropriate in the nineteenth century when only the so-called "cultured few" were represented in secondary schools. When one prescribed then that "everybody" should study certain subjects, everybody meant anybody who was somebody but today the term everybody is coming to mean "everyone."

It is obvious that actual curricular change has not kept pace with changes in educational objectives as our schools have ostensibly moved from serving a select clientele to the future body politic. In some cases educators have shown a remarkable ability to resist new knowledge and research findings. This has been especially true in the area of individual differences, where resistance to innovations of proven value would seem to indicate a belief that it might be easier for youngsters to modify their needs than for the school to change its requirements.

Every year a significant number of basically sound young Americans discover that they are not really wanted, and that neither their teacher nor their curricular experiences seem to pay any attention to who they are, to what they have and what they have not, to what they can do and what they cannot do, but instead impose upon them a nonsensical experience which goes under the name of education.

At his news conference of August 1, 1963, the late President Kennedy asked all American parents to urge their children to go back to school in September and to assist them in every way to stay there. This cure is both inadequate and irrelevant to the real problem of the dropout. Students are not leaving school because they are too short-sighted to realize that more education would benefit them, but because they are learning nothing of value or nothing they perceive as valuable.

The assumption that the cause of dropout lies within the person himself has been challenged by only a few educators who have recognized that in some cases high incidence of dropout may be a symptom of the school's chronic disorder. There is need for each school faculty to examine its own program and procedures, to ascertain whether the institution itself engenders any factors which might tend to encourage dropout. Special attention might be directed toward constructively challenging any fallacious assumptions which operate to reject or squeeze out a segment of those leaving school. The most prominent areas which tend to eliminate pupils show up in the following questions:

Do set standards exist for all students on the assumption that equality of education may be realized through an identical course of study?

Does the evaluation system measure individual progress or communal improvement?

If individuality is excluded as a criterion for marking in deference to a curve measure, can we purport that grades represent individual growth or achievement?

Does scholastic eligibility squeeze out some by denying them the privilege of participation in athletics, newspaper club, and other extracurricular activities because their grades are not in accord with a requisite?

Does this not inadvertently affect holding power and student interest by taking from such students the one thing they relate to in school?

Is discipline a squeeze out?

Is there a social squeeze out by fraternities, sororities, or peer groups in student affairs which can induce dropout by exclusion?

What can be done to modify those factors which might squeeze out some pupils?

Questions such as these are incumbent upon any staff which seriously hopes to diminish the problem.

Curriculum change is not always an easy venture, for there will be those who prefer to introduce noise rather than improvement. The current debate about curriculum seldom demands that the major points of view confront one another. As a result, college intellectuals attack popular education in their journals; administrators defend their programs to the school board; and students of curriculum report their research in uncongenial verbiage.

Part of this disconnection relates to the fact that we suffer from an odd claustrophobia of occupation and groups in American life: the sense of isolation and insulation that seals off historians from journalists, jazz from long hair, Catholics from Mormons, Republicans from Democrats, and television repairmen from everybody. There is need for concern that a discipline like education, purporting to communicate to all, be able to communicate amongst its own.

Arthur Koestler, in a provocative book entitled *Darkness at Noon,* has the chief character, Citizen Rubashov, state the following dilemma of one who has fallen victim to his own political party:

> The party denied the free will by the individual and at the same time expected his willing self sacrifice. It denied his capacity to choose between two alternatives—and at the same time demanded that he should constantly choose the right one. It denied his power to distinguish good and evil—and at the same time spoke pathetically of guilt and treachery.

Perhaps analogy is not amiss at this point. Do we not overwork the language or doctrine of individual differences and yet seldom employ this practice in teaching and evaluating children? Do we not insist that children remain in school because it is good for them when, in fact, for those whose history of failure is constant this is socially sadistic? Do we not tell the student he ought to choose what's right and yet limit his right of choice by giving him no alternative within the curriculum? Is tyranny a word for events on foreign soil or does it include the practices of some public schools? Until potential dropouts are individually helped to succeed, schools will collectively fail.

A Curriculum for the Disadvantaged

Robert J. Havighurst

In writing usefully about school programs which will be valid for the coming decade in the education of the economically disadvantaged, it is important to look ahead at the shape of things to come, and to avoid being turned to stone by the backward look at the ways of the past.

What is the probable social setting in the 1970's for children of the poorest 20 percent of the American population? With considerable assurance we can predict the following:

1. Increased real income and greater stability of that income. Some reform of the welfare system is sure to come very soon to provide a basic family allowance for every poor family. It will operate to keep fathers and mothers together with their children.

2. Higher educational level of low-income parents. The increase in grade-level attainment since the war is reflected in the young adults whose children are now beginning to enter school. Lower-income parents will be better able to appreciate the school experience of their children, to read to them, etc.

3. Pre-school education for at least one year before the age of five. An improved and amplified Head Start program is now ready for widespread use, and teachers trained in one of several programs proven successful will be available in increasing numbers. These successful programs are raising the I.Q. level of disadvantaged children by an average of 10 to 15 points and keeping this gain for three years, at least. In another year or two, we will know whether these children retain their improved learning ability up to the third- or fourth-grade level. If they do, we will be able to employ a curriculum for the intermediate grades which is based on the assumption of very little reading retardation of children in inner-city schools.

4. Improved methods of working in primary grades with disadvantaged children. This is part of the situation we have just described. Once a child from a disadvantaged family has been aided substantially by a pre-school program, he will continue to be aided by primary school teaching that gears in with his Head Start experience.

5. Slowly decreasing racial and economic segregation in the schools. The pattern of residential segregation by race and income which was set in the 1950's and supported by public housing practices will only slowly be overcome by the forces now at work to produce integration in the central city and the suburbs. While we may expect substantial change in the direction of integration, it will not affect large proportions of disadvantaged children during the decade immediately ahead.

6. A gradually increasing gap in material style of life and in social attitudes and values between the middle class and the disadvantaged lower-class group. Though the gap will continue throughout the decade, it will become less noticeable. The "subculture of poverty" which dominates the life style of many poor families today will lose much of its grasp.

To some readers this may appear to be an over-optimistic view of the immediate future, but it seems essentially realistic to me. It is far better for the schools to "tune-up" to the future than to prepare for a disappearing past.

The goal of education for all children, rich or poor, from literate or illiterate families, is the same if it is expressed in general terms. This is to help the child become a competent and happy person, now and in the future, in a democratic, productive, and increasingly urban society. There is no distinction here between social classes. It does not make sense in this society to talk about "turning a lower-class child into a middle-class child" as though this were a good or a bad thing to do. There are common goals of competence and happiness in a productive and socially integrated society. Children will differ individually, because of social group differences, in their progress toward these goals. The school's mission is to help all children move toward these common goals.

There are two important questions to be answered with respect to the curriculum for economically disadvantaged children. One has to do with *methods* of teaching, the other with *content* of the curriculum.

Methods for the Disadvantaged

There is a growing body of data on the relation of reward to learning among children which supports the following propositions.[1]

1. There are differences among socioeconomic groups and ethnic subcultures in the reward systems they teach and use with their children. External rewards (material, or intangible— such as praise) and punishments are to be contrasted with internal (superego and ego) rewards and punishments.

2. In general, external rewards (material or intangible) have greater positive value for disadvantaged or failing children.

3. Appropriate teaching methods can help a child evolve from the external to the internal reward system.

Thus a system of deliberate external rewards (material things like toys, gold stars, edibles) and praise should be employed with disadvantaged pupils.

A Child-Originated Curriculum?

When children do not learn well in school, we naturally ask ourselves whether there is something wrong with the curriculum or the way it is presented to the pupil. There are two contrasting answers to this question. One is that we adults are imposing a limited, rigid curriculum on children and putting their minds in a strait-jacket. The other is that we do not present the curriculum in such a way that the child can understand what he is doing and where he is going.

The first view has had considerable play during the last few years, in a revival of the child-centered curriculum movement which was popular in the 1920's and 1930's. Among its persuasive presenters are John Holt and George Dennison, authors of books recently published. Holt, in his book, *How Children Learn*, says,

> Only a few children in school ever become good at learning in the way we try to make them learn. Most of them get humiliated, frightened, and discouraged. They use their minds, not to learn, but to get out of doing the things we tell them to do—to make them learn. In the short run, these strategies seem to work. They make it possible for many children to get through their schooling even though they learn very little. But in the long run these strategies are self-limiting and self-defeating, and destroy both character and intelligence. The children who use such strategies are prevented by them from growing into more than limited versions of the human beings they might have become. This is the real failure that takes place in school; hardly any children escape. . . . What is essential is to realize that children learn independently, not in bunches; that they learn out of interest and curiosity, not to please or appease the adults in power; and that they ought to be in control of their own learning, deciding for themselves what they want to learn and how they want to learn it.

As expounded by Holt, this proposition seems to apply more to middle-class children than to the economically disadvantaged group. However, Herbert Kohl's *36 Children* appears to present much the same kind of case, based on experience in a Harlem ghetto school.

Kohl describes how he worked for a year with a class of thirty-six Negro slum children who were below average in academic skills. He did get results. There is no reason to doubt this. His method of encouraging them to write about their fears, their hates, and their likes, about the bad and good things they experienced in their homes and streets, loosened their pens and their tongues, added to their vocabulary, and got them interested in school.

What Kohl appears to have done was to attach school learning to the impulses of the children. By helping them to talk and write about the things that were most impelling in their daily lives, he made school relevant to them. To put this into psycho-dynamic terms, Kohl was marshaling the forces of the id on behalf of learning, just as Holt proposes to do. But Holt talks in "safe" middle-class terms about children's curiosity and interests, while Kohl faces the slum realities of children's fears and hates.

But how far can a system based on children's felt needs go? How far can a slum child (or a middle-class child) go toward mastery of arithmetic, of English sentence style, of knowledge of science and history, if he is motivated only by his drive to express his feelings or to satisfy his curiosity, or possibly also by his desire to please his friendly and permissive teacher?

We do not know how far this kind of reward will carry a child's learning. We might guess that it would carry children up to about the seventh-grade level. Therefore, we should ask Kohl and others of this school of thought to prove that their methods will carry children to the eighth-grade level. No such claims appear to have been substantiated, except in the case of socially advantaged children, such as those attending A. S. Neill's school at Summerhill, England. And some observers of this school argue that it can only work with children who have a strong British middle-class superego, and can profit from teaming their somewhat starved id with the superego in the pursuit of learning.

The contrasting view of curriculum calls for more rather than less adult-created structure than the pupil generally gets today, but a structure which is carefully fitted to the student's present knowledge and to his motives. It aims to achieve "a real dialectic of authority and empathy in the classroom," which Donald Barr, headmaster of the Dalton School, [has] called for in his criticism of Holt's position.

The essential element is the pupil's perception of the connection between what he does in the classroom or in his school work and a result which he wants. When this condition is met, the pupil's ego can come into action to guide his effort and reward his success.

Programmed learning is an example, where it is used skillfully. The pupil accepts an assignment to learn a particular lesson or set of facts, and he is informed immediately of every successful step he takes toward this goal.

According to this view, the pupil must accept the notion that he has hard work to do which will require effort on his part in order to achieve the goal that he sees clearly.

Another example is the Mastery Program which Benjamin Bloom has helped to work out in schools in Puerto Rico, a program now ready for general use. The work assignments are divided into relatively small units with frequent tests for mastery. The pupil works for the mastery of his assignment and keeps on working until he has demonstrated mastery. No matter how slow he is, compared with the rest of his class, he achieves mastery before going on to the next assignment. Bloom has found that the slow pupils move along much more rapidly than he had expected. Not only do pupils learn more effectively, they also come to enjoy learning. Bloom says:

> The clearest evidence of affective outcomes is the reported interest the student develops for the subject he has mastered. He begins to 'like' the subject and to desire more of it. To do well in a subject opens up further avenues for exploration of the subject. Conversely, to do poorly in a subject closes an area for further study. The student desires some control over his environment, and mastery of a subject gives him some feeling of control over a part of his environment. Interest in a subject is both a result of mastery of the subject [and] a cause of mastery.

The successful innovative programs for high-school-age students also contain this element of motivation toward a clearly understood goal. For example, the storefront academies that give high school dropouts a chance to prepare for the G.E.D. test and high school diploma equivalency probably are successful because they work with young people who have become convinced that they need more education; they see clearly the connection between their study in the storefront academy and the achievement of this goal.

The Upward Bound and High Potential programs for disadvantaged high school and college youth, where they are successful, seem to combine the element of motivation to succeed with a clearly outlined program of study for a summer or a semester. Such programs can be seen as a long step forward by the student.

Emphases for the Disadvantaged

The argument to this point has been as follows: Economically disadvantaged children have difficulty in the school system for two reasons:

1. Their family environment limits their perceptual, conceptual, and linguistic experience in their early years, thus preparing

them poorly for school. But this family factor is improving, due to the reduction of poverty and the increasing level of education among low-income parents.

2. Teaching methods in the schools have not been well-adapted to the learning styles of economically disadvantaged children. But recent research has shown the way to improved methods of teaching these children.

This line of reasoning suggests that there is no special need for a special curriculum for the disadvantaged child.

Still, there are certain topics and subject areas that might well be given special stress in a school that serves disadvantaged children and youth. These have one or the other of two kinds of value:

1. *To meet specific deficiencies in the life of the child.* For example, it is well established that the diet of children in poor families is very likely to be inadequate, partly because the family lacks money to pay for essential foods and partly because the child and his family lack knowledge about nutrition. Therefore it would seem wise to put special emphasis on the study of nutrition at two levels of the school—the third- or fourth-grade level, with simple and clear rules about diet, and the ninth- or tenth-grade level, with science-based information about nutrition.

2. *To meet self-image needs in the child and adolescent.* Several disadvantaged minority groups have been given shabby treatment in American history and literature, which gets into the school curriculum and tends to undermine the self-esteem of children of these groups when they meet this material in front of their classmates. Three groups have suffered the most from this kind of experience—Negroes, American Indians, and Mexican-Americans.

For the sake of all American youth, the study of these minority groups should be more accurate, truth-based, and positive.

For the sake of minority group members whose forefathers are presented as inferior, cruel, savage, or servile, and who are themselves subject to discrimination in contemporary society, there may be some value in special readings and projects which give them a more positive picture of the past and present status of their own ethnic group.

Conclusion

Thus my conclusions concerning the education of the economically disadvantaged are:

1. We need a pre-school program of at least one year's duration aimed at improving the cognitive and language development of disadvantaged children.

2. Elementary school teachers need to learn more effective methods of rewarding disadvantaged children for effort and achievement in school.

3. Elementary school teachers need to create and maintain an orderly classroom regime in which pupils are convinced that they will be rewarded in the future for consistent effort today.

4. A relatively small adaptation of the ordinary school curriculum should be made to fit specific knowledge deficiencies and self-image needs of disadvantaged children and youth.

Notes

CULTURAL DEPRIVATION AS A FACTOR IN SCHOOL LEARNING/
TABA

[1] A revision of a lecture presented at The Merrill-Palmer Institute, March, 1963.

References

Allinsmith, W. and Goethals, G. W. Cultural factors in mental health: an anthropological perspective. *Rev. educ. Res.*, 1956, 26, 433-438.

Bernstein, B. Language and social class. *Brit. J. Sociol.*, 1960, 11, 271-276.

Deutsch, Martin. The disadvantaged child and the learning process: Some social, psychological, and developmental considerations. Paper presented at Ford Foundation work conference on curriculum and teaching in depressed urban areas. Teach. Coll., Columbia Univer., July, 1962.

Eells, K. Some implications in school practice of the Chicago studies of cultural bias in intelligence tests. Harvard educ. Rev., 1953, 23, 284-297.

Elam, S. L. Acculturation and learning problems of Puerto Rican children. *Teach. Coll. Rec.*, 1960, 61, 258-264.

Guilford, J. P. The structure of intelligence. *Psychol. Bull.*, 1956, 53, 267-293.

Haggard, E. A. Social status and intelligence. *Genet. Psychol. Monogr.*, 1954, 49, 141-186.

Hebb, D. O. *Organization of behavior*. New York: Wiley, 1949.

Hunt, J. McV. *Intelligence and experience*. New York: Ronald Press, 1961.

Jenks, C. Slums and schools. *The New Republic*, 17, Sept. 10, 1962.

Kahl, J. A. Educational and occupational aspirations of "common man's boys." *Harvard educ. Rev.*, 1953, 23, 186-203.

Krogman, Judith. Cultural deprivation and child development. *High Points*, 1956, 38.

Landis, Oneida. Teaching children to think. Yolo County Schools, Woodland, Calif. (Mimeo)

Miner, J. B. *Intelligence in the United States*. New York: Springer, 1957.

Riessman, Frank. *The culturally deprived child*. New York: Harper, 1962.

Sexton, Patricia. *Education and income*. New York: Viking, 1961.

Sigel, I. E. How intelligence tests limit understanding of intelligence. *Merrill-Palmer Quart.*, 1963, 9, 39-57.

Taba, Hilda. *Curriculum development: theory and practice*. New York: Harcourt Brace, 1962.

——. *With perspective on human relations*. Washington, D.C.: American Council on Education, 1955.

NEGROES AND POVERTY/BATCHELDER

References

[1] A. B. Batchelder, "Decline in the Relative Income of Negro Men," *Q.J.E.*, Nov., 1964, pp. 525-48.

[2] G. S. Becker, *The Economics of Discrimination* (Chicago, 1957).

3 David Caplovitz, *The Poor Pay More* (Glencoe, Ill., 1963).

4 E. F. Denison, *The Sources of Economic Growth in the United States* (New York, 1962).

5 L. A. Epstein, "Unmet Needs in a Land of Abundance," *Soc. Sec. Bul.*, May, 1963, pp. 3–11.

6 Charlotte Erickson, *American Industry and the European Immigrant, 1860–1885* (Cambridge, Mass., 1957).

7 C. D. Long, "An Overview of Postwar Labor Market Developments," in *Proceedings of the 4th Annual Social Security Conference* (Kalamazoo, 1962).

8 Edgar May, *The Wasted Americans* (New York, 1964).

9 R. H. Mugge, "Aid to Families with Dependent Children," *Soc. Sec. Bul.*, Mar., 1963, pp. 3–15.

10 Mollie Orshansky, "The Aged Negro and His Income," *Soc. Sec. Bul.*, Feb., 1964, pp. 3–13.

11 ——, "Children of the Poor," *Soc. Sec. Bul.*, July, 1963, pp. 3–13.

12 E. J. Perkins, "Unmet Need in Public Assistance," *Soc. Sec. Bul.*, April, 1960, pp. 3–11.

13 R. L. Plaut, "Increasing the Quantity and Quality of Negro Enrollment in College," *Harvard Educa. Rev.*, Summer, 1960, pp. 270–79.

14 H. W. Reynolds, Jr., "The Human Element in Urban Renewal," *Public Welfare*, April, 1961, pp. 71–73ff.

15 J. J. Spengler, "Demographic and Economic Change in the South, 1940–1960," in *Change in the Contemporary South*, A. Sindler, ed. (Durham, 1963).

16 J. H. Street, *The New Revolution in the Cotton Economy* (Chapel Hill, 1957).

17 Cook County Department of Public Aid, *First They Must Read* (Chicago, 1964).

18 Greenleigh Associates, Inc., *Facts, Fallacies and Future* (New York, 1960).

19 U.S. Bureau of the Census, *U.S. Census of Manufactures: 1958*, Vol. II: *Industry Statistics*, Part I (Washington, 1961).

20 ——, *U.S. Census of Population: 1910*, Vol. IV: *Occupation Statistics* (Washington, 1914).

21 ——, *U.S. Census of Population: 1930*, Vol. II: *General Report* (Washington, 1933).

22 ——, *U.S. Census of Population: 1950*, Vol. II: *Characteristics of the Population, U.S. Summary* (Washington, 1953).

23 ——, *U.S. Census of Population: 1960. Detailed Characteristics, U.S. Summary* (Washington, 1963).

24 ——, *U.S. Census of Population: 1960. Subject Reports. State of Birth* (Washington, 1964).

25 ——, *U.S. Census of Population: 1960*, Supplementary Reports, *Low Income Families:* 1960, PC(S1)-43, 24 Feb., 1964.

26 ——, *Statistical Abstract of the United States: 1964* (Washington, 1964).

27 U.S. Bureau of Labor Statistics, *Consumer Expenditures and Income, Urban United States 1960–61*, Supplement 1 to BLS Report 237–38 (Washington, 1964).

28 ——, *Employment and Earnings*, Sept., 1964, II.

29 ——, "Plant Adjustments to the $1 Minimum Wage," *Monthly Labor Rev.*, Oct., 1958, pp. 1137–42.
30 U.S. Commission on Civil Rights, *The 50 States Report* (Washington, 1961).
31 ——, Report: 1959 (Washington, 1959).
32 ——, *1961 Report*, Book 4, *Housing* (Washington, 1961).
33 U.S. Commission on Race and Housing, *Where Shall We Live?* (Berkeley, 1958).
34 U.S. Department of Agriculture, *U.S. Census of Agriculture: 1959*, Vol. II, *General Report* (Washington, 1962).

Notes

AMERICAN INDIANS: THE MOST OPPRESSED GROUP IN THE UNITED STATES/ROUCEK

1 John Collier, "A New Deal for the Red Men," in W. E. Washburn, *The Indian and the White Man* (New York: Doubleday, Anchor Books, 1964), pp. 392–396.
2 Dick Gilluly, "War on Poverty Fixed on Indians," *Christian Science Monitor* (June 8, 1964).
3 Alden Stevens, "White American Indian," *Survey Graphic*, XXIX (March 1940), pp. 168–174.
4 For details, cf. Clifton E. Olmstead, *History of Religion in the United States* (Englewood Cliffs, N. J.: Prentice-Hall, 1960), pp. 179–182, 415–418.
5 Ray A. Billington, *Westward Expansion* (New York: The Macmillan Co., 1949), p. 668; pp. 651–680 covers Indian-white relations from 1860 to 1887.
6 Gordon Macgregor, *The Changing Indian Warriors Without Weapons* (Chicago: University of Chicago Press, 1944), pp. 116–127.
7 Stevens, *op. cit.*
8 Clark Wissler, "American Indian Tribal Groups," in Frances J. Brown and Joseph S. Roucek (eds.), *Our Racial and National Minorities* (New York: Prentice-Hall, 1937), pp. 37–55. Also Robert F. Heizer, "The American Indian," in Brown and Roucek (eds.), *One America* (New York: Prentice-Hall, 1952), pp. 27–31, and R. A. Schermerhorn, *These Our People: Minorities in American Culture* (Boston: D. C. Heath, 1949), pp. 57–82.
9 Joseph S. Roucek, "The American Indian in Literature and Politics," *Il Politico*, XXVII (1962), pp. 569–585.
10 "U.S. Indians," *New York Times* (May 31, 1964).
11 Dorothea Leighton and Clyde Kluckhohn, *Children of the People* (Cambridge: Harvard University Press, 1947), p. 107.
12 Franklin J. Shaw and Robert S. Ort, *Personal Adjustment in the American Culture* (New York: Harper & Row, 1953), p. 33.
13 E. E. Dale, *The Indians of the Southwest* (Norman: University of Oklahoma Press, 1949), p. 182.
14 Milton L. Barron, *American Minorities* (New York: Alfred Knopf, 1962), p. 154.
15 G. D. and L. S. Spindler, "The American Indian Personality Types and Their Socio-Cultural Roots," *The Annals of the American Academy of Political and Social Science* CCCXI (May 1957), p. 152. Also, A. T. Hallowell, *Culture and Experience* (Philadelphia: Univ. of Pennsylvania Press, 1957), Chaps. 5, 19, 20.

[16] Spindler, *op. cit.*, pp. 154–167.
[17] *Educational Cutdown* (Washington, D.C.: Bureau of Indian Affairs, 1959), p. 9.
[18] *Today's Dropouts, Tomorrow's Problems* (Washington, D.C.: Bureau of Indian Affairs, 1960), p. 2.
[19] Elizabeth E. Hoyt, "Young Indians: Some Problems and Issue of Mental Hygiene," *Mental Health*, XXXXVI, 1 (January 1962), pp. 41–47.
[20] *Ibid.*, p. 44.

Notes

THE MIGRANT: EXPLOITED MAN OF THE YEAR/PALMER

[1] Stan Steiner, *La Raza: The Mexican Americans*, p. 212.

References

Moore, Truman. *The Slaves We Rent.* Random House, New York, 1965.
National Committee on the Education of Migrant Children. *A Policy Statement on the Education of Migrant Farm Workers*, June 6, 1968, New York, 1968.
National Committee on the Education of Migrant Children. *Who Is the Migrant Child?* New York, 1968.
Newsome, William E. "We Open the Doors for Migrant Children." *N.E.A. Journal*, April 1967.
New York Times. "Migrants Returning to Same Shacks and Poverty," March 12, 1967.
Ruehl, Myrtle R. *Where Hannibal Led Us.* Vantage Press, New York, 1967.
Shotwell, Louisa R. *The Harvesters.* Doubleday and Company, Inc., New York, 1961.

THE DROPOUT: FAMILY AFFECT AND EFFECT/STROM

References

Burgess, E. W. "The Family in a Changing Society," *Cities and Society.* Edited by Paul K. Hatt and Albert J. Reiss. New York: Free Press of Glencoe, 1957, pp. 477–482.
Deutsch, M. *Reversing the Effects of Social Deprivation.* Address delivered at the Washington Center for Metropolitan Studies, Washington, D. C., Oct. 23, 1963.
Henry, J. *Culture Against Man.* New York: Random House, 1963, p. 495.
Koestler, A. *Darkness at Noon.* New York: The Macmillan Co., 1941; also The New American Library of World Literature, Inc., 1961, p. 215.

Mead, M. "A Redefinition of Education." *NEA J.* 48, No. 7 (Oct. 1959), p. 16.

Mitchell, J. V. "Self-Family Perceptions Related to Self-Acceptance, Manifest Anxiety and Neuroticism." *J. Educ. Research* 56, No. 5 (Jan. 1963), pp. 236–242.

Niemeyer, J. H. Home School Interaction. NEA Dropout Symposium, Washington, D. C., Dec. 2 to 4, 1963, p. 3.

Stein, M. R. "The Slum: Street Corner Society," and "Suburbia: Dream or Nightmare?" *An Interpretation of American Studies*, Princeton University Press, 1960, pp. 119–134.

Strom, R. D. "Comparison of Adolescent and Adult Behavioral Norm Properties." *J. Educ. Psychol.* 54, No. 6 (Dec. 1963), pp. 322–330.

Notes

A CURRICULUM FOR THE DISADVANTAGED/HAVIGHURST

[1] These propositions are developed more fully in my article on "Minority Sub-cultures and the Law of Effect," *American Psychologist*, 1970 (in press).

References

John Holt, *How Children Learn*. New York: Pitman Publishing Company, 1967.

Herbert Kohl, *36 Children*. New York: New America Library, 1967.

Donald Barr, "The Works of John Holt," *The New York Times Book Review, Special Education Book Supplement*, September 14, 1969.

Benjamin S. Bloom, "Learning for Mastery," *Administrator's Notebook*, April, 1968 (Midwest Administration Center, University of Chicago). See also B. S. Bloom, J. T. Hastings, and G. Madaus, *Formative and Summative Evaluation of Student Learning*. New York: McGraw-Hill, 1970.

Further Reading

In addition to references cited by authors in this Part the following texts may be useful.

Braithwaite, E. R. *To Sir With Love*. Englewood Cliffs, N. J.: Prentice-Hall, Inc., 1960.

An important work of fiction, this book depicts the wholesome influence of a dedicated teacher upon disadvantaged children of another race.

Kozol, Jonathan. *Death At An Early Age*. Boston, Mass.: Houghton Mifflin, 1967.

A moving account of urban education, this book was written by a former teacher in the Boston public schools.

Passow, A. Harry, Miriam Goldberg, and Abraham J. Tannenbaum (eds.). *Education of the Disadvantaged.* New York, N. Y.: Holt, Rinehart, and Winston, Inc., 1967.

A comprehensive collection of readings by some of the most perceptive writers on education of the disadvantaged. Students will find many thought-provoking articles throughout this anthology.

Tiedt, Sidney W. (ed.). *Teaching the Disadvantaged Child.* New York, N. Y.: Oxford University Press, 1968.

In this book, which provides considerable insight into working with disadvantaged children, the reader is referred especially to pages 3–19.

Films of Related Interest

"Children Without" National Education Association, 29 min.

Depicts life for children living in the inner city.

"A Desk for Billie" National Education Association, 57 min.

Documents the life and education of a migrant child.

"Incident on Wilson Street" Anti-Defamation League, 16 min.

Shows the influence of sympathetic teachers upon the lives of children from disadvantaged backgrounds.

Part V

Emerging Professional Issues

All the bright hopes which I entertain for a more glorious future for the human race are built upon the elevation of the teachers' profession and the enlargement of the teachers' usefulness.

Horace Mann
American Educator, 1845

As a profession expands and develops, the roles of its members undergo modification. This is true of education at the moment. One need only walk casually through a contemporary elementary school, high school, or college to note marked contrasts with similar settings only a decade or so ago. Today's teachers communicate by means of overhead projectors at least as much as by chalkboards. Students are frequently grouped in small clusters rather than long rows. A college class may not meet at all for an entire semester, as students pursue independent work in the field or the library. Librarians handle microfilm and computer printouts along with books. The principal—or the college president, or the president of the school board—straddles a calendar of diverse activities more like that of a busy political figure than like those of his predecessors. One could go on and on, in documenting the radically new roles that have emerged in the profession during recent years.

Equally noteworthy are the individuals who occupy these positions-without-precedent. For they are virtually devoid of models. The old adage that **teachers teach as they were taught** appears to have less and less validity as the content, methods, the goals, and the social context of education continue to evolve in new directions.

And yet each person in the profession is, by virtue of the methods through which we appoint people to schools, a product of the system that is already changing before his eyes. He brings with him preconceptions about how things "ought to be"—either more or less like the way they were when he went through school. And with each passing year he tends to grow further away, at least in experience and chronological age, from

355

the students who are the focal point of the educational system. At the same time, he tends, provided he is the sort of individual who is open to new experiences, to acquire perspective, a deepened understanding of the recurrent issues that he faces, and increased skill in the interpersonal and other aspects of his duties. The emerging nature of the new professional in education will be a product of all these factors: shifting societal conditions, new types of people in new positions, and the legacy from the past that these individuals carry with them into their work.

What sort of person is attracted to teaching today?

How great is his commitment? What are his chief goals? What kind of teaching assignment does he seek? How is he like or unlike past American educators in these respects?

A generation gap is said to exist between present-day students and their parents. To what extent does the same gap exist between students and teachers? Between students and administrators?

In what way are teachers similar to other groups of workers who organize for collective bargaining purposes (truck drivers, electricians)? In what ways are they similar to "professionals" (doctors, lawyers) who traditionally have not had unions but have banded together in professional associations?

Some have become concerned that the new collectivism among public school teachers detracts from the energies they devote to their work. Others have made the same charge against students who have organized to change the schools or other aspects of society. How realistic are these concerns?

Teacher Organizations: An Analysis of the Issues

Michael H. Moskow

The recent development of negotiation procedures between school boards and teacher organizations has had a strong impact on the teaching profession and on teacher organizations. Both the American Federation of Teachers and the National Educational Association have developed their own concepts of negotiations, and they have made strong efforts to persuade school boards to conduct representational elections and to negotiate with the designated teacher organizations. To say that competition has been spirited here is to illustrate dramatic understatement.

Although the two organizations have been competing since 1919, the struggle gained new impetus in December, 1961, when the United Federation of Teachers, a local affiliate of the AFT, was elected bargaining agent for 44,000 New York City public school teachers. The UFT received nearly three times as many votes as the NEA's hastily formed contender, the Teachers Bargaining Organization. More important, though, was the fact that for the first time the labor movement gave active support, in the form of personnel and financial resources, to a local of the AFT. Shortly after the victory, the AFT joined the Industrial Union

Department of the AFL-CIO, the major contributor to the UFT.

Since that time, the IUD, headed by Walter Reuther, has been deeply involved in organizing public school teachers and conducting campaigns for collective bargaining. In response to this challenge, the NEA formed a department called the Urban Project to direct its fight against unionization. In the ensuing struggle, large sums of money have been poured into the campaign by both contenders.

NEA Background

The NEA has a membership of over 900,000 consisting of "classroom teachers, school administrators, college professors, college administrators, and specialists in schools, colleges, and educational agencies which are both public and private." Classroom teachers in public schools constitute over 85 percent of the total membership. One of the major beliefs of the NEA, however, is that since education is a profession unique unto itself, membership in associations should not be limited to classroom teachers. Therefore, *all* state affiliates and most local associations accept both teachers and administrators as members.

In line with its concept of professionalism, the NEA uses the term "professional negotiations" to distinguish its efforts at bargaining from the traditional collective bargaining procedures of the labor movement. When an impasse arises, it advocates various forms of third-party intervention, most of which consist of modified types of mediation and fact finding, requiring the bargainers to accept a decision of an impartial arbiter. At no time, however, does it advocate using state labor relations agencies or state mediation agencies since, in their opinion, disputes should always be settled through "educational channels." In extreme cases, when agreement cannot be reached, the Association may resort to sanctions ranging from publicizing unfavorable teaching conditions in a particular school district to a mass refusal to sign contracts by all teachers employed in the district.

In reality, "professional negotiations" is a generic term which the NEA uses to refer to a wide variety of different relationships between school boards and local teacher associations. For example, a local affiliate is considered to have a Level I professional negotiations agreement if the school board has made a written statement, which may be in the minutes of the board meeting, that it recognizes the association as the representative of all teachers in the district or even merely as the representative of its own members. Level II agreements consist of recognition and establishment of a negotiations procedure. If a means for settling impasses is added, the agreement is then considered Level III.

It is interesting to note that the Association classifies as professional negotiations a general school board policy statement which establishes a procedure for recognizing employee organizations, but names no specific representative of the teachers. In addition, dual and proportional systems of representation are considered professional negotiations. On the basis of this inclusive definition, it is not surprising that the NEA can claim over 346 local affiliates that engage in professional negotiations. It does not mention, however, that most of these local groups are merely recognized by the school board as the representative of their members or of all teachers in a district—often a far different thing from the actuality of meaningful negotiations in practice.

Union's Rise

Nationally, the AFT has over 100,000 members, the majority concentrated in large cities. The constitution grants locals the right to determine on an individual basis whether or not administrators shall be admitted as members; but few administrators join, and they are often prohibited from holding office or even voting on motions. Thus, the Federation emphasizes that it is the only organization specifically devoted to the interests of classroom teachers.

As expected, the AFT makes no effort to distinguish its approach to teacher-board relations from traditional collective bargaining. Although it does not advocate strikes as a means of settling impasses, the 1963 national convention passed a resolution (No. 79) which recognized the right of locals to strike under certain circumstances and urges ". . . the AFL-CIO and affiliated international unions to support such strikes when they occur." This resolution is of special importance because previously there had been no official strike policy even though locals had been supported when they went on strike.

Although the AFT has been advocating collective bargaining for over 20 years, it has displayed no clear understanding of exactly what collective bargaining for teachers distinctively entails. In fact, the confusion over the AFT's definition of collective bargaining is quite similar to that exhibited by the NEA on professional negotiations. For example, although the AFT claims to have approximately 12 written agreements between school boards and teachers' unions, only four of them include terms and conditions of employment, while the others are merely recognition agreements. In addition, several agreements do not provide for exclusive recognition; and in two cases, the school boards have signed written agreements with both the NEA affiliate and the AFT local.

It is clear then, that in reality, many of the local affiliates of both organizations, while supposedly negotiating, are doing little more than making statements at open meetings of their school boards. It appears, however, that both the NEA and the AFT are aiming for a procedure whereby the school board and the teachers' organization would jointly determine the salaries of conditions of employment of the teachers. Only when this is achieved will true negotiations take place.

In terms of the effect upon school administration, no significant difference between the approaches of the NEA and the AFT seems discernible. Although there are broad ideological differences between the two organizations, the practical impact of their policies is almost identical. The school superintendent finds great difficulty in distinguishing between the NEA's "professional holiday" and the AFT's "strike." If it is often claimed that the AFT is more militant than the NEA, many local instances have been found to the contrary. When negotiations are conducted by either of the two organizations, essentially the same problems arise, and the participants assume essentially the same roles. And even the general tenor of negotiating sessions seems very similar.

Meanwhile, the battle ranges between the NEA and the AFT for the power and prestige that teachers' loyalties will bring and for the dominance of one broad ideology over the other. That battle is well reflected in the recent debate in the *Record* between Carl Megel,[1] representing the union, and Mrs. Marion Steet,[2] spokesman for the Association.

Who Coerces Whom?

Megel pictures the AFT as a strong defender of teacher rights and liberties. After labeling the NEA a "company union," he then attempts to document his argument that administrator coercion is responsible for most of the NEA membership. He presents examples of teacher contracts and salary schedules which contain clauses requiring membership in educational associations. He quotes from administrator bulletins to teachers, urging them to join educational associations, and he then questions the mystique of a voluntary membership of 100 percent. After giving other examples, he restates the AFT's position on the freedom of teachers to join organizations of their own choosing.

In explaining his criticism of administrator coercion to join educational associations, he claims that, "it keeps teachers weak; it denies them an opportunity for real leadership in an educational democracy." At another point, he claims that "an intimidated teacher is a frightened teacher. A frightened teacher becomes a poor teacher, unable to teach democracy properly to sons and daughters of free Americans."

Mrs. Steet takes up this challenge and, in her usual eloquent manner, makes the best of a bad case.[3] Her central claim is "*not* to justify any coercive or conscriptory membership practices of teacher associations or teacher unions, nor to attempt to prove that there is no coercion of membership in teacher organizations anywhere in the United States." Yet she later asserts that a careful study of Mr. Megel's documents ". . . causes one to doubt seriously whether Megel has uncovered even a small coercion conspiracy against teachers." She does admit, however, that four of the bulletins which Megel presented "do say crassly that teachers are either required or expected to join specific professional organizations."

She then very cleverly puts Megel on the defensive by presenting a well documented case that the AFT engages in coercive practices. Mrs. Steet concludes that,

It should be noted that in all his efforts to round up documentary evidence of membership coercion in professional associations, the author has not submitted a single teacher *contract* within the decade of the 1960s containing a clause requiring membership or "service fees" to any professional association.

Appearance and Reality

Thus, although she claims that she does not try to prove that "there is no coercion of membership in teacher organizations anywhere in the United States," what she ends up doing is, first, to criticize coercion of any kind to join teacher organizations; second, to attack Megel's evidence that there is coercion to join NEA affiliates; and third, to attack the AFT for engaging in coercive practices. She leaves the reader with the impression that there is no evidence to support Megel's contention that coercion is applied to teachers to join education associations, and that if there is any coercion (which she admits is wrong), then it occurs in such a small number of cases that it is of no great concern.

Unfortunately, this approach by Mrs. Steet is somewhat misleading. She would have been on much safer ground if she had said that the NEA realized that there was administrative pressure on teachers to join educational associations in some school districts, but that they were attempting to eliminate this practice. She could have documented this contention by showing that teachers are more active in the Association than they had been in previous years.

My own opinion is that anyone who claims that administrator coercion does not exist simply has not come in contact with classroom teachers. It is quite common for a teacher to be told by his principal or superintendent that he is expected to join the Association. Obviously, pressures of this type will rarely be overt or in written form because the practice of forcing a public employee to join an organization as a condition of employment is almost always considered illegal. This does not mean that informal pressures are any less formidable to the teacher.

Pressures will usually be similar to the type described by the Wisconsin Employment Relation Board in the following case:

> It was found that the superintendent had unlawfully assisted the local education association in obtaining recognition on the basis of signed authorization cards checked by the school auditor, while at the same time, the superintendent told the local union affiliated with the Wisconsin Federation of Teachers to petition the WERB for an election if they wished to secure representation rights.

In a later case the Board held that

> a school district, by the action of its principal in soliciting membership applications and dues and by selling tickets for the convention of the Wisconsin Education Association to the teachers employed by the school district, unlawfully assisted such organization and interfered with the rights of its employees to join or refrain from joining a labor organization.

Even though most pressures will be informal, a surprisingly large number of documented cases exist. For example, if Mrs. Steet doubted Megel's contention, all she had to do was to read a letter in the November, 1964, issue of the *Journal* of the NEA. Addressed to the Educational Policies Commission under the date of 10 September, 1964, it said,

> I am a new teacher beginning my teaching career. As a part of my orientation, I was told that I *must join* my professional organization —the NEA. I have done so. However, I have been unable to find out just what I will receive in return for my membership dues and loyalty (italics supplied).

The 1955 report of the Committee on Government Employee Organization Relations of the American Bar Association contains the report of a study conducted by the NEA in 1952. In a survey of 1,516 superintendents, over 16 percent reported that teachers were required to join education associations.

Further evidence of teacher conscription is supplied in my own survey of 150 public school teachers from three different sections of Pennsylvania. Forty-eight percent of the respondents said there was administrative pressure placed on them to join a teacher association.

When presented with evidence that an administrator is forcing teachers to join, Mrs. Steet's response, typical of the NEA's attitude, is that "professional teachers should and do rebel against such practices. Moreover, the NEA and its affiliates encourage and support teachers in throwing off any such tyranny."

Coercion and Union Shop

Things, however, are not quite so simple. It is unreasonable to expect a teacher to rebel against his supervisor when it may mean his job; it is equally unreasonable to expect the NEA to be with him at the barricades. A bit of analysis may help.

First, for example, it is necessary to separate the problem of *administrative* pressure to join teacher organizations from *organizational* pressure to join teacher organizations. The latter refers, of course, to the union shop issue, a controversy all its own that must be separated from the former problem.

Under the union shop, the majority of employees force a minority of employees to join their organization. Instead of being unilaterally decreed by the administrator, it is a right which an organization of employees had obtained through negotiations. If the majority of employees are opposed to the organization security provision, they then have the right to vote out the organization in a secret ballot election.

The union shop issue is basically one of "majority rights" versus "individual rights." It is often termed the "right to work" issue, but a much more accurate statement is "the right to work at terms that have been rejected by the majority of employees." Although this is a question on which reasonable men disagree, Mrs. Steet assumes that the union shop can never be educationally sanctioned.

Forced membership, however, is not necessarily an evil if it is controlled by teachers. Actually, it can be argued that if teaching is ever to be truly a profession, it will be necessary for teachers themselves to control entrance to the profession. Under these circumstances, forced membership into the teacher's organization becomes only an integral aspect of professionhood. A requirement of this type is far different from coercion by administrators, which usually interferes with the effectiveness of a teachers' organization.

Failing to recognize this distinction, Mrs. Steet lumps together the union shop and administrator coercion and then argues against both as if they were the same thing. Ironically, Megel agrees with Mrs. Steet on this point. His opening sentence is "The American Federation of Teachers maintains that teachers have the right to join professional organizations of their own choice without coercion or intimidation." In a later section of the article he restates that "the American Federation of Teachers has historically supported the right of teachers to join the organizations of their own choosing."

Sisters Under the Skin?

Megel's views and those of the AFT are completely opposed to the attitude of the AFL-CIO. In fact, Megel's arguments are quite similar to those used by the Chamber of Commerce and the National Association of Manufacturers in their fight against the union shop. In arguing for a right-to-work law, the Chamber of Commerce states that "A right to work law guarantees that an employee will have the right to work at his job without being forced by anyone—the government, an employer, or a union—to join a particular union."

As the AFT grows in size and wins exclusive representational rights in other school districts, their present position on teachers' freedom to join organizations will become less tenable. Local affiliates which have won exclusive representational rights will want to strengthen their position and thus eventually obtain union shops. A step in this direction has already been taken in New York City, where the UFT has negotiated a provision that prevents an officer of any other teacher organization from representing a teacher who has a grievance. In the near future, pressure from locals will force a change in the position of the AFT on this issue.

The NEA will find itself in the same situation. In fact, leaders of their local affiliates who were victorious in elections with the AFT have already felt the need to strengthen their position as the dominant organization. The Milwaukee Teacher Association, which won a representational election last spring, has petitioned the Wisconsin Employment Relations Board to deny the Milwaukee Teachers Union the right to a dues check-off and to prohibit the MTU from representing teachers when they have grievances. This type of local pressure will produce a change in the NEA's national policy, and eventually the NEA will have to find some euphemism for the "union shop" and begin to advocate it for "professional" reasons.

Administrator Domination

Unfortunately, the arguments of both Megel and Mrs. Steet are somewhat misplaced. With the advent of collective negotiations, one of the most important issues facing any group of teachers is administrator domination of teacher organizations. In order for negotiations to be effective, teachers must be represented by an organization that is primarily concerned with their own interests. If an administrator controls a teacher organization, there is no guarantee that the best interests of the teachers will be represented at the negotiating table.

The NEA is correct in saying that teachers have a great deal in common with other educators (i.e., administrators and supervisory personnel) because they are working in the same field. They do not recognize, however, that a teacher organization controlled by administrators will not be as effective in meeting the distinctive needs of teachers as will be an organization that is controlled by teachers themselves.

Whenever the subject is mentioned, administrators frequently assume that a personal attack is being made, and an objective discussion of the problem becomes exceedingly difficult. On the contrary, most administrators would never think of attempting to dominate their local organizations. But the fact remains that there are instances where this practice occurs, and, where the threat exists at all, the classroom teacher clearly needs protection.

Since the supervisor has the authority to act in the interest of the employer, there is no assurance, of course, that he will act entirely in the interest of the employees. In addition, because of the great difference between the job of the supervisor and those of his subordinates, their separate interests may not be served best by the same decisions. Maximum benefit for the teacher can only be obtained when leadership of his organization is devoted exclusively to his interest. Thus, when a teacher organization is controlled by administrators, the conflict of interests is most likely to produce an unjust situation for the teacher.

This conflict is illustrated vividly in the not unusual circumstances exemplified in Missouri:

> MSTA [Missouri State Teachers Association] leaders take great care to avoid actions that would result in divisions in the educational lobby. As we shall see later, in 1961, MSTA shied away from taking stands that might alienate school boards or county superintendents. Indeed it seems fair to say that a major reason Missouri has no teacher tenure or minimum salary laws is that the MSTA has not wished to alienate its school board supporters in behalf of its classroom teacher constituency by recommending such proposals to the legislature. Unity strengthens MSTA's bargaining position, but also imposes limits on its objectives.[4]

There are many other cases in which the interests of the administrator and those of the teachers will conflict. Suppose, for example, that the teachers decide it is necessary to invoke sanctions against their school district. If a principal or superintendent were leading the teacher organization, it is inconceivable that he could take such an action against himself; an administrator understandably has too great a vested interest in seeing that the schools remain open and that a large number of prospective teachers apply for jobs in his jurisdiction. Comparable trouble arises when a teacher organization urges the reinstatement of a teacher fired for reasons unacceptable to his peers, but must do its urging through the same superintendent responsible for the contest dismissal.

These examples only appear far-fetched. One result of collective negotiations of all types is that teacher organizations will become much more active, and under these circumstances, it is essential that the organization be controlled by the teachers. If control rests anywhere else, the negotiating power of the organization will be diluted.

A Voice Wholly Lost?

Documented cases of administrator domination of teacher organizations are numerous. For example, in the 1952 yearbook of the American Association of School Administrators, results were reported of a survey on the role of the superintendent in the comprehensive local education association in his community. Out of 3,135 replies, 50 percent of the rural superintendents and 56 percent of the city superintendents reported that they were regular members and participated on a par with other individual members. Over 32 percent of the rural superintendents and more than 20 percent of the city superintendents stated that they were influential members and were consulted on the selection of officers and determination of policies.

Further evidence is supplied in the survey I conducted of 150 Pennsylvania teachers. Sixty percent of the respondents said that their teacher associations were dominated by administrators.

Even if it is not admitted that the NEA is dominated by administrators, it must be recognized that the organization does not speak for the classroom teacher. At its 1963 convention, the Department of Classroom Teachers, which "represents" 85 percent of the membership, voted to invoke sanctions against the state of Utah. It also voted for a resolution that would have forced segregated local and state affiliates of the NEA to admit Negro members or drop their affiliation. On the next day, the delegate assembly voted against both of these resolutions; consequently, they were not put into practice. In effect, even though the classroom teachers were in favor of these two resolutions, the NEA took an opposite stand.

Too, the AFT claims that although 85 percent of the NEA's membership is classroom teachers, their executive committee of 11 members has only two classroom teachers; their board of trustees of six members has only one classroom teacher; and the

75-member board of directors involves only 22 classroom teachers. To the best of my knowledge, the NEA has never denied these allegations. When questioned about the subject, NEA representatives claimed that they have no figures on the subject. Thus, there is no reason to think that the AFT's charges are inaccurate. The crucial problem, then— with which neither Mrs. Street nor Mr. Megel really come to grips—is one of how to prevent administrators from dominating teacher organizations. An outright ban on administrator membership in teacher organizations would be one possible solution to the problem. Given present conditions, however, a more feasible solution would be to permit supervisors to join teacher organizations but with certain safeguards to prevent basic conflicts of interest. Such safeguards would exclude administrators from elective office, from important committee chairmanships, and from voting; they might even entail a provision for having administrators leave the meeting room when a controversial topic is discussed.

Some of these procedures are followed by public employees' unions recognized under President Kennedy's executive order No. 10988. In addition, some private employee unions have provisions to accept supervisors into membership but without eligibility to serve on the executive board or on the negotiating committee.

NEA's Major Failure

Mrs. Steet refers to the "substantial contribution of the professional teacher association to public education and teacher welfare." In one place, she points to the "impressive accomplishment" of the NEA, and later she even refers to the "phenomenal success" of the NEA. In talking about the rate of increase in teachers' pay, she considers the 65 percent increase in salaries and the fact that teacher salaries are now about "16 percent above those in industry" to be "impressive."

It is difficult for me to see how Mrs. Steet can claim such sweeping success for the NEA in improving teacher welfare when the average salary of all teachers in 1963–1964 was $5,963.[5] Teacher salaries were only 1.7 percent above earnings for all employees in manufacturing industries, and average earnings of federal civilian employees in 1962 were 12.6 percent above those of teachers. In 1959, earnings of all teachers ranked

14th among average earnings of eighteen professions. Only social and welfare workers, librarians, clergymen, and dieticians earned less on the average than all classroom teachers in the public schools. In Mrs. Steet's own school district in Philadelphia, the maximum a teacher can earn with a masters degree plus 30 credit hours is $8,750.

Another indication of the NEA's failure is the success of the AFT in winning nine of the twenty representational elections held since 1961.[6] On close examination, the victories prove to be remarkable accomplishments: Not only is the AFT generally lacking as a professional organization, but its affiliation with the labor movement is anathema to many teachers. There seems little doubt that that affiliation has seriously hampered its organizing efforts, yet many AFT leaders still view their labor connection as something close to holy and, consequently, refuse to examine its actual benefits and costs. In any case, the AFT victories can only mean that teachers are dissatisfied with the NEA.

The Union Impact?

. . . This challenge of the AFT has apparently produced many drastic changes in the organizational structure of the NEA. For example, the funds allocated to the NEA's Urban Project, which is responsible for teacher negotiations, have increased remarkably since 1961–1962, when only $28,000 was spent. . . . Consequently, over 10 percent of the NEA's budget is now being spent on teacher negotiations—which indicates that at least financially the Association is becoming more of a teachers' organization.[7]

On the local level, collective negotiations have caused a similar trend. For example, in the districts where representational elections were held and eligibility to vote was determined by an impartial person, principals and other administrators have always been excluded from the unit of representation. This trend can only result in administrators being forced into a secondary role in the NEA. In fact, it could easily result in administrators withdrawing from the NEA.

As it is now organized, however, the NEA can never be an effective organization for representing teachers in negotiations with school boards. The average teacher currently pays $10 national dues, $10 state association dues, and approximately $2 local dues.[8] This dues structure is top heavy. Because the bulk of the funds must be expended at the local level, if the school district is too small for sufficient money to be accumulated, then possibly county or even state associations will have to direct negotiations. At present, the Urban Project has approximately twenty-five staff persons who have been attempting to service from Washington the local and state associations. After two years of traveling the country, the Urban Project staff is finally beginning to realize that its task is impossible. Unable to serve effectively in this way the thousands of school districts in the United States, the NEA has begun to allocate funds directly to state and local associations.

Traditionally, local education associations have been inept in improving teacher welfare. For example, in a 1959 NEA survey of the activities of local education associations, 80 percent of the local associations reported that they sent two or fewer communications to their school board during the past year. Ninety percent of the local associations reported they received two or fewer communications from the school authorities. As expected, 75 percent of the associations reported that they spent the majority of their time participating in social activities.

Organizing for the Future

From all indications, it appears that this image of the local association is changing and that teachers are finally realizing that it is essential for them to form effective organizations. Obtaining funds for education involves a sophisticated power struggle, and teachers are rather late in accepting this fact.

Since teachers have no power to bargain individually similar to some college professors, the role of the teacher organization in this struggle will be crucial. Because teachers can only be protected by an effective organization, it seems probable that the teacher organization of tomorrow will be quite different from either AFT or NEA.

First, it will be structured to function effectively in collective negotiations. Most likely, negotiations will be conducted at the local level, but if they move upward to a county or regional level, then the county organization will control the majority of revenues and full-time personnel. State and national organizations will provide support in the form of consultants and research services; but in large school districts, the local organization will retain full control. In smaller districts, the state organization will play a more important role, and in some states, negotiations will move rapidly to the state level.

Second, the primary function of the organization will be to serve the needs of the teachers. As collective negotiations become more widespread, administrators will be pushed out of any decision-making positions in the teacher organization unless they are completely dedicated to the welfare of the teachers. A very loose affiliation will be retained with organizations of principals and superintendents.

Third, negotiated compulsory membership provisions will be widespread. Not only will teachers be required to join organizations after they have been hired, but in some cases school boards will only be able to hire teachers who are organization members.

Fourth, subject-matter organizations, like the National Council for Social Studies, will continue to be organized on a national basis, and most original contributions in curriculum and study materials will come from national committees specifically organized for the purpose.

Fifth, each local organization that is negotiating will have at least one full-time person, and dues will have to be sufficient to pay for assistance from various specialists such as attorneys and consultants. The rapid increase in the number of full-time executive secretaries working for local teacher organizations indicates that a trend in this direction has already begun.

Finally, as the negotiating organization obtains higher salaries for teachers, its concern will begin to shift toward professional issues on which teachers can act effectively. Such problems as the management of dropouts, the preparation of students for college, and the improvement of guidance systems are illustrations. This shift to a dual orientation has already begun in New York, where the United Federation of Teachers, the exclusive bargaining agent, has expended enormous energies on the "effective schools plan" for long-range improvement of the city's public schools.

The Brown Paper Bag Syndrome: An Educational Anachronism

Mortimer Kreuter

There is a widespread notion that the middle-class origin of most city school teachers somehow gets in the way of effective teaching of the so-called disadvantaged child. I think this is a mistake, or, at best, an unproven hypothesis. Teachers come to the schoolhouse door as eager and able to prepare their children for the tasks before them as the latter's talents and proclivities allow. I know of no teacher who starts her career with the notion that she has been called to guard the gates of the middle-class city. Rather, she wants her pupils to make good in the sense she understands best—academically. Like anyone else, moreover, the teacher enjoys being successful at her job, and her success lies in helping children become more knowledgeable than they were before they entered her classroom—not in thwarting the aspirations of her lower-class pupils. If she fails at her job, if her lower-class children learn more from the streets than the classroom, then I believe we must look for the causes elsewhere than her middle-class origins. I would suggest we begin with the infantile status to which she is reduced, not by the social system from which she comes but by the educational system in which she works.

Teachers in New York City—only lately, unfortunately—are paid fairly decent but not overwhelming salaries, ranging from about \$5,400 to \$12,000 annually, with a middle range figure of about \$9,000.[1] This is at least as good a salary as that of comparable social service professions such as casework, librarianship, nursing, or middle-rank civil service occupations in housing, recreation, welfare, probation or personnel. In its upper reaches, the classroom teacher's salary is equal to, or better than that of senior personnel in the categories mentioned. And yet, teachers talk and act "poor-mouth"; they bring their lunches to school in brown paper bags. Sooner or later, they become entrapped in a brown-paper-bag way of thinking.

I believe that the eating-in habit is a part, or symbol if you like, of the infantilizing process teachers inevitably undergo. Dealing with children in face-to-face contact all day, they work in buildings where the rooms set aside for adult communication are rarely used for that purpose. These rooms also serve as areas for reading, or guidance, or other instructional purposes. It is there, at lunch hour, with the screams of children echoing around them, that the teachers rummage through their bag lunches. Since there is never enough room for whole staffs to eat together, some teachers lunch in one another's rooms, surrounded again by the children's work and books.

This lack of adult interchange, even during the lunch hour, is one of the most debilitating aspects of being a classroom teacher. It hastens the departure of more active individuals to supervisory posts in a more adult world (where, incidentally, the pay is also relatively higher). The flight from classroom teaching into non-teaching positions such as guidance, library, administration, or general organization is a product of the same desire to be part of a more adult scene. There are other ways in which the educational system keeps teachers locked in infantile ways.

Teachers are graded and inspected very much like children. Their private formulations for teaching their classes—their planbooks—are made the subject of weekly inspections. They are also graded on loyalty, dress, deportment, punctuality and attendance, and evidences of growth . . . as are the children. What is worse, the children recognize that their teachers are being checked and graded. One has only to notice how they close ranks to protect a teacher when the principal makes his rounds.

In this never ending world of childishness, teachers become desperate to assert their adulthood. They take courses and trips to improve their minds; they seize every opportunity to organize lavish parties to celebrate the most trivial event: a principal's third or fifth anniversary, the departure of an assistant principal, the leave of a colleague. Significantly, these faculty parties are never held in the school itself but in some large hotel or fine restaurant....

From the standpoint of modern personnel practices, teachers work under sweatshop conditions. They literally have no time to go out to the toilet, and, when they must, they are obliged to summon a next door teacher to keep an eye on the classroom. They must punch time clocks twice daily and file affidavits when ill. A principal I know became a hero to his staff when he broke the time clock in his school, knowing full well that the Maintenance Bureau would never get around to fixing it.

Such instances of check and counter-check are not described to draw out the horrors of bureaucracy. These are too well known. Rather, I want to show that they have a bearing on the content and methodology of teaching in the city schools. I am suggesting that in all our efforts to bring innovation and creativity into the teaching profession, we must first come to grips with the teacher's infantilization at the hands of the system. Unless we get at the teacher's brown-paper-bag mentality, we shall never begin to deal with his professional problems.

That so many of our teachers remain sensibly mature in the face of the process of infantilization, is one of the reasons I regard them as heroes and heroines of endurance. Furthermore, they have built a great union. The United Federation of Teachers, which gives voice to their demands for a share of the decision-making processes of education, should diminish the dependent relations into which they have been forced.

But the brown-paper-bag syndrome is only one aspect of the demoralization of the teaching profession in New York.

In the light of the salary and union advances made over the past few years, it may seem absurd to question the morale of school personnel. And yet I think the question ought to be raised, especially in the light of recent history. Last year 15,000 teachers were licensed and about a third of that number came into the school system. In contrast, the figures of 1941 or 1936 or 1931 show that there were 3,000 applications and only fifty or sixty teachers who were licensed.[2] At that, only five or six on a list of fifty might be given positions. My point is the rather obvious one that a post very easily won can't be worth very much to the winner. The older teachers in the system who, during the economic depression of the thirties, came through the stiffest examinations ever devised, still retain great pride of achievement. They will tell you proudly about the Pulitzer Prize winner in history who flunked his city teaching examination twenty-five years ago. Today's young teacher, on the other hand, may very often come into the field after having failed at several other jobs.

Another point ought to be considered in analyzing the demoralization of the profession. I mean the opening of other markets for college graduate talent. Fields of employment in behavioral and psychological sciences beckon to top college students. Such opportunities existed infrequently, if at all, in the thirties and forties when the top collegiate talent came into the city's schools. Christopher Jencks points out that the demands in human service fields foredoom the schools to a chronic built-in personnel shortage, especially as competition drives salaries up.

Demoralization spreads from another source. Teachers are not only caught in the child's world, they are caught in careers of very limited growth potential. For a substantial increase in status and salary, they must leave the classroom. Otherwise, their only reward for achievement in teaching is to reach the top of the dreary ladder of annual salary increments. Good teachers have the same responsibilities, the same honors, the same check year for year, as bad or indifferent colleagues. There isn't even a way for good teachers to help bad teachers become a little better, except by bootlegging advice and guidance. Teachers are sealed off from each other in their own rooms and rarely get a chance to work together. Young or weak teachers are supposed to go to the administration for help, not to other teachers. Ironically, the collective antagonism of the teaching profession to merit increases may actually encourage individual teachers to stick close to the middle level of achievement.

The system must encourage its teachers to remain teachers. It can do this in part by providing incentives to senior personnel: fewer teaching hours; greater participation in selected supervisory functons; greater monetary reward for teaching; and improved conditions.

Further, the teachers must be brought back into adult relationships. For one example, teaching loads might be reduced to allow teachers to participate in research projects. The teachers' unions must begin to assert themselves not only politically in money matters but also in professional matters. They ought to make a beginning on the issue of screening and upgrading membership (and membership standards).

Both the school system and the teachers' unions must begin to develop a sense of historical continuity with the great teachers of the past so that younger teachers can feel the professional kinship common to practitioners in other fields.

The sense of hero in public education is almost completely lost. And that is an appalling loss. Such men and women were heralded in the past: Angelo Patri of the mental hygiene in education movement; Elizabeth Farrell of the special education field; Leonard Covello of community education. I have known two such outstanding educators: Leon Friend and Maxwell Nurnberg, both of Abraham Lincoln High School in Brooklyn. These two men have probably produced more artists and writers in the New York area than all other high school teachers combined. The list of contemporary "heroes" could also include such brave and independent principals as Elliot Shapiro of P.S. 119, whose courage has become legendary in Harlem, and Edward Gottlieb of P.S. 165, who is in the vanguard of the movement for quality integrated education.

By this time, it will be noted that I have avoided references to slums, poverty, ethnic differences, and learning characteristics, and have concentrated instead on the teachers. That is because I am a city dweller, and every city dweller knows deeply the truth of *plus ça change, plus c'est la même chose* [the more things change, the more they remain the same]. I assure you that twenty-five years ago the poverty was as bad, the slums as rotten, the ethnicity as "different," the learning characteristics about as good as nature and nurture could produce. The major difference between then and now is in the teaching staff. And this difference is the consequence of social and population factors which have led to the school system's decline and the subsequent impairment of the teaching function.

In the period 1946–1960, the lure of the suburbs was very strong among the middle class. A shortage of decent rental housing in the city, coupled with cheap money rates under the Federal Housing Administration and Veterans Administration, pulled out hundreds of thousands of young families. These families clamored for school buildings and more teachers, and were able and willing to pay the costs involved.

That is the first factor. Second, the vacuum of young families departing from New York was filled by Negroes from the rural South and by Puerto Ricans. There was not then, nor is there now, solicitous federal money to minimize the social disruption caused by this in-migration. (Ironically, such money currently is easing the burden placed upon Miami and other southeastern cities by a flood of Cuban refugees.)

Third, all too little is known about the disastrous consequences of former Mayor LaGuardia's bias against new school construction and related capital expenditures. At the present time, the physical deterioration of our schools, which is a result of the lag in school construction in the thirties and forties, is being felt increasingly and, barring massive construction in the immediate future, will probably grow worse in the decade ahead.

With this brief and current look at a declining school system, I should like to take a backward look at a much brighter picture.

New York City was previously an innovative and dynamic school system. It developed a remarkable array of pioneering efforts in such fields as special education of the retarded and handicapped, vocational and technical education, adult and community education, school mental health services, curriculum and materials research, education of the gifted, and arts education. In curriculum alone, for example, it is a well kept secret that many other city and suburban school systems have for decades bought and used the materials and bulletins introduced and perfected in the New York schools.

Another of the chief achievements of the New York system was its separation of the teaching profession from politics. New York City was able from about 1900 on to insist upon a selective recruitment of teachers and supervisors based upon strictly intellectual and technical criteria. This procedure gave teaching personnel both a sense of achievement and worth and genuine professional status. I would wager that New York City has more principals and superintendents who were originally teachers of the humanities, sciences or social studies than any other school system in the country.

In short, among the most significant research areas presented by the New York school system is the situation of the teacher himself. Unless this problem is tackled, it is likely that all the research reports on improving the schools will end up as big black books stacked high in the offices of people who never work with children.

Black Teachers: New Power in the Schools

Susan Jacoby

Black teachers and administrators are beginning
to emerge as a power in the nation's city school systems at a
time when the bitterness of black parents toward these schools is
overflowing. They are being hired and promoted in growing
numbers everywhere, except in the oldest, most rigid bureaucracies such as Boston. Like their white counterparts, black teachers are a part of these systems and have an interest in their
preservation. But they also have a stake in the black community
that is not shared by most of the white teachers. The new black
teacher is more militant in pursuing his interests than Negro
teachers of the past, partly because of the revolution in "black
consciousness" and partly because the teaching profession is no
longer the only option, other than the clergy, for Negroes seeking
to enter the white-collar world.

The opening of school [in the fall of 1968] proved beyond
doubt—if any further proof were needed after the last few years
—that schools in the inner cities are focal points for some of the
most bitter and potentially destructive racial tensions in our
divided society. New York's school strike, which pitted the over-
whelmingly white teachers' union and supervisors' association

against black groups demanding power to hire and fire teachers and principals, was a disaster both for the schools and for the community as a whole. Whites came to use "mob rule" as a synonym for control of schools by local Negro governing boards. Many blacks regarded the union's rallying cry, "due process for teachers," as a simple expression of union determination not to give ghetto residents a say in what goes on in their schools. Between 90 and 95 percent of New York's 57,000 teachers are white. Inevitably, the strike divided the teachers along racial lines. Although some Negro teachers supported the strike and some whites opposed it, sources in the schools said a large percentage of the several thousand teachers who reported for work despite the strike were Negro.

If New York had the most serious conflict surrounding the opening of school, its problems were far from unique. In Boston, police outside the Christopher Gibson Elementary School barred the entry of a black principal "elected" by neighborhood groups and guarded the school system's regularly appointed white principal. A Negro assistant principal—also regularly appointed by the school system—supported the community groups at considerable risk to his job. In Newark, ten white teachers filed suit to prevent the school system from appointing several new black principals, claiming regular promotion procedures had been bypassed.

Amid all of the racial conflict surrounding the schools, black teachers are in a peculiarly sensitive and sometimes painful position. They have "made it" into the middle class; their students, for the most part, come from families that have not made it. "You look at those black children in front of you and you know that this is where you came from," says one black teacher from Detroit. "Those kids are either what you used to be, or what you might have been."

The phenomenon of black self-hatred, documented most perceptively by black writers and social scientists, is still evident in some Negro teachers who express contempt for "lower class" slum children. But the black teacher has been deeply affected by the identity crisis the black power movement has posed for the entire Negro middle class. As a result, he identifies far more readily with black children in slum schools than did the Negro teachers of the past. That identification is one reason most black teachers work in urban school systems. "If the black teacher does not recognize a special responsibility for the progress and achievement of black children, who will?" asks Zeline Richard, a teacher from Detroit who campaigned unsuccessfully for the presidency of the AFL-CIO American Federation of Teachers (AFT) [in 1968]. "I think many black teachers are coming to realize we must be the guardians of the education of all the children in the inner city."

There are other less idealistic explanations for the concentration of black teachers in the city schools. Unlike their white counterparts, most black teachers live in the cities—housing discrimination gives them little choice—and tend to work where they live. It is still difficult for a black teacher to get a job in a suburban school; racial discrimination in hiring is a common practice in many all-white suburban school systems. At the annual AFT convention in Cleveland, it was reported that fewer than fifty Negro teachers were employed by the predominantly white suburban school systems surrounding Cleveland.

Progressive city school officials across the country are aware that one of the main irritants, if not a causal factor, in the bitter New York situation is the fact that more than 90 percent of the teachers are white, while more than half of the students are black or Puerto Rican. Officials are eager to hire more black teachers and administrators, hopeful that such action will help avert similar confrontations in their cities.

Detroit, which has a school system only one-fourth the size of New York's, has nearly three times as many Negro administrators. When Detroit's school superintendent, Norman Drachler, took over the job two years ago, he regarded the task of bringing more black (and young) administrators into the schools as "one of the really critical initial problems that had to be dealt with." In the past eighteen months the number of Negroes on one Detroit teaching staff has risen from 30 percent to 40 percent. More than a third of the teachers in Chicago, three-fourths in Washington, D.C., and half in Baltimore are black. Although the superintendent of schools in Washington is white, most of the other top-level administrators are black.[1]

Black educators are just becoming aware of their growing numerical power and how it might be used to affect the policies of public school systems. On issues not related to race, most black teachers think and behave exactly like most white teachers. Even the most militant black teachers ruefully admit this. William H. Simons, president of the Washington Teachers Union, says,

> The tendency to rely on doing things as they have been done in the past is a characteristic that has nothing to do with the color of one's skin. If all it took were black teachers and administrators to change a school system, we would obviously have the best school system in the world here in Washington. Which of course is not the case.

But many of the most important controversies swirling around the schools are related to race, and here the black teacher, joined by some of the younger white teachers, does depart from the average white teacher.

Community control of the schools, as demonstrated by the conflict in New York, is a major issue that tends to separate black and white teachers, although it would be an oversimplification to assert that all black teachers support community control and that whites automatically oppose it. Many black teachers are just as fearful of what they regard as "parent interference" in the classroom as the average white teacher, although younger teachers of both races tend to be less rigid on this issue. Nevertheless, the evidence from cities with large numbers of Negro teachers indicates that if black teachers are not wholeheartedly in favor of more community control, they are at least less hostile toward it than their white counterparts. Says Keith Baird, a curriculum consultant to the embattled Ocean Hill-Brownsville school district in New York:

> Community control simply means that blacks and Puerto Ricans will have the same say in running their schools that whites have always had. Naturally, that prospect doesn't frighten black teachers.

In general, black teachers are not as fearful as white teachers that their hard-won due process rights will be destroyed if neighborhood school boards have some control over hiring and firing. Many of the white teachers automatically assume that their jobs will be in serious jeopardy if they are subject to the control of a black school board. All of the teachers fired by the governing board of the Ocean Hill-Brownsville district were white, but the fact that more than two-thirds of the new teachers hired by the board were also white was generally ignored. Says Mr. Simons:

> I'm sure it's quite clear to everyone in Washington that we have no intention of letting any local governing board throw out our due

process rights. But we see no reason why this should happen. At the heart of the really violent opposition to community control, there is the assumption that a black neighborhood governing board must be by nature irrational and extremist. If you start with this assumption, then naturally there is no potential for negotiation.

In New York, there are not enough black teachers to exert a countervailing influence to the strong anti-community control stand taken by Albert Shanker and his United Federation of Teachers. The picture is quite different in several other cities and within the teacher union movement.

Historically, Negro teachers in the North, fearful of being "the last hired and the first fired," have been strong union members. At least some of the security younger black teachers feel when they display their militancy is attributable to the protection provided by union contracts against being fired for expressing opinions on political and social issues. The AFT's record on race is a progressive one; the struggling union expelled Southern locals that refused to desegregate in 1956, while the powerful, firmly entrenched National Education Association shilly-shallied on the question well into the 1960's.

Understandably, many black delegates to the AFT convention in August [1968] were deeply disturbed by a strong statement from newly elected AFT President David Selden that he would push for a merger with the NEA. (The NEA has since rebuffed Selden's overtures regarding a merger.) But the most controversial issue at the union convention was school decentralization and increased involvement by representatives of ghetto neighborhoods in running their schools. "The labor movement has forgotten from whence it came," charged Mrs. Richard, referring to the UFT's position in New York. "The fight of black people today is the fight of the labor movement of yesteryear."

The New Caucus, a dissident group of black and young white teachers within the union, had sought to gain a strong endorsement of community control. New York's UFT, anticipating a strike over the Ocean Hill-Brownsville situation when school opened, succeeded in having the words "community control" stricken from the New Caucus resolution. Said Roy Stell, a delegate from Chicago:

> As a black union teacher, you have asked me in voting against this [the New Caucus resolution] to vote against myself. I don't ever want to see the day when my union asks me to go on the picket lines in a strike against my community.

The dispute was papered over by a compromise resolution putting the union on record as recognizing the need for "effective community responsibility and involvement through elected representation in the black, Puerto Rican, and other minority communities of America." The community control issue is a threat to the solidarity of the union, and neither the union leaders nor the dissidents want to see an outright split between black and white union teachers.

The Detroit Federation of Teachers has carefully avoided taking a hard-line stand against community control as the UFT has done. Black teachers account for a third of the Detroit union's membership, and the power of the union—unlike the UFT's position in New York—would be substantially weakened if blacks broke away.

Significantly, the Washington Teachers Union is the only AFT local in the nation that has taken a forthright position in favor of community school boards having a share of power over hiring and firing teachers. Washington and Baltimore are the only large cities in the North where black teachers are in a majority or near-majority. "We teachers have put ourselves on the defensive instead of taking the initiative in regard to community control," says WTU President Simons. "Decentralization and community control could improve education in the large cities, and anything that has even the seeds of improving schooling for children should have the support of teachers. We can protect the rights of teachers through contractual agreements with local boards. And we can work with people if we are only willing to treat them as human beings, regardless of how much formal education they have."

The Washington union supported the city school system's first experiment in community control in an area known as Adams-Morgan, about a mile north of the White House. The Morgan Community School, despite sharp controversy over the project, was one of the few schools in Washington last year where reading scores on standardized tests improved significantly, despite a general decline throughout the system. This fall, the central Board of Education agreed that Morgan's elected neighborhood school board should have expanded powers over staffing, and the union is beginning work on the plan with neighborhood representatives.

Curriculum is another area where the black teacher is beginning to exert an influence in the city school systems. The willingness of large school systems to deal with black history and culture in their curricula seems, regrettably, to have far more to do with the number of black teachers and administrators in the system than with the number of black students. Washington's public school enrollment—now more than 90 percent black—has been more than three-quarters Negro for the past decade. Yet the history of the black man in Africa and America did not receive any particular emphasis and, in some instances, was actively de-emphasized, until the emergence of a strong, militant teachers' union two years ago coupled with a sharp increase in the number of high-level black administrators.

Despite the fact that school appropriations in the nation's capital are controlled by Southern-dominated Congressional committees, some remarkably candid discussions about racial matters are going on in Washington classrooms. The most skilled teachers use the children's interest in racial topics to spur their interest in the conventional subjects the school attempts to teach.

The weekend after the riots triggered by the Rev. Martin Luther King's death, Washington teachers encouraged the youngsters to express their feelings about the riots in compositions and class discussions, and they did not attempt to elicit the moralistic responses schools usually press their students for.

"How did you feel about the looting and the burning?" one teacher asked her sixth-grade class.

"I thought it was all right to loot the white people's stores but not to burn them," replied one girl emphatically.

"Why do you think that?" asked the teacher.

"Because colored people lived over the stores and they got burnt out too."

Another sixth-grader disagreed sharply. "The good stores got looted and burned just like the bad ones," he said. "You can't say that all of the storeowners cheated people. A man on the corner who was always fair to everybody got burned out just like the guys who trick you. It's not right."

The compositions and art work of the children were eventually compiled into a book titled *Tell It Like It Is*, which has been widely quoted and reproduced. "You just don't know," one teacher commented, "how proud these kids were that something they wrote was considered good enough to be printed in a book. Since then we've noticed a greatly increased interest in writing and reading in many of the children, which is an example of how you can take advantage of a pressing current topic to spark their interest in learning. We wouldn't have been allowed to do it ten years ago."

The more conservative teachers in the system are aghast that such activities should be allowed in the classroom. The fact that they are allowed is an indication of a significant change in the school system in recent years—a change that is allowing many teachers to use experiences that are meaningful to the children as a way of interesting them in schoolwork. Black teachers are not responsible for all of the curriculum changes in Washington; some white teachers have been most active in working for curriculum reform that stresses black history and culture as well as the life of the inner-city child. Rather, the presence and pressure of black teachers and administrators have created a climate where such changes are possible. A teaching staff that is 95 percent white is simply not likely to be excited by the absence of Frederick Douglass from an American history book.

In the long run, the most important impact of the black teacher in the classroom may not be in promoting community control or specific curriculum changes, but simply in serving as an image of success for black students in ghetto schools. The same is true for black administrators, especially black male administrators.

The fact that many black youngsters of elementary school age never come in contact with black adults in positions of power and authority is a genuine tragedy in terms of the child's self-esteem —one that few whites can even comprehend. Assume, for a moment, that Scarsdale, New York, were a community of destitute whites and not a wealthy suburb. Suppose the white Scarsdale child saw only three kinds of black people in his neighborhood—welfare workers—who doled out the family's livelihood—policemen, and teachers. Assume that the white Scarsdale child went to school every day and was taught by black teachers and black principals, with never a white face in sight except among the youngsters. It is not difficult to figure out what conclusions the child would reach about which skin color was the source of knowledge and money and power in his world. This is precisely the situation that confronts many black children in the teeming city slums, with only the colors reversed. The question of whether a school that perpetuates such a system can effectively teach black children is an inherently valid one.

Detroit's Superintendent Drachler is deeply concerned about the need to place qualified blacks in positions of authority in the ghetto schools. "If I have a qualified black principal and two openings—one in a white school and one in a Negro school, I'd probably assign the man to the predominantly Negro school," Drachler says. "I think it's absolutely vital that a child in the ghetto see people of his own race who have achieved, and not think that everyone in authority is white. This is not to say that it isn't important to have Negro administrators in white schools, but that, with a limited number of such people, I think they should be used first where the need is greatest."

The idea that only black teachers can effectively teach black children is nonsense. But the chief characteristic of inner-city schools across the nation is they tend to make deprived youngsters feel like failures at the age of six or seven. The real importance of the black teacher may lie in his unique opportunity to bolster his students' self-image. One first grader in a Washington school informed his teacher, as she passed out reading readiness workbooks, "Reading is hard. My brother can't read nuthin'. And he's ten." The teacher looked at the boy and said, "I learned to read when I was your age, and I grew up just a block from your house."

Manager of the Unmanageable: Today's Educational Administrator

John E. Sturm

If there is one group on the contemporary educational scene who is probably justified in experiencing some degree of paranoia, surely it is the administrators. Students have traditionally distrusted them, with the rare exception of the independent school headmaster or the small liberal arts college president who could stay close enough to the student body to be respected, even loved. Now many students have exchanged sulking distrust for open protest against their administrations.

The administrator's own children, always somewhat embarassed by their patriarch's professional calling, today seem to regard him as a virtual liability. The administrator's wife alone remains a sympathetic ear.

Faculty used to regard him with a touch of envy—he who had contrived to leave the "classroom" for the "office" and the privilege of dealing with the school board or the trustees. Today there is scorn where once there was envy. And the initiative often seems to rest entirely with the faculty.

To the public the administrator was once a faceless creature who symbolized the educational system—for good or ill. Community members who "favored" education generally regarded him with some warmth—those who viewed school as a necessary evil were prone to display suspicion if they knew who he was. Today's administrator, in contrast, is a TV and newspaper personality whose face and voice and remarks are known to all, and in the tradition of all celebrities he draws passionate enmity or unrestrained show of support.

His colleagues in business and industry were wont, in the not too distant past, to smile benevolently on his homely non-profit enterprise: the one or two dedicated office typists, the handwritten reports of the teachers, the couple of janitors, the annual cleaning of the building, the commercially printed dance programs once a year, his annual summer bout with the next year's schedule—which he always made up himself. Now these colleagues stumbling upon the language lab during halftime at a basketball game—or coming backstage to see the new lighting and projection equipment that has reportedly made your stage more professional than that of the little theater in a nearby barn—now they look at the administrator with a new kind of disbelief which is only confounded when they drop in to see him about borrowing his videotape equipment only to find that he is spending the week at the state capital. They begin to regard the administrator as someone who heads a rival organization.

Nor is the glimmer of a new professional rivalry confined to local ground. Professors of educational administration in the universities now speak a new language. Formerly much like the practicing administrators, whose ranks they had only recently left, they once drew upon the same body of knowledge and accumulated experience. Today they speak and write in strange tongues learned in the halls of management science, group therapy, industrial cost-effectiveness, governmental staffing patterns, sociological decision-making theory. In vain does the tired administrator pore over their prodigious outflow of books, journal articles, paper abstracts for clues as to how to implement some of the new management systems without overturning the entire heaving structure of which he is the present custodian.

I exaggerate, of course. But these and other winds of change are blowing through the administrative offices of schools today. They represent important challenges to the educational leadership of public and private schools, colleges and universities, for they reflect fundamental types of change with which American school administrators must cope if they are to retain their leadership positions.

It can be illuminating, when considering the changing role of any profession, to review the posture of people who occupied comparable positions in an earlier period. In the case of the administrator, his nineteenth century counterpart provides a particularly instructive model for contrast.

Leadership in Another Era

In nineteenth century America the role of the school was primarily an academic one. The family and church accepted responsibility for most of the social and moral development of young people. In that era educational leaders such as Horace Mann and Chester Barnard strove to make common schools into publicly supported, non-sectarian institutions. This was the age of the academy, of the normal school, and of the emerging American high school. Education was looked upon as a means of bringing immigrants into the mainstream of American life. The tasks of educational leadership involved, by and large, into the building of schools, the preparation of teachers, and the evaluation and reporting of pupil progress—reasonably simple tasks in a simpler age.

The educational leader was also expected to be a curriculum leader. Because the classics were the accepted core of academic preparation for many students, a kind of scholar-principal or scholar-president emerged. It is interesting to research the academic background of early school superintendents in the United States. A great number of them appear to have been authors or classical scholars of a rather high order.

The early administrator was further expected, of course, to deal with personnel problems—that is, he had the responsibility of obtaining and evaluating teachers. An early procedure, approved by state laws, provided that school superintendents should nominate prospective teachers to boards of education, which would then hire or not. This arrangement was originally established to prevent school boards from nominating and hiring friends or relatives to teaching positions. In response to the American tendency to distrust the long-term appointment of public officials, many early superintendents of schools or district principals often stood for election for office.

Principals and college presidents of the nineteenth century were also likely to have the responsibility for hiring and firing members of their faculties. While this procedure was no doubt subject to many abuses, and eventually brought about the rise of teacher organizations and teacher tenure legislation, it probably tended to encourage the administrator's interest in the strengths and weaknesses of individual teachers. Because he also had the supervisory task of helping to improve teaching performance, the early administrator was obliged to meet frequently with teachers in order to assist them and to suggest new teaching methods or procedures.

The administrator's role includes school building, plant maintenance and upkeep. In an earlier time, with lower labor and material costs, the school administrator's responsibility to develop and maintain physical facilities was considerably easier to dispatch than it has since become. Today's specialized architectural and contracting firms, plus the complex machinations of school financing and legal procedures, make this aspect of the modern school administrator's work an extremely time-consuming process. Higher school building costs have had the effect of defeating school bond issues with greater frequency, creating the twin dangers of overcrowded classrooms and limited scope in educational planning.

When schools were considered to be doing an adequate job of educating the young, the school administrator's public relations role was considerably easier than it is today. This was largely the case a century ago when many parents had not had the advantage of a high school education or spoke English only as a second language. Today's fourth and fifth generation parents, many of whom have a college background, require that the administrator deal with a more sophisticated public. It is often cited as ironic that the American public school experiment has worked so well that every citizen can now consider himself an expert in how the schools should educate. As one school principal remarked recently, "If you doubt an adult's ability to discuss school problems, he says, 'Look Jim, I'm an expert—here is my high school diploma!' "

Today's Altered Situation

Viewed against the backdrop of what may seem, in retrospect, the halcyon days of education in this country, the current scene is chaotic for the administrator.

The growth of urbanization, with its developing dichotomy of middle class suburban living versus that of the inner city together with the loss of population in rural areas, has ushered in a whole host of problems of large classes, teacher shortages, old run-down buildings, and woeful deficiencies in financial resources. In urban areas, shifting population patterns have resulted in low standards of school achievement, high dropout rates, juvenile delinquency, and increased parental pressures for school decentralization—especially in predominantly black communities. The school superintendent in such areas may be under a mandate from the school board or state department of education to effect an integration of school populations, while many white parents in the district are likely to favor a "neighborhood" school policy. They vigorously oppose any proposal that their children be bussed to other schools in order to promote a more favorable racial balance.

The urban school administrator has also had to deal with the fact that, at least until recently, teachers have been less likely to want to teach in areas where discipline problems and low pupil achievement were most likely to be encountered. Suburban school systems often have tended to offer higher salary schedules to accompany what appear to be more comfortable working conditions.

Part and parcel of the crush into the cities—and the subsequent crush out again, on the part of those who can afford to leave—is the tremendous rise in the sheer number of individuals now encompassed by the educational system. A great increase in enrollments occurred at the higher education level, just after World War II, when many returning servicemen financed their educations under the federal government's G. I. Bill. This influx of students, together with the subsequent population increase have expanded the physical plants of our institutions of higher learning so substantially that some very large institutions—which have proved challenging to administer—have been created. At the same time, colleges and public schools alike find it increasingly difficult—not to say complicated—to pry additional funds from state legislatures, alumni, the federal government, or private foundations. Thus their services run the risk of deterioration at a time when they are already threatened merely by the gigantic scale of the educational enterprise.

One of the criticisms leveled by students at our larger institutions has been their impersonal nature—large classes taught in large lecture halls by professors whom students never see except standing behind a lectern. Increasing unrest among students of college age, resulting from a disenchantment with the Indochinese war and disillusionment with the traditional affluent American society of the past two decades, has burst forth in riots at many major universities, indicating a willingness to attack the very warp and woof of our institutions of higher learning, causing property damage, physical harm, and instigating disturbance and unrest in the process, in order to obtain what they believe to be a more meaningful education and a redirection of society's efforts away from foreign activities toward domestic programs.

The situation in which a college or high school administrator finds himself under attack by militant groups of students, desiring to liberalize social rules and regulations on the one hand and feverishly trying to restrict university involvement with war or weapons research on the other, is virtually unprecedented in this country. Indeed the whole issue of "academic freedom" has been raised anew during the last decade, when militants on the campuses have urged that the concept is broad enough to cover belief and behavior of all kinds. Often able to enlist a sizable portion of the faculty to their cause, student groups pit themselves against a beleaguered administration which finds itself caught between the demands of at least a part of the academic community for change and the demands of society at large (and the trustees in particular) to hold the line. On some occasions an administration has closed down lines of communication, been unresponsive to needed change, and brought about a confrontation with students as a result. In other cases, university officials have been utterly acquiescent, complying with overnight demands for new faculty and for courses which the faculty themselves regard as educationally unsound.

The result has been a diminution of educational leadership which has backed the administrator into a corner. He must try to please all publics—the trustees, the community, the faculty, the students—many of whom have conflicting goals and objectives. It is indeed no wonder that the college administrator often feels like a juggler who must keep all of the demands in the air at one time, like so many flying balls. If he is not skillful in giving each his equal attention, they are all liable to fall down and crack his head. Unfortunately, this type of administrative performance does not always lead to effective educational leadership!

Many of the same societal conditions which are changing youth's educational aspirations are also affecting the aspirations of teachers. Of tremendous importance in the day-to-day functioning of the modern administrator is the recent rise of contract negotiations by teachers under state legislation. Today's teachers are more militant about rights, job performance, teaching conditions, and the like than ever before. This has been especially evident in city schools, where teacher unions and teacher associations have been competing for membership. One outgrowth of this condition has been a growing polarization between teachers and administrators, the latter being regarded as representatives of the employer (the school boards) and therefore in the camp of the opposition.

A complicating factor in teacher contract negotiations has been the tendency to negotiate away some of the traditional decision-making prerogatives of the administrator. For example, some contracts have established that class size shall be established jointly by consultation with teachers. Such provisions have reduced principals' powers, making it difficult for them to act as coordinators of the total schedule of authority.

Other problems stem from the frequency with which teachers feel free to bypass principals altogether and go directly to the superintendent or school board with complaints and grievances. This practice, according to administrators in the field, is becoming considerably more widespread.

Amid all this, the authority of the city superintendent to implement and influence policy decisions made by school boards has undergone great change. One question here involves whether or not the superintendent should bargain directly with teacher representatives in establishing yearly contracts. This is a time-consuming business. Should it be left directly to the board or to a competent outside negotiator? Where does the superintendent fit in the overall picture of negotiations? Various school districts have used various methods, but one thing tends to emerge—the superintendent finds it more and more difficult to serve as an educational leader and advisor to both sides in an employer-employee conflict situation. In many cases it now appears that he will merely spend much of his time overseeing that contract provisions, which have been negotiated, are fulfilled or that grievances are properly handled.

New Sources of Authority in Education

Cutting across all these issues one can discern a shift in the concept of authority emanating from the administrator or rather from his position alone. This notion of power could exist in an earlier and more stable time, especially a time when a teaching job was valued as a steady means of employment. Today's social and economic conditions, particularly the shortage of qualified teachers in many public schools and two-year colleges, have produced a radically different picture. In many schools it is a seller's market for teachers, and administrators must react accordingly. It is difficult to maintain a position of unswerving authority in these circumstances.

In a similar vein, the administrator can no longer be considered the fount of all wisdom. There is simply too much knowledge and information around for any one person to be master of it all. This is true for teachers as well. The idealized era of education which portrayed the best education to be Mark Hopkins on one end of a log and the student on the other is gone forever.

Moreover, we tend to operate under new group patterns of decision making today—particularly in academic and curriculum matters. The expertise of teachers is likely to be an important factor in the selection of new textbooks or the development of new materials resource centers. At such levels, the authority of the school principal or dean of academic affairs must be tempered by his acknowledgment of the proficiency of the faculty —with the result that yet another shift in educational leadership is occurring. Involvement of faculty here is certainly most practical since it involves added expertise and intellectual power. Unfortunately, not every administrator feels comfortable in this new role of group leader. It is, however, an area which he will avoid only at his own peril.

So it is that, while the average American citizen views these unsettled conditions with wonder or outrage or optimism, as the case may be, the professional educator/administrator is expected to deal with them! One may well imagine that the school administrator often finds himself between the devil and the deep blue sea, attempting to resolve educational problems which have been generated by the society outside the school, but with which the school is expected to deal.

Lipham [1] has drawn an interesting contrast between the modern administrator and the "disruptive movement leader" in which the educational administrator is said to utilize "existing" structures or procedures to achieve organizational goals in order to *maintain* order, whereas the movement leader is more concerned with changing established structures, procedures, or goals. Seay,[2] on the other hand, suggests that today's administrator has the difficult responsibility of deciding when to maintain established structures and procedures and when to initiate change. The one thing that is beyond his power is to *resist* change. During the average tenure of the present-day administrator some changes will become desirable, others will be necessary, and a few, initiated by foresighted leaders, will shape future education processes.

The winds of change are blowing faster in this era than they did in Horace Mann's day, when the job of education to serve society by providing learning for its citizens seemed simpler— when Mann, in one of his final speeches, addressing a group of young prospective teachers, could say, "Be ashamed to die until you have won some victory for humanity."

Some of Mann's pragmatic idealism seems to be reasserting itself among young people entering the profession today. Somewhere in their ranks are the educational leaders of the future. No doubt they will operate rather differently from either their nineteenth century or their early and middle twentieth century counterparts. Perhaps additional administrative personnel will become active—new assistant deans, principals, and superintendents in the middle-management of the educational enterprise. Perhaps new administrative organizational structures will emerge. Perhaps new methods of preparation for administrative leaders will be required. Whatever the challenges of the changing future, it is to be hoped that America's educational leaders will be equal to the task. The author is confident that this will be the case.

Notes

TEACHER ORGANIZATIONS: AN ANALYSIS OF THE ISSUES/
MOSKOW

[1] "Teacher Conscription—Basis of Association Membership?" *Teachers College Record* (October 1964), 66:7–17.
[2] Professional Associations—More Than Unions," *Teachers College Record* (December 1964), 66:203–218.
[3] Mrs. Steet has debated with AFT representatives before my education classes at Temple University on three different occasions.—MHM
[4] N. A. Masters, R. H. Salisbury, and T. H. Eliot, *State Politics and the Public Schools* (New York: Alfred A. Knopf, 1964).
[5] *Editors' Note:* As this book went to press, the latest average, for 1969–70, was $8,552.
[6] *Editors' Note:* Recently the NEA has begun to compete more vigorously with the AFT for rights to bargain collectively as the negotiating organization for teachers. In many school districts today, teacher organizations which are NEA affiliated have begun to win their share of elections to become bargaining agents.
[7] *Editors' Note:* Current NEA budget figures for teacher welfare and unified teaching profession items have risen to approximately 21% as of 1970.
[8] *Editors' Note:* As of the 1970–71 school year NEA dues have risen to $25.00 per year.

Notes

THE BROWN PAPER BAG SYNDROME: AN EDUCATIONAL
ANACHRONISM/KREUTER

[1] *Editors' Note:* As this book went to press the salary scale for New York City teachers ranged from $7,950 to $14,500.
[2] *Editors' Note:* The author here refers to the relatively few vacancies which were filled from a vast number of teacher applicants in New York City during the depression years of the 1930's. Today there are over 60,000 licensed teachers employed in New York City.

Notes

BLACK TEACHERS: NEW POWER IN THE SCHOOLS/JACOBY

[1] As of September, 1970, the new Superintendent of Schools in Washington, D.C. is a young black educator, Hugh J. Scott. He served formerly as Assistant Superintendent of Schools in Detroit, Michigan.   ▶

MANAGER OF THE UNMANAGEABLE: TODAY'S EDUCATIONAL
ADMINISTRATOR/STURM

References

[1] James M. Lipham, 63rd Yearbook, National Society for the Study of Education, Part II, p. 122.
[2] Maurice F. Seay. "Administrative Acts and Their Consequences in Urban Schooling," H. Rudman and R. L. Featherstone, eds. (New York: Harcourt, Brace, & World, Inc., 1968), p. 121.

Further Reading

In addition to references cited by authors in this Part the following texts may be useful.

Ehlers, Henry, and Gordon C. Lee (eds.). *Crucial Issues in Education.* New York, N. Y.: Holt, Rinehart and Winston, 1965.

One of the better treatments of some of the crucial questions which face education today, this text contains a perceptive chapter on desegregation (pages 156–201).

Holt, John. *How Children Fail.* New York, N. Y.: Dell Publishing Co., 1964.

A critical view of educational practices in American schools, this is an eye-opener.

Lieberman, Myron. *The Future of Public Education.* Chicago, Illinois: University of Chicago Press, 1960.

A sound basic treatment of the question of professionalism in education. Despite its having appeared in 1960, this book is especially enlightening on local control of education.

Oaks, Dallin H. (ed.). *The Wall Between Church and State.* Chicago, Illinois: The University of Chicago Press, 1963.

In this, one of the better works on the question of religion and the schools, the reader is referred especially to pages 142–179 dealing with school prayer cases.

Rickover, H. G. *American Education—A National Failure.* New York, N. Y.: E. P. Dutton, 1963.

A formidable critic of American education practices here suggests alternative solutions. A comprehensive comparison of American schools with those of Great Britain (pages 230–305) is particularly illuminating.

Films of Related Interest

"And No Bells Ring" National Education Association, 58 min.

Depicts newer forms of classroom organization: team teaching, small- and large-group instruction.

"Quiet Too Long" National Education Association, 29 min.

Portrays today's new breed of teacher and discusses the current teacher image of militancy and involvement.

"Preparation of Teachers" U.S. Dept. of State, 20 min.

Explores the experiences of two prospective teachers.

"Make A Mighty Reach" National Education Association, 55 min.

Considers a number of the innovations in American schools which give promise of enriching education for today's children.

Appendix / The Professional Literature

The following education journals, several of which supplied articles for this collection, are hereby called to your attention. Although the current national concern over education has provoked articles on education in a wide range of popular and scholarly periodicals, the journals listed here form part of a corpus of professional thought and research in the sociological, philosophic, and historic aspects of education generated by the academic community largely for itself— over and above the attention of the public at large. Each journal has a distinct editorial image. Many contain useful reviews of new books, columns by well-known educators, debates on education issues, and reports on professional organizations.

Any education library or large general library will have copies available, through which you can become familiar with the tone and content of each. They can also lead you to other journals which may have greater appeal for you. For all its shortcomings of long publication delays, traditional editorial acceptance procedures, uneven writing, and—yes—sometimes vacuity of thought, the professional literature is one of the chief channels of communication within the profession —ultimately responsive, as such, to the thinking of the members. It is, therefore, one of the tools with which an educator can affect his profession.

JOURNAL	PUBLISHER	ISSUED
American School Board Journal	Bruce Publishing Company, Milwaukee, Wisconsin	monthly
American Teacher Magazine	American Federation of Teachers, AFL-CIO	four times per school year
The Catholic Educational Review	Catholic University of America	monthly
The Educational Forum	Kappa Delta Pi, an honor society in education	monthly (November through May)
The Elementary School Journal	Department of Education, University of Chicago	monthly (October through May)
Harvard Educational Review	Harvard Graduate School of Education	quarterly
Journal of General Education	Pennsylvania State University Press	quarterly
Journal of Negro Education	Bureau of Educational Research, Howard University	quarterly
Peabody Journal of Education	George Peabody College for Teachers	bimonthly
Phi Delta Kappan	Phi Delta Kappa, an honor society in education	monthly
School and Society	School for Advancement of Education, Inc.	biweekly (October through May)
Teachers College Record	Teachers College, Columbia University	monthly (October through May)
Today's Education	National Education Association	monthly

The Contributors

James Baldwin, internationally known black writer, describes eloquently the problems of Negroes living in modern American society. In 1963 he gave his well-known "talk" which appears in this collection at a seminar before 200 New York City school teachers. Baldwin's works include *Go Tell It on the Mountain, Notes of a Native Son, Another Country,* and *The Fire Next Time.*

Alan Batchelder is currently Professor of Economics at Kenyon College. A former President of the National Education Association, he has written and lectured widely on educational topics.

Robert E. Bills, who is Dean of Education at the University of Alabama, has published widely on educational topics.

R. Freeman Butts, a recognized authority on foreign school systems, is Director of International Studies at Columbia University. He has published extensively on the history of American education.

James S. Coleman, Professor of Social Relations at John Hopkins University, is an authority on the impact of change in American society and has undertaken numerous research studies in this field.

Robert J. Fisher is currently on sabbatical leave in England where he is conducting a study of the British primary school. He is Professor of Education at Eastern Michigan University and the author of several articles in professional journals.

Charles Frankel, a philosopher and a former Assistant Secretary of State, is currently with the Aspen Institute of Humanistic Studies. Among his primary interests is the effect of U.S. foreign policy upon our domestic institutions.

Alexander Frazier is Professor of Education at Ohio State University. His publications reflect an interest in learning patterns and problems.

Richard E. Gross, a member of the School of Education at Stanford University, is co-author of *Educating Citizens For Today.*

Robert J. Havighurst is Professor of Education at the State University of New York at Stony Brook. One of the best known writers on educational topics in America today, he is the author of numerous works including *Education in Metropolitan Areas* and *Society and Education* (with Bernice Neugarten).

Nathaniel Hickerson, Professor of Education at the University of Southern California, writes frequently on quality education for minority groups.

Robert Maynard Hutchins, formerly Chancellor of the University of Chicago, has published many books in the field of education, among them *The Conflict in Education.*

Susan Jacoby is a distinguished writer and reporter for the *Washington Post.* Her pieces on subjects relating to educational and social issues appear in newspapers across the country.

Clyde Kluckhohn, late Chairman of the Department of Anthropology at Harvard University, was a distinguished American anthropologist. His major publications include *The Navaho* (with D. C. Leighton) and *Mirror for Man.*

Mortimer Kreuter is Professor of Education at Columbia University. He has published extensively on teaching in urban areas and on educating the urban child.

Paul Lauter teaches at the University of Maryland in Baltimore. **Florence Howe** teaches at Goucher College. Their dedication to both educational and social change and liberation involved them in Mississippi and the Freedom Schools, Upward Bound and other private and federal experiments in education, and more recently, Resist and the New University Conference. Mr. Lauter is the author of *Theories of Comedy.* Miss Howe is working on a study of the role of women in American life. They are the authors of *The Conspiracy of the Young* and are at work on *Education for Change,* a book about education and politics.

Frederick J. McDonald, a member of the Departments of Education and Psychology at Stanford University, is interested in learning theory and is the author of a text in educational psychology problem solving.

Margaret Mead, the noted anthropologist, is interested in educational processes and their cross-cultural aspects. Her major books include a number of classics, among them *Coming of Age in Samoa* and *Growing Up in New Guinea.* Miss Mead has taught and lectured at many institutions throughout the United States.

Michael H. Moskow, Professor of Economics at Temple University, is an authority on teacher organizations and their contractual negotiations with school districts. He is the author of a number of books relating to this subject, among them *Collective Negotiations for Teachers: An Approach to School Administrators* (with Myron Lieberman).

Gerald J. Pine is Associate Professor of Education at the University of New Hampshire. His articles have appeared in *Phi Delta Kappan* and other educational publications.

Frank Riessman was one of the first psychologists to study and write extensively on problems of disadvantaged Americans. Formerly he served as a psychologist in the Mobilization for Youth Program.

Lloyd E. Robison is Associate Professor of Education at Auburn University. He is the author of a text, *Human Growth and Development*.

Joseph S. Roucek is Professor of Social Science at Queensborough Community College of The City University of New York. One of the first writers to examine the plight of the American Indian from a sociological and educational point of view, he has published widely on the problems of minority groups in America.

Galen Saylor, Professor of Education at the University of Nebraska, is a frequent contributor to educational journals.

Edward Joseph Shoben, Jr., former head of the Center for Higher Education at the State University of New York at Buffalo, has written frequently on student activism and student morality.

Robert D. Strom, until recently Chairman of the Department of Education at Purdue University, has held several positions with the National Education Association. His publications deal with problems relating to the school dropout and the changing American family.

Hilda Taba, late Professor of Education at San Francisco State College, was among the first American educators to be concerned with education for minority groups.

Robert Ulich, former Professor of Education at Harvard University, is an acknowledged authority on religion and education in the United States, as well as on additional issues relating to educational philosophy.

Kimball Wiles, late Dean of Education at the University of Florida, was the author of a number of well-known works on school supervision and educational administration.

Thomas Woody, late Professor of Education at the University of Pennsylvania, was active in research on early American schools and is considered a significant contributor to the literature in history of American education.

The Editors

John E. Sturm combines his interest in American education with a long-time fascination with American history, particularly of the nineteenth century. An Assistant Professor of Education at the State University College of New York at Buffalo, he is especially interested in current problems in educational administration and in the changing nature of the American family. He has recently designed a new course on the latter for prospective teachers.

John A. Palmer, former Chairman of the Department of Foundations of Education at the State University College at Buffalo, is an Associate Professor of Education. President of the local chapter of Phi Delta Kappa, he is active in the American Association of University Professors and serves as advisor to the campus affiliate of Kappa Delta Pi, a national student organization for young people entering the profession.

Index